GHOST DANCING THE LAW

GHOST DANCING THE LAW

The Wounded Knee Trials

JOHN WILLIAM SAYER

Harvard University Press
Cambridge, Massachusetts
London, England
1997

In memory of my grandparents

Emma Lauterbach Kramer, 1895–1990
Fred Louis Kramer, 1896–1994

Copyright © 1997 by the President and Fellows of Harvard College
All rights reserved
Printed in the United States of America

Library of Congress Cataloging-in-Publication Data
Sayer, John William.
  Ghost dancing the law : the Wounded Knee trials /
John William Sayer.
      p.   cm.
  Includes bibliographical references and index.
  ISBN 0-674-35433-8 (alk. paper)
  1. Banks, Dennis—Trials, litigation, etc.
2. Wounded Knee Massacre, S.D., 1890—Claims.
3. Indians of North America—Government relations—1934–
4. American Indian Movement.
I. Title.
KF224.B27S39   1997
973.8'6—dc21   97-1227

CONTENTS

PREFACE

TO ARTICULATE the past historically does not mean to recognize it 'the way it really was,' " wrote Walter Benjamin. "It means to seize hold of a memory as it flashes up at a moment of danger." In the midst of an armed standoff with federal law enforcement officials at Wounded Knee, South Dakota, in the winter of 1973, a group of Oglala Lakota Indians and their supporters rekindled before a watching nation memories of a past that for many had ended with a massacre on that same ground almost a century before. The dangers for Native Americans, of course, had not ended at Wounded Knee in 1890 and did not end there in the spring of 1973 when protesters finally surrendered to federal officials. A year later they were in court, again using history as a weapon, this time in the defense of a long list of federal criminal charges.

The story of those trials represents a piece of the continuing struggle of Native Americans for economic and cultural survival. The central experiences described in this narrative, however, are not exclusive to Native Americans. Stories told in the courtroom during highly publicized political trials have an impact on the public's perceptions of the moral, cultural, and legal issues involved, just as the evolving political dramas outside the courtroom affect the story unfolding inside. While the experience of Native American activists in the criminal justice system and under the media spotlight that followed them there was shaped by who they were, it was also shaped by the legal structures and power relations that have confronted many political activists.

The original research for this book benefited from funds administered by the Graduate School and the College of Liberal Arts of the University of Minnesota. I would also like to extend my appreciation to the Minnesota Historical Society and its archival staff, who put up with me for the better part of a year as I sifted through the boxes of defense committee records and trial transcripts in their care. More recently, the Legal History Program of the Institute for Legal Studies at the University of Wisconsin Law School provided me with time and space to rethink and rewrite the manuscript. Finally, I would also like to thank the people at the Lakota Studies Department of Sinte Gleske University in Mission, South Dakota, for helping me translate a phrase in Lakota used by Russell Means during his trial.

My biggest debt, perhaps, is owed to the thirty trial participants who consented to be interviewed for this project: Dennis Banks, Joe Beeler, M. G. Beeler, Clyde Bellecourt, Vernon Bellecourt, Len Cavise, William Clayton, David Cohoes, Linda Gallant, Leonard Garment, David Gienapp, Doug Hall, R. D. Hurd, Kathy James, William Kunstler, Larry Leventhal, Robert Lyman, Bill Means, Lorelei Means, Ted Means, Fred Nichol, Karen Northcott, Bradley Patterson, Joan Scully, Madonna Thunder Hawk, John Thomas, Ken Tilsen, Rachel Tilsen, John Trudell, and Diane Wiley. Several of them I had known since my own brief association with the Wounded Knee defense committee in the summer of 1973, and they in turn directed me to others on both sides of the issue. All gave generously of their time, and many submitted to one or more follow-up conversations. Of this group I am particularly indebted to Karen Northcott and Ken Tilsen, who helped guide me through the thousands of pages of materials in the historical society, opened up their extensive personal files for review, answered countless questions, and read portions of the manuscript.

I also owe a considerable debt to a number of other individuals. My editors at Harvard University Press, Aïda Donald, Elizabeth Suttell, and Mary Ellen Geer, were helpful, patient, and supportive throughout the process of readying the manuscript for publication. Marian Staats provided me with numerous helpful editorial suggestions. A number of colleagues have provided support and counsel, and have read and commented on various sections of the manuscript: in particular I want to thank Ruth Buchanan, Peter Carstensen, Chuck Epp, Howie Erlanger, Nan Enstad, John Esser,

Marc Gallanter, Susan Geiger, Kermit Hall, Dirk Hartog, David Ingram, Stanley Kutler, Arthur McEvoy, Richard Monette, Paul Murphy, Dan Price, Nancy Shoemaker, and, finally, my friend and colleague Laura Hengehold, for an unending conversation about history, philosophy, and the importance and dangers of writing.

I have tried throughout this project to think critically about the act of writing, about reconstructing and finding meaning in the stories of others' lives, and how that process may either connect us to, or further separate us from, our past. I owe much to the activists and writers who have taken up this task before me, and I have tried to acknowledge that debt, here and throughout the book. Perhaps most of all, my work has benefited from those who have somehow managed to do both, and to do both well.

Madison, Wisconsin
January 1997

INTRODUCTION

People make their own history, but they do not make it just as they please; they do not make it under circumstances chosen by themselves, but under circumstances directly encountered, given and transmitted from the past.

KARL MARX

I was born a Lakota and I shall die a Lakota. Before the white man came to our country, the Lakotas were a free people.

MAHPIUA-LUTA (RED CLOUD)

HAU MITOKAYEPI. I am Russell Means, an Oglala, Lakota." With this traditional Lakota greeting, the Indian activist and alleged criminal Russell Means began the defense of what his attorney William Kunstler had predicted would be the "Indian trial of the twentieth century." Coming at the end of a remarkable time in history, the trial of Means and his co-defendant, Dennis Banks, would in fact turn out to be an extraordinary event. In 1974 these two leaders of the American Indian Movement (AIM), along with other Native American activists from urban areas and reservations, went on trial in federal courts across the upper midwest and plains states for their role in the 1973 protest and siege at Wounded Knee, South Dakota.

The events at Wounded Knee began on the night of February 27, when several hundred Native Americans led by Oglala traditional chiefs and members of AIM arrived at the historic village on the Pine Ridge Indian Reservation. From this place, the site of the 1890 massacre of Lakota (Sioux) Indians by the U.S. 7th Cavalry, the group issued a statement demanding hearings on the United States government's unilateral revocation of the 1868 Treaty with the Lakota and Cheyenne, and an investigation of corruption in the Bureau of Indian Affairs (BIA). The result was a 71-day standoff with federal law enforcement officers that ended with

562 arrests and 185 federal indictments. Yet, when the trials ended in late 1975, there had been only a handful of convictions, with few defendants spending any time in jail.

The siege at Wounded Knee was the culmination of several years of Indian activism, which included symbolic protests at Alcatraz Island and the BIA Office in Washington, D.C., and the rise to prominence of AIM and leaders such as Means, Banks, and Clyde and Vernon Bellecourt. The 1960s marked a new surge of Native American political activity, characterized by one scholar as the move from termination to self-determination.[1] As the Indian movement expanded through the decade, it included legislative lobbying, lawsuits, grass-roots organizing, and finally the more militant confrontational politics that had marked segments of the antiwar and the black power movement. Wounded Knee, the most publicized of the mass protests, provided Indian activists with an opportunity to voice their concerns to a wider audience.

By 1973 the Vietnam War was ending, the student left had already disintegrated, and the black power movement had been driven almost out of existence, leaving the action at Wounded Knee as perhaps the last militant mass protest of the "sixties," and AIM as the last mass-movement national group still engaging in confrontational politics. Many argued that the subsequent prosecutions were aimed at silencing or discrediting the Indian movement's most articulate and militant voices, rather than upholding the law. It was an accusation the government strongly denied. Yet by 1973 the government itself was disintegrating from within. Having adopted a siege mentality long before Wounded Knee, the Nixon administration was lashing out at its critics verbally, and also with force and intrigue. Whatever their motives in seeking to prosecute Indian activists, federal authorities were locked in a battle that would not be confined to the courtroom. This was a struggle not just for the hearts and minds of judges and juries, but for the hearts and minds of the audience outside the courtroom.

Of the seven leaders indicted for conspiracy, Banks and Means were singled out to be tried first. It was they who would speak for those who went to Wounded Knee, the Oglalas on Pine Ridge and their supporters, as well as for the Indian movement as a whole. Although scores of lesser-known defendants went to trial with little public attention, the trial of the two AIM leaders, which began on a wintry January day at the federal courthouse in Saint Paul, Minnesota, drew media and public scrutiny from around the country. There, before an audience of reporters and partisan AIM supporters, the prosecution focused its attention on the alleged violations of law: burglary, theft, assault, arson, and interference with federal officers in the performance of their duty. The government maintained that the proceedings were nothing more than a criminal trial which it intended to conduct according to the accepted rules of procedure—in effect, to try the case according to the expectations of the legal system and the general public. Outside the courtroom, however, the government had another message, one with roots more than a century old: that Banks and Means were renegades who did not speak for all Indians, and that the U.S. Congress, not the courts, was the proper venue for any legitimate grievances that Indians might have with respect to the reconsideration of treaties.

The defense meanwhile raised the whole history of U.S.-Indian relations, including broken treaties, conditions on reservations, and alleged corruption within the BIA, tying it all to government misconduct in Watergate. Throughout the ten-month trial the conflicting objectives of the two sides were shaped and reshaped by legal rules and procedures, by the way the media covered the trials, by events unfolding outside the courtroom that were part of the shifting political and social currents of the mid-1970s, and finally, by the combined histories of the participants themselves.

AIM and the defense committee began organizing a massive defense campaign from inside Wounded Knee and continued these efforts throughout the summer and fall of 1973. While it conducted crucial pretrial hearings, the committee recruited lawyers and legal workers, raised money, and formulated legal and political strategy. In Saint Paul, AIM and its attorneys sought from the beginning to subvert established courtroom practices by challenging the rules and procedures at every opportunity. They continually pushed for more leeway to present a broader story to the jury and to those covering the trial, attempting to expand the definition of who was on trial to include discussions of treaties, poverty, racism, and the struggle for cultural and economic survival. In addition, the defense went outside the courtroom at every opportunity, inundating the media with a continual stream of written and oral press statements on Indian history and current conditions, as well as speaking directly to people in schools, churches, community centers, and private homes.

By late 1975 when Saint Paul and the other trials had ended, the government's overall conviction rate for the cases was less than ten percent. By most measures AIM had won both the legal and the political war. In the wake of Wounded Knee and the trials, funding for Indian programs received more attention in Congress. Many Indians credited AIM with providing them with a stronger voice and opening their eyes to their own history and culture, while many whites said that the movement had helped educate them about history, as well as current conditions. Many of those who had been at Wounded Knee and worked on the trials continued to work for change in cities and on reservations. "The basic fact of American political life—that without money or force there is no change—impressed itself upon Indians as they watched the civil rights movement," the Native American scholar Vine Deloria wrote in 1974, "and the old fear of reprisal, which had plagued previous Indian efforts to change conditions, was partially dissipated."[2]

Yet, despite these advances, by the end of 1975 the Indian movement had lost its momentum. Although local work continued, AIM had ceased to be a force as a national organization. The long trials and the continued surveillance by various law enforcement agencies had drained the organization of time, money, and energy.[3] Even the victories in court and the successful publicity campaign that surrounded the cases were affected by courtroom rules, media bias, and at times the biases of the participants themselves, all of which worked to limit, misinterpret, or misdirect the message that the defense tried to present in and outside the courtroom. The old stereotypes of male warriors or, alternately, "victims" without agency and without hope, and the portrayal of AIM and its attorneys as part of the militancy of the sixties, were images that were often reinforced during the trials at the same time as points were being made concerning U.S.-Indian relations.

AIM, its defense committee, and its supporters had orchestrated one of the most successful mass defense efforts in history and had turned the trial of Banks and Means into a political forum as dramatic as any ever witnessed in a U.S. courtroom. Yet there existed throughout the trials, as there has throughout the whole history of Indian-white relations, a gulf that separated this difficult and complex history from its retelling, from its reception in a white man's world. The defendants were faced with the task of finding a language that would describe the importance of the Native American experience for Native Americans, in words that those who had not lived that history could understand. This is the experience of many people who are thrust into an arena of conflict and judgment controlled by procedural rules and precedents not of their making, a situation where a wrong is rendered unexplainable, a conflict unresolvable, because of the lack of a phrase which could explain the wrong done to one party in the language of the other.[4]

In 1879, Heinmot Tooyalaket (Chief Joseph) of the Nez Percé traveled to Washington to explain his people's attachment to their homeland in Oregon and the reasons they did not wish to sell it. Members of the U.S. Congress listened politely but refused to reexamine the treaties which the

Chief claimed his people had not consented to. Instead Joseph was taken into custody by the military and eventually was transferred to the Colville Reservation in Washington State, where he died without ever returning to his homeland.[5] Nearly a century later, in 1972, a thousand Native Americans from across the country also traveled to the nation's capital, in a caravan known as the Trail of Broken Treaties, to present a twenty-point petition aimed at addressing the problems of the Indian community. The government response rejecting the twenty points, Vine Deloria would later write, "[displayed] a lack of understanding of the history of the relationship between the United States and the aboriginal Indian tribes of the North American continent."[6]

The inability to understand, the unwillingness to acknowledge another version of history, is the first step toward the domination of a people. As Jean-François Lyotard argues, the perfect crime is achieved when the witnesses have been silenced—when a wrong has been done and then the language by which the victims might describe this wrong in their own terms has also been taken from them. Indigenous peoples were often the victims of just such a "perfect crime": they suffered the loss of life, of land, of the means of subsistence, and finally, through schools and churches, the attempt to rob them of their memory, the memory of their language, and their cultural traditions.[7]

Writing of the Holocaust, Maurice Blanchot speaks of a horror so unimaginable that words seem to only trivialize the experience, yet he concludes that words are all we have, an offering to the past and the present, a means to react to "a time so frightful, so dangerous, that any recourse appears justified."[8] Anyone seeking to write the history of the Wounded Knee trials must confront many of the same problems as the defendants confronted in telling their version of their own history, including the history that they themselves were making.[9] For this is not a history exclusive to Native Americans; it is also the experience of Africans enslaved in a foreign land and forbidden to learn how to read or write, or of survivors attempting to relate the horror of the Holocaust to those who ask for proof of its existence. It could be anyone attempting to explain to another in words that convey the intimacy of the wrong done to them, in a language the other can understand. How do the descendants of the original inhabitants of North America explain to another culture the essence for them of the losses, the millions of people dead of disease, starvation, and warfare, the vast continent of land taken from them, the loss of existence itself? How do historians record it when they cannot?

At Fort Robinson, Nebraska, in 1877, the Oglala leader Tashunka Witko (Crazy Horse) was said to have uttered these final words to Indian Agent

Jesse M. Lee: "I came here with the agent to talk with Big White Chief, but was not given a chance. They tried to confine me, I tried to escape, and a soldier ran his bayonet into me. I have spoken."[10] Thirteen years later two hundred more Lakota lay dead, frozen in the December snow near the village of Wounded Knee. Standing near the mass grave of his ancestors in March 1973, Russell Means brought that past into the present for himself, for those who had come with him to Wounded Knee, and for anyone who might hear his voice: "The white man says that the 1890 massacre was the end of the wars with the Indian, that it was the end of the Indian, the end of the Ghost Dance. Yet here we are at war, we're still Indians, and we're Ghost Dancing again."[11]

In 1890 when the soldiers converged on the Dakotas to crush the Ghost Dance, they brought with them an entourage of photographers and reporters to record the spectacle of the last shred of Indian resistance on the great plains. The images that made their way back east were of a final battle with the hostiles and a redemptive victory for the 7th Cavalry. Wounded Knee and the Little Big Horn became tourist attractions, and Cody's Wild West Show replayed the epic battles to the delight of urban audiences across the country. While public policy and popular culture reshaped the surface realities and images of Indian life, past and present, Indian resistance took the form of stories and rituals passed in secret from generation to generation. During the 1960s the resistance had gone public again, but the task of telling stories remained.

The Wounded Knee defendants were faced with the task of communicating their history to a vast unknown audience, an audience that was often the recipient of stereotypical images and misinformation about Native Americans, about the period of upheaval of the 1960s, and about the nature and fairness of the criminal justice system. Further, they had to overcome these biases through media over which they had only limited control. But the task of accounting for this past falls not just to the survivors, or their descendants; it also lies with those who write about the historical events they did not live, who, like the survivors, must attempt to relate to new and skeptical audiences what it was that happened. And historians, too, must communicate through media they do not fully control, confined by their own biases, by the conflicts within the historical record, and ultimately by those same filters of past and present prejudices that readers will bring to the text.

The record that historians must interpret has often been left by those who were forced to struggle over cultural and political meanings according to rules and in languages that were not native to them. Courtroom participants or the historical actors may be confident in their understanding of an event, but that does not mean that they are able to communicate that understanding through the trial transcript or the historical record.[12] "Doesn't anyone speak Injun in this courtroom?" asked a Colorado judge in 1969, when told that the two Native American defendants before her did not speak or understand English.[13] Facing similar obstacles in their 1976 lawsuit to recover tribal lands, the Mashpee Indians of Cape Cod were forced to prove their very existence according to U.S. legal precedents—to demonstrate, in effect, that they were an Indian tribe according to the laws of non-Indians. As the experience of the Mashpee illustrates, courtroom stories are often constricted by rules of evidence that determine what is "relevant," thus privileging one narrative over another.[14]

The legitimacy of one's story may rely on an attorney's ability to navigate the rules of the court, just as one's history may rely on the writer's ability to find phrases and meanings beyond what could be communicated at the time of the events in question. The writer must attempt to comprehend the past in the language of those who lived it, while also uncovering aspects of the struggle which may have been suppressed because of the lack of a contemporary idiom, and for which the intervening times may have offered a new language. Thus the writer, the historian, must find idioms with which to explain the past in words that maintain the integrity of both the past and the present.[15]

In my narrative of the trials, I emphasize the spoken record and people's later reflections on that record. Sources include trial transcripts, legal motions and briefs, jury studies, correspondence, publicity, and information contained in the FBI files pertaining to AIM and Wounded Knee. I contrast this information with national and local coverage of the trials in newspapers, news magazines, and on network television. Finally, I interviewed more than thirty participants, including White House officials, judges, prosecutors, defense attorneys, legal workers, and defendants. It is a historical record that is conflicting and contradictory, within itself and with the memories of those who participated in the events, as in turn those memories are in conflict with each other. The narrative that weaves these conflicting stories together is not intended to provide a single truth, or *the* definitive history of the trials. What I hope to do is amplify voices from the past and identify the structures and procedures that altered or silenced those voices, both as the events unfolded and over the course of time.

Courtroom rules, media bias, and the defendants' strategy all acted as filters on the way the Wounded Knee trials were presented to the public. Interpretations of political or popular trials need to reach beyond questions of guilt and innocence, whether the defendant received a fair trial, or whether the politics of the case affected the proceedings.[16] The symbolism of a highly visible trial can reinforce or challenge popular perceptions of the criminal justice system, but it also can reinforce dominant preconceptions about groups of people, their politics, and the lives they lead. There is strong evidence that the government used its might to silence AIM, legally and extralegally, as it had done with other dissident political groups. The threat to "justice," however, may not be confined to the excessive use of state power; it is not solely a question of due process or free speech, though they were certainly issues in the AIM trials. There must also be concern for the narratives that emerge in the courtroom, the stories about people and events that are shaped by legal language and media perceptions based on class, race, ethnic, or gender bias, stories that in turn shape or reinforce the public's view of history and current events, and the people involved in each.[17]

Defendants and their attorneys may find ways to subvert or circumvent the accepted language and procedural rules of the courtroom—to, in effect, use the system against itself in order to put before the judge and jury testimony that goes beyond the standard questions of guilt and innocence. But getting one's politics before the jury is only one part of the process. Any full discussion of political trials requires substantial information on events outside the courtroom. Only a small percentage of the populace can attend such trials, and a slightly larger number perhaps may get handed a leaflet or attend a public speech. The majority of those interested in the issues being contested in the courtroom must get their information from news coverage, making both the actors and the audience subject to the media's ability to influence public opinion concerning who society's heroes and villains are.[18]

As Todd Gitlin illustrates in his study of the new left in the 1960s, the media are particularly powerful in shaping people's view of the world around them. Through "selections and omissions, through emphases and tones," he argues, the mass media are "a significant social force in the forming and delimiting of public assumptions, attitudes, and moods—of ideology, in short."[19] The "spectacle" constituted by the media, Murray Edelman writes, "continuously constructs and reconstructs social problems, crises, enemies, and leaders and so creates a succession of threats and reassurances."[20] This "spectacle" then is part of the whole of society, an instrument of unification and stability.[21]

Stuart Hall contends that modern media have empowered cultures on the margins of society, making them better able to compete in the ideological struggle, yet he too warns about the dangers.[22] During the "Chicago

Seven" trials, the media portrayed the defendants as counterculture celebrities, focusing on the trial as entertainment, while framing the legal issues as the constitutionality of the federal anti-riot statute and whether the defendants received a fair trial. This, coupled with the judge's restrictive rulings on what could be entered into evidence, severely limited the defendants' ability to turn the trial into a forum on the Vietnam War.[23]

As Gitlin observes, when society becomes increasingly vulnerable to, and dependant on, the media, it becomes almost impossible for a movement both to stay in the spotlight and to maintain its integrity: "In a floodlit society, it becomes extremely difficult, perhaps unimaginable, for an opposition movement to define itself and its world view, to build up an infrastructure of self-generated cultural institutions, outside the dominant culture."[24] Subordinated groups struggling in the public arena, as Lucie White argues, "must create cultural practices through which they can elaborate an autonomous, oppositional consciousness."[25] Self-sustaining autonomous cultural practices, however, may not be enough to enable one to communicate through the barriers inherent in a highly visible political or legal struggle. It is possible for a movement to say too much about its own oppression, providing the very institutions of that oppression with greater access to the terms and desires through which the movement can be motivated and therefore disciplined.[26]

If one views the Wounded Knee trials as a media battle between AIM and the Nixon administration, which had always sought to manipulate and tame the media, AIM and its supporters probably won, but not without costs. AIM had learned to use the media to its advantage in the early stages of Wounded Knee, yet in doing so, they sometimes traded on America's fascination with the image of the male warrior. In Saint Paul, defense committee efforts resulted in successful propaganda and fund-raising campaigns, but AIM and its lawyers were still bounded by their own vision of history and the biases of reporters and the public. The portrayal of the Chicago Seven defendants in the media is similar to that of Banks and Means, each situation a more moderate version of the media depictions of world leaders such as Fidel Castro, Mu'ammar Qaddafi, or Yasser Arafat. In each of these instances U.S. political leaders helped fuel the extreme media characterizations, and in each case the targets of those characterizations, wittingly or unwittingly, played a role in the negative press coverage. "Your eyes provoked us and you'd turned us into stars, we responded to your hopes and expectations," a Palestine Liberation Organization soldier told Jean Genet in 1972, explaining how they had adopted "heroic" and "attractive" poses for the European audience: "But you'd turned us into monsters, too. You called us terrorists!"[27]

The sexual overtones of Genet's account are not accidental. Inherent to these questions of communicating history or political messages to mass audiences are gender dynamics, which played a role in the political development of AIM, in the Wounded Knee defense committee, and in the conduct of the legal proceedings and the press coverage of those proceedings. In Saint Paul the media portraits of the well-known male defendants and their equally famous male attorneys, William Kunstler and Mark Lane, drew on already fixed images of the white male militants of the sixties and the stereotypical Indian warriors of Hollywood films. These same images of masculinity were cultivated by the participants themselves and then accentuated in the media, reinforcing old stereotypes and at times overshadowing more important issues.

The focus on the dress of the defendants, on the militant aspect of their politics, and on stereotypical images of Indians was only partially within their control. The media's predilection for both commenting on the physical characteristics of newsmakers and reporting street actions over courtroom actions, and their bias in favor of the images of Indians that they, like almost everyone else, had grown up with, would probably have played a role in the coverage regardless of how the defendants or their lawyers acted or dressed.[28] At various times during the proceedings, Banks and Means were referred to as "militants," "insurgents," "tall, graceful, bronzed," and "modern day Sitting Bulls." For the defendants and their supporters, men and women, it was often a question of priorities, choices to be made at a critical time based on the alternatives that circumstances presented them with.[29] Those choices—what they said and how they presented themselves in and outside the courtroom—influenced how the press and the public would view the Indian movement, and Indian people as a whole.

Indian women played a significant role in AIM, as activists at Pine Ridge and during the protest at Wounded Knee. They were also, along with a significant number of white women, integral to the work of the defense committee, in some cases while facing trials of their own. Yet the dominant male presence in Saint Paul and the contentious nature of the courtroom proceedings, coupled with the discussions of Indian manhood on reservations and the meaning of women in Indian culture, helped to reinforce certain presumptions and stereotypes concerning women in the movement, which mirrored attitudes toward gender roles in society as a whole.[30] As in other organizations of the left, the Student Non-violent Coordinating Committee and Students for a Democratic Society for example, little was done to counter what was seen as normal with respect to images of women.[31]

Another factor that influenced the media's focus as the trials progressed was the defense's effort to elicit testimony on the history of mistreatment of Indians, including, in the words of one defense attorney, "the totality of government misconduct" as evidenced by its armed response to the Wounded Knee protest. As the trial of Banks and Means progressed into the spring and summer months of 1974, the FBI's mishandling of Wounded Knee evidence, together with the unfolding intrigues in the nation's capital surrounding the Watergate investigations, provided the defense with an opportunity to strengthen its attack on government wrongdoing by tying the courtroom proceedings more closely to the headlines coming out of Washington. Defense attorneys seeking information on strategy and decision making with regard to the use of force and the role of the U.S. military at Wounded Knee subpoenaed the White House tapes, and even discussed calling former President Richard Nixon to the stand after he had resigned in August. At times the effort was so successful that government wrongdoing in general replaced Indian-white relations as the central topic of discussion, in and outside of the courtroom.

Whatever its mistakes, AIM succeeded in putting Indians on the national agenda. The Indian movement that began in the late 1960s in the wake of the civil rights, antiwar, and black power movements may have been a victim of the times as much as a victim of government harassment and its own political errors. One could argue that by the end of 1975, when the trials related to Wounded Knee had ended, no politically left mass movements were still having an impact on a national scale. The women's and gay rights movements were still on the national scene, but they were far from unified, and both had moved away from demonstrations and protests as their primary tactics.[32]

Still, the government's constitutional response to the protest—its decision to prosecute a vast number of political dissidents—played a significant role in curtailing the Indian movement in the mid-1970s, not by winning convictions, but by forcing the political struggle into the courtroom. Although the law is not the final arbiter of social and political conflict, it is a powerful forum that can contribute to the shaping of identities, cultures, and histories. It is an arena where rules and procedures can favor certain interpretations over others, and where one of the parties, the government, may determine the procedures to be followed, as well as the ultimate outcome. To struggle in such arenas, where what is at stake may reach far beyond verdicts of guilt or innocence, to make oneself heard through the barriers of another's rules, another's language, often takes a tremendous organized effort—one that is difficult to sustain over a long period of time, and that may not be able to counter all the wrongs that need to be addressed.

This retelling of the story of the trials also attempts to confront the dual question of what constitutes history and what makes it relevant to the understanding and lives of those who did not live it. In Douglas Coupland's popular novel of the 1980s generation, one of the characters responds to a question from his younger brother, who asks why he would want to visit a memorial to a war (Vietnam) that was over before he had even reached puberty, by saying, "I come here to see a color that I can't see anywhere else any more." The character then thinks to himself:

> They *were* ugly times. But they were also the only times I'll ever get— genuine capital *H* history times, before *history* was turned into a press release, a marketing strategy, and a cynical campaign tool. And *hey*, it's not as if I got to see much real history, either—I arrived to see a concert in history's arena just as the final set was finishing. But I saw enough, and today, in the bizarre absence of all time cues, I need a connection to a past of some importance, however wan the connection.[33]

But who makes these connections? What, or who, determines the relevance of the past to the present?

When Indian activists took to the national political stage near the end of the 1960s, they attempted to rewrite a history that politicians and reformers, artists and writers, had spent a century trying to both mythologize and eradicate. In doing so they made choices concerning what from the unwritten past they wished to reclaim for themselves and what they wished to convey to non-Indians with whom they wished to communicate, either as allies in their struggle or as representatives of the government with which they sought to renegotiate the legal relationships that bound them together.[34] The choices that they made, however, the new history that they wrote, was never totally free from the old images and stereotypes of the past, any more than it was free from the new images and stereotypes of political activists and dissenters being created in the emerging interpretations of the cultural and political upheavals of the period labeled "the sixties."[35]

The narratives that we construct today are as bound by the past and the present as were the actors and events we wish to describe. We objectively sift through the pieces of evidence that we gather and select, determining what are the most important ideas to be transcribed onto the page, all according to our own "encountered circumstances." We may be able to put into words and phrases what we now "see," but it is still left to others to find new silences under future circumstances. This book is an attempt to describe how law and language can shape the past, to present something of what has previously been left out of the historical record. Silences will remain, awaiting future idioms to articulate them in a common language.

THE ROAD TO WOUNDED KNEE

There is a time appointed to all things. Think for a moment how many multitudes of the animal tribes we have destroyed; look upon the snow that appears today— tomorrow it is water. Listen to the dirge of the dry leaves, that were green and vigorous but a few moons before. We are a part of that life and it seems that our time has come.

SPOTTED TAIL, CHIEF,
BRÛLÉ, LAKOTA, 1881

The white man says that the 1890 massacre was the end of the wars with the Indian, that it was the end of the Indian, the end of the Ghost Dance. Yet here we are at war, we're still Indians, and we're Ghost Dancing again.

RUSSELL MEANS,
OGLALA, LAKOTA-SIOUX, 1973

IN JANUARY 1974, Russell Means and Dennis Banks placed a replica of the Treaty of 1868 on the defense table in the federal court house in Saint Paul and kept it there throughout their ten-month trial. For many in the modern Indian movement, the agreement signed at Fort Laramie symbolized all of the treaties and agreements negotiated between Native Americans and the United States from 1778 to 1871.[1] The Treaty of 1868 had promised a permanent peace between the Lakota and the United States, but a century later both sides were still at war.

At Wounded Knee in 1973 the history of the Lakota resistance became intertwined with the modern militancy of the 1960s and the group known as AIM. Traditional leader Frank Fools Crow, an Oglala who had lived his life on Pine Ridge, and AIM leader Russell Means, also an Oglala but one who had spent most of his life in cities, sought to unite past and present and to communicate the importance of that union—the message that the struggle for self-determination and survival of the Lakota had not ended in 1890—to Indians and whites across the country. Wounded Knee in 1973 was as much about history as it was about the conflicts of the early 1970s.

The 1868 agreement was one of the last treaties negotiated by the U.S. government with Native Americans. During the first few decades of its existence, the United States had shifted from "careful diplomacy" with some of its more powerful neighbors to a policy of conquest and colonization based on military and numerical superiority.[2] The Indian Removal Act of 1830 and the forced displacement of tribes from the Ohio and Mississippi valleys signaled the beginning of the end of the treaty-making era. Had it not been for the military strength of the Lakota, the period might have ended sooner. When a commission headed west to seek peace in 1868, it was not the first time the plains Indians had forced the U.S. government to the negotiating table.

The Lakota or Teton Sioux, who had first appeared on the edge of the plains in the early 1700s, had expanded westward out of Minnesota through the Dakota territories to the Yellowstone River and south into what is now Nebraska. Having acquired guns from the French, they became the dominant trappers and traders on the prairie, eventually turning their attention to the acquisition of horses and the hunting of buffalo. By 1850 white travel and trade across the plains had reduced the great buffalo herds, increasing the intertribal warfare among the plains Indians and endangering white migration.[3]

A treaty in 1851 designated boundaries for several plains tribes, including the Lakota, and promised protection from the encroachment of white settlers, government annuities for fifty years, and "a lasting peace between all the nations assembled." The Lakota, however, could not agree among themselves about the treaty's terms, and they ignored the boundaries and went on living much as they had. If the treaty signified anything, it was that the Americans and the Lakota had become the major powers on the plains. Within a few years the two nations were again at war, and renewed negotiations in 1865 brought only more unfulfilled promises of lasting peace.[4]

The commission sent to Fort Laramie in 1868 was yet another attempt to solve the problem of the Sioux. The agreement signed there and ratified by the U.S. Congress in 1869 designated a large area of the plains to be "set apart for the absolute and undisturbed use and occupation of the Indians herein named." The agreement also required the United States to abandon the Bozeman Trail, a road established in 1866 that had brought increasing numbers of settlers and prospectors through the Indian hunting grounds in what is now Montana. For their part, the Lakota finally agreed to some defined boundaries.

These new boundaries included an area of "unceded Indian territory" which stretched from the Missouri River through the western half of what is now South Dakota, into the Big Horn mountains in Wyoming territory, and from the Canadian border south into Nebraska. The western half of South Dakota, including the sacred Paha Sapa or Black Hills, was designated as the "Great Sioux Reservation." It was there that the government intended to establish an agency, issue rations, provide medical care and education, and teach the Indians how to support themselves by farming. The land outside the reservation, including the vast hunting grounds along the Powder River, was to remain in Indian hands only "so long as the buffalo may range thereon in such numbers as to justify the chase."

The terms of the agreement, however, were in dispute from the beginning. U.S. policymakers may have viewed the Treaty of 1868 as a first step toward turning the Sioux into self-sufficient farmers, but at least half the Lakota remained off the reservation on their traditional hunting grounds.[5] While whites believed that the end of the buffalo was inevitable, the Lakota considered the buffalo and the land as one, and any talk of their extinction while the people and the land still existed was meaningless. Neither side could comprehend what for the other were the indisputable truths of life.[6]

In 1870 the Oglala Chief Red Cloud joined a Lakota delegation who traveled to Washington to meet with Indian Bureau officials, members of Congress, and President Ulysses Grant. The delegation arrived on June 1 to great fanfare and ceremony, including a state dinner at the White House that the *New York Times* called "as elegant as that given to Prince Arthur last summer." In discussions over the terms of the two-year-old treaty, however, differences surfaced immediately, and Red Cloud even denied knowledge of the document. What he had agreed to, said the Chief, was peace, after the government had withdrawn its soldiers; now he was ready to commit to further peace, in exchange for the removal of additional soldiers from the plains.

After two weeks of inconclusive meetings, the delegation moved on to New York, where thousands of people lined Fifth Avenue to catch a glimpse of the famous Oglala leader. The next day at Cooper Union, Red Cloud spoke to a packed auditorium of curious citizens and devoted Indian reformers. Pausing after each sentence while an interpreter relayed his words to the audience, he spoke about the difficulty of communicating Lakota desires to peacefully retain their traditional lands to the officials in Washington: "I have sent a great many words to the Great Father but they never reached him. They were drowned on the way, and I was afraid the words I spoke lately to the great Father would not reach you, so I came to speak to you myself; and now I am going away to my home."[7]

The speech was well received, but the appearances in Washington and New York had little effect on Indian policy. The continued dispute over the terms of the treaty was causing many officials to conclude that the era of diplomacy should end. In 1871 a rider to an appropriation bill provided that "no Indian nation or tribe within the territory of the United States shall be acknowledged or recognized as an independent nation, tribe, or power with whom the United States may contract by treaty."[8]

As settlers continued to arrive in Sioux country, reformers convinced themselves that the only way to save the plains Indians was to take their land, making them wards of the state and eventually turning them into fully assimilated U.S. citizens. In 1874, after an expedition led by George Armstrong Custer confirmed the reports of gold in the Black Hills, another delegation was sent to negotiate the sale of the sacred mountains, but several Lakota leaders, including Red Cloud and Crazy Horse, refused to attend the meeting. The government responded by claiming the hills, issuing a directive restricting the Sioux to the reservation, and ceasing any attempts to keep settlers and prospectors out of Lakota lands.

In the spring of 1876, troops were sent to pursue Indians who refused to come onto the reservation, particularly the Hunkpapa of Sitting Bull and the Oglala of Red Cloud. These two bands were soon joined by groups of Miniconjou, Blackfoot, and Sans Arc Lakota, as well as bands of Cheyenne and Arapaho. Near the end of June as Americans gathered for their centennial celebration, the news of a devastating military defeat reached Philadelphia. But the battles won by the Indians over the 7th Cavalry that summer on the rolling hills near Greasy Grass Creek only brought more soldiers and an end to the armed resistance.[9]

On August 15, 1876, Congress directed that all assistance be cut off to the Sioux unless they relinquished the Black Hills and all land outside the reservation. In September, a defeated Red Cloud joined other Lakota in signing the papers that ceded 22.5 million acres of land, including the Black Hills. Later the Oglala Chief said he did not understand what he had signed away, but Indian misgivings about the terms were of little concern to those sent to negotiate the agreement written in English. The commission left after collecting only 10 percent of the required signatures under the terms of the 1868 Treaty, which provided that no cession of any part of the reservation could be valid unless agreed to by at least three-fourths of the adult males.[10]

Twelve years later in 1888, Congress authorized the division of the Sioux Reservation into six reserves and the sale of surplus land for settlement by whites. This time when a commission arrived, they found Red Cloud strongly opposed to the proposal, and officials attempted to bypass him and any organized opposition by dealing with people in small groups. In fact, there was little in the way of negotiations. General George Crook assured the Sioux that they would never again receive better terms and that it was time for them to stop dwelling on the past and start providing for their future. In the end, the Lakota reluctantly agreed to the land cessions and the new reservations.[11]

The Great Sioux Reservation and the unceded territory provided for under the 1868 Treaty had been reduced to six reservations in western South Dakota: Standing Rock, Cheyenne River, Lower Brûlé, Crow Creek, Rosebud, and Pine Ridge. Government officials and reformers alike believed they had done the right thing. The agreement would provide the Sioux with compensation for their land, a secure place to live, and government assistance in the coming years, all of which, it was hoped, would facilitate the peaceful advancement of white civilization.[12] To help ensure against any future opposition by Red Cloud and others, U.S. officials planned to deprive the old chief "of any authority from the Government of any kind or any recognition as a man of any importance."[13]

The promise of a rapid move toward acculturation, however, did not come to pass. Instead the land cessions and relocation onto the reservations had destroyed the Lakota way of life, without any genuine consideration of how they would cope with the attempted transformation. The move toward farming proceeded poorly, and reductions in Indian appropriations added to the worsening situation. "Despair came again," said Red Cloud, whose people seemed on the verge of a total cultural and spiritual collapse.[14]

Then in 1889, rumors reached the Lakota of a god who had come to earth to save his children and ensure a return to the old way of life. In March 1890, Lakota emissaries, including Kicking Bear, returned from Nevada to report that the messiah was real, a Paiute prophet named Wovoka who promised that all Indians who embraced his faith would see the return of dead warriors and the vast buffalo herds to a regenerated earth, where all tribes would live forever in peace and prosperity free of white people. Indians, he counseled, were to cease hostility toward whites and focus instead on dancing the prescribed "Ghost Dance."

Though Wovoka advocated peace and promised the removal of whites by supernatural means, Kicking Bear's powerful oratory took on a somewhat more militant tone. Lakotas were told not to listen to whites who tried to discourage participation in the dance and were given "ghost shirts" that would protect them from the white man's gunpowder, while at the same time enabling Indian powder to "burn and kill" when directed at whites.[15] As reservation crops dried out in the dry winds of summer, the number of Ghost Dancers grew, on Cheyenne River, Rosebud, Pine Ridge, and finally Standing Rock, where Sitting Bull, though he remained skeptical, presided over the ceremonies. The millennium, the Lakota were told, would come in the spring, after a winter of dancing. As the dances grew more intense, the concern of reservation agents reached Washington. Then on November 12, two hundred armed Oglalas reportedly prevented an arrest by Indian police on Pine Ridge. Three days later the Indian agent telegraphed the Commissioner of Indian Affairs in Washington: "Indians are dancing in the snow and are wild and crazy. I have fully informed you that employees and government property at this agency have no protection and are at the mercy of these dancers."[16]

From Pine Ridge, Agent Daniel Royer bombarded the Indian Office with emotional appeals that heightened the concern in Washington and helped fuel the spreading hysteria among whites in the surrounding area. Whatever the threat posed by a few Ghost Dancers chasing away an agent or an Indian police officer, the situation was made worse by the sensational press accounts that prompted fears of renewed fighting on the plains. Heavily armed troops soon arrived to assist Indian police in carrying out orders to isolate the dancers and arrest the principal leaders if necessary.

On December 14, Indian police reported that Sitting Bull was preparing to travel to the Ghost Dance "stronghold" near Pine Ridge, where Kicking Bear, Short Bull, and the most zealous of the Lakota faithful had taken refuge. The next day the Hunkpapa leader was killed by Indian police while being taken into custody outside his cabin on the Standing Rock Reservation. Fearing for his people's safety, Big Foot, with approximately three hundred forty Miniconjou Lakota, left the Cheyenne River Reservation and headed across the Badlands to seek refuge on Pine Ridge. Intercepted by Custer's old regiment on December 28, the starving Ghost Dancers were herded together at Wounded Knee Creek, where three hundred men, women, and children died in an eruption of gunfire while being disarmed the next morning. More Lakota were killed in the weeks that followed, as officials attempted to force others who had fled back onto their reservations.[17]

Whether the Ghost Dance marked a possible return to armed resistance or simply the exercise of religious freedom, as Sitting Bull had maintained, it was quickly transformed into part of the spectacle of the triumph of Christian civilization over the once savage wilderness of the west. When the soldiers arrived on the Sioux reservations to contain the Ghost Dance outbreak, "war correspondents" and photographers traveled with them to record the last gasp of Indian resistance on the plains. Sitting Bull's cabin was removed and reconstructed as part of the North Dakota state exhibition at the 1892 Chicago World's Fair, where Buffalo Bill's Wild West Show opened with a procession led by the Hunkpapa spiritual leader's horse, bearing a rider carrying the American flag.[18] The "battle" of Wounded Knee joined "Custer's last stand" as part of the show's repertoire.

In the decades to come, the cultural war waged on the Lakota by Indian reformers attacked their spiritual beliefs and practices, their social and political structures—everything that constituted them as a people, including their history. Laws, administrative policies, and media stories, as well as art, literature, and "American history," all contributed to the continuing campaign.

By the time the military interceded to curtail the Ghost Dance movement, the period of assimilation and allotment for Native Americans was in full swing. Three years earlier in 1887, Congress had approved legislation that would serve as the basis for federal Indian policy until the New Deal. The General Allotment Act (Dawes Act), which authorized the breaking up of reservations into individual plots, was to be "a pathway for the legal, economic, and social integration of Native Americans into the United States."[19] The act designated 160 acres for each head of a family and 80 acres for each dependent, with the surplus land to be sold for white settlement and development.

Despite protests from Indian leaders, policymakers hoped that the ownership of private property would have a civilizing effect on the Indian and serve as a first step toward U.S. citizenship. Some even hailed the new legislation as the Indian emancipation proclamation. "True ideas of property with all the civilizing influences that such ideas incite," remarked one reformer in 1885, "are formed only as the tribal relation is outgrown."[20] Over the next forty-seven years, 60 million acres, roughly forty percent of all Indian land, was declared surplus and opened to white settlement. Land that continued to be held in trust was often leased to whites, who, it was hoped, would put it to productive use, thus serving as an example for the neighboring Indian tribes. More often, they stripped the land of its natural resources and moved on.[21]

Meanwhile, legislation and administrative directives sought to eradicate all Sioux traditions: hunting, living in bands, the role of traditional leaders, and their migration across a vast territory according to the season. The "disintegration" of their tribal life, argued Secretary of the Interior John Noble, would help the Sioux move toward "civilized habits."[22] Missionaries and educators set about erecting churches and schools, while the government supplied food, clothing, and farming equipment, drew up a list of "Indian offenses," and set up reservation police forces and courts to help impose a system of surveillance and control over the most minute details of reservation life. Traditional Indian dress and ceremonies such as the Sun Dance, a major yearly ritual practiced by many plains Indian tribes, along with other "relics of barbarism," were banned. Use of the Lakota language was discouraged, and Indian children were sent to boarding schools as far away as Pennsylvania.[23]

"Total assimilation," writes Frederick Hoxie, "was a goal that combined concern for native suffering with faith in the promise of America." If successful, assimilation would save the Indian as well as reaffirm the dominance of the White Protestant majority and "the power of the nation's institutions to mold all people to a common standard."[24]

In 1891 the Commissioner of Indian Affairs instructed all Sioux agents to make it clear to their wards that any new resistance would result in "severe punishment, great loss, and take away from them the sympathy of their friends and of all the people of the United States."[25] As the end of the century neared, the destruction of Oglala traditions seemed almost complete. Chief Frank Fools Crow, one of the traditionalists who would inspire the protest at Wounded Knee in 1973, could remember the building of stores and schools by the government and the abandonment of farms for a house in town, as the white population increased around the borders of the reservation. "The flood had begun," said Fools Crow, "and the traditional life-way dam was so weakened it could not hold it."[26]

The eradication of spiritual and cultural traditions, however, was never fully completed. Many reservations, as Hoxie notes, became cultural homelands, where "native identity could be maintained and passed on to new generations."[27] For some like Fools Crow, maintaining those traditions was still tied to old attitudes about the land and to the treaty negotiated in 1868. In 1909 the Lakota petitioned the U.S. government for compensation for a pony herd taken after the victory over Custer. The claim was refused, but the group decided to pursue additional claims under the 1868 Treaty. In 1918 they hired a lawyer who eventually filed twenty-one separate lawsuits on behalf of his clients.[28]

After the turn of the century, different interests began to push individual Indians to sell their allotments, and Congress passed legislation authorizing the removal of trust restrictions from millions of acres of individual plots. When the Allotment Act finally ended, Indians had lost approximately 90 million out of 150 million acres of land. Tens of thousands of Native Americans were now landless, without decent housing or adequate medical care (if indeed they had either in any form), and mired in poverty. On Pine Ridge, where mortality rates soared, the Oglala were kept busy farming, though it remained a nonproductive endeavor.[29] Meanwhile, Congress and the courts debated and redefined Indian citizenship into a version of federal guardianship that applied to tribes as well as individual Indians.[30] By the end of the 1920s the Americanization program had waned, and Indian policy was about to undergo another shift, one that would have a profound impact on the decades to come.

Among the reformers who entered government service as part of the New Deal under Franklin Roosevelt was John Collier, director of the American Indian Defense Association and one of the Interior Department's most outspoken critics. Appointed the new Commissioner of Indian Affairs, Collier was intent on changing the entire direction of federal policy toward Native Americans by returning self-rule to reservation Indians. In the early months of his tenure, the new commissioner placed a moratorium on the sale of tribal land, issued directives regarding religious and cultural freedom, ended compulsory attendance for Indian children at religious services in boarding schools, and gave reservations control over their tribal courts.[31]

Collier's most far-reaching accomplishment, however, was the passage of the Indian Reorganization Act (IRA) in 1934. He and the other New Deal reformers believed that the IRA would restore cultural self-determination to Native Americans and the "bilateral relationship" between Indians and the U.S. government. The act abolished the allotment system, set up a credit fund to provide loans to tribes for economic development, and gave Indians residing on reservations the right to organize tribal governments by adopting a constitution and electing tribal officials. Reformers saw the IRA as a progressive step toward sovereignty, but the promised "self-government" was subject to government rules and guidelines, and, ultimately, to the approval of the Office of Indian Affairs (OIA).[32] In addition, although the new constitutional structures were similar to the traditions of some tribes, they were completely foreign to others. Traditionalists rejected all these measures as another attempt to impose white institutions on Indian tribes.[33]

Despite the criticism, however, the IRA was seen by many Indians as an opportunity for badly needed change. Across the country, 174 tribes voted to accept reorganization, while 78 rejected it. Of the Indians eligible to vote, 39 percent had voted for the act and 25 percent had voted no, while 36 percent who had not voted at all were counted as having voted yes.[34] In 1934 Pine Ridge joined five other Sioux reservations in accepting reorganization; slightly more than 25 percent of the eligible Oglalas voted 1,169 to 1,075 in favor of adopting a new constitution.[35]

On Pine Ridge reorganization brought mixed-blood and "progressive" full-bloods to power, whom traditionalists accused of favoring assimilation and being insensitive to traditional values. The traditionalists, or "old dealers," viewed the new government as culturally alien and a violation of treaty rights imposed on them by the OIA.[36] Oglalas who were now landless and unemployed began to gather around the town of Pine Ridge, the seat of the new tribal council and the OIA. There they subsisted on federal assistance and a few tribal jobs and became a strong voting block in tribal elections. Meanwhile OIA officials branded dissenters as "agitators" and attempted to isolate them.[37]

Oglala traditionalists, however, refused to recognize the new government, insisting that the Treaty Council was the only legal body for making tribal decisions consistent with the 1868 Treaty.[38] Though the new tribal councils had the power to negotiate with federal, state, and local governments, they remained weak and vulnerable to dissent. Reorganization had promised self-government, but the councils were subject to the control and approval of the OIA and were often held accountable for decisions they had no control over.[39] Yet, despite the disruption of inter-tribal relations and the relative powerlessness of tribal governments, the IRA increased Indian participation in the political arena of Indian-white relations and laid the groundwork for the resurgence that would come later. The idea of self-determination was now legitimate, and old and new dealers alike used the OIA's rhetoric to articulate their agendas.[40]

With the U.S. entry into World War II, federal policy toward Native Americans began to shift once again. Thousands of Indians served in the armed forces during the war, only to return to a reservation with limited economic opportunities, and, in some cases, one that was about to be cut off from government services and protections. As the enthusiasm for reform wore off and the country's attention turned away from domestic concerns, Collier fought to maintain a holding action until he finally resigned in 1945. By the late 1940s, many Indians and non-Indians alike believed that the Indian new deal had been a mistake, or at the very least was just outdated. In 1953 the U.S. Congress issued a joint resolution declaring its intent to free Indians from the "limitations and disabilities" of federal supervision and control.[41] The push was on for a return to the politics of assimilation.

The new effort to "emancipate" Native Americans became the policy of termination. What one U.S. senator referred to as the "Indian freedom program" meant the end of all legal relationships between the federal government and Indian tribes. Beginning in 1954 with the Menominee in Wisconsin and the Klamath in Oregon, scores of Indian communities were disbanded and their assets distributed among tribal members, while federal services such as health care and education were discontinued. For most, economic conditions worsened and thousands of acres of land were lost, until the policy was declared a failure and finally ended in the 1960s. To many Indians it had been yet another attempt to assimilate them into the American mainstream and erase their identity. "In everything that it represented," writes Donald Fixico, "termination threatened the very core of American Indian existence—its culture."[42]

Operating concurrently with termination was the government's policy of relocation. Following the war, the economic conditions on reservations prompted many Indians to relocate voluntarily to urban areas in search of better education and employment opportunities. With policymakers once again emphasizing assimilation, the BIA began to encourage and even coerce relocation as another way to address reservation poverty, eliminating costly government programs while integrating Indians into the American society. By the 1970s nearly half the country's Indian population was living off the reservation, but most of them were still living in poverty. In the end, termination and relocation had succeeded only in further politicizing Indian tribes and placing individual Indians in urban centers, where they came into contact with other groups who were struggling for social change during the ensuing decades.[43]

In 1944 the National Congress of American Indians held its first national meeting and began a nationwide effort to promote treaty rights and Indian culture and to unite Indian tribes in their dealings with the federal government. Two years later many tribes began to take advantage of the newly created Indian Claims Commission, and within five years 852 claims resulting from legal wrongs committed by the United States against Indian peoples had been filed.[44] During the 1950s, Mohawks in New York refused to pay state taxes; the Tuscarora forcibly resisted New York's attempts to seize land for a new dam and reservoir; armed Lumbee routed a Ku Klux Klan rally in North Carolina; and several hundred Indians marched on BIA headquarters in Washington to protest termination and "arrest" the Indian Commissioner.[45]

In 1961 several hundred Native Americans representing sixty-five tribes met at the University of Chicago at the invitation of the Kennedy administration. At the meeting the voice of a new generation was heard chiding tribal leaders for their perceived lack of action. A few months later several student leaders met in Gallup, New Mexico, to form the National Indian Youth Council (NIYC). "We were concerned with direct action, Indians moving out and doing something," said Mel Thom, an NIYC spokesperson. "The younger Indians got together in the Youth Council because they didn't feel that the older leadership was aggressive enough."[46] In 1964 NIYC activists joined Indians in the northwest to hold "fish in" demonstrations to support traditional fishing rights guaranteed by treaties signed in the 1850s and now threatened by state prohibitions. A year later traditionalist Cherokees in Oklahoma organized to defy state restrictions on Indian hunting. Over the next few years, Indians from California to Maine organized to protest white use of their land, the education of their children, and what they viewed as other violations of century-old treaties.

"As I look around at the Indian situation," said the Indian activist and scholar Robert K. Thomas in early 1964, "it looks like one big seething cauldron about ready to explode."[47] During the rest of the decade, Indians protested Thanksgiving and Columbus Day holidays and the "theft" and display of ancestral bones and sacred artifacts, called for Indian studies programs on college campuses, picketed movie theaters, and communicated their agendas in books such as Vine Deloria's *Custer Died for Your Sins* and newspapers like *Akwesasne Notes*. A new group of younger leaders was emerging, more impatient and increasingly willing to employ new tactics to redress old wrongs.

By 1969 the civil rights movement had slowed, the black power groups had been suppressed, and the student movement had splintered into small sectarian groups, but women, Chicanos, gays, and Native Americans were gaining momentum. As the policymakers of the Kennedy and Johnson administrations sought to include them in their programs, Indians themselves were becoming increasingly self-reliant in articulating an agenda, which for some meant treaty rights as distinct from civil rights.[48] In 1964 Sioux Indians, claiming authority under a clause in the 1868 Treaty that gave them the right to claim unused federal land, had occupied the abandoned federal prison on Alcatraz Island. Five years later in November 1969, the highly publicized occupation of that same island by young urban and university Indians calling themselves "Indians of All Tribes" helped inspire a wave of public protests across the country.

In 1970, a new organization calling itself "AIM" helped organize a nationwide protest in seven cities against the BIA abandonment of Indians who had relocated to the city. The group also joined treaty rights demonstrations at the Mount Rushmore National Monument. Meanwhile, less spectacular but equally important, there were increases in litigation, lobbying, and electoral political activity. Even the more reserved tribal organizations were becoming increasingly aggressive. On urban streets and reservation roads, in courtrooms and legislative chambers, Indians protested racial discrimination, police harassment, land appropriations, high rates of unemployment, and the erosion of treaty rights. In the forefront of many of these protests was the American Indian Movement (AIM).[49]

AIM had been founded in Minneapolis during the summer of 1968 by four Ojibway from northern Minnesota reservations: Clyde Bellecourt, Eddie Benton Banai, George Mitchell, and Dennis Banks. Banai and Bellecourt had met and organized an Indian awareness program while serving time in Stillwater State Prison. Minneapolis had experienced an influx of several thousand Native Americans during the war and the postwar relocation programs. AIM's original intention was to unify and work with existing Indian organizations that relied on legislative reform and social outreach institutions to improve the conditions of Indians in the city. The group, however, soon moved to a more activist, grass-roots organizing approach.

Complaints about police harassment of Indians acted as an early catalyst for AIM's more activist initiatives. Though Native Americans made up only 10 percent of the population of Minneapolis, they accounted for 70 percent of the inmate population in the city jail. AIM's response was to form a "ghetto patrol" which monitored police radio calls and sped to the scene of an arrest with cameras, recorders, attorneys, and bondsmen. After twenty weekends, the AIM patrol claimed a reduction in the Indian jail population of nearly 60 percent and had helped to establish the Legal Rights Center, a neighborhood law office of criminal defense attorneys dedicated to representing poor people in the predominantly Indian section of the city. AIM also organized funding from the federal government and area churches for a housing project and a "survival school" aimed at educating Indian children about their cultural heritage and helping them cope with urban life.[50]

AIM's efforts to reclaim Indian identity in an urban setting stressed traditional beliefs, treaty rights, land reform, and a return to Indian nation sovereignty, and built on the work of other Minneapolis Indian groups that had begun as early as the 1920s.[51] Though its programs were directed at urban Indians, AIM's leaders still believed their roots were on the reservation and that a focus on Indian spirituality and culture was at the core of their work. The campaign for treaty rights soon linked AIM with other groups and individuals around the country, including the Oglalas on Pine Ridge. In 1972 the murder of an Oglala Indian named Raymond Yellow Thunder in Gordon, Nebraska, ignited the chain of events that would bring AIM to Pine Ridge and eventually lead to the protest at Wounded Knee.

Yellow Thunder had been fatally beaten by two white men, who were charged with second degree manslaughter and released without bail. After his family tried unsuccessfully to get the BIA and the tribal government to request an investigation, Severt Young Bear, the Tribal District Chairman from Porcupine, traveled to the AIM convention being held in Omaha, Nebraska. There he spoke with AIM leaders, who got a resolution of support passed and then headed to South Dakota. After a rally on Pine Ridge and a tense standoff with police in Gordon the next day, local and federal officials promised a full investigation of the murder.[52]

By the 1970s the Pine Ridge Reservation was ripe for a major confrontation. Decades of shifting Indian policies and internal conflicts, coupled with a dwindling land base and worsening economic conditions, had left the reservation one of the poorest areas in the country. White ranchers now leased or owned thousands of acres within the borders of the reservation. Some claimed that the largest landowners were the numerous churches that dotted the landscape. Most businesses, like the Trading Post at Wounded Knee, were owned by whites, while the median annual income for Indians was $800, and conservative estimates put the unemployment rate at 54 percent. Half of those who did work were employed by either the tribe or the BIA; a third of the people were dependent on some type of government assistance or pension. High rates of alcoholism and suicide contributed to a life expectancy of only forty-six years.[53]

After the demonstrations in Gordon, events unfolded rapidly on Pine Ridge. In April 1972, Richard "Dick" Wilson took office as the newly elected Tribal Chairman. According to some on the reservation, Wilson had won office with the help of wealthy whites and then rewarded them with reservation contracts, while at the same time appointing relatives and friends to tribal jobs. By fall critics accused Wilson of failing to call the Tribal Council into session for several months and governing instead by a hand-picked executive council. Wilson in turn banned AIM and Russell Means from the reservation, tried to remove the tribal vice-president for supporting AIM, and allegedly hired a group of men who became known as the "goon squad" to harass AIM supporters and other opponents. Means had joined AIM and returned to do organizing in his home town of Porcupine, and was considering running for tribal chairman in the next election.[54]

By now AIM was receiving both respect and notoriety as a national organization. In the fall of 1972, it joined with fishing rights advocates from the northwest to organize a caravan to Washington to argue for the reorganization of the BIA. The caravan, called the "Trail of Broken Treaties," moved across the country, stopping at reservations along the way to pick up more participants. In Washington they presented a twenty-point program, calling for renewal of treaty rights and treaty making power, reconstruction of Indian communities, and a complete revival of tribal sovereignty. When discussions with officials in the BIA and the Nixon administration broke down, the group took over BIA headquarters and refused to leave. White House officials, who wanted to avoid a confrontation so close to the election, offered the protesters immunity from prosecution and $66,000 in travel expenses, and promised to respond to the twenty points within sixty days if the group left the BIA building and Washington.[55]

On January 29, 1973, the White House released a response to the twenty points signed by presidential assistants Leonard Garment and Frank Carlucci. The letter recognized that Indians needed to "represent their own interests" but rejected the twenty points, stating that the Indian Citizenship Act of 1924 precluded dealings by the U.S. government with Indian tribes on the basis of treaties: "The citizenship relationship with one's government and the treaty relationship are mutually exclusive; a government makes treaties with foreign nations, not with its own citizens. If renunciation of citizenship is implied here, or secession, these are wholly backward steps, inappropriate for a nation which is a Union."[56] The letter also noted that the White House had always consulted Indian leaders on matters "vitally affecting Indian people" and would continue to do so in the future.[57] In the wake of the BIA action, the FBI designated AIM as an extremist organization, shifting its focus from the now decimated Black Panther Party. According to FBI documents, the Bureau was requested by the Justice Department in late 1972 to conduct criminal investigations pertaining to AIM.[58] At the same time, the Office of Economic Opportunity withdrew financial support from the AIM "Survival School" in Minneapolis.[59]

In early February 1973, the murder of another Lakota Indian by a white man, this time in Buffalo Gap, a small town in the Black Hills, brought AIM back to South Dakota. A demonstration in Custer to protest the manslaughter charges and low bail set for the accused murderer of Wesley Bad Heart Bull erupted into a riot, as AIM leaders and county officials negotiated over how to resolve the situation. The fighting between police and two hundred protesters resulted in two buildings being set on fire, numerous injuries, and twenty-seven arrests.[60]

After Custer, AIM moved to Rapid City to help negotiate complaints of racism and civil rights violations with officials of that city and other smaller towns that bordered on the reservation. On Pine Ridge people continued to level corruption charges against Wilson and the local BIA Superintendent, Stanley Lyman. Activists formed the Oglala Sioux Civil Rights Organization (OSCRO), and three tribal council members filed impeachment complaints against the chairman.[61] Some saw Wilson's presidency as exacerbating the old splits between the landless, more assimilated Oglalas in the towns and the traditionalists who had opposed the implementation of the IRA and still held land in the more sparsely populated areas of the reservation. Wilson's allies came primarily from the predominantly middle-aged Oglalas in the towns, while AIM drew its support from traditionalist elders and disillusioned young people looking for a way out of the cycle of poverty and alcoholism on the reservation.[62]

Though the BIA continued to support Wilson as it was bound to do, dissatisfaction with the Oglala leader continued to mount. Wilson contended that he was working to bring much-needed jobs to the reservation, but, in addition to the corruption charges, he was accused of firing AIM supporters from reservation jobs and ordering his "goon squad" to carry out physical attacks on opponents. According to OSCRO members, the BIA overlooked both the questionable financial dealings and the increasing violence. OSCRO also contended that, in the end, Wilson was able to either intimidate or buy the votes of several council members in order to stave off impeachment.[63]

BIA officials saw OSCRO as an extension of AIM, whose presence they believed only increased the tensions on the reservation. Fearing violence, they requested help, and sixty-three U.S. Marshals were assigned to the reservation, joining an undisclosed number of FBI agents. Marshals set up a command post in a BIA building in Pine Ridge to monitor the situation, and, with the help of the BIA police and local law enforcement in Rapid City, they began a constant surveillance of AIM and its supporters. Meanwhile, members of the Marshals Special Operations Group began training BIA police in riot control. By the end of February, the agent in charge of the FBI's area office in Minneapolis, Joseph Trimbach, the U.S. attorney for South Dakota, William Clayton, the director of the U.S. Marshals Service, Wayne Colburn, and representatives of the Community Relations branch of the Department of Justice had all made appearances in Rapid City.[64]

The arrival of the additional marshals triggered a demonstration at BIA headquarters in Pine Ridge, which was originally planned to protest the low rates set by the BIA for rental of Indian land. A spokesman for the marshals told protesters that they were there to protect the lives and property of everyone on the reservation, but few if any of the demonstrators believed him. The next day meetings began in Calico with OSCRO, several traditional chiefs, and other Oglalas. Two days later the groups requested AIM representatives to join the discussions. In the words of one Oglala woman: "We decided that we did need the American Indian Movement in here because our men were scared, they hung to the back. It was mostly the women that went forward and spoke out. This way we knew we had backing, and we would have more strength to do what we wanted to do against the BIA and Dick Wilson."[65]

At 5:50 P.M. on February 27, an FBI agent on the reservation reported that thirty cars were headed northeast on the Big Foot Trail toward the village of Porcupine. Several hundred people had left the meeting hall in Calico, reportedly seeking a larger meeting space in the nearby town. But at the fork in the road, the cars began pulling off into the parking area for the trading post and museum, down the hill from the mass grave of the two hundred Indians killed in 1890. In the minds of many present, Lakota warriors had returned to Wounded Knee.[66]

Shortly after the protesters began settling into the small village, law enforcement officials closed off roads leading to Wounded Knee, with orders to stop and search anyone coming in or out. John Torronez, a field representative for the Community Relations Service of the Justice Department, was handed a two-page document listing the "demands" of those inside:

I. Senator WILLIAM FULLBRIGHT to convene Senate Foreign Relations Committee immediately for hearings on treaties made with American Indian Nations and ratified by the Congress of the U.S.

II. Senator EDWARD KENNEDY to convene Senate Sub-Committee on Administrative Practices and Procedures for immediate, full scale investigations and exposure of the Bureau of Indian Affairs and the Department of the Interior from the Agency, reservation offices, to the area offices, to the central office in Washington, D.C.
III. Senator JAMES ABOUREZK to convene the Senate Sub-Committee on Indian Affairs for a complete investigation on all Sioux Reservations in South Dakota.[67]

The document also listed the people the protesters were willing to negotiate with as: "1. Mr. ERLICHMAN of the White House, 2. Senators KENNEDY, ABOUREZK and FULLBRIGHT—or their top aides, 3. The Commissioner of the BIA and the Secretary of Interior," and gave the government "two options" for dealing with those inside the village:

1. They wipe out the old people, women, and children, and men, by shooting and attacking us.
2. They negotiate our demands.[68]

The protesters claimed that they had "asked for and received complete direction and support of medicine men and chiefs of the Oglala Nation": Frank Fools Crow, Peter Catches, Ellis Chips, Edgar Red Cloud, Jake Kills Enemy, Morris Wounded, Severt Young Bear, and Everette Catches.[69] The document was signed by Vern Long, Pedro Bissonette, and Eddie White Wolf, the president, vice-president, and secretary of OSCRO, and by Russell Means, representing AIM. Leaders of the group further instructed Torronez to communicate to other officials that they were operating under the provisions of the Treaty of 1868.[70]

A South Dakota paper called the takeover a "commando raid" conducted under cover of darkness, and the government responded in similar fashion.[71] By the next day, two hundred fifty heavily armed federal officers had taken up positions around the perimeter of Wounded Knee. The army provided armored personnel carriers and ammunition, Air Force jets flew reconnaissance missions over the village, and representatives from the Pentagon arrived to advise on the situation.[72] The government issued statements to the press, emphasizing that crimes had been committed in the village and that arrests were already being made. Government roadblocks forced reporters who wanted direct contact with the protesters to hike in over back trails at night. People inside, some of whom were Vietnam combat veterans, began digging trenches, building bunkers, and constructing roadblocks on the edge of the village, while at the same time turning the church and a number of private homes into sleeping quarters, communal kitchens, and a medical clinic. The long siege that would last seventy-one days had begun.[73]

While officials in the White House and the Justice Department held daily meetings on the situation, negotiations between the two sides began, broke off, and began again.[74] Officials on the scene called in reinforcements and convened a grand jury to consider charges against those believed to be the leaders of the takeover. In March indictments were issued against Dennis Banks, Russell Means, Carter Camp, Clyde Bellecourt, Leonard Crow Dog, and Pedro Bissonette. Camp was an AIM member from Oklahoma; Crow Dog, the AIM spiritual leader from the Rosebud Reservation in South Dakota; and Bissonette an Oglala from Pine Ridge who had helped found OSCRO.[75]

The protesters and the government forces were not the only armed combatants in the area. There were reports of armed white ranchers patrolling the area, and Wilson's supporters set up their own roadblocks, while threatening to move on the village themselves if the government did not take more decisive action. At one point they even prevented several government officials from entering the village. Wilson called for an "all-out volunteer army of Oglala Sioux patriots" and said the protest was "part of a long range plan of the Communist Party."[76] His charges were echoed by an FBI report that claimed that members of Students for a Democratic Society, the Weathermen, Vietnam Veterans Against the War, Venceremos, and "a black extremist group" were all en route to South Dakota.[77]

On March 10, government forces temporarily pulled back, taking down roadblocks and allowing free access in and out of the village. They waited to see if anyone would leave, but few did. Instead traditional chiefs and others met to proclaim the Oglala people "a sovereign nation by the Treaty of 1868," with the right to negotiate with the United States nation to nation.[78] The proclamation also called for abolishing the current tribal government set up under the IRA. In Washington, Secretary of the Interior Rogers Morton issued a statement calling the demands "vague" and asserting that the Indians inside Wounded Knee did not "represent a constituted group with whom the Government can contract or serve." Morton also asserted that the United States could not respond to "revolutionary tactics, blackmail, or terrorism" any more than it could undo the past: "There is no way I or any other Secretary can undo the events of the past. If it was wrong for the European to move on to this continent and settle it by pioneerism and combat, it was wrong. But it happened and here we are."[79]

Some officials in South Dakota and in Washington insisted that the time for negotiations had passed and urged stronger government action. Included in this group was South Dakota Senator and former presidential candidate George McGovern: "Every reasonable effort at negotiations has failed—every concession made by the Government has been matched with yet another AIM demand. They are seeking violence. The law must be enforced. There is no other way in a society such as ours."[80]

On Pine Ridge people remained divided on the protest, but supporters did collect 1,400 signatures on a petition calling for a referendum on the tribal government. In negotiations, Indians continued to assert their demands that the 1868 Treaty be reviewed and the tribal government be abolished, while government representatives continued to assert that only Congress had the power to change current laws regarding Indian tribes and that it was up to the Oglalas themselves to change their government. Though a tentative agreement to end the siege was reached in early April, it was not until two Indians were killed and a marshal left paralyzed that both sides were moved to reach a final accord to end the long protest.[81]

The sadness that prevailed after Buddy Lamont's death helped convince many inside that the time had come to call it quits. On May 8, the last of the protesters inside Wounded Knee laid down their arms and submitted to arrest by federal officials.[82] With half of the community gone—many having left during the last night—those that remained in the village came together for breakfast, and then gathered around the drum to sing the AIM song one last time and listen to a prayer from spiritual leader Wallace Black Elk. At 7:00 A.M., according to the agreed timetable, members of the Community Relations Service of the Justice Department entered Wounded Knee. By the end of the day approximately one hundred fifty people had been searched, questioned, fingerprinted, and photographed, and sat on a hill near government roadblock number one, waiting for the buses that would take them to Rapid City for arraignment. After seventy-one days, a new phase of the Wounded Knee struggle had begun.[83]

The agreement that ended the Wounded Knee siege promised discussions with representatives of the Nixon White House on the 1868 Treaty.[84] For many participants, treaty rights were central to the protest and would soon become a key element of their defense. On May 17, nine days after the stand-down, several hundred people gathered at Chief Frank Fools Crow's land on Pine Ridge for the first and last of those meetings. Present were many Oglalas, representatives from the other Lakota reservations, and delegations of Cheyenne and Arapaho, as well as the Iroquois Six Nations Confederacy. The federal delegation led by Bradley Patterson, an assistant to White House Counsel Leonard Garment, included representatives of the Justice and Interior Departments. Also present for security reasons were several dozen U.S. Marshals and BIA police officers.[85]

During two days of discussions, Indians spoke of the shrinking land base of the Lakota people and the need for a commission to discuss the return of treaty rights. They also raised issues of water and mineral rights, expressed a desire to abandon BIA tribal governments in favor of more traditional forms, argued for more aggressive prosecution of whites who harmed Indians on treaty lands, and listed the numerous complaints against the tribal government on Pine Ridge. The government, however, stuck by its position that only Congress could deal with treaties and the laws that had modified or superseded them. The representatives from Washington left, promising to return in two weeks.[86]

On May 30, a letter from Leonard Garment was delivered to the group that had gathered at Fools Crow's expecting to meet with government representatives a second time. In the letter addressed "To the Traditional Chiefs and Headmen of the Teton Sioux," Garment reaffirmed the White House position that treaty making ended in 1871 and that only Congress could change or rescind laws passed since then. He urged the chiefs to support Nixon's policies of self-determination and to take their requests concerning treaties to the legislative branch. Further, Garment reminded them, Oglalas had the power to abolish the tribal government in accordance with their constitution. The letter went on to answer specific questions concerning civil rights and the protection of mineral and water rights, setting out specific steps that the administration was taking to ensure the protection of Indian rights and natural resources. Garment requested that the chiefs respond to his letter in writing before scheduling a second meeting, and he warned that further "civil disturbances" would cause Indians to "lose much of the sympathy and support they now enjoy from this Administration, from the Congress and from the public."[87]

In June the Indian Affairs Subcommittee, headed by South Dakota Senator James Abourezk, opened hearings on the reservation and listened to critics of Wilson, the BIA, and the Justice Department and questioned officials on the complaints. Many of the issues raised had already been voiced at Wounded Knee, and the testimony prompted Abourezk's own critical comments of the BIA and conditions on Pine Ridge.[88] At the same time, newly released statistics from the Bureau of the Census revealed that Indians were the poorest minority in the country, lagging behind others in every economic category.[89]

A letter dated June 9, signed by Matthew King, Chairman of the Teton Sioux Treaty Council, and Chief Fools Crow, expressed "great anger and dismay" over Garment's letter, reaffirmed their position on treaty rights, and promised more resistance. The letter written by King pointed out that the 1871 legislation referred to by Garment clearly stated that no valid treaty made prior to March 3, 1871, was "invalidated or impaired" by the new legislation. "We are not asking for the negotiation of new treaties or the changing of any existing treaty," wrote King, "we are merely asking that the treaties that already exist be enforced." The letter also called for the return of all federally controlled land in the Black Hills, expressed skepticism about government proposals to protect reservation mineral rights, and adopted a wait and see attitude toward Garment's promises to enforce civil rights on the reservation. Finally, arguing that it is "an established rule of law that acts done under a claim of right are not criminal," King urged that all criminal charges arising out of the Wounded Knee protest be dismissed.[90]

By the time the "Trail of Broken Treaties" arrived in Washington in 1972, the Nixon administration believed it had already developed a progressive position toward Native Americans. The President had repudiated the much-maligned termination policy in a message to Congress in 1970 and called instead for a policy of "self-determination." Nixon's support had also facilitated the return of 48,000 acres of land to the Taos Pueblo Indians of New Mexico, including the sacred glacial pool called Blue Lake, which had been appropriated for the Carson National Forest in 1906. Many Indians were willing to give the administration credit for its early initiatives, while others remained skeptical of its long-range intentions and commitment with respect to mineral rights and proposed educational programs.[91] But whatever the White House might have planned with respect to future Indian policy, the attentions of the President and Garment, the aide who had helped facilitate the new enlightened attitudes, were soon turned toward another more pressing problem for the White House, one that would have an unforeseen impact on the upcoming trials of the Wounded Knee defendants.

When protesters entered Wounded Knee in February 1973, the recently inaugurated, second-term President was riding high with a 68 percent approval rating from the American people. By summer, however, things were beginning to fall apart. Inflation was on the rise and higher prices on food had spawned a consumer boycott of meat, in which 25 percent of the population participated. By the fall, growing oil shortages had added to the crisis. Many in the country, including members of Congress, were also angry about the dramatic increase in the U.S. bombing attacks over Cambodia, despite the Vietnam peace accord. Worst of all for Nixon, the Watergate conspiracy was beginning to unravel.

In a letter to Federal Judge John J. Sirica, the convicted Watergate burglar James McCord said that pressure leading to guilty pleas and perjury on the part of some of the burglars had come from high up in the Nixon administration. On May 11, three days after the stand-down at Wounded Knee, the presiding trial judge in the Pentagon Papers case, William Matthew Byrne, Jr., revealed that he had twice been contacted by the White House. The next day he dismissed the charges against Daniel Ellsberg, because of government misconduct. Five days later, on May 17, Senator Sam Ervin gaveled to order the Senate Watergate hearings, a daytime television spectacle that some would compare to the Army-McCarthy hearings of 1954. By July, after watching Dean, Haldeman, Ehrlichman, and Mitchell parade before Ervin's committee, the American public dropped Nixon to a 40 percent approval rating—and that was only the beginning.

While the government continued to insist that those accused of crimes at Wounded Knee must be prosecuted, the press and public remained divided over the impact of the protest. A Harris Survey released on April 2 said that ninety-eight percent of those polled had heard about the "takeover." Fifty-one percent said they sympathized with the Indians inside Wounded Knee, as oppposed to only twenty-one percent for the federal government. Twenty-eight percent indicated that they were not sure. Sixty percent of those polled also rated U.S. government treatment of Indians as "poor."[92] Press coverage during the aftermath of the takeover, however, was not always favorable to the protesters.

Several newspapers, including the *New York Times,* reported on the "wreckage left by militant Indians and their supporters" in what it termed the "bizarre seizure" of the village.[93] One South Dakota paper called for government compensation for the "victims" of the "militants' occupation" while condemning aid given to those inside the village; another suggested that the government should have ended the occupation much sooner. The *Saint Paul Pioneer Press* asked for swift prosecution and prison sentences for those found guilty, and called the occupation "a high handed gang seizure of other people's property, homes, businesses and supplies."[94]

Newspapers quoted Indian leaders and others who were critical of the protest, including Senator Abourezk, who, in a speech at Wounded Knee near the end of May, criticized the use of violence as a means of bringing about social change.[95] Meanwhile the FBI publicized its conference for law enforcement officials, judges, and prosecutors, on "Extremists and Terrorism," held in Rapid City.[96] South Dakota papers carried stories about the discontent on the Rosebud Reservation and the talk of a possible takeover there, and reported on the continued presence of U.S. Marshals on Pine Ridge.[97] Still, stories like one in the *Rapid City Journal* acknowledged the increased awareness of Indians by Rapid City Central High School students as a result of Wounded Knee and a speech by given by Dennis Banks prior to the protest.[98]

For Native Americans, the political struggles that erupted in the 1960s were linked closely to issues that were a century or more old. In a sense, an element of the new Indian resurgence was an effort to recapture their version of that history. In the mid to late nineteenth century the Lakota, as other Indian nations had before them, became central actors in a political drama. As Stephen Cornell observes: "While they seldom were involved directly in decision making, they often set the terms on which decisions were made."[99] In the 1960s and 1970s, Indians, like African Americans, students, women, gays, and others, were making an attempt to be actors on the political stage, to move from just influencing the terms to participating fully in the decisions that affected their lives.

Both the press and the public would have more opportunities to form opinions on the new Indian movements and the issues they raised. From the Treaty of 1868 and the land cessions that followed, to the alleged corruption of tribal leaders and the failed policies of the BIA, the continuing political debate would be carried out in several arenas, including a federal courtroom in the upper midwest. For the next two years the defense team representing those charged with crimes at Wounded Knee would attempt to use the courts as a forum to review more than a hundred years of Indian history, linking past injustices to current mistreatment, while targeting a government that was already being shaken by allegations of corruption and wrongdoing.

THE BUILDUP TO THE TRIALS

I was real apprehensive of what I saw in the beginning, not at the attorneys but at the situation . . . I was not afraid of a poor defense, but I was afraid that the political struggle would be lost because of now being tied to the courts.

DENNIS BANKS,
AMERICAN INDIAN MOVEMENT,
APRIL 1989

If we are going to be involved, we should be involved as prosecutors, not as part of the general executive branch of government trying to address social issues, or racial issues, or political issues.

R. D. HURD,
FORMER ASSISTANT U.S. ATTORNEY,
SEPTEMBER 1988

ON FEBRUARY 29, 1973, Saint Paul attorney Ken Tilsen received a phone call from a lawyer in New York who had been contacted by someone in Milwaukee. Fifty people, Tilsen was told, were in jail in Rapid City on charges connected with Wounded Knee, and someone was needed to help get them released. Though skeptical about the report, given the number of attorneys he had heard were already on the scene, Tilsen flew to Rapid City where he spent the weekend conducting bail hearings. At a meeting Sunday evening, Tilsen questioned the priorities of approximately twenty lawyers who had just returned from the reservation, where they said they had been busy in negotiations with the government and discussions with the media. Tilsen remembers being furious and suggesting that it was time for them to begin "acting like lawyers."[1]

As an attorney known for representing antiwar activists, however, Tilsen knew that defining what it meant to "act like lawyers" in the midst of an ongoing political struggle was not always easy. Throughout the remaining months of the siege, numerous lawyers did fulfill their traditional roles as advocates: they attended arraignments and bond hearings, assisted in negotiations with the government, and filed lawsuits challenging the use of the military at Wounded Knee, the government blockage of food shipments into the village, and alleged civil rights violations by the Pine Ridge tribal chairman and law enforcement officials.[2]

When the scene shifted from protest to pretrial hearings, however, the traditional definition of a legal advocate was further stretched; attorneys shaped and reshaped their roles and responsibilities within the context of a diverse, multicultural defense committee, representing a highly politicized group of Native Americans who faced hundreds of state and federal criminal indictments. Lawyers continued to make court appearances, research defense issues, and draft motions, but they also engaged in fundraising and publicity for the committee and bowed to their clients' wishes concerning the direction of their defense.

Decisions concerning what legal tasks the Wounded Knee defense team was responsible for and the nature of that responsibility involved political as well as legal strategizing. The lawyers and legal workers who worked with the defense committee were committed to following AIM's lead in planning the defense, but AIM leaders were not always of one mind as to what that direction should be. If they were to be ready for trial by the end of the summer, people with a variety of experiences, egos, and cultures would have to learn to work together as an organized, cohesive unit and agree upon a theory of defense that was both legally and politically coherent. Facing all these complexities, the defense team developed its early organizational groundwork during the siege, and the entire pretrial period was critical for the defense.

Representatives from the Justice Department in Washington and the U.S. Attorney's office in Sioux Falls were also on Pine Ridge shortly after the takeover began, monitoring the situation, advising the marshals, interviewing witnesses, handling the processing of those arrested, convening grand juries, and attempting to negotiate an end to the situation. William Clayton, the U.S. Attorney for South Dakota, acting on rumors that the BIA building was the target of a proposed takeover, had arrived almost two weeks prior to Wounded Knee: "It was common knowledge that some of these people had been to Alcatraz, they had been to Custer, they had been on the Pine Ridge Reservation prior to that, and the trading post at Wounded Knee. They had been to Gordon, Nebraska. There was a whole series of incidents . . . It was a very turbulent time in my opinion."[3]

The area around Wounded Knee was considered an area of civil disorder and thus off limits to the public without government permission. Arrests of people attempting to get in and out began almost immediately and would soon number in the hundreds. The U.S. Attorney had a small office and staff in Rapid City—there were only three or four assistant U.S. attorneys for all of South Dakota—and offices outside the state were asked to help handle the situation. The staff was increased in Rapid City, and at least one attorney was on duty in Pine Ridge throughout the siege. Most of the time that assistant was R. D. Hurd, the man who would head the prosecution team for the conspiracy cases.[4]

Decisions on early arrests, charges, and the convening of grand juries were under the direction of the U.S. Attorney. Justice Department officials handled negotiations and advised the marshals and the FBI. According to Clayton, neither he nor Justice officials ever considered the possibility of not bringing charges. Though the defense would later claim that decisions on arrests came from Washington, Clayton maintains that such decisions were routinely handled by his office.[5] U.S. attorneys reviewed the evidence assembled by the FBI and submitted it to the grand jury, which handed down the first indictments against the leaders of the takeover in March.[6]

When they had finished, the indictments against all defendants encompassed eight sections of Titles 18 and 26 of the U.S. Criminal Code. Offenses charged included impeding or obstructing federal officers during the lawful performance of their duties incident to a civil disorder, assaulting a federal officer, transporting firearms for use in a civil disorder, using firearms in commission of a felony, being in possession of unregistered (illegal) firearms, robbery, various combinations of burglary and larceny, destroying a motor vehicle, reckless disregard for the safety of a human life, and conspiring to commit one or more of the charged offenses.[7]

Though many defendants were released without bond, the U.S. Attorney maintained a hard line on bail for those viewed as leaders in the protest. Russell Means, arrested in April, sat in jail until the end of May before his $125,000 bond was raised. Labeled as "armed and dangerous" and fearful of spending any time in a South Dakota jail, Dennis Banks slipped into Canada, where he remained until his $105,000 bond could be posted. In court, Clayton and defense attorney Mark Lane argued about bail for AIM spiritual leader Leonard Crow Dog, with Lane insisting that he was a religious leader who had never touched a gun in his life and Clayton stressing the seriousness of the charges and Crow Dog's position as a leader of AIM.[8]

Though the U.S. attorneys regarded their decisions on prosecution as legal and not political, Hurd and the others recognized the importance of communicating to the public that crimes were being committed at Wounded Knee:

It was important from the standpoint of the publicity that the takeover was receiving, to make sure that insofar as possible that we took the position that we were interested in criminal offenses, and that the political or social problems . . . should be addressed in a form other than through the FBI or through a prosecutor's office . . . Our function is crime and if we are going to be involved, we should be involved as prosecutors, not as part of the general executive branch of government trying to address social issues. To the extent that you want to project that publicly, that is somewhat of a political decision.[9]

In the months to come the government would press its position with respect to the criminal charges, but the ability of the defense to intertwine legal and political issues in and out of court kept the prosecution on the defensive and vulnerable to countercharges of misconduct toward Native Americans in general and Indian activists in particular.

On Memorial Day weekend in 1973, a group of lawyers and legal workers gathered in Rapid City with members of AIM, OSCRO, and their supporters to begin planning for the defense, as well as for upcoming treaty discussions with representatives of the Nixon White House. A sign-up sheet for the weekend listed fifty-four people in attendance, from sixteen different cities in eleven states.[10] Many had been inside Wounded Knee during the protest, among them a Rapid City Indian named Ramon Roubideaux, who at the time was general counsel for AIM and a key participant in the negotiations that ended the long siege. But Roubideaux was an exception; from the beginning local attorneys had refused to represent the protesters. Many of the out-of-state lawyers had been recruited by the National Lawyers Guild (NLG or "Guild"), including two who arrived from Boston by van, bringing a file cabinet and a stack of law books. Others were contacted by the American Civil Liberties Union, or came simply on their own initiative for a variety of independent reasons. A few, like William Kunstler, whose clients included the "Chicago Seven," Stokely Carmichael, Dr. Martin Luther King, and the Berrigan brothers, had been contacted directly by the defendants.[11]

AIM leader and defendant Carter Camp, a Ponca Indian from Oklahoma, and Wallace Black Elk, a Lakota spiritual leader from the Rosebud Reservation, were intent on educating the predominantly white lawyers, legal workers, and law students in attendance on Indian culture and spirituality.[12] Some questioned whether this was the best use of time at a legal meeting and expressed a need to talk more concretely about how lawyers would relate to AIM politically and legally, but key Indian representatives responded that the best way for whites to do that was to understand the importance of Native American traditions for those who had been at Wounded Knee. Several whites agreed and thought that Black Elk's presentation set a tone of commitment and respect for Indian values that was critical to a successful defense.[13] The unspoken struggle for space on the agenda was among the legal, the political, and the cultural, three components that would become intertwined, if never totally integrated, throughout the defense effort.[14]

At the first general session on Saturday afternoon, intense debates occurred over how the cases would be handled. Members of the NLG argued for a committee under the direction of the Indian defendants to oversee the defense of all the cases. Other lawyers, experienced in political cases but accustomed to working independently, advocated separating the defendants and assigning particular defendants to particular lawyers. The committee approach won out, along with the suggestion that lawyers volunteer their time, with money raised going to bail and material resources for the defense. In the wake of these decisions, several lawyers withdrew from the defense effort.[15]

That evening Ken Tilsen led a discussion of the cases, including the state charges arising from the protest at Custer, South Dakota, in early February and the tribal court charges filed in connection with Wounded Knee. He also summarized the civil suits challenging the government's treatment of Indians on Pine Ridge and its handling of Wounded Knee. Discussions took place on whether to change the venue of the trials and where to go, and on motions to dismiss based on the composition of the grand juries, bad faith, and selective prosecution, as well as the unconstitutionality of several statutes.[16] By the end of the weekend, a general plan for proceeding with the legal work had been established, and several people in attendance had made commitments to work on specific tasks. The massive national defense effort, now known as the Wounded Knee Legal Defense/Offense Committee (WKLDOC), referred to as "Wickle-dock," had taken on a loose organizational structure and begun the push toward pretrial hearings.[17]

Perhaps the strongest organizational presence at the meeting (besides AIM's) was exerted by members of the NLG, which had been involved in the protest from the beginning. The NLG had been founded in 1936 to combat the attacks of the American Bar Association on New Deal legislation and programs; in subsequent years Guild lawyers battled the House Committee on Un-American Activities for clients such as the "Hollywood

Ten," defended people charged under the Smith Act in the 1940s and 1950s, worked with the civil rights movement during the 1960s, represented the Mississippi Freedom Democratic Party, and became involved with the Vietnam antiwar and Black Power movements. Numbering about 5,000 members nationwide, the Guild began recruiting volunteers to make short-term commitments to the Wounded Knee defense almost immediately after the protest began. Within days NLG lawyers from Denver, Minneapolis, Berkeley, New York, Boston, and Madison, Wisconsin, began showing up in South Dakota or offering to do legal work at home.[18]

An NLG press release on March 9 expressed support for AIM and the action at Wounded Knee, and a nationwide mailing that same day announced a fund-raising effort for current and anticipated legal expenses. By May, when it was apparent to everyone that a long-term defense effort was necessary, the NLG already had a functioning communications network and some definite ideas about what should be done organizationally.[19]

After the weekend meeting NLG members discussed how the Guild would live up to its commitment to the Wounded Knee defense, without draining resources from its ongoing efforts in defense of the inmates charged in the takeover of the state prison at Attica, New York, in 1971.[20] At a national meeting in early June the organization divided the country into two groups, urging members east of the Mississippi to make a commitment to the Attica defense and those to the west to work on Wounded Knee. Discussions also took place concerning the lack of organization in WKLDOC, specific legal work that needed to be done, publicity, committee security, and political questions raised by the dynamic of white lawyers getting involved in Native American struggles. The NLG formally committed itself to the support of AIM, the people of Pine Ridge, and the defense committee, and several more members made commitments to travel to South Dakota.[21]

In early June WKLDOC moved into the first in a series of semi-permanent quarters—several houses that were part of a college fraternity near downtown Rapid City. From this location several long-term volunteers and countless short-termers began in earnest the job of constructing a defense. Though discussions and arguments would continue through the summer, a rough division of responsibilities was taking shape. Ramon Roubideaux, by virtue of his position as AIM'S attorney, headed up the defense committee. Ken Tilsen, who had won the respect of many defendants by his forceful representation during the siege, became the day-to-day coordinator for all the cases, civil and criminal.[22] By this time he had decided to take a year off from his practice in Saint Paul. He rented an apartment in Rapid City and spent the weekdays there; on weekends he would drive back home to Saint Paul, where his wife, Rachel, was now running his office. Tilsen remembers putting about 200,000 miles on the car that year: "I used to drive with the windows wide open so I could scream and holler and sing along to these crazy country western songs."[23]

Tilsen was joined by Joe Beeler, an ex-federal public defender from Chicago, who headed up the recruitment of non-NLG lawyers and would eventually take over coordination of all the nonleadership cases.[24] Mark Lane, the author of *Rush to Judgment,* directed investigations and evidence gathering from a house on the reservation and took responsibility for the Custer cases. Len Cavise, an attorney from Washington, D.C., came from the National Office of the NLG in early summer, bringing with him his Wounded Knee organizational responsibilities. Others who arrived to make long-term commitments included lawyers and legal workers who took responsibility for everything from tribal court cases to office administration and brought some stability and continuity to the loosely organized committee.[25]

With the constant comings and goings of invited and uninvited volunteers, security was a continuing problem. Distrust of strangers who arrived without connections necessitated keeping the details of some investigations "secret" and occasionally resulted in suspicions that someone was an "infiltrator." The issue was partially resolved in several ways. First, a hierarchy evolved; a group consisting of a few AIM leaders, plus attorneys Tilsen and Beeler, made ex-officio decisions and then took them to the whole committee.[26] Second, the committee tended to operate on a "need to know" basis. Different subgroups would not necessarily know what the others were doing, leaving the leadership to keep track of the different facets of the defense. By fall the committee had initiated the use of security checks, though they were not always strictly adhered to and did not prevent the infiltration of at least one undercover agent.[27]

The process of arriving at a formal structure and work assignments came slowly. Decisions were being forced on the committee on a daily basis; tasks for a particular day were often decided early over breakfast; and nightly discussions of what to do and how to do it were endless, only occasionally structured in the form of weekly committee meetings. The chief topics at meetings, aside from the legal work itself, were the questions of WKLDOC responsibility for ongoing problems on Pine Ridge and security within the committee. People from the reservation and AIM members, including Russell Means, the AIM leader most in contact with the committee, were often present. Although many of the Indians would remain relatively silent during the legal discussions, several did push for greater involvement on the reservation, while many whites argued for restricting WKLDOC to Wounded Knee, Custer, and related legal matters. Others countered that the problems on Pine Ridge were related, particularly the complaints of harassment and other infringements on people's civil rights by the so-called "goon squad" and by what many regarded as overly aggressive FBI agents.[28]

The permanent presence of the investigation subcommittee on Pine Ridge, which was gathering, among other evidence, documentation on reservation living conditions, provided easy access for people seeking legal help for problems, but the limited resources of the committee could not always address these situations. It was difficult for many of the committee members to resist trying to find remedies for all the problems they confronted on a daily basis. The debate over defining what was "Wounded Knee related" began in May and remained unresolved throughout the existence of WKLDOC.[29]

The AIM or reservation presence on the committee would be a source of stability and inspiration, as well controversy and conflict, in the months to come. AIM leaders clearly saw the need for the defense committee, but it often seemed as if the leadership could not agree upon a plan for working with the committee or an overall strategy for its own defense. Rivalries among the most visible leaders contributed to the disagreements, but the central difficulty, of course, was that neither AIM nor anyone else had dealt with the necessity of such a massive defense effort before.[30] Dennis Banks, considered by many the most thoughtful of the AIM leaders, became concerned with the lack of political direction in the defense when he returned to South Dakota in mid-summer, but admitted that beyond identifying the problem he had little to offer in the way of leadership himself:

> I was real apprehensive by what I saw in the beginning, not at the attorneys but at the situation, because . . . none of us knew what direction we should really take. There was no leadership and I was part of the blame for that, Russell was part of the blame for that and then the attorneys themselves . . . I had never been charged with thirteen major crimes before in my life. I had never worked with committees, or a whole raft of attorneys before, or a legal defense team before . . . I was not afraid

of a poor defense, but I was afraid that the political struggle would be lost because of now being tied to the courts.[31]

Members of the NLG who had past defense experience with political groups were probably the most conscious of trying to relate to the AIM leadership politically, and many, like Tilsen and Cavise, always believed that the politics of Wounded Knee had to be part of the defense. They grew frustrated when it became obvious that AIM was not in a position to provide continuous political leadership to WKLDOC or to always follow through on a task it had taken on. Others on the committee were less politically minded, and those who had a romanticized view of Indians because of their perceived spiritual superiority were disillusioned upon witnessing any dissension among the defendants. Friction between factions within AIM often played itself out in the committee, and committee members seeking to influence the direction of the defense would occasionally play on these differences, lobbying one faction or the other on a particular committee issue.[32]

The more organizationally minded committee members often had to balance or work around the large egos of the "movement legal heavies" when the jockeying for position with the defendants and the press interfered with committee decisions and tasks.[33] Sometimes disagreement over someone's role would be played out in a long discussion over work assignments or individual participation. The fierce commitment to collective decision making by some members resulted in a measure of democracy, as well as the numerous and lengthy meetings.[34] The process was often necessary and helpful, but "long-winded lawyers" also became the subject of joking among Indians working with the committee. "It took them two and three times as long to say anything," commented Ted Means, "especially the lawyers; they'd take a three hour meeting to discuss something that normally would only take fifteen minutes." In the minds of some in AIM, the dynamics of WKLDOC were an argument for the necessity of an upper-echelon leadership group within the defense.[35]

AIM was caught between carrying out its political program and trying to defend itself in court. Along with supporting WKLDOC, it was continuing to organize in Indian communities around issues such as treaty rights, police harassment, and economic conditions. For many, Wounded Knee had brought the issue of treaty rights to the forefront of Indian-government relations, and AIM's goal was to build on that momentum to get Indians to think of themselves as a nation rather than as separate tribes. Plans were in the works for an international treaty conference to be held some time in 1974.[36]

The geographical diversity of its leadership also contributed to AIM's problems. Means had ties on Pine Ridge and Banks was now determined to stay, but others, like Clyde Bellecourt from Minneapolis, and Carter Camp and Stan Holder from Oklahoma, returned to their respective homes and local political work for portions of the summer. This, coupled with the ongoing travel for speaking and fund-raising events, made getting the leadership together a difficult task.[37]

The continual presence of defendants and Indian supporters had two immediate effects on WKLDOC. First, it further taxed the already strained resources for food and space, causing some to question whether the committee should be providing meals and sleeping space for anyone not there on official business. Second, it forced each group to deal with the most prominent cultural differences of the others. The volunteers would have had a hard enough time adjusting without the presence of any defendants. WKLDOC was a diverse group, composed of experienced and inexperienced lawyers, law students and legal workers, left politicos and apolitical romanticists, some who saw themselves as part of the struggle, and others who saw themselves solely as litigators; thus the situation was ripe for conflicts of politics and life-styles.

The volunteers came from all parts of the country, from different class backgrounds with different life experiences, and found themselves eating, sleeping, and working together with total strangers. By the end of June, twenty-one people from six states were in residence in Rapid City.[38] With only a small working budget, living and working accommodations, which often were the same place, left much to be desired. Len Cavise described the experience as "white kids getting no salary, no free time, no independence and no privacy, but each of whom was treated to the utter exaltation of being involved in something important."[39]

Legal work was farmed out to people with law libraries. Office equipment was borrowed, donated, or purchased with committee funds when available. People cooked, washed, and kept house collectively. In the first office in Rapid City, volunteers shared beds—sometimes by choice, sometimes by necessity—slept on the floor, and pitched tents on the lawn. Some attorneys who could afford it stayed in motels or rented apartments; the more hospitable ones invited committee members over in the evening to watch the Watergate hearings and eat ice cream.[40] For some, a motel room was not far enough away from the chaos. Several who had made long-term commitments cut short their stay; some followed through on promised work at home, while others left the committee altogether.[41]

The differences between whites and Indians manifested themselves in several areas, not the least of which were food and drink. Partly because of life-style and partly because of limited finances, the defense committee prepared a lot of meatless meals. The few complaints of the meat eaters were usually ignored, except when the meat eater was Russell Means or another AIM leader who happened to be in for a meal. Stories abound among ex-committee members, like the one Ted Means tells about his brother: "The committee had that office on Main Street and they had a kitchen down around the corner and up the alley, where they'd eat and we went over there because they said they were having burgers, and we went up to eat and my brother Russ, you know he was pretty hungry, and they were good sized burgers. We got our plates and we went to sit down to eat and he cut into the burger and it was green. He said, 'Jesus, it's spoiled meat.' All the time they were split pea burgers."[42]

Less humorous were the early misunderstandings over the use of alcohol. Alcoholism is one of the most serious problems on Indian reservations, particularly among the men. Several white lawyers who didn't know about the problem, and believed they were helping relations between WKLDOC and its clients, went out drinking with a client only to be told later, often by an Indian woman, that it was an activity that should not be encouraged. Late in 1973 and again in 1974, committee offices chose to ban the use of alcohol, a rule that was sometimes difficult to enforce.[43]

Part of the problem was that the AIM presence on the committee was not consistent. Different people came and went, bringing with them different attitudes toward the white legal volunteers and different ideas about what the committee should be doing. Madonna Gilbert, a 33-year-old Minneconjous Lakota from the Cheyenne Indian Reservation in South Dakota, and Lorelei DeCora, a 19-year-old Winnebago Dakota from Sioux City, Iowa, two defendants who had been inside Wounded Knee, were asked by Russell Means to help with the defense and serve as liaisons with WKLDOC. Both women had earned respect within AIM for their work during the siege, and their presence around the committee served to bridge the often difficult gap between cultures. Each made it a point to have some individual contact with committee members, learning why people had come and openly expressing their appreciation of the legal support.[44] Means himself was the AIM leader most in contact with the defense work in the summer of 1973, and he was capable of providing needed leadership, though at times he was as quick to criticize the work of the committee as he was to praise it.[45]

The tension between Indians and non-Indians was further exacerbated by the comings and goings of short-term legal volunteers. Every time a defendant visited the WKLDOC office there were new faces to deal with. Yet, as defendants and supporters came and went, they began to show their respect for the faces that were becoming familiar. The presence of the defense committee investigative team living and working on the reservation also helped demonstrate the depth of the commitment that many were willing to make to the defense.[46] Equally important was WKLDOC's commitment to take leadership from its clients. Many long-term committee members worked at understanding and respecting Indian beliefs and values even if it proved frustrating at times. There would be clashes throughout the trials, but, as Ted Means says, "We were always able to accommodate."[47]

One of the conflicts in WKLDOC involved differences over the role of women. AIM leadership tended to be male and elitist, as did the leadership of WKLDOC. The white male left was well known for its sexism, and, though groups such as the NLG had begun to struggle with this issue in the early 1970s, it was far from being resolved. Even male lawyers who represented progressive clients were often used to giving the orders for others to follow, whether the others were secretaries, younger lawyers, or legal workers. In fact the NLG itself had only recently opened membership to law students and legal workers, and the latter only after heated debate. When Native American traditions and AIM's internal politics were added to this dynamic, questions of who cooked, what was cooked, who washed dishes, who typed, who worked on what motion, who represented whom in court, and who slept with whom could easily become political conflicts involving ethnicity and gender.[48] AIM leaders could not understand why a lawyer might do his own typing or help cook a meal. Some of the lawyers didn't understand it either.[49]

Neither AIM nor WKLDOC, however, was merely a replica of left movement groups in the late 1960s. Questions of sexism had arisen at Wounded Knee, but as Mary Crow Dog explains in her autobiography, *Lakota Woman*, women in the Indian struggle saw their priorities as different from those of white women.[50] Gender relations within AIM could not be judged by the same measure as those in groups such as SDS. "For Indian feminists," wrote Native American activist and scholar Rayna Green in 1980, "every women's issue is framed in the larger context of Native American people." At the same time as white women were rejecting many of the middle-class traditions that had been prevalent in post–World War II America, Green argues, Indian women "insist[ed] on taking their traditional places as healers, legal specialists, and tribal governors."[51]

WKLDOC was able to build on the experiences of SNCC in the south and SDS's community organizing projects in the north, where activist women had developed organizing skills and self-confidence even as they confronted the sexism of the mostly male leadership in those organizations. Many credited women for spearheading the dissent on Pine Ridge, and women like Decora and Gilbert had emerged as influential activists within AIM after Wounded Knee. The presence of these two Indian women, together with the long-term commitment of several white women lawyers and nonlawyers who gained more strength and respect the longer they stayed, helped educate white and Indian men as time went on. The legal proceedings never lost their male tone, but behind the public persona of AIM and its defense committee, women, defendants, and committee members were moving into positions of influence and leadership.[52]

Much of the summer of 1973 was spent raising money. AIM leaders were continually on the road during and after the protest to raise funds and publicize the upcoming trials. When Wounded Knee erupted, Vernon Bellecourt launched a speaking tour which eventually took him to Europe, where he articulated Indian grievances, raised money for food and medicine, and generated letters of support from different countries.[53] Other recognized leaders, particularly Banks, Means, and Clyde Bellecourt, traveled the country speaking to whites and Indians, raising money for the defense effort as well as their own support.[54] Money remained tight, however, with large amounts of it still going for bail. More people were coming to hear the now-famous speakers and offer moral support than were willing to make financial contributions. In July Vernon Bellecourt made another swing through Europe, but, although his visit helped to set up support committees in Belgium, Denmark, Germany, France, Britain, Sweden, and Italy, the trip was not as financially successful as his earlier one. In a telephone interview from Europe, Bellecourt commented, "We don't need sympathy, we need hard money support."[55]

To assist in these efforts WKLDOC began publishing a regular newsletter, detailing the state of the defense and the needed resources. The mailing list of several hundred individuals and organizations also included a list of friendly press contacts across the country. Regular press releases attempted to keep the media informed and interested in the cases. Local support groups organized fund-raising events, while in Boston a group of supporters and NLG members who had worked with WKLDOC in South Dakota formed the "Wounded Knee Information and Defense Fund," which attempted to coordinate efforts in the northeast and nationwide.[56] If communications were weak anywhere, it was between WKLDOC and the reservation. Few on Pine Ridge had telephones, and, though the committee distributed a "Clients' Newsletter," word of mouth was the primary source of information throughout the legal proceedings.[57]

Recruitment also remained an ongoing task; by fall, the committee had turned to lining up trial lawyers for the coming year. Next to the NLG, the organization that contributed the most attorneys to the defense was the National Association of Criminal Defense Lawyers (NACDL). Beeler, a member of the organization (which was not known for its radical politics), sent a telegram requesting help to the annual meeting in August 1973. After several phone calls and letters the NACDL sent a delegation to South Dakota and pledged to recruit lawyers for the upcoming trials. At the time he sent the telegram, the most Beeler had dared to hope for was the donation of some badly needed law books.[58] By the end of the month thirty-five NACDL attorneys had made commitments to WKLDOC, and Maryland attorney Robert C. Heeney was on his way to South Dakota to discuss the committee's needs and report back to the membership.[59]

Coordinating all the recruiting and ongoing legal work took considerable patience and perseverance. Tilsen and Beeler, the two senior lawyers in residence, divided up the legal tasks and assigned work to others on the committee, including some who would never set foot in South Dakota. Portions or all of a pretrial motion or a civil complaint, such as the challenge to the firing of several tribal secretaries who had openly expressed sympathies for AIM, were being prepared by lawyers outside South Dakota. Tilsen or Beeler would edit the document and then file it in the appropriate court.[60]

By August the committee was at work on the change of venue motion, its first major undertaking and clearly the most pivotal to date. Though there were some who believed the trials should be held close to Pine Ridge, the majority of the committee and defendants felt that the climate of racism was so extreme near the reservation that the proceedings had to be moved out of western South Dakota, if not out of the state altogether. Tilsen enlisted the help of friends and friends of friends, and had telephone conversations with the sociologist Jay Schulman, who along with Richard Christie had developed the innovative jury survey techniques that became a mainstay of political trials by the end of the decade and a staple in many trials by the 1980s.

Schulman, however, was too involved with the Attica cases to travel to South Dakota in order to engage in any direct consultations. Tilsen and company were left to survey attitudes in western South Dakota more or less on their own, spending as many hours on the phone consulting with the absent experts as they did conducting the survey. A questionnaire was devised, and volunteers called a sample of phone numbers from each exchange, asked to speak to the oldest adult in the household, and then went through a list of questions designed to extract people's attitudes concerning Indians in general and Wounded Knee in particular. In the fall, working from jury lists, the committee surveyed the eight counties that constituted the Sioux Falls area in the eastern part of the state.[61]

In hearings before U.S. District Judge Fred Nichol, defense committee lawyers used the surveys and press coverage to demonstrate that the so-called leadership or conspiracy defendants could not receive a fair trial anywhere in South Dakota. The U.S. attorneys introduced their own opinion poll to back up their assertion that all the defendants could receive a fair trial in the state. They also claimed that the polls demonstrated more prejudice against the government outside South Dakota than there was against the defendants inside the state.[62] U.S. Attorney Clayton argued that if there was doubt, the only way to know for sure was to start picking a jury and see what happened: "We always believed that they could have had a fair trial in South Dakota, that we should have selected the jury from the panel and then if it developed that these people said they were prejudiced, and couldn't be impartial . . . then the court could decide to move it to a different location."[63] But Judge Nichol, a lifelong resident of South Dakota, was keenly aware of the negative feelings toward AIM and in particular its well-known leaders. Nichol ordered the previously consolidated trial of Banks and Means, along with the cases of Camp, Holder, and Leonard Crow Dog, transferred to Saint Paul.[64] At the same time, judges for the nonleadership cases and the Custer cases agreed to transfer those cases to Sioux Falls. Now only some tribal court cases arising out of Wounded Knee would go to trial on or near the Pine Ridge Reservation.[65]

Judge Nichol also granted the defense's request to have the prosecution produce statements, photographs, logs of government radio conversations during the siege, and other physical evidence in the government's possession. The only discovery request Nichol denied was for a list of government informants.[66] On other matters, the judge postponed ruling on the admissibility of the 1868 Treaty, denied motions to dismiss based on inadequacies in the indictments and irregularities in the selection and proceedings of the grand jury, and took under advisement the defense motion to declare the defendants indigent pending a review of WKLDOC's financial statements.[67]

Near the end of November, Nichol presided over the last of the pretrial hearings in the Banks-Means case. At issue were more motions to dismiss, including one alleging bad faith prosecution and harassment by federal officials. Defense attorneys questioned former Attorney General Richard Kleindienst concerning the government's alleged use of indictments as a way to force the protesters into negotiations. Kleindienst admitted that there had been discussions with the U.S. Attorney in South Dakota but denied that the Justice Department had directed any of the specific decisions on the indictments. Clayton, who followed Kleindienst to the stand, insisted that the only orders that had come from Washington were to dismiss the indictment against *Boston Globe* reporter Thomas Oliphant, who was charged with participating in an airdrop of supplies into the village.[68]

After several days of testimony Nichol denied the motions, including one arguing that under the terms of the 1868 Treaty the government had no jurisdiction over crimes committed on the reservation.[69] Yet the defense's relationship with Nichol seemed positive by the end of the pretrial hearings, and some in WKLDOC, though certainly not all, were confident that they would receive a fair trial from the South Dakota federal judge.[70] Their experience with South Dakota's other federal district judge was another story, and it demonstrated how influential a trial judge could be on the conduct and outcome of the upcoming trials.

Bond reduction hearings before Judge Andrew Bogue had been contentious and often unsuccessful for the defense. During pretrial proceedings in September, Bogue questioned WKLDOC's representation of all the defendants, claiming that it might be a conflict of interest. Nichol had expressed similar concerns to Banks and Means, but was quickly satisfied that they understood the situation.[71] Bogue, however, required WKLDOC to send letters to all the defendants, detailing the possible conflicts and problems of joint representation (including "the problem of ideological attorneys"), and requesting them to execute a waiver attesting to their understanding of their rights to independent counsel, their desire to be represented by WKLDOC lawyers, and their agreement to waive any future challenge.[72]

In the fall Bogue again questioned the quality of the representation for the defendants, but a defense motion to get the judge to recuse himself was denied. Administrative considerations which led to the assignment of visiting judges to try some of the cases finally removed Bogue from the trials, at least temporarily.[73] By the end of October, about the only positive aspect of the relationship from the perspective of the defendants was Bogue's order directing the Pine Ridge tribal officials to stop interfering with WKLDOC investigations on the reservation.[74]

Outside the pretrial hearings, defense committee activities took some unusual twists, and the definition of its "work" continued to be stretched. In a bizarre episode in mid-August, WKLDOC briefly turned the tables on the FBI when it filed assault charges against one of its agents. According to committee members, FBI agents, who had rented rooms just down the street from WKLDOC, had been seen noting license plate numbers and taking photographs in front of the committee houses. The next day volunteers photographed the agents, while noting down the license plate numbers of their cars. WKLDOC claimed that one volunteer was assaulted when an agent tried to take his camera away, and another person was pushed on the steps of the county courthouse where committee members had gone to file charges. The assistant county attorney took the complaints and finally agreed to file charges for one of the assaults after an hour-long meeting with a delegation of WKLDOC attorneys who had descended on his office to discuss the shortcomings of South Dakota justice.[75] On the reservation, AIM distributed a "wanted poster" for the missing FBI agent which read, "This fugitive is armed and must be considered dangerous," and offered a reward of a case of beer for his return.[76]

A week later WKLDOC was on the offensive again, filing suit in federal district court to charge the FBI with "threatening, assaulting and interfering with activities of attorneys and legal workers" of the defense committee. The suit asked for injunctive relief and $600,000 in punitive damages, alleging surveillance, harassment, shouted obscenities, threats of physical harm, assault and battery, false arrest, and false imprisonment by FBI agents.[77] The investigative team on the reservation distributed a WKLDOC leaflet titled "Arm Yourself With Legal Knowledge," which explained people's rights concerning the FBI.[78] Tribal Chairman Wilson countered by having Lane and three other investigators evicted from the reservation by Tribal Council resolution. Nine BIA policemen served the eviction and took photographs of the committee members and a reporter from the *Minneapolis Tribune* who happened to be on the scene.[79]

Toward the end of August, WKLDOC issued a statement detailing alleged attacks by the "goon squad" and charging federal officials with inaction: "The FBI, BIA police, and the Justice Department have yet to make one statement or move to curb the monthly attacks."[80] In a speech to the IDS Men's Club in Minneapolis, Joseph Trimbach, the FBI agent in charge of the midwest region, denied the charges, calling them "trumped up" and "absurd."[81] In separate rulings, Judge Bogue granted an order directing officials of the tribe not to interfere with defense committee investigations but denied the request for an injunction against alleged FBI harassment of the defense committee, saying that "a plaintiff who seeks an injunction, must come into court with clean hands," and ruling that WKLDOC had initiated the conflicts with the FBI.[82] Meanwhile, the Justice Department announced it had created a unit on Indian rights but denied that it was in response to events in South Dakota.[83]

Near the end of December South Dakota newspaper editors selected Wounded Knee as the state's story of the year.[84] By now AIM had developed a reputation for manipulating the media, but some within the organization continued to distrust the press and counseled against becoming overly reliant on it.[85] AIM had certainly learned how to attract attention, but by late fall a combination of media bias, confrontations with law enforcement officials, and internal dissent within the organization had resulted in as much coverage of the Indian movement's internal dynamics as of the substantive issues facing Native Americans across the country.

At its national convention at White Oak, Oklahoma, in early August, AIM selected Dennis Banks as its National Director and pledged to continue its campaigns for treaty rights, the repeal of the 1934 Indian Reorganization Act, and the dismantling of the BIA. A pamphlet setting out the program was prepared and distributed by WKLDOC along with other materials on the cases. Shortly after the convention AIM celebrated its spiritual roots with a traditional Sun Dance on the Rosebud Reservation.[86] But this was the first time the AIM leadership had been together all summer, and Banks in particular continued to worry about the lack of leadership for the upcoming trials.[87]

Then in late August, a dispute of unknown origins erupted in which Clyde Bellecourt was shot by fellow AIM leader Carter Camp. News of the event had an immediate and devastating impact on the spirits of many in WKLDOC, leaving them wondering about the people whom they had looked to for political leadership and were trying to defend. Many of the volunteers had felt closer to Camp because of his familiarity with the politics of the new left.[88]

Bellecourt, of course, was well known and respected as one of the founders of AIM. As he lay in intensive care, AIM and WKLDOC tried to explain, both to themselves and to eager reporters, what had happened. At a time when the defense was preparing for pretrial hearings, violence within AIM claimed the headlines and gave credence to the rumors of splits within the organization. Stunned AIM leaders attempted to link

Camp with government harassment and infiltration, portraying him more as a victim than a villain.[89]

In September the papers were still carrying stories about the collapse of AIM. Bellecourt, recuperating in a Minneapolis hospital, refused to cooperate in the prosecution of Camp, saying, "I spent $14^1/_2$ years of my life in jail and I won't put another man in jail if I can help it."[90] But the story and other public criticism kept making news. South Dakota Senator George McGovern referred to AIM leaders as "violent lawbreakers" and "rip-off artists."[91]

A few weeks later on October 18, Pedro Bissonette, a leader of the civil rights movement on Pine Ridge, was shot to death by a BIA policeman on the reservation. The BIA claimed the officer was defending himself while trying to execute an arrest warrant. Many were convinced otherwise. Bissonette was respected by everyone involved in Wounded Knee and was expected to be a key witness in the trials. His death brought depression and outrage, weakened the defense effort, and threatened to plunge the reservation into more violence. AIM leaders called for mass demonstrations, but Tribal Chairman Wilson promised he would use force to keep them off the reservation.[92] Four days after Bissonette was killed, two BIA policemen were shot and wounded by unknown assailants. Russell Means denied charges that AIM members were involved. Monitored by BIA police officers, Bissonette's funeral procession detoured off the reservation to allow Banks, barred by a tribal court order from attending the funeral, to pay his last respects.[93]

The tension on the reservation and the controversy over the circumstances surrounding Bissonette's shooting continued through the fall. Wilson echoed the assertions of federal officials when he said that Bissonette "was not killed because he was AIM." U.S. Attorney Clayton promised an investigation, but AIM was skeptical that anything would come of it. Banks, on a speaking tour of college campuses, said in Michigan: "The government will thoroughly investigate the matter, but thoroughly do nothing." Whatever the outcome, nothing could compensate for the loss of a man who many felt was one of the movement's most important leaders.[94]

To some following the events in the press, stories about Bellecourt, Bissonette, and the legal problems of other AIM leaders helped substantiate the FBI's characterization of the organization as "the violence-prone AIM." Russell Means and Vernon Bellecourt were arrested on warrants issued by the South Dakota Grand Jury investigating the February riot in Custer. The charges included assault, conspiracy to commit arson, and participation in a riot.[95] In September, three AIM members, including Means's brother Bill, were arrested in Minneapolis for possession of drugs. In mid-October, not long after he was released from the hospital, Clyde Bellecourt was sentenced to fifteen days in jail on an old disorderly conduct conviction. Meanwhile, Banks made news just for pleading not guilty to ten charges connected with the Custer riot, including arson, assault with a deadly weapon, injury to a building, and conspiracy.[96]

Negative publicity, however, did not keep the crowds away from AIM fund-raising events. At a Wounded Knee support rally on the University of Minnesota campus, more than 3,000 people heard black activist Angela Davis and others charge the government with attempting to destroy AIM by any means, including the judicial system. Across town an anti-AIM rally sponsored by the John Birch Society drew only 200. There, Johnson Holy Rock from Pine Ridge charged AIM with causing the divisions on that reservation.[97]

Articles in newspapers also reported on living conditions on reservations, complaints about the government's Indian policy from leaders not connected with AIM, Russell Means's campaign for Chairman of the Pine Ridge Tribal Council, protests against police brutality in McLaughlin, South Dakota, and AIM's efforts to establish closer ties with more moderate Indian groups.[98] Yet stories about Native American poverty always seemed to be competing with the media's close scrutiny of the messengers of the unpleasant news, and coverage continued to portray Indian activists as people who were separate from most Indians and frequently in trouble with the law. In November the *New York Times* credited AIM with getting the public's attention and instilling a newfound "sense of pride and purpose" in many Native Americans, but argued that six months after Wounded Knee, the Indian rights movement had vanished as a result of internal bickering, legal tangles, and other problems unique to Indians.[99]

From the government's perspective, it may have seemed as if Indian activists were still ahead in the battle for public sympathy. In Minneapolis, Federal Judge Miles Lord ordered the Office of Economic Opportunity to return the funding to the AIM survival school that it had cut off after the occupation of the BIA office in Washington in late 1972.[100] In Washington the BIA came under heavy criticism from Senator Henry Jackson and others during confirmation hearings on the appointment of Morris Thompson to be director of that agency. On the Navajo Indian Reservation in Arizona, BIA officials were trying to defend themselves against charges of discrimination in hiring and awarding government contracts on the reservation during hearings before the U.S. Commission on Civil

Rights. After considerable testimony, the Commission likened conditions on the Navajo reservation to those of a third world country.[101]

Equally problematic for the government's image were the weekly revelations from Washington that continued to move the general public closer to outright distrust of its political leaders. Congress battled the President over the White House tapes, Vice President Spiro Agnew pleaded "nolo contendere" to a single count of tax evasion and resigned, and the firing of Attorney General Elliot Richardson and Watergate Special Prosecutor Archibald Cox provoked waves of protest. By November Nixon's approval rating had dropped to 27 percent, and many were calling for his impeachment. However, it was a federal judge, not the media, who would decide how much testimony about Indian policy would be allowed in the courtroom, and it was still anybody's guess whether Watergate would explode into a substantial enough issue to have an effect on the prosecution of a group of Indian dissidents.

The social conflicts and political confrontations of nineteenth-century France, Michel Foucault observed, "prompted those in power to treat political misdemeanors in the same way as ordinary crimes in order to discredit them." Slowly, over time, Foucault wrote, "an image was built up of an enemy of society who can equally well be a revolutionary or a murderer, since after all revolutionaries do sometimes kill."[102]

The protests at the BIA offices in Washington and at Wounded Knee had provided AIM with a public platform, which it had used to articulate the grievances of Native Americans around the country. But now most of its leadership and a significant portion of its members were under indictment. In speech after speech, Means and others attempted to connect the government mistreatment of Indians with the criminal prosecutions: "The federal government is prosecuting me more severely than other defendants. The state is doing the same to Banks on the South Dakota charges. They are working together to make examples of us. It is a strategy intended to destroy AIM as an organization dedicated to obtaining Indian rights. They want to discourage other Indians from seeking their rights."[103] The government, however, had a ready response to questions about its prosecution of the Indian activists: "The defendants were not engaged in the possibly innocuous acts of leafleting and picketing, but with acts of anarchy intended to shake loose the very foundations of an organized society maintaining public order."[104]

Prosecutors expressed confidence in their case at the end of pretrial hearings, and not without reason. The early 1970s had seen a resurgence of calls for law and order in statehouses and the nation's capital. Hurd admitted to reporters that these were not normal cases, but added that "there is nothing unusual about the charges filed against the defendants."[105] Two Native Americans had died at Wounded Knee, and several law enforcement officials had been wounded, one seriously. There was ample evidence for government claims that the defendants had committed crimes and threatened the public order, whatever their political motives might have been.

The defense was also confident; in seven months it had put together a well-organized defense team, including a number of highly skilled trial attorneys. Banks, who had worried a great deal about the defense and his own trial, was now "more than comfortable" with the situation. William Kunstler told reporters that "for the first time in generations an American jury would have the chance to pass on what has happened to the American Indian." AIM counsel Ramon Roubideaux said the trial would demonstrate how the American Indian had been "depressed and deprived of his property" throughout history.[106] Nonetheless, what constitutes a threatening situation or reasonable resistance to it is determined by those who are seldom placed in those situations.[107] In the federal courtroom in Saint Paul, much would still depend on Judge Fred Nichol.

Although the defense had won favorable rulings on discovery and a change of venue, these were decisions based on standard legal arguments of due process and undue bias. The more substantive legal and political issues for Native Americans—arguments in support of defense motions for dismissal that raised the issues of reservation poverty, government mishandling of Indian resources, harassment by law enforcement officials, and the jurisdictional provisions of the 1868 Treaty—had all fallen on deaf ears, at least for the time being. As the criminal process moved to the trial stage, testimony on the issues that meant the most to the defendants would come up against even stricter rules of admissibility, and the ever-present press would be on hand to evaluate and report on their success.

"The law governing the use of speech in legal rituals—the law of evidence," writes Lucie White, "has devised an arsenal of doctrines for guarding against the voices of . . . subordinate groups."[108] In 1976, the year after the Wounded Knee trials ended, the Mashpee Indian community on Cape Cod sued in federal court to recover lands taken from them between 1834 and 1870, without the required government consent. The defendant, the town of Mashpee, responded by denying that the Mashpee were a tribe and therefore that they were outside the protection of the federal law and without standing to sue. After the judge instructed the jury that the Mashpee must demonstrate their tribal existence according to the particularly narrow definition adopted by the Supreme Court in 1901, jurors found that they constituted a "tribe" during some periods but not others, and the suit was dismissed.[109]

As Torres and Milun observe in their article on the case, the Mashpee's testimony of its "lived experience" never quite fit the definition established by the legal precedent. In effect, they had been forced to petition the courts to allow them to exist, according to rules that determined both the form and the measure of that petition. The requirement that the story be told in a particular way elevated one version of the events to a noncontingent status. The conflict between systems of meaning, that of the Mashpee versus that of the state, they write, "is really the question of how we can 'know' which history is most 'true.'"[110]

During the kind of highly visible and politicized trial that was being predicted for Saint Paul, the struggle for meanings—the "history" of Wounded Knee to the Native Americans who had gone there, versus the definitions of what constitutes criminal acts according to the law—would be fought out in the media, as well as in the courtroom.[111] Highly publicized political trials can become forums for challenging legal language and conventions, but they may also serve to legitimize the status quo, or worse. In 1969, media coverage of the Chicago Seven trial created caricatures of antiwar protesters and did little to aid the campaign to end U.S. involvement in Vietnam. In 1973, as the Watergate investigations began to cast doubt on federal officials charged with enforcing the law, the government had a heavy stake in reassuring the nation that the institutions of justice had not been reduced to caricatures in the face of serious challenges from within or outside the system.

For all his favorable rulings toward the defense in pretrial hearings, Fred Nichol was still a federal district judge, bound by his training as a lawyer and the long-accepted rules and procedures of the federal court system. And he was bound as well by the bias and prejudices of any white male who had come of age well before the upheavals of the 1960s. Russell Means and Dennis Banks knew these prejudices well, but they had a team of legal experts on hand to help them navigate their political issues through and around the rules, to resist the conventions of legal process. In the spotlit arena in Saint Paul, both the defendants and their lawyers would have to confront and convince the others sitting in judgment—the 99$^1/_2$ percent of Americans who were not Indian, but were present in the courtroom as jurors and reporters, and on the outside as interested spectators.[112]

THE SAINT PAUL TRIAL BEGINS

It's one thing to stand in a bunker against armed federal agents. But the courts are more deadly than Wounded Knee. They have a stamp of legitimacy about them and can destroy without a drop of blood being shed.
WILLIAM KUNSTLER, JANUARY 1974

I N JANUARY 1974, as the "Indian trial of the twentieth century" was about to begin in Minnesota, Bob Dylan launched his first U.S. concert tour in nearly a decade. When he spat out the ten-year-old line, "Even the president of the United States sometimes must have to stand naked," the crowd of 18,000 in Chicago Stadium let out a roar. As the defense began selecting a jury in Saint Paul, they were undoubtedly hoping for a panel with similar sentiments. As winter tightened its grip on the upper midwest and news of the worsening economic conditions—high unemployment and inflation, coupled with the energy shortage—was added to the weekly Watergate revelations, you didn't need a Dylan audience to find people receptive to criticism of their public officials, particularly if you were in the Minnesotan's home state.

Situated on the Mississippi River just downstream from its twin city, Minneapolis, Saint Paul had emerged in the mid-nineteenth century as the transportation center for the midwest portion of the country beyond Chicago. In the 1840s it was known for its river travel and trade, but it became increasingly industrialized and was a center for railroad transportation by the end of the century. At the same time, Minneapolis had become the "queen flour city," the home of a large state university, and the cultural center for the region. In the east it was hailed as the "Paris of the plains."

Such publicity brought a flood of immigrants of Scandinavian, German, and Irish descent to the state, and a century later the Twin Cities and their surrounding suburbs had a combined population of over 1.4 million. By 1970 both cities were part of the state's rich history of liberalism and activism, and served as home for more than 50,000 college students on several campuses in the metropolitan areas. Many of these students had formed the core of the anti–Vietnam War movement during the 1960s. There was also a chapter of NLG which provided legal support to movement groups and had recruited a number of volunteers for WKLDOC in 1973.

Minnesota's activist reputation dated back to the early part of the century, when the Non Partisan League took root, and continued with the formation of the Farmer-Labor Party in the 1920s and the election of Floyd B. Olson in 1930, a governor who unabashedly took the side of labor in disputes with the state's industrial giants. Though Olson's brand of populism did not quite take hold, a more moderate form of liberalism was carried on by Hubert Humphrey and those who followed in his footsteps, such as Eugene McCarthy, Walter Mondale, Orville Freeman, and Saint Paul Mayor Lawrence Cohen.

The state's Indian history was of equal importance to those about to pick a jury for two Native American defendants. The Anishinabe (or Ojibway) and the Dakota Sioux had hunted, fished, and gathered wild rice and maple syrup on the lands that became Minnesota long before white settlers pushed into the area. Like Indians in South Dakota and elsewhere, they had been forced to relinquish vast portions of their homeland and settle on reservations scattered throughout the state.[1]

In 1862 a group of Dakota who were unhappy over the loss of their traditional lands, and suffering the effects of a hard winter and belated distribution of promised food, struck back at white settlers, killing several hundred. The 38-day conflict, eventually ended by federal troops, became known as the "Great Sioux Uprising of 1862." General Henry Sibley called the Dakota "outlaws and villains," and Governor Alexander Ramsey referred to them as "visiting bands of murderers." Three hundred were sentenced to death before a military tribunal that had provided for little in the way of due process or actual fairness. President Abraham Lincoln's intervention saved most of those condemned, but thirty-eight were executed in a mass public hanging at Mankato on December 26, 1862. Thus ended Minnesota's Indian trial of the nineteenth century.[2]

Attempts at assimilation in Minnesota followed a path similar to that of other states. Indians seeking to participate in government off the reservation were told that to vote they must be "civilized," and in 1917 the state's Supreme Court ruled that the Indian could accomplish this by "taking up his abode outside the reservation and there pursuing the customs and habits of civilization."[3]

By the time of the rebirth of Indian activism a century later, there were more than 30,000 Ojibway on seven reservations in the northern half of the state and about 1,000 Sioux on four reservations in central Minnesota. In addition, there were about 500 Winnebagos and a few scattered others. Faced with poor economic conditions and encouraged by the BIA, a number of reservation Indians had headed for the Twin Cities after World War II. On the reservations the Ojibway bands evolved a strategy of legal action and negotiation with the state over treaty rights that yielded some accommodation and success. Meanwhile, in the cities the struggle for Indian rights spawned the American Indian Movement in 1968. By 1974 AIM had chapters in both cities and had held a national meeting on the Leech Lake Reservation in the northern part of the state.

Because of all these factors, WKLDOC early on listed the Twin Cities as a possible site for all of the trials. Almost immediately after Judge Nichol ordered the leadership trials transferred to Saint Paul, Diane Wiley, a former researcher at the University of Minnesota, put together a team of forty volunteers to conduct an opinion survey in the area. Jay Schulman and Richard Christie, who had served as defense consultants in jury selection for the Harrisburg Seven, Camden Twenty-five, and Gainesville Eight trials, helped direct the effort. A list of questions was drafted (for example, "What have you read or heard about Wounded Knee?"), and people were trained to conduct telephone interviews. From the data provided by these 576 interviews, the group developed a sociological demographic profile of the approximately 700,000 registered voters in the nine-county area from which potential jurors would be drawn. The whole process, which began in late October, was finished just as the trial opened in January.[4]

When the findings were compared with a similar study done in South Dakota, Minnesota's liberal heritage and the difference in geographical distance to the events of 1973 were clearly demonstrated. People in South Dakota were more familiar with both Wounded Knee and the defendants, Banks and Means, and had a much more negative opinion of the two AIM leaders. The findings also demonstrated that South Dakotans were more hostile toward Indians in general and AIM in particular.[5] The surveys clearly supported Nichol's decision to move the trial to Minnesota. More important, the results provided the defense with some ideas for questions to ask prospective jurors—how to identify and evaluate their biases and ultimately determine who would make the "best" juror from their perspective.[6] Still, Schulman remained concerned about the lack of Native Americans in the Saint Paul division; only 5,000 were registered to vote in the area, making it unlikely that any Indians would serve on the jury. Schulman described the situation as an "enormous edge" for the prosecution.[7]

In addition to the survey work, defense preparations included setting up a structured defense committee which was divided into specific subcommittees, with assigned tasks and responsibilities for each volunteer. The subcommittees coordinated their work with WKLDOC in Sioux Falls, where people were preparing for the start of the nonleadership Wounded Knee trials and the Custer trials, which were scheduled to begin shortly after the start of the Saint Paul trial. In coordination with WKLDOC, AIM's new national office orchestrated demonstrations, printed publicity, held press conferences, and arranged speaking engagements by AIM leaders and visiting celebrities.[8]

On the government side, Assistant U.S. Attorneys R. D. Hurd and David Gienapp, who had been involved with Wounded Knee from the beginning, were responsible for prosecuting the case in Saint Paul. They were assisted by Earl Kaplan, an attorney from the Justice Department, and U.S. Attorney Clayton, who divided his time between Saint Paul and his office in Sioux Falls. Hurd, the senior of the two if only by a few years, acted as lead counsel. Both Gienapp and Hurd had spent 80 percent of their time on the case during the latter part of 1973, but they were almost lost in the spectacle of the opening week.[9]

On January 8 at 10:00 A.M., in an atmosphere of pomp and circumstance, the trial of Dennis Banks and Russell Means finally opened in courtroom number three of the Saint Paul Federal Courthouse. Outside, supporters of the defendants, including a group of Oglala traditional chiefs and elders from Pine Ridge, marched and listened to speeches, including a welcome from Mayor Cohen, all under the watchful eye of specially assigned U.S. Marshals.[10] Wounded Knee had made celebrities of Banks and Means, but two of their attorneys, William Kunstler and Mark Lane, also shared the media spotlight. Kunstler represented Means, along with Ken Tilsen, who had practiced in Saint Paul since 1951 and was best known for his defense of the "Minnesota Eight," a group who had conducted a raid on a local draft board. Lane was assigned to Banks, along with Minneapolis lawyers Doug Hall and Larry Leventhal, both of whom had ties to the Indian community. Also present was AIM general counsel Ramon Roubideaux, the only Native American attorney.[11]

Kunstler told reporters that he hoped much of the case would be tried "through the media and the people," and the defense wasted no time in staging events geared to attract those two audiences. More than 2,000 attended a rally on the University of Minnesota campus the night before the opening of the trial and listened to AIM leaders and other celebrity speakers.[12] Banks, too, made it clear that the defense did not intend to limit the trial to the confines of the courtroom: "Let the public determine who is guilty at Wounded Knee. I am positive that when the public sees the evidence, they will have no choice but to declare that the U.S. government is guilty."[13]

The crowd that gathered outside the courthouse the morning of January 8 included film crews from all three networks, reporters from major newspapers, a correspondent from Tass, the Soviet Union news agency, and a German television film crew shooting a documentary on AIM. The Soviet report charged that "the trial was specifically staged by the authorities in order to suppress the patriots and preserve the disgraceful racist order in the country."[14] U.S. papers carried stories of the Wounded Knee "insurrection," referred to the defendants as leaders of the "insurgents" or "militants," recalled that Banks had been labeled a "war chief," and noted the defendant's braids and "colorful" dress. On January 12, the *New York Times* spoke of the "potential drama" of the trial, summarizing the central question as whether the defendants "are to be treated as common criminals or modern day Sitting Bulls," while describing Banks and Means as "tall, graceful, bronzed, almost the epitome of Indianness."[15]

The defendants continued to assert that they were being prosecuted because of their beliefs and that they intended to put the government on trial for past injustices toward Indians. "We are not on trial," said Means; "the United States of America is on trial for violating the treaties."[16] At the same time, prosecutors continued to maintain that the case would be "tried on the issues in the indictment." In a press conference held the first day, Hurd denied that the government charges were a veiled attempt to destroy AIM: "In no way should this be considered a prosecution of AIM or any group of individuals," said the Assistant U.S. Attorney, but rather a prosecution of "alleged crimes by certain individuals."[17]

WKLDOC had begun distributing a "Wounded Knee Trials Press Packet" to the media before the opening day of the trial. The packet contained a

summary of the indictments and disposition of the pretrial motions, biographical sketches of the lawyers, copies of some recent news stories, an
article on jury selection by Schulman, and a "Statement by a Lakota
Woman Who Participated in Liberation of Wounded Knee." The packet
also contained information on AIM, the situation on Pine Ridge, and the
importance of the treaty issue to the defense, as well as a "suggested reading
list" on Indian history and culture.[18]

Presiding Federal Judge Fred J. Nichol was also receiving his share of
publicity. Appointed to the federal bench by President Lyndon Johnson
on the recommendation of Senator George McGovern, Nichol was the
Chief Judge of the South Dakota District at the time of Wounded Knee.
Newspapers detailed the career of the judge, who was born, raised, and
educated in the state, calling him an "up-by-the-bootstraps midwesterner"
and a "friendly establishment liberal." Also noted was his reputation among
South Dakota attorneys as "super fair," a liberal interpreter of individual
rights, but "tough as nails" on sentencing once someone was convicted.
Reports also mentioned that Nichol had admitted that although he had
always opposed mixed marriages between the races because of fears for
the children, he now viewed the situation differently.[19] The publicity surrounding Nichol's liberal reputation helped provide the proceedings with
a stamp of fairness and legitimacy, at a time when many of the country's
institutions were under attack and in a trial where one of the main themes
of the defense was to expand on many of those critiques.

Nichol was no stranger to cases where the politics of Indian-white relations were involved. In 1971, he had presided over the trial of several
Native Americans who had occupied the naval air base in Minneapolis and
had ruled against the admissibility of treaties as a defense. Now in the final
pretrial hearing, Nichol denied another motion to dismiss and put aside
until later motions seeking a ruling on the admissibility of the 1868 Treaty,
as well as the defendants' contentions that under its provisions the U.S.
federal courts had no jurisdiction over Sioux lands. Though he described
himself as personally sympathetic to Indians and to the treaty issue, Nichol
was still not convinced that the treaty was relevant in the upcoming criminal trial.[20]

Nichol did rule that the defendants were indigent and thus entitled to
have the federal government pay part of the costs of the defense. The
defense had filed affidavits claiming that WKLDOC was virtually penni-
less. Four of the six defense lawyers were to be paid $30 an hour inside
the courtroom and $20 an hour outside. The four said that they would
share the fees.[21] Some critics charged that Nichol's decision was a misuse

of taxpayers' money. A few weeks later, the Chief Judge of the Eighth Circuit Court of Appeals limited the courtroom pay to $12.50 an hour, adding that after the finish of the trial the attorneys could apply for a rate of $17.50.[22]

Inside the packed courtroom, seating arrangements had been worked out ahead of time. Forty seats were set aside for the media, ten each for the prosecution and defense, and an additional thirty-seven seats for AIM supporters, which were drawn by lot. U.S. Marshals controlled entrance into the building, as well as access to the floor of the trial. A metal detector screened everyone entering the courthouse, including trial participants. The marshals also escorted people into the only two elevators that could now stop on the floor of the trial, and they patrolled in and around the courtroom. The Saint Paul Police Department, which had conducted training on Indian culture, assigned officers to patrol the outside of the building. The city's Human Rights Department even set up a 24-hour telephone hotline to try and quash rumors before they got started. One early rumor was that Ted Means, Russell's brother, had been shot and killed on Pine Ridge.[23]

Midway through jury selection, Kunstler complained to Nichol that the heavy security measures were a common government tactic in political trials, geared to prejudice the jury against the defendants by making them and their supporters appear to be dangerous people. Hurd responded by saying that the defense was to blame for encouraging people to come to Saint Paul for the trial. Nichol expressed sympathy for the defense's position, noting that while he assumed there would be no trouble, the marshals probably assumed there would be. But Nichol also pointed out that reporters had been complimenting the marshals on how courteous they were, and he expressed his own admiration for their work. The judge refused to do away with the security, but he did modify it somewhat for trial participants.[24]

Though Kunstler's complaints did not lead to significant changes, the discussion demonstrated early on how it was possible to turn almost any issue into a political forum in the midst of a trial and how the prosecution and the judge would try to respond. In an exchange between the defense attorney and Hurd and Nichol, Kunstler alluded to the trial of Daniel Ellsberg, the break-in at the office of Ellsberg's psychiatrist, and what he characterized as the attempt to bribe a federal judge. The government, Kunstler argued, would "stop at nothing to win these cases." Nichol responded by noting that in most of the cases cited the defendants had been acquitted, but Kunstler was prepared with an answer:

MR. KUNSTLER: Judge, they may win with the juries eventually, because jurors are becoming wiser to the ways of the world and the ways of the government, but they are tied down in a trial for months and years. These defendants have been tied down since the indictments. That's the winning aspect. Everyone thinks that the jury's verdict is the victory. The jury's verdict is just that they go free, but the real loser is the defendant. AIM should be out organizing, AIM should be out doing its job, not tied up in a courtroom . . .

These are the latest victims, that started with the anti-war movement, priests and nuns, Vietnam vets, now American Indians. Whoever comes up in a dissenting way is then cut down through the judicial process, and the victories at the jury's hands are not a real victory at all. They keep people from going to jail, yes; that they do, but they tie down enormous resources, enormous assets, and I think it's all done deliberately. I know it's done deliberately. I don't think any sane thinking American can think any different of the grotesque use of the courts in the last four and a half years . . .

Why this trial, Your Honor? Why not every trial in this building, have this type of security? What's so different about Russell Means and Dennis Banks or the American Indian Movement that they are treated thusly? I think, Your Honor, some judge has to say: This is ridiculous and prejudicial, and I hope you're that judge.

THE COURT: Well, thank you. You do indicate, though, that Mr. Means and Mr. Banks, to the extent that you've indicated, the same procedure was followed in all these other trials. They were treated the same way.

MR. KUNSTLER: By the same government, Your Honor, for the same purpose. They were all grotesque criminal prosecutions, conspiracy prosecutions brought by the federal government. Of course it's the same, that's what we're complaining about . . .

MR. HURD: I wanted to object to the remarks of counsel relative to the bugging of the psychiatrist's office or attempting to bribe federal judges, on the ground that it's irrelevant and immaterial to whatever issue is being raised at this time and this place. Beyond that, the only response that I would have, Your Honor, is that I have observed the security, and that I have not gotten the impression that defense counsel has gotten from it.

Relative to why this case has more security than the normal case, the defendants and their counsel have been telling us that this is going to be the Indian trial of the century. There has been a great deal of publicity of thousands of people coming in town for this trial . . . I also have been engaged in this case from the outset and it is not a political trial, in my view.[25]

As they had with the numerous pretrial motions, the defense was determined to keep the pressure on the prosecution in and outside the courtroom.[26] During the first weeks of the trial, however, their success was uneven, and both the judge and the media remained skeptical about the numerous charges of government misconduct. The defense's preparedness, however, was not in doubt; by the end of jury selection it was clear that the months of pretrial organization and the early victories before Nichol were paying off.

One hundred thirty-three panelists, drawn randomly from voter registration lists, were assembled for jury selection, which began on January 8. The group was divided equally between men and women; their average age was forty-two. A week into the selection process, the defense questioned the fact that the first fifty-seven prospective jurors were all white, pointing out that their survey and the 1970 census showed that 1.7 to 1.8 percent of the population for the fifteen counties that constituted the district were nonwhite. Commenting on the statistics, Means quipped, "The jury wheel had a flat tire." Nichol questioned Federal Clerk Harry Sieben about the method of selection and satisfied himself that there had been no attempts to prejudice the pool.[27]

Nichol began by summarizing the charges and then cautioned the assembled panel that the indictments were not proof of guilt, that the government had the burden of proving the defendants had committed crimes; he noted also that if they were selected as jurors, they would not be able to discuss the cases with anyone or read press reports of the trial. He then explained the procedures for jury selection and the purpose and nature of the questions he would be asking, in an effort to elicit information "that would bring out any bias or sympathy or any prejudice against either side, if there is such bias, prejudice or sympathy."[28]

Exercising his discretion under federal rules, Nichol ruled that he alone would question the prospective jurors, allowing the prosecution and defense to submit lists of potential questions for him to consider. The government's 49 questions were fairly standard for a criminal case, dealing with prior knowledge of the incident at Wounded Knee; a panelist's familiarity with defendants and their attorneys; personal history, including nationality and political affiliations; and any prior experience with law enforcement, juries, or the judicial process. The defense's list of 157 questions, however, contained several on Indian history, AIM, Wounded Knee, and an individual's right to protest and dissent. Working from the two lists, Nichol came up with 65 to 70 questions, the answers to which he reasoned would provide enough information to both sides from which to make decisions on challenging a prospective juror for some disqualifying cause or for the exercise of their preemptory strikes at the end of voir dire.[29]

To aid in these decisions the defense had assembled a team of experts, including specialists in speech, voice, and body language, plus an Indian spiritual leader. The cast also included Schulman and Wiley and a rating system based on their findings from the survey. Talking to reporters, Schulman referred to the survey as "a systematic way of determining the sociological makeup of an area, and then who of that area would make a fair and open minded member of the jury." But he admitted that they were not always right, citing a juror they liked in the recent Berrigan trial who had held out for conviction against the other jurors.[30] In addition to relying on the survey data and the expert opinions, the defense circulated the names of the panelists among their local supporters and interviewed anyone who knew someone on the list.[31]

Inside the courthouse, Nichol methodically questioned each of the 133 prospective jurors, while ruling on challenges from both sides.[32] The first few questions to each panelist were designed to establish who could serve without hardship to themselves or their families. Fifty people were excused for family obligations, often because they had young children, or for job-related reasons. At one point the defense questioned the district court policy of excusing mothers of children under ten years old because it released a number of young adults. According to their pretrial survey, the bulk of the district's population was age 35 and under.[33]

Nichol then questioned each panelist about whether he or she could follow his instructions on the law and about his or her attitudes toward Indians, as well as the panelist's knowledge of the case, the defendants, and the lawyers for each side. In the end twenty panelists were dismissed for cause, in most instances because they could not accept that defendants did not have to prove their innocence or even testify in their own behalf. "Well, if they are entirely innocent they probably wouldn't even be here," said a 37-year-old foreman, expressing the sentiments of more than one panelist. Several admitted that their views were strong enough to outweigh the judge's instructions on the issue of presumption of guilt.[34]

Central to Judge Nichol's questions on bias toward Indians was what he called the "sixty-four-dollar question," asking panelists how they would feel if their son or daughter wanted to marry an Indian. Few on the panel admitted to being prejudiced or said that any sympathy they might have toward Native Americans would interfere with their judgment if selected. In addition, Nichol questioned panelists on Wounded Knee, discovering that few had followed the protest on a daily basis. Said one prospective juror, "I'm really indifferent about the whole thing," adding, "I try to stay as indifferent as I can."[35]

Some on the panel did not know what the initials BIA stood for; most did not have Indian friends or even acquaintances. Many admitted that what they did know about Indians came from television and movies, and that they had ambivalent views about the preferability of retaining traditional culture versus assimilation. Only occasionally had a panelist engaged in any extensive reading on the subject, such as the few who had read Dee Brown's *Bury My Heart at Wounded Knee*.[36] After two weeks of questioning, one newspaper commented that little direct prejudice had been uncovered, but that what was becoming apparent was "fairly widespread ignorance of the American Indian, his culture and his history."[37]

The defense's endeavors to investigate each panelist paid off at least once, when they challenged the statements of one woman who had claimed to be a regular churchgoer. The defense was told that the woman had not been to church for two years because the minister was active in antiwar activities and race relations. When confronted with the information, she admitted that she had stopped attending because services had turned into discussions of racism and the Vietnam War. After arguments from both sides, Nichol granted the defense a challenge for cause.[38]

Such probing into a prospective juror's background went too far in the opinion of the U.S. attorneys trying the case. Hurd argues that Nichol allowed too wide a latitude in the number of questions asked and the areas of inquiry. After a day or more of questioning, in Hurd's opinion, one wound up with two kinds of panelists: those who wanted to be off the jury and those who wanted to be on, with each, after a time, able to figure out the answers that would achieve the desired result. Either way, he says, you wound up with a bad jury.[39]

While Nichol asked the questions, each side met nightly to discuss the panelists, but the process for the defense continued to stretch beyond what was considered normal by the average trial attorney. Armed with statistics and opinions, expert and otherwise, the defense team grabbed every available minute—during recess, during lunch, and every evening after court adjourned—to discuss and debate the prospective jurors. Part of what people hoped to do with the data derived from the surveys was to provide a context to help determine whether a panelist was giving truthful answers to the questions posed concerning knowledge of Wounded Knee or attitudes toward Indians. They also had formulated profiles of who might make a sympathetic or at least an impartial juror on the basis of age, occupation, residence, religion, and other demographic data. But Schulman and others admitted that they were still exercising a lot of guesswork, and not everyone trusted their system. Science battled intuition, and data ran up against spirituality as people tried to decide whom to strike from the panel.

This process provided the trial team with its first opportunity to work together as a unit. Discipline was needed to keep comments short and maximize time. In any unresolved disputes, the defendants had the last word. Of the two, Means, influenced by the spiritual leader Phillip Deere, often expressed the strongest opinions. Sometimes the data of the social scientists or the experience of one of the longtime criminal lawyers persuaded him that his instincts might be wrong, other times not. In the end, the defense as a whole was pleased with the final selections. Hurd, however, thought that the elaborate process was all for show and that he and Gienapp made fairly accurate guesses as to whom the defense would strike.[40]

By February 5, eighty-seven panelists had been excused for hardship or disqualified for cause, as the defense and prosecution pared the list down to the group from which the final selection would be made. The thirty-eight possible jurors and eight possible alternates from which they made their final selections were slightly younger and more urban and suburban than the original panel. The twelve jurors and four alternates that emerged from this group had an average age of 32, with eight under the age of 30. According to reporters who kept track of their answers to Nichol's questions, none had followed the events at Wounded Knee, though most were aware of the takeover. Only seven had heard of either Banks or Means or any of their lawyers. Four had said that they received their news from television rather than newspapers. The press also noted that one of the alternates was one-eighth to one-quarter Indian.[41]

The prosecutors made no public complaint about the jury, but privately they believed that the panel was not as good as they had hoped, because of the number of strikes Nichol had allowed the defense. Hurd thought they could still win but was not as confident as he had been: "Given the manner of selection, I thought we had done as well as we could."[42]

Privately and publicly, the defense was pleased with the results. Both defendants told the press that they felt it was possible to get a fair trial from the jurors selected. Means was quoted as saying that he believed that the jury was better "than any Indian could get in South Dakota."[43] Both he and Banks, however, said that their predictions were conditional on the admissibility of the 1868 Treaty into evidence. Banks stated: "If the jurors who are seated keep an open mind about the treaty issues, the probability of our receiving a fair trial will be 60–40. If the treaties are not presented before this panel, we might as well have the trial in South Dakota."[44]

For the defendants, getting the treaty issue before the public was as important as getting it before the jury. At a meeting of the defense committee and a broader coalition of volunteers at the AIM center, Banks told the 150 people in attendance that their continuing goal was to figure out ways to use the trial for maximum attention, and that the defense must not lose the visibility and momentum it had captured during the first two weeks. He reminded the group of the three demands of the "Trail of Broken Treaties" in Washington, D.C., in 1972: establishment of a treaty commission, repeal of the Indian Reorganization Act, and removal of the BIA from the Department of the Interior. The trial, said Banks, was an opportunity to educate the public on these and other issues. Distribution of press packets, mailings to colleges, radio feeds, and speaking engagements at community centers, high schools, and churches all continued as jury selection progressed.[45]

Meanwhile, Russell Means had put himself and perhaps his movement on the line by entering the race for Pine Ridge tribal chairman against Dick Wilson. Across the country, the closely watched campaign was being billed as a referendum on AIM, the BIA, Wilson, and the takeover of Wounded Knee.[46] On January 24 Oglalas went to the polls, giving Means 667 votes, Wilson 511, and enough scattered votes to other candidates to force a runoff. Even Wilson, who had referred to AIM supporters as "renegades" and "lawbreakers," acknowledged that he was surprised by the strong support for Means. For AIM the vote was a vindication of their protests, and they tried to publicize the results as much as possible.[47] In the changing political spectacle that AIM was now caught up in, however, such credibility could be short-lived.

Back in Saint Paul the defense sought to publicize conditions on Pine Ridge with a massive motion to dismiss that was admittedly geared more to the press and public than to the judge. According to Tilsen, the strategy behind the motion was to write and distribute a single document that set out the situation on the reservation.[48] Under the headline "Motion Claims

Terror Dominates Reservation," the *Minneapolis Tribune* carried the story on page two and described the motion and the 250-page supporting affidavit as drawing "a picture of a police state atmosphere designed to protect a political machine run by the tribal government on the Pine Ridge Indian Reservation of South Dakota."[49]

The supporting affidavit prepared by Lane and the investigative team on the reservation cataloged the complaints that AIM and others had made throughout 1973: the lack of protection from the BIA and FBI against "goon squad" harassment and intimidation; FBI surveillance and infiltration; and an overall government conspiracy to destroy AIM.[50] Two weeks later, WKLDOC lawyers filed a lawsuit seeking an end to all Wounded Knee prosecutions and accusing federal, state, and tribal officials of conspiracy to deny Indians their civil rights. The suit named President Nixon, U.S. Attorney Clayton, South Dakota Governor Richard Kneip, and Tribal Chairman Wilson as defendants and charged that they had "instituted and maintained a reign of terror, including but not limited to murder, mayhem, assault, bribery, extortion, intimidation, and other acts of physical or psychic violence."[51]

The defense strategy of intertwining politics and law to keep the focus on the government was not always successful, however. A week into the trial, it was learned that FBI agents had visited the editorial offices of the *Saint Paul Pioneer Press.* The FBI claimed that it had just stopped by to let the paper know that it was available to answer questions about the Bureau's role in the case. Kunstler, however, charged that they were attempting to intimidate the press; he compared the situation to the Ellsberg case and demanded a hearing on the matter. But Nichol, noting that the defense had been contacting the media "to a considerably larger extent" than the government, seemed irritated that the issue was even raised and quickly set it aside.[52] The press seemed equally unwilling to pursue the matter beyond getting comments from the parties involved. The executive editor of the *Pioneer Press,* John Finnegan, stated: "I didn't view the meeting as the FBI trying to influence us, nor would they."[53]

The local media were on hand to report on appearances by Kunstler before the Saint Paul Press Club and at a local Jaycees dinner, where he received a standing ovation.[54] The New York attorney told the Jaycees that the government often used criminal prosecutions to destroy groups who questioned its power: "We have the illusion that the law is just and fair and equitable. But it's a very manipulative system. It's used now as a very sacred kind of executioner—replacing the hangman's noose and the axe— that doesn't show blood."[55] Attacking the conspiracy laws, Kunstler told the audience: "If they can't get you doing it, they'll get you for trying to do it, they'll get you for thinking about it." Interviewed after the speech, several members of the "clean, trim middle-class audience" said that they respected the defense attorney even if they didn't agree with him. Some were clearly impressed with both the man and his message, making comments like, "When you hear the wild man talk he doesn't seem as wild as he does in the press," and "I think the government has built him up to look like a radical."[56] Also in attendance was Judge Nichol, who admitted to a growing respect for Kunstler. Back in court, Nichol complimented Kunstler on his conduct thus far in the trial and recessed the proceedings so that Kunstler could return to New York to defend himself against disbarment proceedings for his actions in a previous trial.[57]

WKLDOC also continued to orchestrate appearances by nationally known celebrities including comedian and activist Dick Gregory, who drew crowds of reporters and supporters at a fund-raising party at the Guild for Performing Arts.[58] The same week Marlon Brando, known for his support of Indian causes and a reported contributor to the protesters inside Wounded Knee, made an appearance in the courtroom; he embraced Banks and Means during a recess and then emerged with press and onlookers in tow to make a brief statement: "Those on trial are the American people, I should say more specifically, the American conscience." Reporters followed the actor around Saint Paul as he made various personal appearances, including a stop at the WKLDOC office.[59]

The prosecutors were aggravated by the media-event atmosphere almost immediately. In and outside of the courtroom, they argued that it had no place in the proceedings: "We kept thinking of this as a criminal trial, but it became very difficult to maintain that during the course of the trial. We kept wanting to talk about the trial and we'd have delays to wait for Marlon Brando to come so he could watch. We had delays in trial because Russell Means had a speaking engagement he didn't get back from."[60]

The government, however, did not totally concede the political ground to the defense. In the latest of an ongoing exchange of letters, Leonard Garment, now Counsel to the President, wrote Chief Frank Fools Crow on January 8, the opening day of the trial, once again setting out the White House position on treaties with the Sioux.[61] Garment pointed out that Sioux legal claims were currently being reviewed by the Indian Claims Commission, and that if Fools Crow had questions about the way these claims were being handled he should contact those attorneys "who have long been retained by the Oglala Sioux people to represent them in these law suits." He reminded Fools Crow that he was not the official voice of the Oglala, a position, Garment noted, that would be determined in the upcoming elections. Garment also outlined the White House position on the 1868 Treaty, stating that it was still "a valid legal document, with its obligations still in force except insofar as any of them have been changed by the Congress, by the parties, satisfied by litigation or expired."

In a list of answers to specific questions accompanying the letter, Garment cited federal case law which established the jurisdiction of the United States over Indian people and upheld certain "specified instances" of challenges to the terms of the 1868 Treaty. A series of decisions in the Court of Claims on cases brought by attorneys for the Sioux in the 1930s and 1940s were cited by Garment to back up his assertions that the U.S. government had fulfilled all its obligations under the treaty concerning law enforcement, education, land allotments, and economic help. Further remedies, said Garment, would have to come from Congress. He also contended that the assignment of U.S. Marshals to Pine Ridge was in keeping with pledges under the treaty to help maintain peace on the reservation. Finally, though Garment acknowledged that the federal government had been guilty of "shameful conduct" toward Native Americans, he urged Fools Crow to look to the future, adding that he had "no desire or inclination to defend the past two centuries of treatment of Indian peoples."[62]

When prosecutors distributed the letter along with a Justice Department press release, defense attorneys complained to Judge Nichol that U.S. Marshals on security duty were handing out the letter outside the courtroom. The contents of the letter were set out in detail in both the *Minneapolis Tribune* and the *Saint Paul Pioneer Press*.[63] Two weeks later, in court and before the press, U.S. Attorneys emphatically denied the defense charges that there was a conspiracy to crush Indian activism. Responding to the defense's massive motion to dismiss, Clayton and Hurd filed a formal answer and supporting affidavits totaling 330 pages, which contended that the defendants did have access to the reservation and denied accusations of false arrests, illegal seizures, and surveillance.[64]

The prosecutors also helped fuel the continued close media scrutiny of AIM's internal dynamics. As jury selection ended, the prosecution revealed that it had a letter allegedly written by former AIM leader Carter Camp, which had been discovered by the FBI in a Rapid City apartment in September 1973. The apartment had been occupied by members of the defense committee prior to the move to Sioux Falls. The letter, written by the man accused of shooting Clyde Bellecourt that summer, indicated that Camp might testify for the prosecution. But while AIM denounced Camp as a provocateur who advocated violence, Hurd said that he had no intention of calling him as a witness. In a hearing on whether the FBI had received any information about defense activities, the manager of the Rapid City apartment building testified that the FBI had requested that she keep an eye on the occupants of the apartment, but no evidence emerged that any information other than the letter had been obtained by federal officials.[65]

With testimony about to begin in Saint Paul, the legal and political stakes were rising for both sides. Vietnam and Watergate had political leaders scrambling to shore up public faith in the institutions of government; to that end the belief that the justice system remained untainted by scandal and capable of dealing with the situation was crucial. Yet, although many people were becoming cynical about their public officials, the majority were still not receptive to the broader critique of government that AIM and others were trying to articulate. In fact, as the Watergate investigation zeroed in on the abuse of power by a few individuals, it diverted attention away from issues of class, race, and inequality.[66] Americans were sympathetic to the plight of Native Americans, but they could still separate that sympathy from an acceptance of the movement that had made them aware of the situation in the first place. By 1974 people were looking for a restoration of order and stability, and few in the country had the energy to embrace a social movement that could be seen as countering those desires.

Too often those who oppose the status quo, Todd Gitlin observes, "can achieve media standing only as deviants."[67] If large numbers of white middle-class kids could be portrayed as deviants, or even traitors, for opposing a war that had killed thousands of young Americans, it was even easier to do so with a relatively small group of Indians who had engaged in a three-month armed standoff with hundreds of federal law enforcement officials in western South Dakota. Treating political dissidents as celebrities was only a short step away from turning them into caricatures and delegitimizing their political issues. AIM had been successful in using the media as a forum, but its leaders had also been characterized as militants, insurgents, war chiefs, and modern-day Sitting Bulls. Press coverage of their activities seemed evenly split between issues of Native American rights and sovereignty, on the one hand, and militant rhetoric and confrontations, on the other. As Gitlin notes: "Political news is treated as if it were crime news—what went wrong today, not what goes wrong every day. A demonstration is treated as a potential or actual disruption of legitimate order, not as a statement about the world."[68]

As jury selection was coming to a close, the news of Wilson's narrow victory over Means reached Minneapolis. During the campaign Wilson had continued to label his opponent a radical and a communist. "I am strongly against armed revolutionaries who threaten to burn and destroy, to force their ways on innocent people," the tribal chairman told reporters. Means, meanwhile, had promised to abolish the "white man's" tribal government and return to traditional forms of governing. Such rhetoric dominated the press coverage of the campaign and often overshadowed the more substantive investigations of the issues.[69]

A few days before the election, a *Minneapolis Tribune* article provided some documentation on the leasing of Indian land on Pine Ridge that gave credence to one of AIM's original complaints at the time of Wounded Knee. The article pointed out that the complicated ownership of the now divided land parcels under the Allotment Act—830,000 acres, with 7,000 owners and 45,000 separate ownership interests—made it difficult to determine who owned what; therefore the BIA, which was required to get permission before leasing the land, often did not do so. The burden was on individual Indians to come forward to object and possibly receive some money for the leasing.[70] The press also reported that an audit looking into allegations of corruption in the tribal government failed to prove or disprove the claims. The report did note, however, that the tribal government lacked financial controls and that service programs did not receive all the money allocated to them.[71] Such stories were rare, however, and what little coverage the press provided on the Pine Ridge election usually consisted of one-line charges and countercharges.

On February 8, Oglalas cast 1,709 votes for Wilson to 1,530 for Means. The next day newspapers reported allegations of voter fraud, and also that white ranchers and merchants on or near the reservation were happy about the results.[72] Calling the election an "illegal travesty," Means told the press that he would request a recount. During the runoff Means had complained of irregularities and charged state and federal officials with conspiring against him, when his brother Ted was arrested during the campaign and no bonding companies would agree to post his bond.[73] Wilson, who had characterized the election as a contest between democracy and violence, immediately ordered all Means supporters who were not Oglalas off the reservation within ten days, adding, "that includes some long haired lawyers."[74] The newly reelected Tribal Chairman told an eager South Dakota press that it was a "historic occasion": "[The vote] came down to whether the Oglala Sioux, serving as a weather vane for the world, would endorse government by violence, threat, and destruction or whether we would pursue progress through our imperfect system of democracy."[75]

Despite the evidence of fraud, and despite the fact that Means had lost by fewer than 200 votes, doing better than any of his critics had predicted, front page headlines such as "Means may have lost more than election" preceded articles speculating on what effect the "bitter defeat" would have on AIM's credibility and the ongoing trials.[76] Means's status as a movement celebrity had drawn the press to the Pine Ridge election, but the message the media conveyed about that campaign was not necessarily the one that Means wished to convey. As both sides knew, this could also be the case with coverage of the upcoming trial testimony in Saint Paul.

Still, the jury's interpretation of what they were about to see and hear could differ greatly from both the media's and the participants' perceptions of what was relevant. Media fascination with personality does not necessarily reflect the view from the jury box; legal moves or rhetorical flourishes that make headlines do not always win "not guilty" verdicts, any more than they ensure that the desired political point will be conveyed.[77] To use the courtroom as a political forum and win acquittals, the defense had to find ways to keep several different audiences interested and focused on issues that could not be easily dismissed as merely colorful or deviant. In early February it might have seemed as if Banks and Means had the government on the run, but they were still in court, charged with serious crimes; and, as jury selection had demonstrated, that circumstance created presumptions about the Indian movement and its leaders that could be difficult to overcome.

THE OPENING STATEMENTS

The evidence is going to show that these defendants together with their co-conspirators, in order to attract public attention to claimed grievances and demands and extort confessions from the United States . . . decided to seize the community of Wounded Knee, South Dakota, by force of arms.

R. D. HURD, ASSISTANT U.S. ATTORNEY, FEBRUARY 1974

The prosecution . . . opened up with a statement that we'd asked the Senate to investigate the conditions that were imposed by the federal government upon our people. To this we plead guilty.

DENNIS BANKS, FEBRUARY 1974

ON THE MORNING of February 12, Judge Nichol carefully explained to the jury the procedure for opening statements and their intended significance, cautioning them that what they were about to hear was not evidence and should not be considered as such. The opening statements would be the first opportunity for each side to speak directly to the jury about the merits of the case and, as in any trial, constituted a crucial stage in the battle for the hearts and minds of the jurors.[1] But now the moment was perhaps more crucial than usual, for Dennis Banks and Russell Means had both been granted the right to speak on their own behalf.

Common trial procedure dictates that opening statements should not be arguments, but rather an opportunity for each side to inform the jury about what it believes "the evidence will show."[2] Prior to the start of court, Nichol directed defense attorneys to make certain their clients understood the rules. Though the judge promised he would be more liberal with the defendants because they were not lawyers, he warned that he would not tolerate arguments from them.[3] Still, even under such admonitions, it was possible to act as an advocate, to explain to the jury not just what evidence would be presented, but what one expected that evidence to prove, that is, "what the evidence will show."[4] Further, although the prosecution might object to something the defendants said, they could not subject those statements to the close scrutiny of cross-examination. The two Indian activists who wanted to use their trial as a forum to tell an alternate version of a piece of history had been provided with a rare opportunity to present themselves to the jury without having to take the witness stand.

U.S. Attorney William Clayton led off for the prosecution by reading the grand jury indictments containing the full charges against the defendants: that "on or about the 27th day of February," defendants Banks and Means did "willfully, knowingly, and unlawfully" break and enter the trading post and "take and carry away" firearms, ammunition, food, and other items; did on the 8th of March assault with a gun FBI agent Joanne Pierce; did on the 28th of February steal a 1970 Dodge automobile belonging to Cleve Gildersleeve; did "act to obstruct, impede, and interfere with U.S. Marshals and agents of the F.B.I. who were engaged in the lawful performance of their official duties incident to and during the commission of a civil disorder," which "obstructed, delayed, and adversely affected commerce and the conduct of a federally protected function," by preparing and locating trenches, bunkers, and roadblocks at Wounded Knee "which were manned by persons armed with guns"; did on the 6th of March possess Molotov cocktails which had not been registered as required by law.[5]

Clayton then turned over the reading to Hurd, who began by setting out the conspiracy counts in the indictment: that "beginning on or about February 28, 1973 and continuing up to the date of the return of this indictment," defendants Banks and Means "willfully, knowingly and unlawfully did combine, conspire, confederate and agree with each other and with Clyde Bellecourt, Pedro Bissonette, and Carter Camp, Indians, being co-conspirators not named as defendants herein, and with persons unknown to the Grand Jury, to commit offenses against the United States."[6] The offenses as read by Hurd listed all the individual charges that had been read to the jury by Clayton. The Assistant U.S. Attorney then read the other parts of the conspiracy: "in order to attract public attention to claimed grievances and demands and to seek to obtain concessions from the United States," the defendants and co-conspirators planned to forcibly take possession of the trading post; to unlawfully obtain and cause to be obtained "firearms, ammunition, foodstuffs, automobiles and other things to the Grand Jury unknown" for use in preventing law enforcement officials from carrying out their duties; did "seize and caused to be seized" homes at Wounded Knee "to be used for shelter and eating and for organizing security patrols"; did select and organize guards and patrols, set up or cause to be set up roadblocks, and construct trenches and bunkers, which could be "used for the purpose of directing gunfire at law enforcement officers lawfully engaged in the performance of their official duties."[7]

Hurd then read the overt acts included in the grand jury charge: that on February 27, Means and Bissonette drove in a caravan of motor vehicles from Calico to Wounded Knee; that they along with others "prepared a list of demands of the coconspirators to be delivered to officers and employees of the United States"; that on the 28th of February Means, Bissonette, and Camp each met with Joseph Trimbach, Special Agent in Charge for the FBI, and that Means delivered to Trimbach "a list of persons held by defendant and his conspirators"; that on or about the 1st day of March, Means held a conversation with Trimbach; and finally that on or about the 28th of February, Means, Camp, Bellecourt, Banks, and Bissonette "constructed and caused to be constructed trenches in and around Wounded Knee . . . seized and caused to be seized the Sacred Heart Catholic Church . . .[and] broke and entered and caused to be broken and entered the Wounded Knee Trading Post in Wounded Knee, South Dakota."[8]

The last two counts read by Hurd charged the defendants with assaulting and wounding FBI agent Curtis Fitzgerald with a gun on the 11th of March and U.S. Marshal Lloyd Grimm on the 26th of March, while each was in the performance of his official duties.[9] The actions enumerated in the indictment lent specificity to what the government had been telling the press and public from day one about Wounded Knee: that numerous and serious crimes had been perpetrated against people and property inside the small South Dakota village in the winter and spring of 1973; and more important, that a few individuals had conspired and instigated the commission of those crimes. To each of these actions, Hurd said, the defendants had pleaded not guilty.

Concerned about the effect of what Banks and Means might say, Hurd cautioned the jury that these statements were neither evidence nor argument, but merely a "narrative" of what each side intended to prove in the case. Then repeating the charge in the indictment, Hurd told the jury that the government would present evidence that would prove the defendants seized the village of Wounded Knee by force of arms to attract public attention to their grievances, and to make demands upon and extort favorable responses from the U.S. government. He then retraced the events of Wounded Knee, emphasizing the seizing of private homes and property, the shooting at law enforcement officers and private citizens, the demands and ultimatums issued by the protestors, and finally telling the jury that the events that began with the meeting in Calico through the takeover and long siege of Wounded Knee were all under the leadership and direction of the defendants, Banks and Means and their co-conspirators. Hurd also contended that because hostages had been taken and people had been shot at, the government response of constructing roadblocks was intended to "stabilize the situation."[10] Hurd ended by re-emphasizing the use of force and suggesting that the negative effect of the takeover was far-reaching: "They continued to fortify the town of Wounded Knee and continued to fire upon law enforcement officers and thus the evidence will show that the confrontation and civil disorder was to obstruct, impede and interfere with firemen and law enforcement officers and virtually impede Congress and other federally protected functions."[11]

U.S. Attorney Clayton then took the floor again to finish the government's presentation. He continued to enumerate the many crimes that he said the state would prove—the holding of townspeople and several U.S. Postal Inspectors as hostages, the constructing of roadblocks, the exchanges of gunfire, the making of Molotov cocktails, the theft of an automobile—and spent several minutes giving details about the wounding of U.S. Marshall Grimm, emphasizing that "fragments of those bullets went into an area of his spine," leaving him paralyzed from the waist down, and the shooting of FBI agent Curtis Fitzgerald, where the bullet had "severed the arteries in his right wrist." Clayton contrasted the violence attributed to the defendants with what he said were the efforts of the government to bring about a peaceful solution and protect "the innocent residents, those who had lived there many years of their lives." Law enforcement officers who went into the village at the end of the siege, said the U.S. Attorney, would testify regarding the fortifications and destruction left behind by the occupants. He ended with the same straightforward manner that he and Hurd had used throughout, telling the jury that what the government had just presented was not evidence but a "road map" for them to follow as the trial proceeded.[12]

"Hau mitokayepi. I am Russell Means, an Oglala, Lakota."[13] Thus did Means begin his opening statement to the jury in mid-morning on February 12, shortly after Clayton had concluded the government's presentation and Nichol had once again cautioned the jury that the statements were not to be treated as evidence but merely as "an outline of what the individual defendants believe the testimony will show so far as they are concerned." The contrast between Means, who opened for the defense, and the prosecutors who had just ended could not have been more striking. Means's appearance and oratory dramatized the political and cultural conflicts between the prosecution and the defense that had been evident throughout the pretrial preparations and jury selection. The AIM leader told the jury that he would discuss the case at hand, but that it was not a case of the United States versus Banks and Means but rather "the United States of America versus the Oglala people and all Indian people."

Means sought to turn the tables on the government by serving notice once again that it was the government that should be on trial for a century or more of crimes against the Indian people. Beginning each point with the traditional phrase "we will introduce evidence," Means targeted the U.S. Attorney's office, the Department of the Interior, the BIA, and the FBI as he recounted a litany of government misconduct that included harassment and intimidation, domination of tribal governments, attempts to erase traditional religion and beliefs, and government inaction in addressing wrongs, both historical and current. The Oglala Lakota had always lived by a communal government, respecting traditional chiefs and head men, said the AIM leader, adding that the BIA-backed puppet government of Dick Wilson did not represent the people of the Pine Ridge Reservation. Echoing historical divisions, Means argued that the town of Pine Ridge, seat of the BIA and the tribal government, "in no way represents the people of Wounded Knee" and the other small communities on the reservation. Means told the jurors that Oglalas still believed in the Treaty of 1868 and still struggled to maintain their traditional culture. The U.S. government, he charged, is "in a concerted effort and conspiracy to destroy our culture through the concepts of cluster housing, through the concepts of missionary schools, through the concepts of government schools."[14]

As Means began to explain that to the Indians treaties were regarded as sacred documents, Judge Nichol interrupted, reminding him and the jury that he had not yet ruled on the admissibility of the Treaty of 1868 and that the jury in fact might never see it.[15] "I will try to get back to where I was at," commented Means, after an exchange of several minutes between the judge and defense attorneys. Prefacing his next remarks by saying that he would try to explain Indian philosophy and connect it with why he and others went to Wounded Knee, Means told the jury that the conspiracy charge was a "charge for what we think." The AIM leader then presented a portrait of Indian life, contrasting the traditions and beliefs of his people with those of the white jurors. Comparing what he called the mutual respect between different groups of Indians with white attitudes, Means said, "We do not have missionaries to change Crows to Sioux." The core of the Indian value system, explained Means, is the belief that all things came from the earth: "All living things come from our sacred mother earth, all living things, the green things, the winged things of the air, the four-leggeds, the things that crawl and swim, and of course, the two-leggeds . . . It is our philosophy that because all living things come from one mother, . . . we have to treat one another with the respect and reverence that we would our own blood relations."[16]

The second essential element of the Indian value system, Means told the jury, is knowledge. He spoke of the knowledge that Indians knew "eons before Christopher Columbus got lost," that everything is round, the stars, "sun moon trees," people, the drum, the sweat lodge, and the sacred pipe. "And so the spirituality of the red man is why we welcomed with open arms the man from across the sea, the European," said Means, "in every instance we welcomed him."[17]

Means then traced for the jury the circumstances that led himself and others to Wounded Knee, starting with an account of the Treaty of 1868, the document that for him and Banks was the cornerstone of their defense. The defense would prove, Means asserted, that the treaty was "continually abrogated illegally" and "continually violated" by the United States, as were other Indian treaties, despite a legal status equal to that of the U.S. Constitution. Likening the Indian movement to the early Christian movement, Means related how he and others had tried to get the government to intervene after the tribal court had issued restraining orders preventing him from attending meetings and religious events or any gathering of more than three people on the reservation. But, said Means, when he complained to the U.S. Attorney, seated at the prosecution table, about this violation of First Amendment rights, he was told that it was an internal matter for the tribe. And all their letters to the President and to Congress, he told the jury, had gone unanswered.[18]

Turning to the loss of Indian manhood on the reservation, which he attributed to years of inactivity, Means told the jury that in the 1970s there were only five "options" for an Indian to express his manhood: participate in athletics, put on a uniform and join the armed services, grab the bottle, mistreat his wife, or cut his hair, put on a tie, and "become a facsimile of the white man." The Indian leader's narrative about a rebirth of manhood through activism said much about the public presence of AIM members as warriors. Now, said Means, there was a new way to express Indian manhood: "the American Indian Movement, to express our Indianness in the Lakota way." Means told the jury that he had once cut his hair, but that in the traditional Lakota way if a man cuts his hair, he is in mourning: "When I had my hair cut, I was mistaken for a Chicano, a Hawaiian, a Pakistanian, everything but an American Indian. I am very proud to be

Lakota, and when I walk down the street, I want people to know I'm Indian."[19]

Finally, Means told the jury and packed gallery about the protest at Wounded Knee. Again using the phrase "we will introduce evidence," Means told the jurors that the people the government referred to as "hostages" were people who had refused to leave Wounded Knee. The trading post, he charged, had been operating illegally for twelve years, keeping people on the reservation in economic bondage through the trader system, while violating the Truth in Lending Act, usury laws, and postal regulations. The incident involving the assault on agent Joanne Pierce, said Means, was provoked by the government forces. He also charged that the FBI and the U.S. Marshals had been illegally invited onto the Pine Ridge Reservation by Richard Wilson, without the consent of the Tribal Council. The BIA and Wilson's tribal government were corrupt, Means contended, citing a man who had worked in the realty division of the BIA for twenty-three years and now, together with his children, was the largest landowner on the reservation. He also charged that the BIA police were used to harass and intimidate critics of the tribal government. While traders and government employees were acquiring land illegally, Means continued, Indian people were denied the right to make decisions concerning Indian land. He related that during Wounded Knee 50 percent of the eligible voters on the reservation signed a petition calling for a referendum vote on the continuation of the current tribal government, but that it was rejected as insufficient by the Solicitor General of the Department of the Interior because it did not include eighteen-year-olds—even though in the last tribal election the same department would not let eighteen-year-olds vote. The damage to the buildings in Wounded Knee, he asserted, was from the thousands of rounds of government fire. Defense testimony, Means told the packed courtroom, would put all these facts into evidence.[20]

The occupation of Wounded Knee, Means said, was not the work of outside agitators, but of the Oglala people trying to seek redress for their grievances and equal enforcement of the laws. Reminding the audience that he was an Oglala, he asserted that AIM was called in only as a last resort: "Once again, I remind you that we went to the tribal council; that we went to the Bureau of Indian Affairs; that we went to the federal judge; that we went to the United States Attorney; and each time, the door was slammed in our face."[21]

Finally, Means returned again to the Treaty of 1868. The Indians had lived up to the treaty, he argued, and AIM in taking over Wounded Knee was asking the government to live up to its part. "All we have ever asked of the United States of America is to live up to their own laws," said Means, adding: "They made the laws, we didn't." He then turned the point into a plea for treaty rights: "It is my sincere belief that if I do not have treaty rights then my unborn and my children might as well right now become white people and forget, forget the traditional values and traditional ways because if we don't have treaty rights, we don't have any rights at all."[22]

Looking for common ground with the jurors, Means once again compared the Indian movement with the early Christian movement, saying that both groups were persecuted for their "spiritual beliefs." He concluded by quoting what Chief Joseph of the Nez Percé had said in the agreement with the government over his surrender—something, Means told the jurors, that in effect he was asking of them:

Give me the right to choose my own teachers;
give me the right to practice a religion of my fathers;
give me the right to travel and come and go as I please; give me the right
    to trade with whom I please, and do business with whom I please;
give me the right to follow the ways of my fathers;
and I will obey every law or submit to the penalty.[23]

As Means returned to the defense table, his attorney, William Kunstler, rose and embraced him. After the noon recess, Hurd (trying to combat what he saw as a calculated attempt to dramatize the moment) objected to Kunstler's embrace: "Assuming that this was an honest emotional response to an argument which apparently was designed to evoke such responses, and not merely for the dramatic effect of it, I think it is inappropriate behavior for an attorney in the courtroom."[24]

Both Kunstler and Lane protested Hurd's objection, and Judge Nichol let the matter pass without a ruling, but the episode was a prelude for the conflicts that were about to explode during Dennis Banks's upcoming opening statement. Banks began by holding aloft a copy of the Treaty of 1868, and telling the jury that he was sorry that they might never get to see it. Then, echoing the prosecution's opening that had charged the defendants with taking over Wounded Knee to dramatize complaints and force action from the government, he pleaded "guilty" to the charges of trying to get the Senate to investigate "the conditions that were imposed upon our people." Dropping the traditional "the evidence will show" phrase that Means had used, Banks's opening statement began more as an argument: he explained to the jury that he was pleading guilty to seeking action because "the policy of the BIA was one of total disruption against the Indian community." The BIA and the Department of the Interior, the AIM leader charged, "have been responsible for much of the misery, much of the poverty, and the early deaths that happened on the reservation."[25] Banks argued that such government policy went back to the 1880s; he read from a report of the Commission of Indian Affairs that was made part of the Congressional Record on September 28, 1886: "The Indian must therefore be taught how to labor and that labor may be made necessary to his well being. He must be taken out of the reservation through the door of the General Allotment Act, and he must be imbued to the exalting egotism of American civilization so that he will say 'I' instead of 'We,' and 'This is mine' instead of 'this is ours.' "[26]

Calling the protest at Wounded Knee "an event that was destined to change the course of Indian history," Banks was about to change direction when Nichol interrupted him. The AIM leader, who had still not said anything about what the evidence would show, had just used the phrase "my testimony" when Nichol reminded him and the jury that this was not testimony or evidence but an "outline." Banks then told the jurors that the reason for the change of venue to Minnesota was the racism toward Indian people, and toward AIM in particular, in South Dakota. As Banks began to quote a statement to that effect by Judge Nichol, saying that the people of South Dakota "would rather line us up and shoot us all dead," the judge interrupted again, commenting, "I never said that." Nichol attempted to say more, but Banks would not yield the floor and tried to continue his statement. Nichol, visibly frustrated, finally ordered the marshals to take custody of the defendant: "Mr. Banks. Marshal, will you take him and sit him down. Now, Mr. Banks, if you want to make an opening statement under the same rules as Mr. Means did, you may, but I am not going to permit you to make an opening statement of this nature."[27]

During a conference at the bench, Nichol told the attorneys that Banks was misquoting him and that the change of venue had nothing to do with the defendant's guilt or innocence and was not evidence toward motivation; he sustained the prosecution's objection to Banks's statements. First Lane and then Kunstler attempted to argue the point further, but Nichol cut them off, saying that he didn't want to hear any more argument. In fact, Banks's quote of Nichol had not been far off. At the start of the trial, a South Dakota newspaper had quoted Nichol regarding the change of venue, referring to a doctor friend of his who had told the judge what to do with the defendants: "just line those people up against the walls and machine gun them."[28]

Calm prevailed in the courtroom for only a few moments. Banks began to address the jury regarding the statements they had made during jury selection about their lack of knowledge of treaties, the BIA, and Indian heritage and culture. Hurd interrupted, requesting a conference at the bench during which he objected to Banks's statement as "clearly argumentative" and "an attempt to personalize the opening statement." Defense attorney Doug Hall responded by arguing that Banks's comments were "preliminary to his discussion of motivation and intent in the movement from the Calico meetings into Wounded Knee," making it legitimate material for an opening statement. Nichol, however, concurred with Hurd and sustained the objection.[29]

Banks then resumed his opening in the style Means had previously used. Prefacing a series of allegations against the government with the phrase, "our evidence will show," he told the jurors that the defense would prove that they, the jurors, were qualified to be Area Director of Indian Affairs; that the BIA only began responding to recommendations by Indians after the formation of AIM in 1968; that Buddy Lamont, an Oglala who had fought in Vietnam, was killed "defending the Oglala Sioux Nation" at Wounded Knee; that Indian people still believe in "the Indian way of life"; that Oglalas "begged AIM for assistance"; that the tribal government refused to let the traditional Sun Dance be held on the reservation in 1973; and that Indians on Pine Ridge continued to lose their land because of "mismanagement" and "irregularities." The government had charged them with "disruption and obstruction," Banks continued, but the evidence would show that the obstruction that occurred came from Washington, not from the defendants: "Our evidence will show that it is true that obstruction has occurred but it has never been committed by the American Indian Movement. It has never been committed by Dennis Banks or Russell Means or any of the traditional Oglala Sioux; that the obstruction came from Washington, that the obstruction came from the Department of Interior: that the obstruction of Indian rights came from the Bureau and its area offices."[30] Banks went on to tell the jury that the defense would cross-examine prosecution witnesses and through them demonstrate that the Oglala Sioux were deprived not only of their traditional rights but of their civil and human rights. "I cannot say that I was not at Wounded Knee," Banks continued; "I am guilty."[31]

Then moving on to the murder of Raymond Yellow Thunder, Banks charged the BIA with failing to respond to the request of the family for an investigation of Yellow Thunder's murder in Gordon, Nebraska. The accusation drew objections from U.S. Attorney Clayton and another admonishment from Judge Nichol. This time Lane protested, saying that such evidence would be presented, but Nichol countered that evidence of events in Gordon would not be accepted. Lane, however, continued to argue that such evidence would be the basis for showing how Banks became involved with the Oglala on Pine Ridge, but a visibly angry Judge Nichol would have none of it:

> COURT: I don't want to sit here and listen to another argument . . .
> Please sit down.
> LANE: Except the Court—
> COURT: Mr. Lane, I'm going to ask you to be removed . . . if you and
> Mr Kunstler are going to keep taking exception to my rulings.[32]

Lane and Kunstler both objected, and Nichol had the marshals remove them from the courtroom, threatened to have Tilsen and Banks removed when they protested, and then called a recess during which he denied a request by Chief Fools Crow to read a statement or give an Indian prayer in the courtroom. "I won't let my courtroom be turned into a circus," responded a still angry Nichol, adding that he felt he had been "leaning over backwards" to accommodate the defendants.[33]

During a conference in chambers, however, Nichol was persuaded that Lane was taking exception to the manner of Clayton's objections and not to the judge's ruling. True to his reputation, the judge quickly cooled off and explained to the jury that the old federal rule, since changed, had necessitated that attorneys make such objections for the record, adding, "I guess I wasn't listening very carefully." Nichol told the press later that he felt he was a little hard on the defense attorneys when he found out what they were trying to do, but added, "it may help to clear the air in the future."[34]

Beginning with the legalistic phrase, "the evidence that we bring forth here will attempt to prove the following facts," Banks resumed his opening statement, outlining the steps that brought him to Wounded Knee, telling of the meeting at Calico, the "dictatorship" of Tribal Chairman Wilson, the role of women in leading the dissent on the reservation and their demands for action, and his days as a Minnesota Chippewa on the Leech Lake Reservation. He recalled for the jury that his mother had been refused assistance by the BIA and later died an alcoholic. It was the same "unresponsive BIA" on Leech Lake and on Pine Ridge, Banks told the jury, and the same BIA that was established in 1849 under the Department of War: "We'd reached a point in history where we could not tolerate that kind of abuse any longer, where these women, these parents, these mothers who couldn't tolerate the mistreatment that goes on on the reservations any longer, they could not see another Indian youngster die, they could not see another Indian man meet death, whether he was in Chicago or Nebraska or Buffalo Gap."[35]

Banks then, like Means before him, turned to the subject of treaties. With Nichol's caution on their pending admissibility in mind, he told the jurors that treaties were relevant because they spelled out certain "mutual agreements" and "boundaries that were made in good faith by Indian chiefs."[36] And then just as quickly Banks shifted his focus again, this time to the negotiations at Wounded Knee and the distrust that developed toward the government negotiators. They had requested to meet with specific White House officials but were turned down, he said, adding: "there's nobody left in Washington who we trust."[37]

Banks told the jurors as he had in the beginning that he and his co-defendant were "guilty" of asking for investigation of the BIA, and that this request was part of recommendations made by the National Congress of American Indians as far back as 1936. "And year after year after year," said Banks, "the same recommendations, the same suggestions have come from Indian groups that these people in Oglala at the Calico Community Hall were asking." If he was guilty of obstruction, Banks went on, then there had to be a place in the trial to explain what the Oglala women felt about the "disruption" of their lives at the hands of the U.S. Marshals, the FBI, and the BIA. These groups, said Banks, had interfered not just with the Oglala, but with all tribes. The evidence, he said, would show many violations prior to Wounded Knee: "Wounded Knee represented to the Oglala Sioux and to Indian people all across the country, that last desperate attempt to bring about justice." Not only did Indians from all over country respond, he contended, but so did people from all walks of life. "People came there," said the AIM leader, "because the Oglala Sioux women had cried loud enough so that their pleas were heard all across this planet." The importance of Wounded Knee, said Banks, "is that Indians and non-Indians alike came together and created that last desperate attempt; an attempt to bring Indian heritage, Indian ideas back." Continuing in a more argumentative tone, he added that contrary to what the government charged, he and Russell Means had never forced people out of their homes, but rather were invited into people's homes at Wounded Knee.[38]

Turning to the Sun Dance, Banks related for the audience how he had participated for the first time in this traditional Lakota ceremony. The AIM leader revealed deep feelings for Indian spirituality and the Lakota heritage, as well as the attitudes toward gender embedded in that spirituality and heritage:

> The Sun Dance, which is a very sacred religious event where men war-
> riors offer themselves to the Great Spirit to seek a vision, . . . there must
> be fasting, . . . we must give up water, . . . we must prove to Mother
> Earth and all the female objects of this planet, to all the female things,
> that we would like to share some of the pain. The men warriors would
> like to share some of the pain that our mothers had when we were born.
> The piercing of the skin is a reminder to me that I truly owe myself to
> Mother Earth and to all the female things of this planet . . . and when
> the flesh was torn from me I suddenly realized what a great sin, what
> a great injustice it would be to lose the Oglala Sioux religion.[39]

Lakota religion, Banks told the jury, was suppressed during the 1920s and
1930s, which forced the traditional chiefs to go underground with the ceremony. "Nothing will be underground any more," said Banks, as he
brought to a close his opening statement:

> Wounded Knee represented a last pint or a last blood transfusion. It was
> unfortunate that three Indians have died but they died knowing, and
> all of us who were at Wounded Knee, and those people who called us
> to Wounded Knee will go the Spirit world knowing that the unborn
> generation will be given that opportunity to live the life that they choose
> and not the life that somebody else dictates.[40]

Means and Banks had been both passionate and eloquent in their expression of Indian sorrow and rage, as they recounted their own lives and the
history of Native Americans, particularly the Oglala of Pine Ridge. Both
continually attacked the government, discussing the events leading up to
the protest, the broken treaties that gave rise to the reservation system,
and the conditions that existed at places like Pine Ridge. Perhaps most
important, both men, particularly in their discussions of Indian culture and
spirituality, had demonstrated that although they may have been rightly
called militants, they were also articulate and thoughtful leaders, respectful
of tradition, of family, of religion, and of law. By the end of the day, however, there were still silences in the narrative. Though given a fairly wide
latitude by Nichol, both men had been interrupted by objections and were
faced with curtailing what they had intended to say, or rearranging it into
phrases dictated by court procedure and the judge's rulings.

There were also silences imposed by the participants themselves. Banks
and Means had spoken from their experience as Indian men, about coming
of age under difficult circumstances and gaining political maturity during
confusing times. Those experiences, put into words before a packed court-

room, reinforced the traditional masculine images that were seen in much of the trial coverage. In his statement Banks had given credit to the women on Pine Ridge, calling them the "real warriors of Indian society." But he likened their pleas for help to those of his mother; his narrative spoke mainly of their grief in watching their children die and depicted their only response as asking the traditional Oglala leaders and AIM to take some action. Neither Banks nor Means spoke of the women who had been arrested at Wounded Knee, or of those who were still active in AIM and on the reservation. Both men had discussed the Lakota traditional belief in Mother Earth, of honoring women in traditional ceremonies for what is owed to all "female things of this planet." These were moving and important descriptions of traditional Indian beliefs, but they were not narratives that reflected the equally important changes that were taking place for women on Pine Ridge and within AIM and the defense committee, changes that mirrored those beginning to take place in the whole of American society.

AIM leaders were rightly looking to their heritage, but there were aspects of those traditions with respect to the honoring of women that had been forgotten, and still others that were being left behind by the women who had helped build the movement. As Mary Crow Dog, a protestor at Wounded Knee, would later write concerning Lakota tradition: "There is a curious contradiction in Sioux society. The men pay great lip service to the status women hold in the tribe. Their rhetoric on the subject is beautiful. They speak of Grandmother Earth and how they honor her."[41] Crow Dog then asks: "Honoring us for what? For being good beaders, quillers, tanners, moccasin makers, and child-bearers."[42] This is "fine," she writes, but as her story points out, and as she and others demonstrated at Wounded Knee, women were integral to the protests that erupted on Pine Ridge and elsewhere, as full participants in those actions. Women within AIM may have been fulfilling roles that they had chosen, what Rayna Green terms "complementary, mutual roles" based on tradition, and necessary when "community survival is at stake," but the images presented to the public did not fully reflect the importance of those roles.[43] Nor did they reflect other changes that were occurring in Indian country. As part of the political revival spawned by the IRA and the Community Action Programs of the 1960s, Indian women were also becoming more involved in tribal governments as elected officials and as appointed employees.[44] The opening statements of Banks and Means, coupled with the confrontational nature of the drama unfolding in the courtroom, had done little to counter stereotypes in the larger society or the political left of woman as wife, mother, spiritual model, or behind-the-scenes supporter of the political battles that raged in the early 1970s.[45]

Although the conduct and rhetoric of the defendants and their attorneys contributed to absences in the courtroom record, the biases and priorities of the media were perhaps the central factors in the reconstruction of that narrative for the audience outside the courthouse. While the opening statements of both sides should have been the focus of the trial that day, the story that dominated the television and radio coverage that night and captured the headlines the next morning was that of the radical attorneys being removed from the courtroom.[46] Under the headlines "Lawyers Ousted at Wounded Knee Trial" and "Judge Ousts 3 'Knee' Attorneys," the Twin Cities' two morning newspapers, like papers elsewhere, recounted almost word for word the dispute between Nichol and attorneys Kunstler and Lane, with Kunstler drawing most of the attention. The opening statements were relegated to the inside pages, summarized in a few paragraphs with a couple of one-line quotes from Means, most often his comments about Indian manhood. The *New York Times,* focusing on the confrontation and on Mean's comments about manhood and the possibility of more protests, headlined its coverage: "Wounded Knee Trial Opens with Revolt Warning."[47]

It was not the first time the press had opted for the sensational in its coverage of the trial, nor would it be the last. With headlines like "St. Paul Wounded Knee Trials Delayed When Means Fails to Show Up" and "Attorneys Clash, Audience Applauds at AIM Trial," South Dakota papers had already displayed a tendency to focus on clashes between attorneys or conflicts involving the defendants.[48] Elsewhere the press had spoken of Wounded Knee as an "insurrection" and of the defendants as leaders of "insurgents" or "militants," with one paper noting that Banks had been called a "war chief" and another remarking on the "potential drama" of the trial.[49]

From the beginning, the trial had been treated as a spectacle and the federal courtroom as an arena of conflict, where looks, actions, and the sounds of words, rather than the ideas they conveyed, were often the focus of attention. Press coverage of AIM had not stopped at the courthouse door, but depictions of the trial inside often characterized the proceedings and the participants as if the arena were still the grassy plains of the upper midwest or the concrete plazas of an urban university. The defense committee did distribute a pamphlet containing the opening statements of the defendants, and one local newspaper ran a story several days later on the trial tactics of the defense which reviewed sections of the defendants' statements.[50] But as testimony in the trial finally began, press coverage of the opening statements could have provided a more substantive look at what the participants expected to present to the jury. The media, however, had opted for the story of the country judge versus the big city radical attorneys and their militant clients.

THE GOVERNMENT'S CASE
GETS DERAILED

Part of the function of the prosecutor's office is not just to prosecute crimes, but to select the crimes that you're going to prosecute based on your requirement to deter other conduct . . . whether you're talking about organized crime or organized civil disobedience, . . . the leadership is usually what you look for.

R. D. HURD, SEPTEMBER 1988

[The] basic theme was that the conditions on Pine Ridge were existing because of the active support of the government . . . so that government misconduct, . . . the FBI abuse, the marshal's abuse, the BIA abuses, . . . were an integral part of the defense from day one.

KEN TILSEN, OCTOBER 1989

ON THE AFTERNOON of February 12, 1974, the prosecution called its first witness in Saint Paul. Two days later the head line in the *Minneapolis Tribune* read "Jury Hears First Claims on Treaties." The basic assumption in the prosecution's case was that even if Russell Means and Dennis Banks did not directly commit crimes at Wounded Knee, they had conspired with others to commit those crimes and then directed people in carrying out the plans of that conspiracy. But placing Banks and Means at the head of a conspiracy was also the central contradiction in the government's case, because it forced them to distinguish an agreement to break the law from the exercise of free speech and political leadership.

Under the law, the existence of such a common purpose or agreement could be inferred from surrounding circumstances, as long as the prosecution could also show that at least one of the conspirators had committed an overt act in furtherance of that agreement.[1] To accomplish this the government planned to use a variety of witnesses, including Wounded Knee residents and clergy who would tell of being forced out of homes and churches, being held captive by armed guards, and having witnessed theft and destruction inside the village. In addition, several U.S. Marshals, FBI agents, and other government officials would describe the armed standoff and the wounding of three law enforcement personnel. All witnesses, when possible, would testify to situations that put Banks and Means in leadership roles during the occupation to demonstrate to the jury that they were in charge of carrying out a plan to further the commission of crimes, or, under the nonconspiracy charges, that one or both defendants had done something to aid and abet the commission of an offense.[2]

According to the prosecution, the conspiracy defendants were singled out not for political reasons, but because they were more culpable than others. The analogy was to the older man who leads a teenager into committing a crime. "They lured a lot of people along with them just in the heat of the moment," Gienapp contends. Too many people were involved to charge them all with conspiracy, adds Hurd, "so you try to identify those people who were primarily responsible in organizing the conspiracy." The prosecutors were confident that if they could get their evidence before the jury and keep it focused on the issue of guilt, the chances for a conviction were good.[3]

Yet the same evidence that could demonstrate that the defendants were in charge while crimes were being committed—portraying them as spokesmen or designated negotiators, recalling an overheard conversation or rereading the contents of a press statement—could also open the way for the defense to elaborate on the reasons for the protest in the first place. To this end defense attorneys intended to use cross-examination not just to discredit the government's witnesses, but to tell an alternate story. According to Tilsen, two basic points would be raised at every opportunity: one, that Oglalas, led by their traditional leaders, went to Wounded Knee to make a statement in response to oppressive conditions on Pine Ridge imposed by the tribal government and supported by the BIA and the Justice Department; and two, that the overreaction of federal law enforcement officials at Wounded Knee was representative of the history of mistreatment of Indians in the United States. In Tilsen's words, the defense wanted to stress the "totality of government misconduct" right from the beginning. Every "examination and cross examination, every statement" had to fit the theory.[4]

To help orchestrate their strategy the defense organized an "evidence collective," consisting of lawyers, legal workers, and law students. Working out of Tilsen's office, people catalogued and cross-referenced witnesses, places, and events so that all available information could be quickly connected up and checked on for use in cross-examination. The collective met together daily, with one or more of its members also attending the meetings with the attorneys and defendants at the end of each day in court. In addition, volunteers took notes on each day's proceedings, indexed the daily transcript, and wrote up a summary of the testimony for the lawyers and defendants to review the next morning.[5]

For the defendants, demonstrating that the government had consistently violated the Treaty of 1868 was a key element in demonstrating the history of government misconduct toward the Lakota. The first opportunity to raise the issue came when prosecutors called Cleveland Nelson, Director of Natural Resources for the BIA on Pine Ridge, to set out some basic facts concerning the reservation.[6] Over government objections, defense attorney Larry Leventhal used the current boundaries set out in the map to elicit testimony as to what the boundaries of the reservation had been under the Treaty. Responses to questions first from Leventhal and then Kunstler established that large parcels of land on Pine Ridge were owned by whites, that 50,000 acres had been taken by the government for use as a bombing range, and that the total area of land removed from tribal control over the years was more than half the total area of South Dakota.[7] Cross-examination of another witness explored the contention that Dick Wilson's invitation to U.S. Marshals to come onto the reservation also violated the Treaty.[8] Though Nichol refused to admit the Treaty into evidence, the defense had made their point—that, in the words of one news report, "the rights guaranteed to the Sioux have deteriorated since the Fort Laramie Treaty was signed in 1868."[9]

Within a few days a pattern had developed: government witnesses gave relatively short, direct testimony and then were subjected to a much longer cross-examination, during which defense attorneys, one representing each defendant, would try to elicit inconsistencies or direct contradictions with prior statements; in addition, when an opening presented itself, they would ask questions concerning treaty violations, conditions on the reservation, and government mistreatment of Indians, past and present. After several witnesses testified to events preceding Wounded Knee—including an undercover agent who said he heard Vernon Bellecourt promise a Rapid City audience that a "revolution" was coming—the jury heard the first testimony on the takeover itself.[10]

John Hardy, a BIA fireman, said that gunfire damaged his truck when he responded to a fire alarm at Wounded Knee the night of the takeover.[11] Then Wayne Romero, a Pine Ridge BIA police officer, told of watching the car caravan move into Wounded Knee, hearing gunfire, and being shot at when he went to investigate.[12] On cross-examination Romero admitted that the caravan was occupied by people from the reservation and contained few outsiders. Several questions about connections between the BIA police and U.S. Marshals and possible connections between the witness and Dick Wilson were disallowed as being beyond the scope of what had been covered on direct examination.[13] Nichol also cut short questions concerning the alleged "goon squad" and indicated that he would start getting more restrictive on what could be included in cross-examination.[14]

The defense, however, challenged Nichol's admonition almost immediately. Delmar Eastman, the head of the BIA police on Pine Ridge, pointed out the relative positions of forces at Wounded Knee on a map and then was confronted with more questioning by Leventhal on the boundaries of the reservation indicated by the map and those designated under the 1868 Treaty. After another debate outside of the jury's hearing, the map was admitted into evidence, with the current boundaries intact. Nichol did explain to the jury that those boundaries were still in dispute but that he had not yet decided on the admissibility of the Treaty.[15] Moments later he ruled that questions concerning the roadblocks allegedly set up under Wilson's direction and the government's failure to live up to the agreement that ended the siege were also beyond the scope of proper cross-examination; he then engaged in what one newspaper termed a "heated exchange" with Lane, before finally complaining that cross-examination seemed designed to get the attention of reporters rather than the jury.[16]

However much Nichol reprimanded the defense, however many questions he ruled outside the bounds of cross-examination, defense attorneys kept pushing the limits of cross-examination and challenging the judge's rulings. U.S. Marshal and demolitions expert James Propotnick described the heavy fortifications and booby traps discovered inside Wounded Knee after the siege ended, and the defense brought out the fact that marshals had been assigned to Wounded Knee before the occupation had begun and that 80 to 100 were on the reservation by early May.[17] Another witness testified to the placement of bunkers and then was asked about the government's allegedly preventing food from coming into the village.[18] A former legal aid attorney testified that rifles he had been transporting in the trunk of his car were retrieved by Means and alleged co-conspirator Pedro Bissonette a day before the takeover. At the time, said Gary Thomas, they told him that something was going to happen at Wounded Knee, and later he heard gunfire coming from the direction of the village.[19] But on cross-examination, Thomas also testified over government objections that Dick Wilson had threatened his life in front of witnesses and that the FBI had taken no action on his subsequent complaint.[20]

*   *   *

As the trial moved into its third month, cross-examination of a key prosecution witness led to the first serious reprimand of the government by Judge Nichol. On March 1, Father Paul Manhart, a Catholic priest from Pine Ridge, testified to the presence of weapons, exchanges of gunfire, and having been imprisoned by Means in the basement of his church, all during the first night of the takeover. Over defense objections Manhart described the damage done to the church and the items taken from its altar. Though the defendants had not been charged with theft from the church, Nichol ruled that the prosecution had the right to prove there was a civil disorder in progress, which was relevant to the charges of interfering with federal officers in the performance of their duties. The defense, to no avail, argued that under the 1868 Treaty the church was an uninvited guest on the reservation and thus had no right to complain.[21] Calling the priest a "prisoner" in his own church, newspapers termed Manhart's statements the first "emotional" testimony concerning the "victims" of the takeover.[22]

The next day Kunstler asked Father Manhart about a petition signed by residents of Wounded Knee calling for the government to "cease and desist from firing upon our guest members of the American Indian Movement." Looking at a copy of the petition, Manhart admitted that the majority of names were Wounded Knee residents, but said he believed that many of the signatures were forgeries. Defense attorneys, however, noted that the petition, which had been provided by the prosecution, appeared to have been altered and inquired as to the whereabouts of the original, which had been in the hands of the FBI since it was presented to the government on March 3, 1973. FBI agents called to the stand out of the presence of the jury could not establish the chain of custody of the original, and the government was forced to admit that the copy given to the defense and prosecution had in fact been altered.[23]

Nichol said that he was "greatly disturbed" about the handling of the petition: "I used to think the FBI was one of the greatest bureaus that ever came down the pike," said the Judge, adding, "I think it's deteriorated and I don't care how many FBI agents are here in Court listening to me."[24] Though he could not bring himself to accuse the FBI directly, Nichol did say that he could not help feeling that there was something deliberate in the manner in which the document had been handled. Hurd insisted that the mistake was due to the sheer volume of evidence the bureau had collected, and he promised to review the files for any other documents that came under the court's discovery order. The next day Nichol explained the situation to the jury and had the original petition and the altered version given to them to examine so as to better understand Manhart's testimony.[25] The priest's reappearance on the stand prompted another exchange, this time concerning questioning about Manhart's attitudes toward Indian religion and AIM. Nichol sustained the government's objections, exclaiming: "As I've said several times, the American Indian Movement is not on trial in this case."[26]

To add to the judge's concerns, several jurors reported that they had received a pamphlet in the mail entitled "Renegades, the Second Battle of Wounded Knee," a publication of the John Birch Society. Five jurors had received the pamphlet, which criticized AIM and the protest, while others had received a second pamphlet entitled "Atheistic Communism." The material, which jurors said they had not read, was turned over to law enforcement authorities.[27]

The next morning an agreement was reached for a search of the FBI files over the coming weekend. The files reportedly consisted of 5,239 volumes, containing 315,981 documents or "serials," many several pages long. Under headlines like "Judge Accuses FBI of Distorting Evidence" or "Judge Blasts FBI on 'Knee' Evidence," the morning papers reported that Nichol was visibly angry and noted his comments on the FBI. For the defense it was not just a matter of tampering, though that would give credence to their charges of misconduct, but the petition itself was important because it demonstrated that 70 of 100-plus residents of Wounded Knee seemed to corroborate AIM's claim that it had been invited onto the reservation and that law enforcement officials had been asked to leave. At the end of court on March 7, Nichol was visited by Hurd and Philip Enlow, an FBI agent in the Minneapolis office, who assured the judge that, although there had been problems due to the volume of material, there had been no intentional tampering with evidence. Said Enlow after the meeting: "In no way has the FBI attempted to hide or conceal anything in connection with his court orders or evidence the defense has a right to have. There was a misunderstanding in the handling of the case, and as soon as we found the error, it was corrected and the court was so notified."[28]

While Hurd and Tilsen looked through the FBI files pursuant to the judge's order, Joseph Trimbach, the Special Agent in Charge of the Minneapolis FBI office, paid Nichol a visit on Saturday. Trimbach, a key supervisory figure at Wounded Knee, repeated the assurances given earlier concerning the FBI and the evidence in its possession. To reporters afterward, Trimbach said only that they had "discussed many things" and that officials in Washington were aware of the situation: "well they know about it and naturally they are concerned."[29] On Monday Tilsen told the judge that they had looked through 200 documents out of a possible 315,000 over the weekend and found 100 that should have been turned over to the defense pursuant to discovery orders. Hurd agreed, but insisted that the documents were not important. At Trimbach's invitation, Nichol went to see the files for himself and commented afterward that "there was an awful lot of stuff to look at."[30]

For a defense team that wanted to put the government on trial for past and current mistreatment of Indians, there was now an immediate issue of potential misconduct which they hoped the judge, jury, and media would connect with events in Washington. At the same time, the government hoped that Nichol's firsthand view of the massive amount of evidence that it had to sift through in complying with his discovery orders would soften his view of their situation. Amid reports that Kunstler was preparing a motion to dismiss, Banks and Means both told reporters that they did not want a dismissal unless it was based on the 1868 Treaty. "When we are found innocent," said Means, "the government will have to live up to its treaty obligations and if it doesn't there will be Wounded Knees all over the place."[31]

Meanwhile prosecutors tried to get their case back on track, with more witnesses providing accounts of hearing gunfire, being forced from their homes, seeing guns and food taken from the trading post, and the occupation of the church. Pastor Orville Lansberry and his wife Emma both told of hearing a knock at the door in the middle of the night and the command "open up or we'll shoot," and then hiding first in their basement and later in a gully while praying that they would get away, and then finally fleeing their home by car. As dramatic as the testimony was, however, it provided no direct evidence against Banks and Means, and the defense spent little time on cross-examination.[32] The headline in the *Sioux Falls Argus Leader* read, "Elderly Pastor, Wife, Relate Night of Suspense, Threats, Escape from Wounded Knee" and was accompanied by a long article, but other papers were less impressed with the Lansberrys' testimony.[33]

Other witnesses did provide accounts of speeches or commands given by Banks or Means, along with other evidence that they were in leadership positions, but on cross-examination the defense elicited testimony on treaty rights, mistreatment of Indians, the gunfire coming from government positions during Wounded Knee, and the question of whether people had remained in the village when they were given the opportunity to leave. Sometimes inquiries were disallowed, such as the questioning of a trading post employee on the finances of her employer.[34] On occasion the defense would not even cross-examine people whose only testimony was hearing gunfire and seeing items taken from the trading post.[35]

After several days of testimony by Wounded Knee residents, the prosecution shifted to questioning a series of FBI agents and U.S. Marshals who vividly described exchanging fire with the occupants of the village.[36] On cross-examination the defense asked questions concerning details of the exchanges, government surveillance prior to the protest, who was giving the orders at Wounded Knee, and the witnesses' knowledge of treaty rights and the Indian Civil Rights Act.[37] The prosecution kept raising objections, and Nichol ruled against questions concerning Indian history, the FBI hierarchy, and an alleged U.S. Marshal sniper team; but he did allow testimony describing government fire power, including military equipment: automatic weapons and their accuracy, the size of M-1 and M-16 ammunition, the availability of shotguns, pistols, and grenade launchers, and the use of armored personnel carriers.[38]

When Tilsen asked a U.S. Marshal whether the marshals and the FBI considered themselves the equivalent of the cavalry at Wounded Knee in 1890, Hurd laughingly objected to the question and drew an angry rebuff from Means, who shouted: "People were killed in 1890, what is funny?" Nichol threatened to adjourn the session, and so many tried to speak at once that the court reporter could only note, "this is impossible to report." The next day, with the jury present, Nichol cautioned Hurd to control his laughter, saying that he guessed he had "bawled out the wrong people." Hurd apologized, saying his laughter was out of nervousness and was directed toward Tilsen's question and not to the 1890 event itself.[39]

Shortly after that exchange Hurd again found himself the target of defense questions when government witness William Leavitt took the stand. Leavitt, a rancher and one of the volunteer firemen who had answered the fire alarm the night of the takeover, testified that he was shot at and that he witnessed the vandalizing and looting of the trading post. But on cross-examination he was first asked about his affiliation with the John Birch Society and then confronted with statements he had made to Hurd during the siege, to the effect that if the government did not do something soon, someone would dynamite Wounded Knee. Leavitt denied the dynamite part, but did admit to conversations with Hurd and to the formation of a "protective association" by white ranchers with livestock on or near Pine Ridge. Over objections by the prosecution, Leavitt also admitted reading the pamphlet "Renegades," the same one that had been sent to several jurors. Nichol ruled the testimony admissible to show possible bias on the part of the witness.[40]

Under questioning by Leventhal, Leavitt admitted that at the time of Wounded Knee he owned several thousand acres on the reservation, plus additional land leased to him at anywhere from $1 to $10 an acre. An argument ensued over questions pertaining to provisions in Article 12 of the 1868 Treaty, which required signatures of three-fourths of the adult Sioux to transfer land from the reservation. The prosecution objected to the questions as irrelevant, contending that since Leavitt no longer owned the land, the legality of the leasing practices would not influence his testimony. Finally, Leventhal was allowed to ask if the witness was aware of the provisions and of who had signed his deed, the judge ruling that such knowledge could be evidence of possible bias on the part of the witness. Leavitt said that he was not aware of the provisions, that there were many signatures on his deeds, and finally, that he was not aware of AIM's criticism of the leasing of reservation land.[41]

In response to one question, Leavitt claimed that Indians on Pine Ridge had good housing and the "best education," causing Means to put his head down on the table and laugh, which drew another reprimand from Nichol.[42] Other questions such as "What percentage of the Indians living on the reservation live in homes that have running water and inside toilets?" and "Do you know what the average income is per family on the reservation?" were objected to as "irrelevant and immaterial and outside the scope of cross examination" and disallowed by the judge. After Leavitt exited, Hurd acknowledged that Leavitt had in fact mentioned the possibility of someone dynamiting Wounded Knee, that he had counseled Leavitt to do nothing, and that he had reported the conversation to the FBI though he was not concerned about it.[43]

Meanwhile, defense attorneys had learned that law enforcement officials might have engaged in illegal electronic eavesdropping during the protest. Nichol recessed the proceedings and set a special hearing to take up motions to suppress evidence and to dismiss the case, outside the presence of the jury. Newspapers previewed the upcoming hearing with headlines like "Alleged Wiretap at Wounded Knee Could End Trials," or "Much Evidence Withheld, Knee Defense Charges."[44] Just to make certain that no one missed the connections to current events, Kunstler announced in court that Daniel Ellsberg, whose case had recently been dismissed because of government misconduct, would arrive the following week should his testimony be needed in the motion hearing.[45]

While prosecutors and defense attorneys battled over the evidence inside the courtroom, WKLDOC continued the steady stream of press releases on the courtroom events, AIM activities, and conditions on Pine Ridge. Publicity often included requests for contributions and encouraged letters of support directed to Judge Nichol and others. Information and brochures on the "Native American Speakers Bureau" were sent to the local and national media, community organizations, college campuses, and individuals around the country. A "client newsletter" was also distributed in an effort to keep the large number of defendants regularly informed on what was happening in all the trials.[46] In addition, members of the defense committee would talk daily with the reporters who were covering the trials, developing a dialogue over time. Defense attorneys provided previews of what to expect as they headed into the courthouse in the morning and highlighted certain aspects of the proceedings for reporters at the close of each day. Prosecutors also talked to the press, but they put out few press releases and denied making an organized effort to influence or shape press coverage.[47]

AIM used the anniversary of the Wounded Knee protest as a catalyst for commemorations and fund-raising events in Minnesota as well as South Dakota. The Native American Theater Ensemble performed a benefit at the Guthrie Theater in Minneapolis, and various Twin Cities women's groups held a rally and dinner in support of Indian women which drew several hundred people. On the campus of the University of Minnesota, an "Indian Solidarity Day" rally in support of Banks and Means drew 1,500 people. A WKLDOC newsletter announcing the event called on people to support the now familiar AIM demands: the establishment of a congressional committee to examine Indian treaties, repeal of the 1934 Indian Reorganization Act, and the removal of the BIA from the Department of the Interior in order to end the conflict between corporate interests and the management of Indian lands.[48]

At Wounded Knee two hundred people gathered for a commemorative ceremony. Since the protest, AIM had made an effort to keep a presence on the reservation, and some who had come to Pine Ridge during or shortly before the protest had stayed to organize around treaty rights and other issues. Means and other Oglalas also filed suit in federal court against Dick Wilson, charging "fraud, illegalities, and misconduct" in the recent Tribal Council elections. The suit, seeking injunctive relief, cited intimidation of candidates and voters, hundreds of illegal votes, destruction of voter registration lists, and lack of assistance by federal officials in monitoring the election.[49] Stories in South Dakota papers showed Wounded Knee residents still split on the protest, and South Dakota Representative James Abnor used the anniversary to call for compensation for the "victims" of the takeover.[50]

Meanwhile, the Indian Claims Commission set compensation for the 1877 appropriation of seven million acres of Lakota land, including the Black Hills, at $17 million. The Commission said it would next determine whether the government through its Indian programs over the years had already repaid the sum directly or in kind. Several Sioux tribal leaders, however, indicated that they wanted some 200,000 acres, including the Black Hills, returned.[51] Legislation pending in Congress promised to provide Indian tribes with greater self-government and additional funds for education. Recent government reports showed Indian children with lower test scores and higher dropout rates at every level. South Dakota Senator James Abourezk grudgingly admitted that Wounded Knee had made it easier to get an Indian aid bill through Congress: "As destructive as it was," said Abourezk, "it did create a lot of awareness of the trouble between Indians and the federal government."[52] During a speech in Saint Paul, however, the state's other senator, George McGovern, again criticized AIM's "armed occupation" and praised U.S. Marshals for their "incredible restraint" during the protest.[53]

Two other events outside the courtroom demonstrated AIM's continuing problem of conflicting public images. When Patricia Hearst was kidnapped by a radical group calling itself the Symbionese Liberation Army, Banks and Means were asked by reporters for their views on the situation. The two defendants, charged with holding people against their will, took the opportunity to call for Hearst's release and offered to help with the negotiations.[54] At almost the same time, Clyde Bellecourt and his brother Leonard were arrested in Minneapolis for allegedly trying to steal a sausage from a local grocery store. The AIM leader denied the charges, alleging police harassment, while noting that he had been arrested forty-seven times since the formation of AIM.[55]

In Saint Paul prosecutors were on the defensive for the next several weeks, as the defense attempted to demonstrate that the government had violated its own laws in an effort to convict the Wounded Knee protesters. Though the revelations of what had happened seemed minor, the hearing itself became almost a replay of the Watergate investigations. Throughout the hearing the FBI and the prosecutors seemed to be their own worst enemy: announcements were followed by retractions; a new revelation seemingly surfaced every week, until one small infraction—listening to some telephone conversations on an extension phone—became, like the now famous burglary, a story of intrigue and negligence, if not wrongdoing.

Joseph Pourier, a Bison State Telephone Company employee from the reservation and the first witness to take the stand, testified that he had restored telephone service to the Wounded Knee trading post during the siege at the request of the government and at the same time had installed a party line hookup at a government roadblock, making it possible to listen in on conversations to and from the trading post. The request, made five days after the takeover by U.S. Marshal Tommy Hudson, was for the stated purpose of making negotiations easier. Pourier also said that the extension was no different from any other party line found throughout the reservation, but acknowledged that he was uncertain about whether he had informed the people inside Wounded Knee of that fact.[56]

After one witness revealed that the written request for the installation had been destroyed and another said she had heard Dennis Banks's voice coming from a speaker at the government roadblock, defense attorneys noted that the Justice Department had assured them that the FBI was not tapping phones and that legal matters had been discussed on the phone in question. The implication was that the government had not just illegally monitored phone conversations of criminal suspects, but had deliberately eavesdropped on private conversations protected by the attorney-client privilege.[57]

In rapid succession the prosecution turned over one document that indicated there had been an official request for a phone tap, accompanied by Hurd's assurance that although the request had been approved it had not been implemented, and an internal FBI memo discussing phone monitoring at Wounded Knee on March 3, 1973. Hurd also admitted that, contrary to his assertions two weeks earlier, there had been four, not three, informants present at the meetings prior to the protest.[58] Additional witnesses were questioned about equipment attached to the phone at the roadblock and about a receipt for the purchase of items that could have been used to install a listening device labeled "Emergency purchases, Indian Activities, Wounded Knee, SD."[59]

Joseph Trimbach, the official directly in charge of FBI activities at the beginning of the protest, took the stand only to receive Fifth Amendment warnings against self-incrimination almost immediately. Confronted with two memoranda indicating that five conversations had been listened to and that officials were expecting a court order sanctioning eavesdropping, Trimbach said that he must have known about the telephone installation, but had forgotten about it when he assured Judge Nichol on March 9 that there had been no electronic eavesdropping involved in the case. He also repeated his earlier assurances that the FBI's failure to turn over materials pursuant to the discovery order was just an oversight and not intentional. Trimbach acknowledged that the Attorney General had refused the U.S. Attorneys' request for summaries of information on FBI informants, but denied that any informants had attended meetings with defense lawyers.

A visibly angry Nichol ordered a search of the FBI files for any further evidence of eavesdropping or the existence of informants, saying that if the government refused, the case would be dismissed. According to the Supreme Court, he said, the existence of a "surreptitious invasion by a government agent . . . into the legal camp of the defense does violate the protection of the sixth amendment."[60] When questioned about written responses to requests from Hurd which bore his signature, Trimbach insisted that he had not seen them, but that it was commonplace for assistants to handle matters in his name. Nichol quipped that he had just received a birthday greeting from former Agent in Charge Richard G. Held and that he "was crushed to find out" that Held "may not have written the letter at all."[61] Testimony finally ended on day three with Trimbach once again denying knowledge of preparations for a legal wiretap, while asserting that listening on an extension telephone was not a wiretap under the meaning of the law.[62]

Afterward Hurd told reporters that people inside Wounded Knee knew that the telephone was on a party line and that they had no right to expect privacy.[63] The defense, however, attempted to capitalize on the situation with a barrage of publicity. A letter from Sioux Falls WKLDOC on behalf of all the nonleadership defendants to U.S. Attorney Clayton officially requested disclosure of surveillance and eavesdropping, listing offices and other places where "clients had or have a reasonable expectation of privacy."[64] Daniel Ellsberg told a Twin Cities audience that the government was behaving as it had during his trial, "with its attitude of acting above the law." Several newspapers drew parallels to the circumstances of Judge Matthew Byrne's dismissal of the charges against Ellsberg and Anthony Russo for their role in the release of the "Pentagon Papers."[65] One Twin Cities newspaper, however, described the ongoing hearing as having the "demeanor of a piece of staged entertainment, rather than a serious quest for the truth."[66]

A few days later, with Judge Nichol again in the audience, Kunstler spoke to the Saint Paul Rotary Club and railed against government wrongdoing, linking the attacks on the left with Watergate and making comparisons with Nazi Germany. "This once great country," said the New York attorney, "has been reduced to a nation of cheats and liars and burglars." Afterward Nichol was quoted as saying that he agreed with "a great deal" of what Kunstler had said: "We are in trouble in this country, and the judiciary, just as he says, may be the last bastion of freedom."[67] When questioned whether his presence at the speech was possibly prejudicial to the government, Nichol replied no, and reminded reporters that Kunstler had said similar things in the courtroom.[68]

As the hearing moved into its second week, people continued to sift through the evidence on file in the Minneapolis FBI office. Tilsen reported that the files on Means and Banks alone consisted of 1,008 serials in 17 volumes and 901 serials in 12 volumes respectively, with each serial possibly consisting of more than one page. He argued, however, that the problem was not quantity, but rather the FBI's refusal to turn over anything other than a "specific item asked for with such detail as to make it impossible for them to refuse the request."[69] Tilsen also contended that the government's resources were far greater than those of the defense, but under questioning by Gienapp he acknowledged that the defense had already received hundreds of documents, including witness statements, photographs, audio tapes, and films, pursuant to the pretrial orders.[70]

Then, in the middle of the testimony of the BIA electrician who installed the telephone at the government roadblock, prosecutors turned over copies of notes taken by U.S. Marshals with respect to the monitoring. When asked why the notes had not been available earlier, Gienapp replied that the agents in charge of complying with the discovery orders didn't know that the notes existed. Nichol quipped, "You see, that's the disturbing thing, we're always finding out that the head of the bureau or the guy at the top never seems to know anything," to which Gienapp replied, "Well, that's true, your honor."[71]

On the stand a succession of government officials denied any knowledge of calls being monitored; asserted that it was unintentional; argued that listening on an extension was not technically eavesdropping; admitted listening but denied hearing anything of a legal nature; and finally, argued that the monitoring was justified because it yielded information about possible booby traps inside the village. One agent termed the monitoring a necessity during a "state of war."[72]

As the defense leveled more accusations against the FBI, Hurd flew to Washington to confer with Justice Department officials on the question of informants in the defense camp. A tape of a BIA radio communication contained a reference to mail being read, and then the government revealed that it had a copy of a letter written by Banks to AIM attorney

Ramon Roubideaux.[73] Meanwhile seven FBI agents had been going through the mass of documents for three weeks with few results, but defense attorney Doug Hall said he was "suspicious, if not confident, that there are other goodies in that pile that they haven't turned over."[74] Tilsen called the case untriable, Kunstler termed it the "theater of the absurd," while Gienapp insisted that the government was doing the best it could and asked, "How many 71-day crimes around the country are there where there are massive forces on both sides, where negotiations are going on during the time of the crime?"[75]

On March 28, while Hurd was en route back to Saint Paul, Attorney General Saxbe filed a brief asking the U.S. Circuit Court of Appeals in Washington to uphold President Nixon's refusal to turn over five tapes to the Senate Watergate Committee. That night the assistant U.S. Attorney reported to Nichol that the Justice Department had overruled the FBI and would comply with the judge's order concerning informants. In court the next day, Hurd announced that the files would now be searched for evidence of an invasion of the defense camp, material that was exculpatory, and evidence that might have been the result of electronic or telephone interceptions. Hurd said it was the first time the U.S. Attorney General had authorized such an order, while Judge Nichol expressed his regrets at the state of the state: "I deplore the necessity in a democracy to have a so-called spy system or an informer system, but unfortunately, I guess we've had one for some time, whether we like it or not."[76]

Over the next two weeks more government officials took the stand, prosecutors searched through the massive quantity of paper, and the press speculated on what might turn up pertaining to who had listened to what conversations, pursuant to whose orders, and on the possibility of a dismissal. Names of people connected with the growing Watergate investigation, Attorney General William Saxbe and FBI Director Clarence Kelley, began to appear in reports on the trial.[77] The press coverage, however, was far from uniform. The *Saint Paul Pioneer Press* defended the use of the party line to gather information on "booby traps and land mines" planted by the protesters: "Considering the violence and dangers which prevailed at the time, it would have been surprising if law enforcement officers had ignored those telephone conversations when lives were at stake."[78]

Testimony in court and discussions in Nichol's chambers led to more disclosures, admissions, and denials. A formal request for a legal wiretap had been made and turned down, and the affidavit in support of the request had indeed been signed by Joseph Trimbach. Hurd submitted his own affidavit stating that the search of the FBI's "confidential source files" had yielded no additional evidence that would either help or hurt the defense, or any evidence that an informant had penetrated the defense camp.[79] Clayton testified that he had not authorized a wiretap at Wounded Knee, as Trimbach's affidavit indicated, and Hurd then said that he had forgotten seeing the request for a wiretap in the files and that had he learned of the Trimbach affidavit in mid-March, but that in his opinion it was not covered by the subpoena issued for the FBI agent. Finally, FBI agent Philip Enlow asserted that the missing page of the affidavit containing Trimbach's signature must have been the result of a clerical error.[80]

In a reportedly heated exchange in chambers, Nichol criticized the U.S. Attorneys concerning Trimbach's previous statements, while defense attorneys suggested that the FBI official had committed perjury.[81] Back on the stand, Trimbach admitted that he must have seen his own affidavit, but that he had not prepared it, did not remember signing it, and must have forgotten it all when he testified earlier. On cross-examination he said he did not know why a page of the affidavit had been cut in half and then taped back together, or why it appeared that pages had been stapled and restapled several times. Hurd suggested that it had been done for the purpose of making copies.[82] Following Trimbach, there was testimony that the FBI had purchased ninety cassette tapes during the occupation and that U.S. Marshals had requested and received keys to the Pine Ridge telephone building, supposedly to protect it from AIM.[83]

"Memory Fails Me—Trimbach," read the front-page headline in the *Saint Paul Pioneer Press* the next day. It was indicative of the press coverage. The day after Trimbach's testimony the prosecution turned over a letter from a Justice Department official written during Wounded Knee, indicating that he thought the eavesdropping on the party line was illegal.[84] But Nichol ruled against calling Saxbe, Kelley, or former acting FBI Chief L. Patrick Gray, and he allowed Assistant Attorney General Henry Peterson to file an affidavit in lieu of taking the stand. In his affidavit Peterson admitted discussing the use of the party line with FBI officials, seemingly contradicting witnesses who claimed no knowledge of phone monitoring.[85]

Additional government witnesses also denied the existence of an electronic tap and justified the limited monitoring with testimony about the concern for land mines planted inside Wounded Knee.[86] Carl Belcher, Chief of the General Crimes Section, Criminal Division of the Department of Justice, insisted that the listening on the phone was legal and that it was intended to simplify negotiations, but admitted that it was never used for that purpose. Belcher also claimed that he was not aware of any internal memo questioning the legality of the monitoring. FBI Agent Roy K. Moore said he was not told about the phone when he arrived at Wounded Knee and only learned of the application for a wiretap after it was turned down. He also said that the information on booby traps had not come from the monitoring.[87]

M. Mark Felt, Acting Associate Director of the FBI at the time of Wounded Knee, also testified that the information on booby traps came from live sources and not the telephone. But he also said that it was agent Moore who had first told him about the eavesdropping, contradicting what Moore had just testified to. Felt also insisted that in general the bureau did not conduct illegal wiretapping, which brought several questions concerning past FBI activities from Kunstler. Afterward Nichol characterized Moore's testimony as "clearly less than candid" but refused the defense's request for the names of informants referred to by Felt, stating that it was not relevant to the hearing. He did, however, issue a subpoena for the "confidential source" that had just been named in a story in the *Minneapolis Tribune*. The "source" turned out to be an AP photographer who had been questioned by law enforcement officials as he left Wounded Knee, but provided them with little information other than hearing about plans for an "Indian Nation" and seeing weapons.[88]

After listening to arguments from both sides and a reaffirmation by Hurd that no evidence given to the prosecution had resulted from a wiretap and that he had not learned of the eavesdropping at the extension phone until March of 1974, Nichol deliberated his decision overnight.[89] In an hour-long reading of his findings the next day, he concluded that the defendants did not know the line was a party line, that the phone was not used for negotiations, and that someone in the government had eventually concluded that the eavesdropping was illegal; thus he ruled that any evidence acquired as a result of it was inadmissible. He also called the government's response to discovery orders "dilatory" and "considerably weaker than it should have been," but said that he could not find that it was willful or the result of "bad faith on the part of the FBI." Rather, said the judge, it was a combination of negligence and the sheer volume of material that had been gathered: "I must conclude that the government misconduct in the instant case does not stoop nearly to the depths of that in *Ellsberg*."[90]

Nichol saved his sharpest comments for the FBI, saying that the bureau was guilty of "repeated negligence" and that the many revelations in the hearing had brought him "to the brink" of dismissing the case.[91] But, said the judge, "accused individuals must be brought to trial or our institutions for the maintenance of societal order will collapse." Dismissal was a "last resort," he said, to be used only when a judge found himself "powerless to provide a criminal defendant with a fair trial." Finally, saying that he was "acutely aware" of the government's "compliance, or lack thereof," with his discovery orders and "the rules of law," Nichol ended with a warning: "If further misconduct occurs on the part of the government, I would certainly consider a renewed motion by the defendants. It is my deepest hope and expectation that such a renewal shall not be necessary."[92]

Press reports highlighted what one paper referred to as Nichol's "severe reprimand" of the FBI and the prosecutors.[93] Clayton said the decision was not a "mortal wound" and was not "unexpected." Prosecutors believed that the defense had successfully made "a mountain out of a mole hill."[94] Kunstler, however, claimed that they had "conclusively proved" their case and expressed disappointment with Nichol: "We challenged him to go the last mile and he wouldn't do it, we still have to wait until the federal judges catch up with the American people." The defendants, however, maintained that they wanted the trial to proceed to a jury verdict and vowed to continue to "bring out the fact that there is misconduct in all of the federal government."[95]

Near the end of March, an editorial appearing in two South Dakota papers invoked an often repeated theme of the 1960s, when it criticized speeches by Kunstler and Means made in Denver in which they invoked the coming bicentennial by calling for a new revolution by 1976. Kunstler reportedly told the audience, "It is better to die in the streets than to go down without a whimper." The editorial rebuked any call to violence as outside of the ideals of the American Revolution: "Striving for social change within the framework of these principles is one thing. Overt action of the kind envisioned by Kunstler and Means is quite another."[96]

What many in the press did not yet seem to grasp was that many Native Americans were not concerned with living up to the ideals of the American Revolution, and that AIM was not the only group willing to articulate that view. In South Dakota, the Black Hills Sioux Nation Council rejected an Indian Claims Commission offer of $17 million in compensation for the Black Hills and another $450,000 for gold taken out of the area before 1875. The group announced plans to petition Congress for the return of the land. In Washington, a representative of the National Congress of American Indians testifying before a Senate subcommittee criticized the Justice Department for not adequately protecting Indian resources. At the same time, Indians from several states were meeting in Billings, Montana, to discuss the protection of natural resources on Indian land.[97]

In Saint Paul the release of an internal Justice Department review of Wounded Knee lent additional credibility to the protest. The so-called White Paper suggested in part that protest actions on a reservation "could be justified . . . as a forceful exercise of Indian self-determination in Indian territory." It was perhaps a further indication of Nichol's shifting attitude toward the government that he ordered the report to be made available to the defense, despite protests from Earl Kaplan, the Justice Department representative at the trial, and then added, "If they don't like it they know what they can do about it." The judge also wondered out loud why the government had done virtually nothing when Indians occupied the BIA building in Washington in 1972 and so much when they occupied Wounded Knee a few months later.[98]

The hearing on the suppression and dismissal motions in Saint Paul had lasted four weeks. In the end there was no evidence that the attorney-client privilege had been breached by electronic surveillance or by an informant; there was only a party line and the telephone at a government roadblock. But the eavesdropping on the extension phone, like the burglary at the Watergate complex, was no longer the issue. Many, including Judge Nichol, suspected the FBI and Justice Department of trying to cover up another relatively minor infraction, or perhaps even something more sinister that was yet to be revealed. FBI Director Clarence Kelley knew the mood of the country in the spring of 1974, as he traveled outside of Washington seeking to improve the image of the Bureau.[99] As the President's attorneys battled special prosecutor Leon Jaworski over the release of White House tapes, defense attorneys and reporters in Saint Paul speculated on what they might contain relative to Wounded Knee.[100]

The *New York Times* noted during the hearing that the government had been under almost constant attack since the trial began.[101] Although prosecutors would present some strong witnesses in the weeks to come, they would never regain the offensive, in or outside the courtroom. The defense had planned it that way, and everywhere Russell Means and Dennis Banks spoke they reiterated their now familiar theme: "It's really the United States that's on trial, not us."[102]

6 MONTH FIVE AND COUNTING

You have to bring some levity into the proceedings . . . and sometimes a little drama and I think we did that.
WILLIAM KUNSTLER

It's like a road show . . . if a road show starts to get tired you change your scenery a little bit, that's what we were trying to do.
DENNIS BANKS

W E INTEND to continue with the plan we've had for the trial," U.S. Attorney William Clayton told reporters after the wiretap hearing.[1] The prosecution, however, now faced a judge who was becoming increasingly skeptical about the government's case. Within moments after testimony had resumed, Nichol again blasted the "arrogance of the FBI" in connection with another late disclosure of information. The prosecutors would struggle with their case for another three months.

It was violence in a Sioux Falls courtroom, however, not the intrigues in Saint Paul, that grabbed the headlines as April came to a close. The trial for five of the nineteen defendants indicted in the Custer riot was proceeding with jury selection when it erupted into a riot of its own. The events began when defense attorneys refused to proceed, pending the outcome of an appeal in a dispute over the selection process. South Dakota State Judge Joseph Bottum reprimanded the attorneys for what he termed their contemptuous behavior, and jailed one—Indian attorney Ramon Roubideaux—for contempt. The defense in turn accused Bottum of attempting to "squelch the political, racial and ideological overtones" of the trial and portray demonstrators as "common criminals."[2]

The next morning when a number of spectators refused to stand as he entered the courtroom, Bottum dismissed the jury, had several spectators removed from the courtroom, and finally recessed the proceedings.[3] The following day legal workers, defendants, and spectators, including Russell Means and Vernon Bellecourt, again refused to stand. Said Means: "I've stood in other courtrooms, that's not the point. I cannot in good conscience stand before that man . . . I'll stand every time the judge in Saint Paul enters the room."[4]

When attempts by Means and others to negotiate a compromise failed, Bottum called in riot-equipped police to clear the courtroom. Club-swinging officers engaged spectators, including several clergymen, defendants, and legal workers, arresting several and sending many to the hospital, including one of the defendants. Outside demonstrators marched, chanted, broke windows and doors, and stormed through the courthouse protesting the arrests. Later, AIM held a rally in support of the defendants that was attended by several participants from the Saint Paul trial.

Kunstler filed a motion with Nichol asking him to restrain Bottum, but the judge denied the request. AIM declared a "national emergency" and requested Indians from around the country to come to South Dakota. Banks contrasted his trial with the situation in Sioux Falls, but Means said that Indians couldn't get a fair trial in Saint Paul either. Earl Callahan, the Sioux Falls Police Captain, said he hoped people would not "soak up all the propaganda being put out by Indian leaders." Meanwhile, thirteen people were charged with rioting and assault, though many claimed that police gave no warning before rushing into the courtroom.[5]

In Saint Paul the day after the riot, Banks and Means remained seated when Judge Nichol entered the courtroom, a gesture he ignored. Then, as prosecutors resumed calling witnesses before a jury that had not heard testimony in six and a half weeks, another controversy erupted. "Someone better tell them to get off their high pedestal," said Nichol, referring to the FBI, as Hurd belatedly handed defense attorneys a copy of a signed statement given by the witness currently on the stand. In a sharp exchange with the judge, Hurd said that he had just been given the statement and noted that the defense already had a summary of what the witness had previously told authorities. But Nichol termed it "complete disrespect" for the court: "If that's the kind of arrogance that's going to exist down there in that Minneapolis office of the FBI, I can do something about it, and one of the things I can do about it is dismiss this case entirely on the ground of government misconduct, which apparently appears to be deliberate."[6] Then, turning to Hurd, Nichol said he was aware that he was making his remarks in front of the jury and that the prosecutor could make any motion he wished to. But Hurd declined to move for a mistrial, saying only that it was the government that was not receiving a fair trial, not the defendants.[7] Newspapers characterized Nichol's remarks as the "sharpest yet" directed toward the FBI. Headlines like "Nichol Angered Again at FBI, Hints Dismissal" headed press coverage of the controversy, rather than the testimony of the Wounded Knee resident on the stand.[8]

The next day Hurd argued that the judge's openly "hostile attitude" toward the FBI and the press coverage of those remarks were making it increasingly unlikely that the government would receive a fair trial. He also cited press quotes of Nichol expressing agreement with Kunstler's public criticism of the FBI's campaign against black liberation groups. "I don't give a damn," responded Nichol, "I agree with much of what he says." Nichol added that he had expressed his feelings concerning the "deterioration" of the FBI directly to Clarence Kelly while attending a conference in Saint Louis. Later when Hurd reported that several more FBI reports had just turned up in Sioux Falls, he had to respond to more criticism: "I don't enjoy trying a case where I have egg on my face every day."[9]

On the stand when the eruption over her missing statement occurred was Wounded Knee resident Jean Fritze, who, along with her husband Guy and their thirteen-year-old daughter Adrienne, provided additional accounts of the now familiar story of gunfire, looting, armed guards, and the fortifications constructed around the village. They also said that they had seen the defendants with pistols, that Clyde Bellecourt had said that the takeover was "Russ's show," and that they saw Banks wearing one of Mr. Fritze's sweaters.[10] The press, however, seemed more interested in Nichol's agreement to issue a subpoena for any White House tapes that might contain conversations regarding Wounded Knee than it was about the day's testimony.[11]

Meanwhile in Sioux Falls the situation remained tense. Weeks earlier the Custer and nonconspiracy Wounded Knee trials had opened to less than packed courtrooms, with no visiting celebrities or network news cameras in attendance.[12] Though the city of just over 81,000 did not have the history of progressive movements that existed in Minnesota, the defense committee had developed at least cordial relations with city officials and various community organizations, primarily church groups.[13] Now as WKLDOC and AIM experienced a backlash in the wake of the riot, one committee member likened the city to an "armed camp." City officials and the local media continued to blame AIM for the riot, and Judge Bottum refused to declare a mistrial or remove himself from the case.[14] The *Rapid City Journal* called the refusal to stand in the courtroom a "planned show of disrespect" toward the judge and the courts, which could "inevitably lead to erosion of the system." The president of the South Dakota Bar Association agreed, characterizing the episode as "a deliberate attempt to override our system."[15]

AIM in turn declared South Dakota a "war zone" and announced plans for a boycott of tourism in the state. During a morning recess in Saint Paul, Means passed out a statement which referred to the recent actions of "hostile settlers" and said that Indians would stop cars entering the state.[16] In another editorial, the *Rapid City Journal* called the proposed boycott a setback to Indian-white relations and an action that would hurt Indians: "The state of South Dakota and many Indians in it have demonstrated a willingness to take a positive approach to economic stability with dignity for its Indian population. That effort should not be destroyed by activist elements which offer no positive alternative."[17]

The war of words continued with Lane calling South Dakotans "the most racist people in the country." The Lieutenant Governor denied the accusation and demanded an apology from Lane. The Sheriffs Association, the local bar association, and the newly elected mayor of Sioux Falls all announced their support for Judge Bottum. Governor Richard Kneip called AIM members "terrorists" and "hoodlums," and accused them of creating a "climate of fear, hatred and reprisal." Madonna Gilbert responded to Kneip, listing complaints against the state and noting that prior to the "police riot" in Sioux Falls, AIM had requested a meeting with state officials on the judicial system. Though she admitted that thus far her trial had been fair, Gilbert argued that it was difficult for Indians to receive a fair trial anywhere in the country "due to the racism and ignorance of white people."[18]

AIM also accused local prosecutors of a double standard of justice, citing the failure to prosecute assaults on Indians. Said AIM leader John Trudell, "We will no longer tolerate the harassment of drunken white courage." The County Attorney denied Trudell's claims and offered statistics of prosecutions to prove his point. He also refused to convene a grand jury to look into the courthouse riot, accusing AIM of thriving on intimidation and not being representative of Indians in the state. Instead, Trudell was charged with damaging a tavern sign.[19] A *Sioux Falls Argus Leader* editorial pleaded for calm and acknowledged that there were injustices against Indians, while suggesting that the majority were not radicals.[20]

Jury selection resumed in the Custer trial under heavy security, with only family members and reporters allowed into a makeshift courtroom in the civil defense building.[21] Across town in the federal courthouse, the first trial of nonconspiracy defendants from Wounded Knee had begun. Charged with larceny and burglary of the trading post were Madonna Gilbert and Lorelei DeCora, the key liaisons between AIM and WKLDOC through much of 1973, and Tonia Ackerman, an Indian woman born in Canada who had worked with AIM in Saint Paul. All three defendants, who were now living on Pine Ridge, had chosen to waive their right to a jury and proceed before Judge Warren Urbom. The defense was anxious to start with a victory and was confident it could receive a fairer trial from the Nebraska federal judge than from a South Dakota jury.[22]

The two defense attorneys, Albert Krieger and James Shellow, had both volunteered through the National Association of Criminal Defense Attorneys. Though less political in their relationship to the cases than their counterparts in Saint Paul, they too set out to put the government on the defensive.[23] It may have helped that the lawyers representing the government were not full-time prosecutors; faced with more cases than his staff could handle, Clayton had appointed four South Dakota attorneys to handle the nonconspiracy trials.[24]

One of the early prosecution witnesses was Wounded Knee Trading Post owner James Czywczynski, who many believed had profited by charging high prices and heavy interest on credit, while underpaying the Indians who made crafts for resale in the store. The prosecution opened Czywczynski up to questions concerning his finances by having him testify about the value of items allegedly stolen from his store. With his attorney and reporters listening closely, Czywczynski asserted his Fifth Amendment privilege against self-incrimination ninety-five times to inquiries from defense attorneys regarding the financial arrangements of his business.[25]

The only other story from the trial that made page one news was the birth of a baby girl to Lorelei Means. The proceedings were so low-key that the defendants were not even present during much of the testimony, preferring instead to spend their time organizing on the reservation. "The courtroom stuff was up to the lawyers," said Gilbert; "I didn't worry about it."[26]

In Saint Paul, Joseph Trimbach retook the stand to testify that he had met with Means during the first hours of the takeover and received the list of demands that contained the AIM leader's signature, along with a list of "hostages." The testimony, which included a reading of the demands, established Means and two of his alleged co-conspirators, Pedro Bissonette and Carter Camp, as leaders, but also brought out reasons for the protest. On cross-examination defense attorneys rehashed the circumstances of the wiretap affidavit, attempting to show that Trimbach had committed perjury during his earlier testimony. On re-direct examination Hurd asked questions aimed at pointing out that given the chaos of the first weeks of the takeover, it would have been possible for Trimbach to request a wiretap and then forget about it.[27]

Trimbach was followed by Agnes Gildersleeve, a seventy-year-old Chippewa Indian who helped operate the trading post. Described in the press as a "spunky elderly woman" or "feisty little Chippewa Indian woman," her often humorous testimony landed her on page one.[28] Gildersleeve, a Wounded Knee resident since 1934, even had Banks and Means laughing at themselves when she spoke of their constant "posing" for photographers during the siege. On the more serious side, she described how people had been forced to vacate their homes and told to consider themselves "hostages and political prisoners." During her testimony, the prosecution introduced a letter signed by fifty Wounded Knee residents criticizing AIM and the occupation and stating that the protest had set Indians back fifty years. Gildersleeve also said that when she asked Banks why they had attacked innocent people, he had responded, "You had the food, you had the guns, you had the ammunition, we needed it and we took it."[29]

On cross-examination the defense attempted to show that Gildersleeve had not been harmed and that directions such as being told to lie on the floor were actually for her protection during incoming fire. Other questions, aimed at demonstrating that she was unduly prejudiced against AIM, did not always achieve the desired result. When asked if it was true that she believed AIM was a communist organization, as she had stated in a letter, Gildersleeve replied, "Yes sir, their guard told us that they adopted communist tactics, Chinese tactics and the Negro tactics, and that composes AIM." She was equally direct concerning the takeover: "I resented the loss of that store, of the museum, and the garage, and all that was left of my home."[30]

Despite her criticism of AIM, Gildersleeve admitted that Banks was "nice" to her and had helped her retrieve an antique clock that had been taken from her home. She also said that she felt that the federal government should be doing more for reservation Indians, and that she had told Senator Abourezk that if the government had taken care of Indian people, the protest might have been prevented. But overall Gildersleeve remained firm in her negative opinion of AIM's tactics throughout cross-examination: "I'm not prejudiced against their organization, but what they stand for only: destruction, and razing . . . rioting and things like that."[31]

Gildersleeve's testimony may have helped the prosecution, but attention to it was short-lived. While making an appearance at the trials in Sioux Falls, Means was arrested under a new indictment for his role in the Custer protest. Judge Nichol ordered him returned to Saint Paul, but would not intercede to get Means released without bond on the South Dakota charges. Still in custody, the AIM leader wore his jail uniform in court to protest Nichol's decision. The angry judge refused to explain the situation to the jury, saying that Means had the option to wear street clothes and chose to dress as he did.[32]

Testimony resumed with an FBI agent who had entered Wounded Knee posing as a telephone repairman and then continued with Mrs. Gildersleeve's sister, Amelia Clark. Both witnesses echoed the earlier descriptions of bunkers, weapons, and damage to the village; Clark also described being held hostage.[33] Suddenly in the middle of Clark's testimony, Means stood up and announced, "I fired my lawyer, I'll now represent myself."[34] As Nichol urged caution, Means replied, "I'm aware that I am dealing with years of my life." Banks then announced that he too was firing his lawyers, and Means told Nichol that the action was taken to protest the judge's "bias and prejudice toward Indians" and to demonstrate that his treaty rights were "inviolate." The case, said Means, was a "racist travesty on justice." Then, over Nichol's objections, the defendants defiantly ordered their lawyers to leave the courtroom. The judge just as quickly told them to stay, and then in the midst of heated charges and countercharges ordered them to be retained by the marshals when all but Hall and Leventhal headed for the door.[35]

By noon the next day a compromise had been reached. Over the strenuous objections of the prosecution, Nichol granted Banks and Means co-counsel status for the purpose of conducting cross-examination of certain witnesses. Hurd again insisted that the government was not receiving a fair trial and accused Nichol of "bowing to intimidation and threats."[36] The defense attorneys maintained that they were only responding to a decision that the defendants had made on their own. During a late-night meeting they had turned down a mistrial offer and agreed to the compromise, because they were already convinced that the present jury would vote for acquittal.[37]

The result was also in keeping with the defense strategy of trying to give the jury a sense of who the defendants were as people. It was a version of an old criminal law adage: that juries don't convict friends. If a trial goes on long enough, Ken Tilsen explains, the jury begins to regard the defendants and their lawyers as part of their everyday life—if not friends, at least not the enemy. "You can convict symbols," says Tilsen, "but it's harder to convict real human beings."[38] Banks and Means had been allowed to present long, impassioned opening statements, and now jurors would hear them question selected witnesses.

With Means wearing a new sweatshirt emblazoned with the words "Custer had it coming," the prosecution pressed on. Wounded Knee resident Mary Pike told of the takeover of the church and Banks sleeping in her house; when she was allowed to return home from the church basement, she said, "they had taken over my home, my kitchen." On cross-examination she admitted that she had not been harmed, that she played the piano and sang for Means, that Bissonette was "very nice" to her, and that an Indian woman who said something mean to her was reprimanded by another guard.[39] Greta Big Owl followed with similar testimony and insisted that she thought the petition asking the government to leave was a sign-up list for food.[40]

Still, the prosecution remained on the defensive. Documents from a Senate committee given to the defense by a reporter fueled more discussions concerning defense claims of a government conspiracy to destroy AIM and the illegal use of the military during the protest. The material included memos detailing FBI investigations of AIM prior to Wounded Knee; communications between the Defense and the Justice Departments; and discussions of Colonel Volney Warner's role in the negotiations to end the siege. Hurd was again placed in the position of explaining why the documents had not been made available earlier. When Nichol asked, "Aren't you getting kind of tired of explaining your own negligence in some of these matters?" Hurd responded, "No, Judge, I'm getting used to it, as a matter of fact."[41]

The next day, in what one newspaper called "another series of foul-ups by the prosecutors," Nichol ordered the testimony of Alexander Richards struck from the record because an FBI report of the statement given by Richards, which contradicted portions of his testimony, had not been turned over to the defense prior to his testimony. Richards, who had been inside Wounded Knee, testified that Means had told people to take up positions at bunkers and directed the firing at law enforcement positions.[42] Hurd said he thought he had given the statement to the defense and complained that he was "getting ganged up on all the way," with Means responding, "It's your buffoonery that is causing you to get ganged up on."[43] The *Minneapolis Tribune* commented that Hurd seemed to be throwing himself on the mercy of the court rather than challenging defense maneuvers and court rulings, and characterized his demeanor as a shift from "urbane urban prosecutor" to "underdog country lawyer from South Dakota."[44]

Keeping the pressure on the prosecution meshed with the early strategy of putting the government on trial, and the continued slip-ups on the evidence just created more openings, particularly as the judge and the press became more receptive to charges of misconduct. According to Larry Leventhal, this also strengthened the contention that the defendants and others at Wounded Knee were victims rather than "perpetrators of crimes."[45] Yet it was still possible for the defense to go too far; after one exchange over cross-examination Nichol could be heard shouting: "I'm damn sick of this kind of treatment!" during a meeting with defense attorneys in his chambers.[46]

On May 28 Banks and Means made their debuts as co-counsel, and their respective approaches to cross-examination received as much attention from the press as the testimony of the witness they questioned. Everett Little White Man, an Oglala and a BIA policeman on Pine Ridge, added little to previous descriptions of gunshots and looting, and his testimony concerning the discovery of Molotov cocktails and ammunition in the trunk of a car that had been stopped coming out of Wounded Knee was ruled inadmissible because it could not be connected to the defendants.[47] His cross-examination, however, was front page news, complete with descriptions of the defendants' "contrasting styles." Banks was characterized as cautious and careful, while Means was likened to "a buffalo turned loose in a trading post—aggressive, tough and intimidating." The cross-examination began with an exchange with Nichol that seemed to typify the event:

NICHOL: Do you have some questions?
MEANS: A lot of them.
NICHOL: I was afraid of that.

Means was indeed aggressive, addressing the witness by his last name and each time stressing the words "White Man," making it sound like an accusation aimed at the clean-cut BIA policeman. One of his first questions was whether White Man was a descendant of the BIA officer who had assassinated Crazy Horse. Nichol at first ruled against the question and then changed his mind, admitting that everyone probably wanted to know. The answer, "I never followed my family tree that well," was indicative of the witness's lack of knowledge of Oglala history and culture, which Means harped on through most of his cross-examination. When White Man admitted that he knew little of the 1868 Treaty and the history surrounding it, Means taunted, "And you claim to be an Oglala Lakota?"[48] Other examples of Means's questions included the following:

> As a captain of police and a college graduate, before you were reassigned or given special assignment to Pine Ridge Agency, did you read up on any of the laws of that tribe?
>
> In your role as a BIA policeman . . . do you take pride in surrounding and starving and shooting Indian people?[49]

Although these and other questions from both defendants on traditional religion, the 1868 Treaty, and trading post finances were disallowed, the defendants successfully illustrated how Indian history was being lost over time.[50] Banks was even able to turn the appearance of an Air Force physician who had treated a U.S. Marshal's wounds into a discussion of medical care on the reservation. During cross-examination Banks pointed out the notation "VIP" written on the marshal's medical chart and asked how many Indians had been treated at the Air Force base and how many of their charts had been marked VIP. The answer, of course, was none.[51]

But the actions of another AIM leader almost upstaged the drama provided by the defendants. John Trudell, the newly elected National Chairman of AIM, was carried from the courtroom after he leaped two rows of seats, shouting that the trial was illegal and ending up right in front of a startled Judge Nichol before the marshals could corral him. The incident, which came during cross-examination of Officer White Man, was the focus of the coverage in some newspapers.[52]

In Sioux Falls the first nonleadership defendants to go to trial were acquitted without the defense having to call a single witness. After three weeks and a dozen witnesses, the government had rested, only to have Judge Urbom rule that the charges were not supported by the evidence. This brought to nine the number of cases ending in dismissals or acquittals without a single guilty verdict.[53] In contrast to what was happening in Saint Paul, the prosecutors and defense attorneys exchanged compliments with Judge Urbom on his handling of the proceedings. Both sides had even agreed to move the remaining trials to Urbom's hometown of Lincoln, in order to keep him on as the presiding judge.[54]

More important, negotiations were in progress that could lead to a resolution of the remaining cases. One hundred fifteen cases would be dismissed in return for pleas of guilty from five defendants. The special prosecutors, who were only being paid $75 a day by the Justice Department, had become discouraged when they realized that the trials would go on for long periods of time and that convictions would not come easily. Further, the defense had overwhelmed them with pretrial paperwork and the false idea that there were an unlimited number of lawyers to try the cases. It was something that WKLDOC deliberately "flaunted," said Beeler, trying to look "invincible" even if they were having trouble finding a lawyer for the next trial.[55]

Clayton proposed the deal to the Justice Department in a teletype dated June 5, saying that "the ten remaining burglary and larceny cases arising from the seizure of recently stolen property from cars stopped at road blocks leading out of Wounded Knee are unprovable" and that the chances of successful prosecution of the eighty-six Civil Obedience Act cases were "extremely slim."[56] Meanwhile lawyers and legal workers met to discuss the proposal with clients on the Rosebud Reservation in South Dakota, where a Sun Dance was being held.

Beeler and other WKLDOC members were in favor of the deal because they thought the five cases on which the prosecution wanted pleas would probably be lost anyway. But some in AIM wanted the treaty issue to be heard and were less concerned about the possibility of someone going to jail. Urbom, however, had agreed to hear the issue of jurisdiction under the treaty, and though resistance remained, the five defendants in question eventually agreed to plead nolo contendere pursuant to the agreement.[57]

Despite the appearance of invincibility, the lack of money and other resources was also a factor in the defense's desire to strike a bargain with the prosecution. Even if the remaining Wounded Knee case were dispensed with, it was doubtful that any deals would be struck in the Custer cases. Testimony in those trials began in June, with the introduction of film footage of what newspapers called the "brutal battle"—scenes of burning buildings, wrecked squad cars, and club-swinging police. Meanwhile at a conference in Wisconsin, AIM discussed the upcoming treaty conference and other issues but acknowledged that the defense committee was still a major priority. Leaders also blamed agents provocateurs for infiltrating AIM and causing trouble, and pledged stronger security to combat the problem.[58]

As the arguments and interruptions continued in Saint Paul, it was Nichol who increasingly seemed to be the focus of attention, as the press remained poised to report on which side the judge would criticize next. The fifth month came to a close with a recess because Nichol feared a demonstration. Kunstler, accompanied by Banks, Means, and a number of supporters, had descended on the Minneapolis office of the U.S. Attorney to ask that an indictment be sought against Joseph Trimbach for perjury and illegal wiretapping.[59] Back in the courtroom, FBI agents and U.S. Marshals, along with a few Pine Ridge residents, testified about gun battles and injuries to officers, as the prosecution tried to hammer home the point that law enforcement personnel were at times risking their lives in the spring of 1973. At the same time the defense used cross-examination to try to shift the blame for the undeniably dangerous situation back on the government.[60]

Testimony once again bogged down in arguments over what was admissible and then was upstaged by Means, who had to be carried from the courtroom by five marshals after calling a witness a liar. Means later apologized to get his contempt citation expunged, but then told reporters that Nichol had "blackmailed" him into making his statement of regret. "Means has said worse things about me than that," responded the judge. Nichol did, however, cancel the planned one-day recess that would have enabled the defendants to attend the upcoming treaty conference in Mobridge, South Dakota. He also had sharp words for Kunstler, who Nichol believed could have corrected Means's press statements.[61]

In another newspaper interview the judge also expressed his continued concern over events in Washington, saying that constitutional safeguards were "falling before the torrential force of presidential power." With an apparent eye toward the FBI, Nichol added, "Law and order works both ways—on those who obey the law, as well as those who enforce it."[62]

Heeding the call for law and order with a note of humor, the defendants attempted to arrest FBI agent Gerald Bertinot as he left the witness stand. Bertinot was one of the agents who testified in the wiretap hearing that he had listened in on telephone conversations from the Wounded Knee trading post. As he passed the defense table, Banks rose and announced: "We are placing this man under citizen's arrest." The agent was quickly spirited out of the courtroom but was pursued through the building by AIM supporters, until U.S. Marshals and other agents were able to escort him out through a skyway that had been closed to the public during the trial and into a waiting car. Nichol warned the defendants about their actions, and an angry Hurd complained that it was all "a show for the press," adding, "I'm getting sick of this stuff." Said Kunstler, "That was the funniest thing I've ever seen, an agent sneaking out of the courtroom pursued by Indians; it was like something out of the Keystone cops."[63]

The next day, however, Kunstler again clashed with Nichol as he cross-examined an FBI agent about the direction from which some gunfire had come. The judge cut off the questioning and ordered all the attorneys into his chambers. Press reports on the episode speculated about the reasons for Nichol's anger—his health, and the possibility of fatigue from the five-month-old trial.[64]

The disagreements within the defense committee over how to respond to Nichol mirrored discussions within many left legal circles over judges and juries in political trials. Defense attorney Doug Hall felt that Kunstler and Lane were pushing too hard, but Kunstler maintained that as a matter of practice a defense attorney should exploit overreactions or other weaknesses of a judge:

> It de-mystifies the court and I think that's very important, because the judge is up there as the authority figure in the courtroom and to the jury probably represents something just short of God . . . I think it's good to take him off the pedestal, if you can to show the jury that he's really just a man, who happens to be a federal judge by the nomination of some senator and the approval of the Senate Judiciary Committee . . . and that he may not be the smartest in the world, he may not have the best grasp of the law, he may not be a paragon of virtue, he may not be a paragon of patience . . . you have to show the jury he's not a God.[65]

Otherwise, said Kunstler, a comment or even an expression from the judge while someone is testifying can carry great weight with the jury. Yet, in the nonleadership cases where the defense had chosen to try the cases to Judge Urbom instead of a jury, there had not been the kinds of clashes between the judge and defense attorneys that were occurring in Saint Paul. There was also concern among some that if Nichol's health worsened he might declare a mistrial, possibly putting a retrial before a less favorable judge. One proponent of this view was Hall, who had counseled his colleagues from the beginning that he believed they would get a fair trial from Nichol. By now Hall had assumed the role of unofficial mediator between Nichol and the defense camp, occasionally attempting to smooth over the clashes occurring in the courtroom.[66]

The prosecution clearly felt that Nichol was being pushed around, as did the judge himself, who believed as did Hurd that the defense wanted him to react like Julius Hoffman, the judge who had presided over the Chicago Seven trial and had cited Kunstler for contempt numerous times. Hurd argued that Nichol's rulings sometimes reflected the judge's fears of being labeled a racist or another Hoffman.[67] Indeed, Means had already referred to the judge's "racism" in and out of court, and Nichol acknowledged that the comments bothered him. But the judge also said that he felt intense pressure coming from the prosecution as well. In addition, letters commenting on the case and the judge's role were pouring in from around the world; the majority were in favor of the defendants, with the exception of those from South Dakota. Referring to the letters from his home state, Nichol says, "I didn't get very many compliments."[68]

The day after the exchange between Kunstler and Nichol, enough calm had settled over the courtroom that a remark by Leventhal that he would proceed with an "abundance of caution" drew laughter from the defense table and a smile from the judge. Several witnesses, including Joseph Trimbach, testified about being stopped at Indian roadblocks and being escorted in and out of Wounded Knee by armed guards. On cross-examination they were met with questions about the identities of the Indians involved and their knowledge of treaty law and the Indian Civil Rights Act.[69] Then Gene Graham, one of four Postal Inspectors stopped by armed men as they entered Wounded Knee, testified that their car keys, credentials, and other papers had been taken, and that they had been tied up and held at gunpoint for two hours in the trading post. Graham also described a lecture they received on Indian history and culture, given by AIM religious leader and alleged co-conspirator Leonard Crow Dog.[70]

The other inspectors involved provided similar testimony and claimed that they had been engaged in an effort to resume postal service to the village. The defense believed that the charges were a strong part of the prosecution's case; there was even a photograph showing the inspectors lined up, hands on their heads, flanked by armed guards. Defense attorneys attempted to challenge the identifications of the guards and brought out the fact that the inspectors were also armed, suggesting that their mission was to spy on activities inside the village, not to resume postal service as they contended. They also asked questions about Crow Dog's lecture, again putting the 1868 Treaty and the 1890 massacre into evidence.[71]

Following the inspectors, FBI agent Larry A. McGee was the first of several witnesses to testify about the circumstances of the shooting of agent Curtis Fitzgerald. On cross-examination the defense questioned witnesses on the exact nature of Fitzgerald's wound and how it occurred, implying that the agent might have accidentally shot himself while firing at a fleeing

U-Haul van during a high-speed chase. They also pointed out that people in the van would not have known who was in the car and then turned to questions about the presence of armed "goon squad" members and white ranchers, asserting that law enforcement had done little to curtail these groups and that they could have been responsible for some of the shootings the defendants were charged with.[72]

The press was split on the effect of government witnesses and the defense efforts to undercut their testimony. Some reporters had begun to comment on the length and cost of the trial—one estimating it at $2,130 per day, not counting the salaries of government employees—placing the blame on the defense and its "painfully slow and drawn out" cross-examination.[73] Yet the media also noted the prosecution's failure to link Banks and Means directly with the assaults on Fitzgerald or anyone else.[74] Despite the postal inspectors and the vivid descriptions of shootings, car chases, and other dangerous conditions, the prosecution had presented little, if any, direct evidence linking the two defendants with the specific crimes in question. Even Judge Nichol had commented on the lack of evidence connecting the defendants with the alleged assaults.[75]

Part of the continuing problem for the prosecution was that there was always a more interesting story to pursue. Former Deputy Attorney General (now Federal Appeals Court Judge) Joseph T. Sneed, Chief of Staff for Wounded Knee in the Justice Department, was called to discuss the Department's concern about the dangerous conditions and a decision to reinstate government roadblocks outside the village. But Sneed also wound up answering questions about who made decisions regarding negotiations, the use of force and the military, and conversations with John Ehrlichman and other officials in the White House and the Departments of Justice and Interior, including Attorney General Richard Kleindienst. Sneed admitted that there was a conscious decision not to involve Nixon, saying people believed "that it just wouldn't be very helpful to the President to get directly involved in Wounded Knee at that juncture."[76]

During the continuing debate over what questions constituted proper cross-examination, Hurd accused the defense of engaging in a "fishing expedition." Still, in an overly long trial, intrigue was intrigue, and even Nichol raised a question about the appointment to federal judgeships of two key officials involved in responding to the protest: "I don't know how all these Wounded Knee attorneys in the Department of Justice got elevated to federal judge right after Wounded Knee, but there must have been some reason."[77]

Outside the courtroom, AIM continued to attract the attention of law enforcement officials and the press. Means was involved in an altercation at a private country club in the Rosebud Reservation town of Mission, where he and others had gone to investigate reports that the club was refusing to serve Indians. The BIA claimed that Means had initiated the physical contact, but the AIM leader insisted that officials tried to remove them forcibly when they attempted to eat lunch at the club restaurant. While the press reported the charges and countercharges, Means stayed on Rosebud where a tribal court ruled that the federal law enforcement officials had no authority to arrest him, an order the government ignored. Intervention by Judge Nichol saved Means from what could have been a lengthy detention awaiting a hearing on the charges, but South Dakota Representative James Abnor asked the U.S. Attorney to seek revocation of Means's federal bond. Abnor said he had received several complaints about the "outbreaks of lawlessness by Indian agitators," but he claimed that only a few Indians were causing trouble and that if the courts dealt with them, peace would return to South Dakota.[78]

In Saint Paul, AIM announced the opening of the Red School House, which was to be a model for Indian "survival schools." Across the river in Minneapolis, pressure on city officials concerning police activities in Indian neighborhoods resulted in the appointment of a mayor's advisory council on Indian relations.[79] On the Standing Rock Reservation in South Dakota, AIM hosted a gathering of representatives of seventy tribes to discuss strategy for pursuing the fight for treaty rights. One of the proposals to come out of the weekend-long meeting was for the International Indian Treaty Council to seek membership in the United Nations. Several tribal chiefs in attendance announced their support for AIM's stand on the enforcement of treaties. Afterward participants met with federal officials on land and health issues in Aberdeen, South Dakota, while AIM representatives traveled to Washington to speak with the Commissioner of Indian Affairs about proposals for more training for BIA police officers. Back in South Dakota, officials noted that tourism in the state was down for the month of June, but did not mention the AIM boycott.[80]

In Sioux Falls, after deliberating for nearly fifteen hours, the jury in the first Custer trial found all three defendants guilty of rioting where arson was committed.[81] The next day word circulated that the plea bargain agreement on the nonleadership cases was apparently dead. U.S. Attorney and Justice Department officials in Washington claimed that the defense had rejected the offer.[82] According to Tilsen and Beeler, the FBI scuttled the proposal by making false representations to the Justice Department. Their assertion centers on two FBI memos sent to Justice, one stating that the dismissals would have a negative impact on the Bureau's operations "in both the intelligence and criminal fields in curbing the militant activities of A.I.M.," and a later memo claiming that U.S. Attorney Clayton had advised the Bureau that "as far as his office is concerned the Wounded Knee Defense has rejected the criminal plea bargaining proposal made by the government."[83]

Whoever was to blame, the trials would now continue before Judge Urbom in Lincoln. In the WKLDOC office there, Katherine James, a 21-year-old legal worker, was coordinating the defense of the remaining cases in federal court; no lawyer had come forward to replace Beeler, who had left the committee a few weeks earlier thinking that the plea bargain arrangement would be accepted. At the same time, nine people charged with felony, riot, and assault for their part in the courthouse riot made their first court appearance in Sioux Falls.[84]

On June 27 Means spent an entire day in Sioux Falls courtrooms, on the charges stemming from the Rosebud altercation and the courthouse riot. "I'm just tired of going to jail all the time for just no reason," the AIM leader said.[85] A few days later, as the temperature soared to 101 degrees, Means was back in Saint Paul where the trial had entered its seventh month. The prosecution's plans to put forward testimony that might have strengthened their case hit a snag when one of two Indian undercover agents who had been inside Wounded Knee refused to testify. Once inside the village, James Northrupp, a Cherokee Indian, had switched allegiances, telling AIM leaders that he wanted to be a double agent. The government was also having trouble locating a second informant who had not been heard from and was scheduled to testify in a few days.[86]

Government witnesses who did appear continued to fall short of placing the defendants close to the commission of crimes. The defense believed that the repeated testimony that placed Banks and Means in meetings and making speeches might help the conspiracy theory, but, along with providing opportunities to raise political points, it also took the defendants off the front lines. Before voting for conviction, the theory went, juries wanted to be shown that a defendant had committed a particular criminal act.[87]

One example of this was the testimony of Reverend Wesley Hunter, Executive Director of the Association of Christian Churches, who had been in Wounded Knee in early March. Hunter described Banks, Means, and other AIM leaders giving orders, attending meetings, encouraging people to stay until the situation was resolved, and being key people in negotiations with the government. On cross-examination he spoke of their dedication to Indians and the demands for Indian rights. Hunter also stated that many at Wounded Knee were not members of AIM and affirmed that the organization had been invited onto the reservation. When questioned by Lane about Pine Ridge housing conditions, he answered, "My impression of them was that it would be very difficult for a human being to live in those during the South Dakota winters."[88]

Following Hunter's testimony, Judge Nichol listened while the prosecution presented its case for revoking Means's bond. The reasons given were the "explosive" situation in South Dakota and Means's propensity to get into conflicts with law enforcement officials. Defense attorneys, however, accused the U.S. Attorney of bowing to political pressure: "If only Russell Means would go away," said Tilsen, "there wouldn't be any Indian problem in South Dakota." But Hurd responded angrily to the charge: "We are not asking that this court do more than enforce the rules that this court has already laid down." Nichol expressed sympathy for the government's position but denied the motion. He did, however, set further restrictions on Means's movements, requiring him to clear his travel plans with the court.[89]

John Ehrlichman's conviction on four counts of perjury conspiracy to obstruct justice in connection with the break-in at the offices of Daniel Ellsberg's psychiatrist gave the *Saint Paul Pioneer Press* the opportunity to contrast those proceedings with the progress of the Saint Paul trial. The paper commented on the "histrionics" of the AIM defendants and characterized the time taken in their trial for recesses, hearings, press conferences and speeches as evidence of "pettifogging, grandstanding, irresolution, and sloth" and as taking the focus away from what it should be, deciding guilt or innocence.[90]

In a speech before the Saint Paul Jaycees, Kunstler criticized the *Pioneer Press* editorial for "feeding the public misinformation and half truths." But he praised the reporters covering the trial and the press's handling of Watergate, noting that it was important for people to have a "healthy skepticism" about government.[91] In a reply to Kunstler, the *Pioneer Press* said that it had implied both sides were at fault for delays, not just the defense, that the paper did not expect "blind faith" from its readership, and that Kunstler's comments demonstrated a low opinion of the general public.[92]

*   *   *

In the courtroom the prosecution was nearing completion, with a series of witnesses telling about the wounding of a Deputy U.S. Marshal who had been left paralyzed from the waist down by gunfire that the government claimed came in an ambush-like attack from a bunker inside Wounded Knee. After several marshals told of being fired upon without warning, however, prosecutors detoured to bring on an unrelated and controversial witness, a move that triggered another courtroom confrontation and may have lessened the impact of the testimony on the shooting.[93]

Wounded Knee resident Nancy Hussman, the wife of one of Dick Wilson's alleged "goon squad" members, John Hussman, testified that she saw Means in the trading post while Molotov cocktails were being made. Hussman said that she heard Means order their construction, and watched while the defendant held up a vase and said, "Save these, these could be used for Molotov cocktails." A little later, she testified, Means issued the order: "Clear the store, the pigs are coming." Hussman also said she had seen Means with a rifle at the trading post and Banks in and around the church, which she described as a "mess."[94] At one point Hurd and Lane got into a shouting match that again made the papers. In response to a statement by Hurd that Pedro Bissonette had tried to shoot a BIA policeman, Lane yelled, "That's an absolute lie!" Hurd shouted back, "That's the absolute truth!"[95]

Outside the courtroom, Hurd complained to the press about Means's continued tardiness and claimed that the defendant had deliberately bumped into him the previous day. Nichol, he said, had told the defense attorneys to control their client. Hurd also accused the defense of deliberately delaying the trial to keep Means from facing his other charges, a statement that sent Lane complaining to the judge.[96]

In court Kunstler and Lane took turns trying to discredit Hussman's testimony with questions about her and her husband's friendship with Wilson and her appointment to a tribal job; they suggested that the witness had fabricated her story about Means in order to help her husband with his pending criminal charges. Hurd denied that any promises had been made to either the witness or her husband, but Lane pressed the point until a heated exchange erupted between Kunstler and Hurd which quickly involved both defendants and Nichol, who threatened to hold Means in contempt. In fact it may have been Banks, who received permission to address the court on Means's behalf—"We are not showing contempt, nor do we intend to"—who saved his co-defendant from being removed from the courtroom. After a momentary calm, Lane continued to probe the activities of Hussman's husband, lengthening an already long cross-examination, until Nichol again attempted to cut him off. After another exchange, Lane was jailed for contempt.[97]

The next morning the *Minneapolis Tribune* noted that the incident almost overshadowed Lane's "effective cross-examination of a witness who has given some of the most incriminating testimony in the trials."[98] The question was, overshadowed in whose eyes? In the *Sioux Falls Argus Leader*, under the headline "Defense Attorney Lane Held in Contempt in Long Heated AIM Trial in St. Paul," Lane's trip to jail dominated a story which also reviewed past conflicts during the trial. Another paper reported that Lane appeared exasperated because he could not shake the witness's damaging testimony. The defense attorney circulated a press statement from his cell, reportedly written on paper towels, saying that he believed that Nichol was "essentially a fair and good man," but one "who comes from and returns to a state terminally afflicted with the cancer of racism."[99]

As expected, the appearance of U.S. Marshal Lloyd Grimm, wheeled into court by another marshal, helped evoke sympathy that the government no doubt hoped would transfer to its overall case. Permanently confined to a wheelchair, Grimm recounted the events that led up to his shooting near the end of the seventy-one-day siege. "It felt like my feet never came down," said Grimm, who went on to describe the details of his paralysis.[100]

As they had with the witnesses that preceded him, defense attorneys questioned Grimm closely on the direction of the gunfire. Though he believed that the shots had come from one of the bunkers inside the village, Grimm admitted that he did not know who had fired the shots and that it was possible he was mistaken about the direction from which they came.[101] The defense was convinced that the shots had not come from inside the village, but they were also concerned about the impression Grimm's appearance would make on the jury. Defense lawyers engaged in a relatively gentle cross-examination, hoping only to instill in jurors the idea that the marshal had been shot by someone other than those inside Wounded Knee, such as the white ranchers or "goon squad" members who were in the area around the time of the shooting.[102]

On Wednesday, July 24, the ninety-eighth day of the trial, the government prepared to rest its case. The last of the evidence consisted of film footage and photographs taken inside Wounded Knee beginning the first night. The photographs showed the fortifications around the village and the state of the buildings at the end of the siege. A compilation of news film from ABC and CBS news broadcasts in March and April, which Hurd introduced and narrated, captured the chaos of the first few days, some gunfire, and the looting of the trading post. The films also showed both defendants in leadership roles, including clips of Banks explaining why people had come to Wounded Knee and Means saying that "sometimes there has to be violence to force the white man to listen."[103]

Six and a half months after the trial opened and after presenting fewer than sixty days of testimony, the government rested. As the defense prepared motions for acquittal based on insufficient evidence, illegal use of the military, and lack of jurisdiction under the 1868 Treaty, the participants summed up the case so far. "I'm pretty happy," said Hurd, "I think we presented a prima facie case and that the jury will convict on all ten counts." Means told reporters that he expected the defense case to be much shorter, saying, "We won't bumble and fumble as much and as long."[104]

The story on the front pages, however, was the news that the President had lost his battle over the White House tapes in the Supreme Court. Three days later the House panel voted to send the Articles of Impeachment to the full House. Once again the defense was talking to the press about obtaining the tapes.[105] But in Sioux Falls, where three Custer defendants had just been sentenced to jail terms of one to seven years, Nixon's problems provided little consolation. WKLDOC was looking for a new city in which to hold the next trial, without much success. An opinion survey conducted in Hughes County, which included the state capital, Pierre, revealed that 74 percent of those interviewed thought that Indian militants were responsible for the property destruction during demonstrations in February 1973, and most thought that the responsibility of a jury was to find them guilty. To add to the committee's headaches, Means was arrested again, this time trying to intervene in a fight in Valentine, Nebraska.[106]

In Saint Paul Hurd continued to assure the press that he believed the government's case would hold up: "I think it should be clear to anybody that Means and Banks were in leadership roles during the occupation . . . and were responsible for acts of their co-conspirators."[107] A week later, however, Nichol dismissed several of the ten remaining charges against the defendants, including burglary, auto theft, and possession of firebombs.[108] The defense had argued for a dismissal of all charges based on a clause in the 1868 Treaty which provided that the Tribal Court "shall have jurisdiction over all offenses when committed by a member of the Tribe and non-member Indians."[109] Nichol, however, agreed with the government's long-held position that since 1868 Congress had enacted legislation which had either "amended or abrogated" the terms of the Treaty. Included in that superseding legislation was the Major Crimes Act, which gave the federal government jurisdiction over thirteen specific offenses committed on reservations. The Treaty, said Nichol, did not deprive the federal courts of jurisdiction over counts in the indictment based on that legislation. And, citing a 1912 Supreme Court case, Nichol noted that Congress's power to amend treaties was well established: "The Tribes have been regarded as dependent nations, and treaties with them have been looked upon not as contracts, but as public laws which could be abrogated at the will of the United States."[110]

Nichol also ruled that there was enough evidence to send both the theft and the conspiracy counts to the jury. Conspiracy, said the judge, requires an agreement which need not be express or formal, and at least one overt act committed by a co-conspirator in furtherance of the conspiracy; he noted that the law required only circumstantial evidence for such a showing. Nichol concluded that testimony existed from which an agreement "may be inferred," as did testimony regarding the actions of the defendants and their co-conspirators.[111]

The judge then acquitted both defendants on the charges of burglary of the trading post. Following South Dakota criminal statutes, as he was bound to do under federal law, he found that the necessary requirements—namely, fraud or secrecy—which had to be intended under the wording of the indictment were not present. There was no evidence of fraud, said Nichol, adding that the looting of the trading post had been anything but secret.[112] In addition, he acquitted the defendants on possession of the Molotov cocktails (because no evidence had linked either defendant to the items in question), and on the theft of an automobile (because prosecutors had failed to present evidence that the car's value was in excess of $100, as required under the statute).[113]

In perhaps the most controversial part of the ruling, Nichol also acquitted the defendants on counts IV and V, attempting to "obstruct, impede or interfere" with U.S. Marshals and agents of the FBI "engaged in the lawful performance of their official duties." Here the phrase "lawful performance" was the key to the judge's findings. As Judge Urbom had earlier, Nichol found that the use of military equipment and officers at Wounded Knee constituted a "posse comitatus" under federal law and had been initiated without either the required congressional authorization or the needed exception, namely a presidential declaration that a civil disorder existed.[114]

On the basis of testimony first heard in Lincoln and repeated before Nichol, the defense contended that the FBI had requested troops, but that the White House, desiring to keep Nixon and the Army officially out of the situation, attempted to bypass the law by quietly supplying the law enforcement personnel at Wounded Knee with military equipment and advice.[115] The key military official on the scene was Brigadier General Volney Warner, the Assistant Division Commander of the 82nd Airborne, who at the time of Wounded Knee was a Colonel and Chief of Staff of the 82nd, and the Pentagon's liaison in South Dakota. On the stand, Warner claimed that he was only present at Wounded Knee in an advisory capacity: "I had no command, I did not regard AIM as the enemy of the United States, there was no effort being made to kill anybody inside Wounded Knee, there were no federal troops employed in that action."[116]

Warner also maintained that his presence helped defuse tensions and keep the marshals in check, and he insisted that there had been a conscious decision not to involve the military. But he admitted that he had been in numerous meetings with officials on the scene and in regular contact with Washington. Two additional officers verified the nature of the equipment and supplies and the existence of a chain of command from Warner to the Pentagon that included Fred Buzhardt, Counsel to the Secretary of Defense, and Alexander Haig, Nixon's Chief of Staff, but at the time of Wounded Knee the Vice Chief of Staff of the Army.[117] The equipment maintained by the military while in use during the siege included fifteen armored personnel carriers, clothing, rifles, grenade launchers, flares, and 133,000 rounds of ammunition, for a total cost, including use of maintenance personnel from the national guard of five states and pilots and planes for aerial photographs, of over half a million dollars.[118]

The prosecution argued that advice and borrowed equipment did not constitute military involvement, but Nichol ruled that the presence of two high-ranking officers to counsel officials directing the operation, along with all the military hardware, amounted to Pentagon involvement in a civil disorder and was enough to constitute the illegal use of the military under the federal statute. Thus, as the defense had argued, federal officers were not in the "lawful performance" of their duties as alleged in the indictment. Nichol was careful to note that he was not accusing anyone of engaging in criminal conduct on the reservation. He also refused to acquit on the assault charges, stating that those particular indictments required only that the officers be engaged in their statutory duties and that there was no requirement that those duties be lawful.[119]

As Nichol read his decision, the White House, citing confidentiality and presidential privilege, announced that it would not respond to the May 2 subpoena for tapes involving conversations about Wounded Knee. It would be one of the President's last acts of defiance. The next day, Thursday, August 8, Nixon resigned, leaving Vice President Gerald Ford to preside over the White House, the Justice Department, and the rest of the mess in Washington. The prosecution's case had ended with several acquittals and speculation about the possibility of calling the ex-President to the stand.[120]

One key to the success of the defense thus far was an ability to work together despite the diversity of the vast legal team. In and out of the courtroom, despite the sometimes volatile combinations of egos and cultures, the defense team hung together in the common purpose of winning the cases legally and politically. Though there was disagreement, as in the discussions over how to deal with Nichol, the legal workers, law students, and lawyers had forged a working relationship with one another and with their clients, to whom they remained willing to bow in disputed situations. Both Banks and Means contributed ideas about defense strategy throughout their trial. Although their differences surfaced occasionally, according to Banks they worked well together most of the time: "There were periods of time when Russ and I were very close and that closeness continues today . . . But there were times during the trial when he and I wouldn't even speak to each other for two, three days at a time."[121]

Among the lawyers, Kunstler and Lane led the public attack, but Tilsen provided the practical glue that held the case together, always directing people's attention toward the task at hand. Outside Saint Paul, attorneys from the NACDL were willing to take any case assigned to them, and with few exceptions worked well in trial.[122] The conflicts that had arisen in 1973 over the role of legal workers and law students still existed, but not without change. By now a number of nonlawyers, primarily women, had made long-term commitments to WKLDOC and had gained the respect of most defendants. In Lincoln legal workers coordinated the defense and often prepared the cases for trial, long before attorneys arrived on the scene. Without the nonlawyer volunteers, WKLDOC would not have existed outside of Saint Paul.[123]

By August, however, the length of the Saint Paul trial and the sheer volume of the other cases were beginning to tell. The old adage that juries don't convict friends may have been working on behalf of Banks and

Means, but whoever coined the phrase could not have imagined the massive amount of legal work that still confronted WKLDOC and AIM in the summer of 1974. The Saint Paul case had become a magnet for both publicity and talent, but neither was necessarily transferred to the proceedings in South Dakota or Nebraska. "There were lawyers floating in and out of Saint Paul, volunteering to help out for a week or so, which was kind of dumb because we had five lawyers in court every day," said a former law student volunteer, "and nobody volunteering to go to Lincoln for a week."[124] In August, meetings were held in Saint Paul to discuss the "desperate financial state" and the shortage of lawyers in the other cases. Outside the Twin Cities, where some individuals had double workloads in the absence of a group to specialize in a given area and committee members sometimes resorted to shoplifting food and other essentials to get by, resentment toward the resources in Saint Paul was growing.[125]

Some in AIM even questioned the commitment of their long-time legal allies. At an August NLG meeting in Minneapolis, John Trudell challenged the Guild's commitment to the Wounded Knee and Attica defenses, and told the group that they needed to listen more closely to Indians and blacks to better understand their oppression. The speech sparked heated debate within the organization that had been involved in Wounded Knee almost from the beginning, and the convention resolved to step up recruitment for the remaining cases.[126] By the end of the prosecution's case in Saint Paul, the defense was quietly confident of victory. But if the expected success in that case turned out not to act as a catalyst for a renewed commitment of resources from somewhere else or the dismissal of a significant number of cases by the government, WKLDOC and AIM could still lose the war.

THE DEFENSE CASE AND THE GOVERNMENT'S REBUTTAL

We do not know anything about conspiracy. The Indians are guided by the Great Spirit and our sacred pipe ... If there's a crime against looking for justice, where do we go to find justice here in America?

GLADYS BISSONETTE, AUGUST 1974

As far as I'm concerned, Russell Means and Dennis Banks and the rest of the AIM leadership belong behind bars for the years they have ripped off, cheated, lied [to], and stolen from their own people.

LOUIS MOVES CAMP, AUGUST 1974

I N THE EARLY 1970s as the American Indian Movement surged into
the national spotlight, well-worn paperback copies of two books
about Indians were circulating among friends and making their way
into college classrooms. *Bury My Heart at Wounded Knee* and *Custer Died for
Your Sins* educated many Americans about the past while serving notice
that Native Americans were still actively engaged in a struggle to reclaim
that history and to redress a long list of grievances, past and current.[1] On
August 13, seven months after jury selection had begun, authors Dee
Brown and Vine Deloria each took the stand on behalf of AIM leaders
Russell Means and Dennis Banks.

For many in the country, these writers were already considered authorities on Indian history, the current status of government policies toward
Native Americans, and the state of Indian-white relations within the
country. When Nichol ruled that each man could testify as an expert witness, Deloria on the Native American position on treaties with the government and Brown on Indian history, his ruling helped to legitimize their
testimony and validated the knowledge gained by readers of their books.
As each author testified to his knowledge of Indian policy, broken treaties,
and current conditions on reservations, many of the contentions made in
the opening statements of the defendants were given greater authenticity.

The Indian movement had used the popularity of books such as Brown's to push its concerns into the public arena; now this was being done in court, with the stamp of legal legitimacy.[2]

The testimony began with Deloria, a Lakota and a member of the Standing Rock band in North Dakota, who was led through a discussion of the ideas in his books as a way of explaining the importance of treaties, culture, and religion, and the adverse effects that non-Indian groups such as anthropologists have had on Native American traditions.[3] When a motion was made to offer a copy of *Custer Died for Your Sins* into evidence, an admission by Leventhal that the defense possessed only a paperback copy drew applause from the audience. Then, when Hurd complained, as the defense had earlier, that he had not received a copy of the evidence in advance, Kunstler responded, "We could only afford one copy."[4] The exchange brought another round of laughter, but as Leventhal tried to elicit Deloria's opinion on the Native American interpretation of treaties, Hurd's objections turned serious.

Not all Indians interpreted treaties in the same way, argued Hurd, and therefore one Indian writer was not in a position to testify for all Native Americans. With the jury out of the courtroom, Deloria asserted that while Hurd was correct as to the existence of differences of opinion, there was a general sense among Indians that they had rights under treaties, just as U.S. citizens had rights under the Constitution. The issue was relevant to the motives of the defendants, Kunstler argued, adding that there already was evidence in the record that both Banks and Means held to traditional views of treaties, which was what Deloria was trying to explain. By questioning Deloria concerning his discussions with Oglalas and the foundation report he had completed on legal and historical considerations of the Treaty and Sioux political history, Leventhal laid the evidentiary basis for the witness's testimony as an expert on what treaties meant to Native Americans, and what the 1868 Treaty in particular meant to the Sioux.

The central issue for Native Americans, said Deloria, was the "relationship to the land"—that the lands around them formed a universe and that sacred lands were at the center of that universe. Treaties, the author noted, were regarded by Indians as a religious covenant rather than a legal document, and the Treaty of 1868 was regarded as just such a covenant.[5] Then, after more objections and more arguments and counterarguments concerning admissibility and relevance, a piece of history found its way into the record. Complete with its replica seals, ribbons, and signatures, an exact copy of the Treaty that the Sioux signed at Fort Laramie in 1868, authenticated by the National Archives, was marked as defense exhibit

P-8 and admitted into evidence. "Thank you very much, Your Honor," said Banks at the moment of acceptance.[6]

Moments later, Hurd and Leventhal argued about whether Deloria could be asked his opinion concerning provisions of the Treaty pertaining to law enforcement on the reservation and other matters. Although that and other questions were kept out as calling for legal conclusions (matters of law to be determined by the judge), Deloria was able to indicate what issues different provisions of the Treaty did address. Finally, after more legal wrangling, Nichol accepted the witness as an expert for the purpose of answering one question proposed by Kunstler: "Do you have an opinion as to how the 1868 Treaty is generally understood by the Sioux?" "Yes," answered Deloria. The Sioux, he said, took the words of the Treaty literally.[7] Though he was an attorney himself, Deloria's opinions concerning the Treaty's current legal standing and its relevance to issues of land use and reservation boundaries were also ruled inadmissible. He was, however, able to testify to the Sioux's continuing efforts to win back control of the lands promised to them under the Treaty. These were efforts, said Deloria, that were spearheaded by "mostly full blood traditional chiefs who have pursued the treaty fight as long as I can remember or document."[8]

On cross-examination Hurd began by telling Deloria that he too had read *Custer Died for Your Sins* and enjoyed it. The U.S. Attorney again questioned the unanimity of Indian opinion with regard to spiritual beliefs and treaties, to which Deloria responded, "Yes, but the belief is still there; my father is an Episcopal missionary and he believes in both religions."[9] Asked whether he had ever advocated the use of violence as a means to change, the author invoked the Fifth Amendment after being cautioned by the judge. As Deloria left the stand, Nichol said, "I might say personally I was glad to have heard your testimony."[10]

Next came Dee Brown, a non-Indian, who was the author of perhaps the most widely read book about Indian history. As Kunstler began to question Brown about why he wrote his book, Hurd quipped, "Again I get the paperback," then moments later objected, "I keep suspecting there's a back door on this that I don't see." Inviting yet another legal discussion out of earshot of the jury, Nichol responded, "Come up to the desk and we will find out whether there's a back door or not." Brown was eventually allowed to say that he had wanted to respond to the "blood and thunder" books about the west and Indians that he had read as a boy.[11] With the defense referring to the author's college degrees and his twenty-three years of research and teaching experience, and with Kunstler responding almost incredulously to one of Hurd's objections, "But this is testimony from an historian, Your Honor," Brown was finally qualified as an expert on portions of Indian history. The designation allowed him to give testimony similar to Deloria's on the meaning of treaties, including his opinion on the United States' record on noncompliance: namely, that the federal government had violated and was still violating almost all of the treaties that it had made with Native Americans.[12]

Hurd continued to object, blocking some answers and getting parts of others stricken from the record if not from the ears of the jurors. Though he was allowing considerable latitude to the defense, Nichol continually cautioned the jurors that Brown's comments on many matters were not conclusions of law, but rather opinions with which they were entitled to disagree or to "give it such weight as they feel it deserves."[13] Over and around constant objections and cautions, however, Brown was able to present some of the history of Lakota efforts to enforce their treaties with the U.S. government and the effects of white expansion on Native Americans: "It was a matter of life: the treaty provided certain areas of land, which was necessary to sustain the particular tribe, and unless the treaty was followed, the tribe was in danger of dying."[14] "Did they use normal channels?" asked Kunstler with respect to enforcement. "Yes," replied Brown over Hurd's objection, using the example of Sitting Bull and others to echo Banks and Means's chronicle of the events on Pine Ridge presented in their opening statements: "They wrote letters to Washington, which were never answered that I know of."[15] His opinion on the effects of "massacres" perpetrated by whites was initially kept out—"I don't want to get into massacres, which I personally feel were on both sides," commented Nichol in sustaining an objection from Hurd—but Kunstler continued to rephrase the question until Brown was able to give his opinion concerning the overall effect of this history on Native Americans into the 1970s. There still existed among some, he said, a fear that they were "in great danger at all times of being wiped out," and if there had been a shift away from these fears in recent years, it was at least in part a result of the recent increase in Indian activism.[16]

On cross-examination Hurd conducted his own exploration of history, which emphasized legal reforms that had led to compensation for lost land and treaty claims now pending in the courts. On occasion the defense expert had to admit that he was not completely familiar with Indian history after 1900. But when Hurd tried to press him on this lack of knowledge with respect to government efforts to remedy past treaty violations, Brown responded, "Well, I know that most of South Dakota does not belong to the Lakota Indians."[17] Hurd did get the witness to acknowledge that not all Indians had the same view of the 1868 Treaty and that Brown had no idea why the defendants had acted as they did.[18]

On redirect examination, Kunstler tried to explore the possible justification for actions in pursuit of treaty rights. After numerous objections he was allowed to ask Brown if, as a historian, he believed there were situations in which it was "historically justified for people to resist oppression, even to resist it with force." Brown replied in the affirmative, but added that "every example has to be considered on its own."[19] Hurd took recross-examination to press the point even further, with Brown answering one question by saying that "there are times in a people's history when the only way to survive is by violence." Moments later Brown replied no when Hurd asked if a group, having failed in its attempt to impeach the President, would be justified in seizing the city of Saint Paul to force his ouster.[20]

The next morning Frank Kills Enemy, an eighty-year-old lifetime resident of the reservation whose grandfather had been one of the signers of the 1868 Treaty, took the stand. Kills Enemy detailed conditions on the reservation before and after the Indian Reorganization Act of 1934 and talked about the importance of the sacred pipe, of trust, and of what the 1868 Treaty meant to the Sioux. The government, he said, had never fulfilled the provisions of the treaty, such as promises regarding education and health care. Again Hurd raised objections, arguing that the testimony was just the opinion of one individual, and again Nichol overruled him, saying that the statements went to the question of motive.[21]

Anita Agnes Lamont, whose mother and grandparents had survived the 1890 massacre, followed Kills Enemy to the stand. Wounded Knee in 1890, she said, was an event she had discussed with her son Buddy, who had gone to the village in 1973 and had been killed by gunfire from government positions in April. Mrs. Lamont was allowed to speak briefly about events prior to Wounded Knee, including the arrival of the marshals on Pine Ridge in February, but the prosecution successfully objected to questions about her son's funeral.[22]

Toward the end of the second day, the defense witness who would make the biggest impression on the packed courtroom took the stand. Gladys Bissonette, age fifty-six and another lifelong resident of the reservation, had been active in OSCRO and inside Wounded Knee for the full seventy-one days. During her eight hours on the stand, she provided testimony on the events that led her and other Oglalas to stage the protest at Wounded Knee.[23] Bissonette described in "vivid detail," as one newspaper put it, life on the reservation after Dick Wilson took over as Tribal Chairman, the efforts to remove him, the numerous meetings to decide upon a course of action, and the frustration after calls for help went unanswered by federal officials. She spoke of battles within the Tribal Council, protest demonstrations, and Wilson's reprisals through administrative decisions and physical intimidation: "I can show you files and files and files of complaints, grievances, that have never been investigated on the Pine Ridge Reservation." The Oglala chiefs had invited AIM onto the reservation, Bissonette insisted, because they had no other choice.[24]

Bissonette also depicted life inside the village during the occupation, describing sleeping and eating conditions and what she called the "horrors" of the siege, namely the almost continual barrage of government flares and bullets. Again she insisted that people had no other choice and that in hard times she would remember the history of her people: "As I remember back on the days when they had unarmed our ancestors, killed them and let them freeze to death, there were no mercy for the children. There were no mercy for the women. That's the very first thing that had come to my mind during that fire fight. I knew this had to be the last. I didn't care for myself because I knew what I was standing up for. I was standing up for justice for the Indian people."[25]

Bissonette brought tears to the eyes of several people in the audience when she, herself in tears, spoke of the death of her nephew, Buddy Lamont. As she described her reactions, Lamont's mother, who had just testified, rose from her seat in the audience, saying, "It had to be my boy, why did the government have to kill my son?" Mrs. Lamont was led from the courtroom, and Nichol recessed the trial for the day.[26] Back on the stand the next morning, Bissonette repeated her assertion that it was the traditional chiefs' decision to call on AIM, stating that Russell Means had no choice but to follow his chiefs.[27] Bissonette, who had acted as cook inside the village and had been involved in the negotiations with the government, also spoke of shortages of food and medicine, particularly milk for babies, and of how they coped when the government turned off the gas used for cooking: "The government negotiator Frizzel said, 'Oh, we're letting food and medicine in,' but this is why Wounded Knee was; because we were always covered with lies. There were things—I could sit here and talk forever and tell you about all the happenings on the reservation."[28]

In the meetings to decide on strategies for negotiations with the government, Bissonette said, only Oglalas were present; even Banks was not allowed to attend. She also said that the 1868 Treaty was an important part of those discussions. Adding credence to the defense claims of other armed people in the area, she spoke of a firefight during which a call from the marshals came over the shortwave radio, saying they were receiving fire from a point outside the perimeter of the village. Bissonette said that the village was receiving fire from the same place. When challenged on her identification of the voice on the radio, she said that the caller identified himself as a marshal, then added, "and besides that I know there are no boys in Wounded Knee who have that southern drawl." In response to another question about who else was around at the time, she replied that Banks was present, "but he was asleep." The comment drew laughter from the audience, and apparently even amused the judge, who cautioned the audience on laughing but noted, "There's been so much testimony throughout this trial that every time an important moment comes up, it turns out that Dennis Banks appears to have been asleep."[29]

Toward the end of his direct examination, Lane asked Bissonette if she had seen evidence of a conspiracy or plan to violate the law during meetings inside Wounded Knee. "No," Bissonette responded, "we do not know anything about conspiracy. The Indians are guided by the Great Spirit and our sacred pipe. So we look into whatever we think is right . . . We do not intend to break any laws. We do not intend to commit any crimes. If there's a crime against looking for justice, where do we go to find justice here in America?"[30] Hurd successfully had all of her answer after the word "no" struck, but the words had already been spoken.[31] Women had been considered by many the backbone of the Wounded Knee protest, and many had hoped this would be emphasized in the defense's case. Bissonette's testimony was as dramatic and poignant as people had expected it to be,[32] and Hurd's efforts to cast doubt on it by pointing out that problems existed on the reservation prior to Wilson's taking office seemed to backfire as Bissonette answered his questions straightforwardly:

> HURD: There's been a liquor problem on the reservation for many
>   years, hasn't there?
> BISSONETTE: Oh, yes. That's the way the white man brought us up.
> HURD: And you have had some firsthand experience with that
>   problem, haven't you?
> BISSONETTE: Oh, yes.
> HURD: And you have drunk on the reservation, haven't you?
> BISSONETTE: Oh, yes.
> HURD: And you have been in possession of liquor on the reservation?
> BISSONETTE: Oh, yes.
> HURD: So this is nothing new or shocking? The fact that people do
>   drink on the reservation and have liquor on the reservation?
> BISSONETTE: Not until I became concerned about the Indian people

... I sobered up and opened my eyes and saw how the people were getting bought off through liquor, which is happening right today on the reservation.[33]

Asked if she didn't think the BIA had taken steps in recent years to solve those problems, Bissonette replied that things were getting worse and then related the comment of a BIA worker concerning the Pine Ridge Christmas party in 1973, that "the place looked worse than a bar." In a similar vein, Hurd confronted her with improvements in health care facilities and education, but each time Bissonette challenged his assessment that conditions had improved. "They have plenty of cough syrup and aspirins," she responded, ridiculing his assertions with respect to the Indian hospital. Bissonette also spoke of what she termed favoritism shown toward mixed bloods and of the discrimination against full bloods or traditionalists such as her father, who was, in her words, "an old treaty man."[34] When she asserted that violence on the reservation was caused by the onslaught of marshals and not by AIM, Hurd reminded her of the occupation of the BIA building in Washington. "Well, I think that any time any Indian does anything," replied Bissonette, "it comes out in the news media purely strong and purely bad." Then when Hurd asked if there wasn't an obligation to protect federal property, Bissonette responded with her own question: "I would like to know why they would shoot us Indians down just to save a building; take human lives to save a building. How greedy can you get?"[35] When several in the audience applauded the remark, Nichol warned them about the outburst.

Responding to questions, Bissonette admitted that she had joined the caravan to Wounded Knee thinking that she was going to Porcupine for a meeting, but once inside she decided to stay to work for the removal of Wilson and the enforcement of treaty rights. Even when she denied knowledge of events that the defendants themselves admitted, such as the taking of food from the trading post, Bissonette seemed credible. With her hand on the sacred pipe, she swore that she had no knowledge of thefts from the trading post: "All I know is there was food brought to the Catholic Church where I was." None of the women involved in Wounded Knee had been indicted by the government for conspiracy, and as Hurd neared the end of his cross-examination he tried to get Bissonette to admit that she was not involved in decision making. But away from the spotlight of the media coverage many women in OSCRO and AIM had fulfilled leadership roles, and Bissonette insisted that she was involved in the negotiations, even though, she said, she did not make decisions to set up roadblocks, make Molotov cocktails, or take prisoners of war, adding, "Nobody made a decision to do that."[36] She did, however, affirm Means's "negotiate or kill us" statement at Wounded Knee: "I also made the same statement, because we were tired of running." Did that indicate violence? Hurd wanted to know, referring back to her earlier statements that those who went to Wounded Knee did not want violence. The violence between Indians and the government did not begin with the protest in 1973, Bissonette responded; "we've been at war with the government all our lives."

When Bissonette finally stepped down after a day and a half on the stand, the defense huddled briefly, and then Means rose from his seat and addressed Judge Nichol: "Your Honor, we believe that the story has been told and that we stand on our treaty rights. The defense rests."[37] Banks then rose to concur: "Just for the record, the defense for Dennis Banks rests also." As reporters scurried to file their stories, Nichol dismissed two more counts of the indictment, and the shocked prosecutors requested an extended recess to prepare their rebuttal. Quoting from testimony of the defense witnesses, the media paid little attention to the constant legal arguments over what was admissible or to Hurd's cross-examination. Press reports and hallway conversations were dominated by discussions of Bissonette's direct testimony and speculation over the defense's decision to rest after only three days.[38] Lane told reporters that the decision was made only after the defense saw how powerful Bissonette's testimony had been: "I've been a lawyer 24 years and I've never seen a witness like that." Lane's statements, however, were apparently intended to add extra emphasis to the meaning of the testimony. Others in the defense camp admitted privately, if not publicly, that the decision had been made a week earlier.[39]

Banks and Means had already had a chance to address the jury in their opening statements and through their cross-examination of witnesses. No one in the defense camp believed that anything would be gained by putting them on the stand and subjecting them to cross-examination by the prosecutors. Believing that the government's case was not particularly strong, the defense team opted to fill out their side of the story as strongly as possible, without trying to contradict what they believed to be untruths or inconsistencies in the prosecution's case. Kunstler told reporters that "anything else would have been superfluous." And Hurd summed it all up by saying, "It clearly shows that they are relying on a theory of criminal acts being justified because of past abuses."[40]

Hurd was half right. In the early 1970s sociologists studying criminal trials began to document the importance and difficulty of telling stories in the courtroom to jurors, spectators, and reporters. Defense committees in political trials, including WKLDOC, were early beneficiaries of this information. As a growing number of recent studies have argued, telling the truth from the witness stand is not necessarily enough if the teller of the story and the listener do not share the same sets of norms, assumptions, and life experiences.[41] Finding a commonality between defendants and their audience, including the jury, can be particularly difficult in political trials.[42] By the time the prosecution had rested, Banks and Means had probably done as much as they could to reach the jury with their message.

The genius of the defense's decision not to put Banks and Means on the stand went beyond even the nontraditional legal strategies of the time. Throughout the trial the defense had spoken of Indian history and its spiritual and cultural traditions, treaty rights and the conditions on the Pine Ridge Reservation, and what they believed to be unconscionable and illegal government policies. Yet the focus of the stories being told was often the strong personalities of the participants. The decision to keep Banks and Means off the stand helped to depersonalize the proceedings for the first time since the trial opened. The importance of the historical and contemporary "facts" presented in the testimony of Deloria and Brown was not just that they were presented by well-known authors, but that these were narratives that had been sanctioned by publication, by favorable book reviews, and finally by the designation of "expert opinion" from a federal judge.

"Within a white supremacist culture," writes bell hooks, "to be without documentation is to be without a legitimate history."[43] The names of the defense witnesses who followed the two famous authors to the stand, Kills Enemy, Lamont, and Bissonette, were not known outside of the Pine Ridge Reservation, but their testimony provided human faces and voices in connection with the legal and historical narratives that had been presented—voices with a resonance that the more famous defendants, with their often stereotypical media images, could not provide.

Some press reports, of course, gave as much space to Brown's comments about violence as they did to his interpretations of treaties.[44] Others reduced Lamont's appearance to that of a grieving mother, a characterization that was no doubt partly a defense calculation and partly an all too classic portrayal of Indian women. But the testimony of the three Pine Ridge residents taken together could not be reduced to victimization or pleas for sympathy, for they had all told stories of the resistance that Brown and Deloria had spoken of, stories that reached back into Indian history for more than a century. Even the *Saint Paul Pioneer Press,* which a month earlier had accused the defense of reducing the trial to a tale of "pettifogging, grandstanding, irresolution, and sloth," called Bissonette's appearance on the stand "the most dramatic testimony of the trial."[45] The *Times* gave the defense some of its lengthiest trial coverage, citing the testimony of all five witnesses. Leventhal, whose focus was the treaty issue, believed that the testimony examining the Indian position on treaties was particularly important. Kunstler thought that the defense had presented evidence of a good First Amendment protest, one he likened to the Boston Tea Party: "Our people were very good and presented another side to why they were there, and what had happened and what it was all about. I think the jury really understood at the end that this was a massive protest, very dramatic, taking over an historical site that had great significance to Indian people."[46]

The defense witnesses had told stories that somehow resonated in the lives of non-Indians, stories that were not confined to the "powerful warrior" images of the two men on whose behalf they were speaking. Though the moment did not last long, the defense had done more than successfully execute a theory of criminal defense. For a brief but sustained period of three days, witnesses had moved the proceedings from spectacle to historical forum and had begun to explain to others what too often seemed unexplainable.

While the government organized its rebuttal testimony, a delegation of Oglalas prepared to travel to Washington to present the President with a resolution passed by the Lakota Treaty Council demanding enforcement of the 1868 Treaty. In Canada, Banks spoke with a group of Indians called the "Ojibwa Warrior Society," who had taken over Anicinabe Park in Ontario, land they claimed had been illegally sold to a nearby town in the 1950s.[47] A *New York Times* article describing the increased demands by Indians around the country for independent status credited AIM with contributing to the new feelings of "Indianness" and having more of an impact than the government was willing to admit. The article was not uncritical of AIM, but commented that the government's attempts to destroy the movement by jailing its leaders had not been effective thus far.[48] Not to be left out, the government released a report on the military's role at Wounded Knee, calling its presence a moderating influence on the actions of U.S. Marshals and the FBI.[49]

In Saint Paul the events that unfolded over the next few weeks would bring more charges of government misconduct, a subject which, in the wake of Nixon's resignation, was wearing thin for the audience in and outside the courtroom. On Wednesday, August 22, a week after the defense rested, the government came back with a surprise rebuttal witness, the 22-year-old son of Ellen Moves Camp, one of OSCRO's key activists. During several hours of testimony as the stunned and angered defendants listened, Louis (Louie) Moves Camp, a member of AIM who with his mother had been at Wounded Knee, linked one or both of the defendants to nearly every crime they had been charged with.

Moves Camp testified that he saw guns at the meeting in Rapid City prior to Wounded Knee and that he had heard Means tell people they were going to take over the village. At the trading post, he said, he witnessed Means telling people to "rip everything off," and he saw both defendants in possession of items from the store. Moves Camp swore that $1,000 had been taken from the safe and given to Banks and Means, and that he had heard one or both of the two leaders give orders to take people hostage, to build bunkers, and to make Molotov cocktails. He also claimed to have seen Means fire a rifle in the direction of government positions and reward the person who said he had shot an FBI agent who was chasing the U-Haul van. Finally, he told the jury that there was a security meeting one morning attended by four of the conspiracy defendants, including Banks and Means, to discuss where people should go that day. Later that day, Moves Camp continued, it was reported that a marshal had been shot and upon hearing the report, Means said that he was "very happy."[50]

In a relatively short period of time, Moves Camp did what the prosecution had been unable to accomplish during months of testimony—provide evidence to the jury of Banks's and Means's acts of wrongdoing. Page one stories in Minnesota and South Dakota detailed Moves Camp's testimony under headlines like "Witness Rips AIM Leaders." Some noted that Moves Camp appeared nervous, particularly when making eye contact with the defendants and with AIM members in the audience. Several quoted the comments of the angry defendants and their attorneys. "A complete fabrication," Means told reporters at the end of the first day. Hurd said that he had only learned of the availability of Moves Camp two weeks earlier.[51]

The drama of Louie Moves Camp was just beginning, however. AIM and WKLDOC were in a momentary state of shock when he took the stand, but just as quickly shock turned to anger and then action. By as early as the afternoon recess, the defense believed they had the witnesses and documentation to counter what some were beginning believe was an FBI-concocted story. First to arrive in Minneapolis for the defense's expected rebuttal was Moves Camp's mother, Ellen.[52]

On the stand, Moves Camp now faced cross-examination by Kunstler. In the course of heated exchanges between the young witness and the New York attorney, Kunstler caught Moves Camp in the first of what would be a series of contradictions and misstatements. At one point, as he was repeatedly asked about what had been said at the Rapid City meeting, Moves Camp blurted out, "You're trying to put words in my mouth," and Kunstler shot back, "I think that's already been done by others." As Kunstler continued to pick at the details of Moves Camp's testimony, trying to pin him down on times, places, dates, names, and specific statements, a flustered Moves Camp became more hostile. Several times Nichol attempted to calm down both the witness and the defense attorney.[53]

Just as Nichol called the noon recess, Ellen Moves Camp, who was reportedly in a state of anger and disbelief over her son's accusations, made a surprising and dramatic appearance in the courtroom. From the back of the courtroom Moves Camp headed toward the front, shouting, "Your Honor, I want to talk to my son," and then to Louie, "What did they do to you so you're lying?" Nichol ordered marshals to take her into custody, as she reached the jury box, crying: "Don't do it. They're lying to you. They're going to bury you. You're lying, Louie. Leave me alone. You marshals, FBI, what are you doing to my son?"[54] Ellen Moves Camp was ushered out of the courtroom and then fainted in the hallway in the presence of the defendants and other AIM members, who attempted to prevent the marshals from taking her. But Nichol ordered her arrested and accused defense attorneys of staging the whole incident. The judge was reportedly so angered that he communicated through a marshal that the attorneys should leave and return to his chambers later to meet with him. During the meeting that followed, Nichol could be heard from the hallway shouting and pounding his desk, as he berated the defense. The defense attorneys, however, insisted that they had not instigated Moves Camp's outburst. Back in court Nichol told the jurors, "We've had too many of these dramatic events occur during this trial," while directing them not to hold the episode against the government or the defense.[55]

After a meeting with Mrs. Moves Camp in Tilsen's office, at the suggestion of a third party who had been sitting next to her right before the outburst, Nichol retracted both his arrest warrant and his statements accusing the defense of engineering the episode.[56] Nichol told reporters he should not have been so quick to assume that the event was planned, though, he added, that did not mean that he believed Moves Camp or her son any more or less than any other witness. Moves Camp told the press that she had apologized to the judge for her outburst, explaining that it was something that just happened when she heard the lies her son was telling. Everything she had heard Louie say so far was a lie, she continued, adding that he did not sound like himself and that he was using words and phrases that he did not normally use, such as "Indian" instead of "red skin."[57]

Preceding Louie Moves Camp's return to the stand was Edgar Red Cloud, the 77-year-old grandson of Chief Red Cloud who had fought the U.S. Cavalry in the nineteenth century. Speaking through an interpreter, the lifelong resident of Pine Ridge said that he had not heard of OSCRO, had not invited AIM to the reservation, and did not know about Wounded Knee until after it happened. "It may have been good for people who done it," said Red Cloud, "but for us on the outside, we're hurt by it." The defense asked no questions on cross-examination.[58]

Back on the stand, Moves Camp began sparring with Kunstler almost immediately, accusing the attorney of having tried to confuse him by bringing his mother into the courtroom earlier. The remark provoked a derisive reaction from the audience, and an angry Nichol ordered the marshals to remove all persons with AIM insignias "any place on their body."[59] After a short recess Nichol complimented those in the audience who had been "well mannered" throughout the trial, but he cautioned everyone to maintain order in the courtroom. Then, speaking of Ellen Moves Camp's appearance in court, he expressed his regret about the "traumatic experience" and requested that the jury "erase it from their minds," adding that he intended to investigate the incident further. "If you're going to blame anybody for it, why don't you blame me," said Nichol, "I'm supposed to be in charge of this courtroom." He then recessed the court for the day, saying it would be unfair to continue the proceedings "at this time."[60]

The next day Kunstler's cross-examination of Moves Camp exploded into what one newspaper called "the most serious disruption of the eight month trial."[61] Kunstler began the morning session with questions that suggested that Moves Camp had made contradictory statements about who had ordered people to take things from the trading post. He then asked Moves Camp if he had taken anything from the trading post, suggesting that the witness had struck a deal with Hurd. The questions again provoked heated exchanges between the witness and the defense attorney until it began to sound all too familiar to anyone who had watched the Watergate hearings unfold:

> MOVES CAMP: I'm not saying that it's not so, it's the best of my rec-
> ollection right now . . . yes, and I thank you for refreshing my
> memory.
> KUNSTLER: You're perfectly welcome.[62]

After a recess Kunstler asked Moves Camp if he was sure that officials from all the countries he had listed the previous day had been at Wounded Knee, including both East and West Germany. When the witness answered affirmatively, Kunstler asked if he realized that the event he described was the first time East and West Germany had agreed on anything. The question drew laughter from the audience, and an already impatient Judge Nichol ordered the marshals to clear a particular row of the audience. As marshals began to forcibly evict a row of AIM members, including both Bellecourt brothers, a struggle ensued during which one marshal sprayed both a spectator and a fellow marshal with Mace. A visibly angered Kunstler berated Nichol for his order: "All this because of a laugh?" Nichol responded by asking the defense attorney if he wanted to join the others in being arrested, and Kunstler, throwing a pencil across the courtroom, replied, "I don't care whether I do or not, Judge." As marshals moved to comply with Nichol's arrest order, Kunstler rose, arms in the air, saying, "Take me away." Lane, echoing Kunstler's words, was arrested moments later. After several more exchanges involving Banks, Tilsen, and Hurd, Nichol excused the jurors, who had witnessed the entire episode, and adjourned court for the weekend.[63]

Outside, defense attorneys stated that they would not request a mistrial, while Banks compared Nichol to Judge Bottum, the South Dakota judge who had ordered the courtroom cleared in Sioux Falls. Inside, Artley Skenadore, the Saint Paul AIM leader in charge of courthouse security for the defense, told Nichol that he had ordered the wrong row removed. Nichol reportedly replied, "Why didn't you tell me at the time?" From the county jail, Lane complained that he had been injured in the eye by a marshal and promised to talk about what he termed "South Dakota justice" in his summation to the jury. A jailer told reporters, however, that Lane had no visible signs of injury. The drama of Moves Camp's testimony was almost lost in the even more dramatic spectacle of the jailing of the two famous defense attorneys. Newspapers were divided on how effective Kunstler's cross-examination had been. All pointed out discrepancies in the testimony, but the *Saint Paul Pioneer Press* termed it all "sleep producing."[64] That night as Leventhal visited with his colleagues in jail, they heard a young black man call from a nearby cell, "Say, if you guys are such hotshot lawyers, what are you doing in here?"[65]

The next day Tilsen drove Nichol over to the jail to visit Kunstler and Lane. After negotiations, which included two New York attorneys who had arrived to represent Kunstler, who was already under attack from the New York state bar, the parties agreed on a joint statement of regret but refused to apologize to each other, publicly or privately. Nichol acknowledges that he was aware of the situation in New York and did not wish to cause Kunstler additional trouble by proceeding with the contempt citation.[66] Regarding the agreement, Tilsen told the press that there was little choice—either agree or take time for a hearing on contempt charges. After his release, Kunstler told reporters that the judge had "lost control of himself." Despite Kunstler's reputation as a troublemaker in court, it was his first overnight stay in jail for contempt.[67]

On Monday, Nichol read the statements of regret signed by himself and the attorneys to the jury, and then cautioned them not to hold the episode against the defendants.[68] Moves Camp then returned to the stand to face more cross-examination by Kunstler, who used the witness's FBI statement to point out contradictions between it and his recent testimony. Moves Camp expressed surprise that Kunstler had the statement and requested a private meeting with the judge to inquire about it. This time Kunstler drew smiles from jurors when he raised the question of representatives of communist countries at Wounded Knee. The witness, however, stuck to his story, insisting that the groups had been there and that someone had presented a check to Means. Moves Camp did say that he agreed with the traditional view of the 1868 Treaty and that when he joined OSCRO he thought it was an important organization which he hoped would end "goon squad" harassment. Finally, Kunstler questioned Moves Camp concerning the date of his departure from Wounded Knee, noting that witnesses would testify that he was in California in April. But Moves Camp insisted he did not leave the village until May.[69]

Taking over from Kunstler, Lane continued the questioning about Moves Camp's stay in Wounded Knee, asking him about the specific times he said he witnessed the actions he ascribed to the defendants and about the specific dates of a fund-raising trip he made to California. Two witnesses who would provide the defense with crucial testimony regarding Moves Camp's whereabouts during the events he claimed to have witnessed were already en route to Minnesota. Responding to more questions from Lane, Moves Camp denied that his testimony was a tradeoff for getting rid of his five pending felony charges. As Lane began to probe where the witness had been staying prior to his testimony, Hurd objected, causing Lane to quip:

"Every time R.D. tries so hard to keep something out, we know it's relevant; we just don't know what it is."[70]

At a conference at the bench, Lane asked Hurd if the witness had been arrested in Wisconsin, possibly for rape. Hurd acknowledged the arrest but said he believed it was for public intoxication, nothing more substantial, and that he would check on the particulars.[71] Hurd then took the stand to testify that he had made no deals with Moves Camp to dismiss charges in return for his testimony, though he admitted that Moves Camp was facing a possible twenty years in prison. The brief testimony concluded the prosecution's rebuttal.[72]

While reporters and other spectators debated the effectiveness of Kunstler and Lane's cross-examination, Moves Camp met with his mother and brother in Nichol's office.[73] Afterward both mother and son spoke to the press. In the office used by the prosecutors, with two Justice Department attorneys and four marshals looking on, Louie Moves Camp read a five-page statement to the press, expanding upon the criticisms that he had made against AIM on the witness stand: "As far as I'm concerned, Russell Means and Dennis Banks and the rest of the AIM leadership belong behind bars for the years they have ripped off, cheated, lied [to], and stolen from their own people."[74] Only then, he told the press, would Indians realize how badly they had been treated by the two leaders. He also called Means a "hypocrite," but conceded that he believed that Banks was basically a "good man." Moves Camp told reporters he had left AIM because he believed that the organization was hurting the American Indian more than it was helping.[75] Noting that her son had on new boots and new clothes, Ellen Moves Camp told the same reporters that she was convinced that the FBI had told Louie what to say and asserted her intention to take the stand to refute his statements. "I love my son, but I can't turn on my people," Moves Camp said; "I have to do what I am going to do to prove that they are liars."[76]

The defense was convinced that the FBI had put Moves Camp up to his story and that Hurd, if not directly involved, had used the witness without checking on his story simply because he knew that his case was in trouble.[77] Said Tilsen later: "He [FBI agent Price] brings Louis to Hurd and Hurd is so desperate, he's losing this case, it's lost, and this FBI agent brings him to him and he just gobbles it all up without using any good judgment."[78]

Hurd admits that he thought Moves Camp was a dangerous witness because he wasn't sure what he would say on the stand once he got there. But he also believed that at least a portion of what Moves Camp said was probably true and that it was up to the jury to decide on his credibility.

By that time, Hurd did think that the prosecution had not received a fair trial and that it would be difficult to get the jury focused on guilt or innocence with respect to specific crimes charged: "I figured we needed to let the jury hear that evidence and judge his credibility. If they believed him, I thought it would obtain a conviction for us. If they didn't believe him, I didn't think we were any worse off than we were already."[79]

The next day, the defense paraded one last celebrity before the waiting press corps as Harry Belafonte, accompanied by his family, watched part of the court proceedings and spoke to reporters. "What's really on trial here is the validity of AIM," said the entertainer and longtime civil rights advocate.[80] Inside the courtroom, Jay West testified that Moves Camp had been in California from mid-March to sometime in June when he and West drove back to Pine Ridge together. The period of time in question covered many of the events that Moves Camp said he had witnessed at Wounded Knee, including the assaults on Fitzgerald and Grimm.[81] Ellen Moves Camp testified that her son had left the village in March, but on cross-examination by Hurd, her credibility was shaken when she denied seeing guns, bunkers, or anyone firing shots from inside the village or taking food from the trading post. "You're sure you were there?" asked Hurd, showing her a group photograph taken at the trading post which included people carrying weapons that Moves Camp said she never noticed. Even Nichol suggested at one point that she could change her testimony if she wanted to.[82]

Ellen Moves Camp's testimony had not helped the defense, but another witness testified that he too had seen Louie Moves Camp in California in April, and two more said that Moves Camp was very worried about his pending charges in South Dakota.[83] Testimony by defense attorney Tilsen and an affidavit filed by Kent Frizzell put the defendants outside of Wounded Knee before officer Grimm was shot, also contradicting Moves Camp's testimony.[84] The next day, even South Dakota papers were reporting that the witness was in trouble; headlines read, "Witnesses, TV Logs, Newspaper Photos Attack Credibility of Trial Witness" and "Moves Camp's Veracity Comes Under Scrutiny."[85] Testimony, however, was far from over.

Outside the courtroom the defense was conducting its own investigation as to the circumstances of Moves Camp's arrest in Wisconsin. Lane's earlier questions had been prompted by a telephone call that Tilsen's wife, Rachel, had received from the wife of a county attorney in Wisconsin, who said that Moves Camp had been accused of rape while in the custody of FBI agents. The story that Lane uncovered was that Moves Camp had been lodged at a dude ranch in western Wisconsin with two FBI agents for the two weeks prior to taking the stand and had in fact been accused of raping a young woman he had met at a bar. One of the agents, David Price, had been assigned to the Pine Ridge Reservation and was well known to the defense.[86] After an evening of dinner and drinks, the two agents had left Moves Camp with a woman who he said wanted to stay with him and returned to the motel. The next day the woman filed a rape complaint with local law enforcement officials. After discussions with the woman and apparently with Agent Price, officials had decided not to proceed with the complaint.[87]

Under pressure from defense attorneys, who continued to ask questions they already knew the answers to, Hurd finally acknowledged that back on August 28, Moves Camp had been questioned about an alleged rape, but he denied that there had been any attempt to cover up the incident or any attempt to put pressure on Wisconsin law enforcement officials to quash the complaint. Nichol ruled that the defense had the right to question witnesses concerning the activities of the FBI and to ascertain their effect, if any, on Moves Camp's testimony.[88] But another bizarre episode involving the FBI interrupted that testimony almost before it began.

In the process of questioning a witness, Kunstler, having noticed a side door to the courtroom continuing to open and close, silently motioned to the judge and then walked over and yanked the door open. To the delight of a laughter-filled audience, two FBI agents who had apparently been listening to the testimony practically fell into the courtroom. Under questioning from Nichol in his chambers, both agents denied they were trying to circumvent rules providing for the sequestering of any potential witness. Nichol satisfied himself that the agents were not potential witnesses themselves, though one had been at Wounded Knee, and that they had not intended to pass on information concerning Ronald Williams's testimony to Agent Price, who was to take the stand later.[89] The defense, along with some members of the press, was far from satisfied. Kunstler recalled for reporters that the FBI had been caught eavesdropping on defense lawyers and their clients during the "Gainesville Eight" trial of antiwar activists in Florida the year before.[90]

When Price's partner, Agent Ronald Williams, was finally able to testify, he verified that Price had been in contact with Wisconsin officials concerning the rape allegations, but denied that he heard Price tell Moves Camp "not to worry."[91] Williams was also quizzed about the circumstances of Moves Camp's custody, but Hurd brought out on cross-examination that the protection was what the witness had wanted and that he was free to go at any time. Williams acknowledged that they had intended to keep Moves Camp close in order to determine his sincerity, suspecting at first that his willingness to testify might be a trick.[92]

Wisconsin County Attorney Robert Lindsay denied on the stand that anyone had pressured him, insisting instead that after questioning the complainant and four others who claimed to have witnessed the two having consensual sex, he had determined that there was insufficient evidence to go forward with the rape charge against Moves Camp.[93] But Lindsay refused to answer a series of questions about what he had told his wife about the case, invoking the privilege of spousal immunity. Mrs. Lindsay had allegedly told Lane that there was a possibility of seven felony counts against Moves Camp and that her husband was angry that the FBI had taken him out of the state immediately after the incident. Though Lindsay gave no answers, the questions had been asked and heard by everyone, including the jury. Other River Falls law enforcement officials backed up Lindsay's contentions, though one, a police sergeant, admitted that he had been told that Moves Camp was an important witness and that he did have a conversation with someone "higher up" in the FBI. The River Falls Chief of Police, however, refused to respond to a subpoena.[94] In an interview the county attorney insisted that it was "likely" a jury would have acquitted Moves Camp of the charge of rape.[95]

Finally, David Price, the agent who had had contact with the Wisconsin authorities, took the stand. Price admitted that he had told Moves Camp not to worry and that he had also told Wisconsin officials that Moves Camp was an important witness. However, he denied Lane's accusations that he had pressured officials or that he was holding the rape charge over Moves Camp's head to make sure that he would testify. Price claimed that although he had talked several times with Hurd, he had not told the prosecutor about the rape allegations. He also contended that Moves Camp had received no money other than the standard witness and relocation fees.[96]

The jury heard three more witnesses and had two documents read to them, putting the final chapter on the Moves Camp affair and the trial itself. The defense brought in George Gap, an Oglala from Pine Ridge, to say that Edgar Red Cloud was not considered a hereditary chief of the Oglalas because he was part Cheyenne. Louie Moves Camp's wife, Gaylene Roach Moves Camp, testified that her husband had told her he was only in Wounded Knee a week or so and that the government had promised him money, a house, and the dismissal of his charges if he would testify. Hurd retook the stand to say that he had instructed the FBI to approach Moves Camp with "caution" and insisted that the money Moves Camp had received, $1,990.50 in all, represented the standard witness fees and relocation expenses, which he eventually turned down. He denied that Moves Camp's relocation would have brought an end to the prosecution of his South Dakota charges. With one final denial by Hurd, this one concerning whether he had any prior knowledge about the veracity of his witness's testimony or had known when Moves Camp was or was not in California, it all came to an end, eight months and 150 witnesses since jury selection had begun in January.[97]

Newspaper coverage speculated on the credibility of the prosecution's "star witness" and used phrases like "the most bizarre aspect of the surprise studded trial" to describe the latest twist in the proceedings. The defense claimed complete success in discrediting Moves Camp, while Hurd, conceding that his witness's credibility had been shaken, contended that his statements had corroborated the testimony of several other witnesses.[98] Few in the press seemed to care anymore. The *Times*, which had devoted considerable space to the defense's case just a month earlier, ignored the Moves Camp episode, except to cover the arrests of Kunstler and Lane. Network television cameras had left long before that. Even Kunstler's dramatic closing statement to the jury would receive less coverage than his own overnight stay in jail. In two weeks the trial had gone from historical forum to Watergate II, complete with questions on what prosecutors knew and when they knew it, and witnesses who refused to answer questions under oath or invoked the now familiar phrase: "to the best of my recollection."

To a public now saturated with images of misconduct at the highest levels of government, the escapades of a couple of FBI agents during a trial somewhere in the midwest could not have mattered much. It all might have made for great television if watching Watergate had not become a full-time job by the spring of 1974, draining most people of whatever appetite they had for intrigues and conspiracies. Across the country people were already trying to do what the former President had pleaded with them to do months before: put Watergate behind them. The "unseen animals" that Howard Baker had once invoked were no longer crashing around in the forest; the trees had been clear-cut and the animals had all been rounded up—all but one, anyway. On the eve of jury summations in Saint Paul, newspapers across the country carried the same page one story: "Ford grants Nixon full, free and absolute pardon . . . for all offenses against the United States."

THE 8 CLOSING ARGUMENTS

This case, believe it or not, is a criminal case, and the issue in a criminal case is the guilt or innocence of these defendants . . . It is not a philosophical dispute as to whether or not crimes may be committed in order to right past wrongs or bring about an ultimate good.

R. D. HURD, SEPTEMBER 1974

He'll tell you this is just a criminal trial, not a political trial . . . Just a criminal trial; just as Socrates was condemned in a criminal trial, and Jesus was condemned in a criminal trial . . . They're all just criminal trials.

WILLIAM KUNSTLER, SEPTEMBER 1974

OUR LONG national nightmare is over," the newly sworn-in President declared on August 9. A month later, with the pardon of Nixon and the appointment of Nelson Rockefeller as Vice President, it looked to many to be business as usual in Washington. Now it was Gerald Ford who was trying to put Vietnam and Watergate behind him, to heal "the wounds of the past," he told Congress and the nation. Ten days after his inauguration the President offered a program of conditional amnesty—"earned reentry"—to those who had challenged the Vietnam War by refusing military service. But as Ford spoke of "clemency" and "mercy," it appeared that he was offering something less than the "full, free and absolute pardon" he had granted to his former boss. Only 6 percent of the 350,000 who were eligible applied for the program. One resister spoke for many when he said: "They can cram it."

Had Banks and Means or any of the others who had gone to Wounded Knee been offered clemency for their "crimes," they probably would have responded similarly. No offer, however, was forthcoming from the White House. When R. D. Hurd walked to the podium on September 10 to begin his summation in Saint Paul, neither he nor the Nixon/Ford Justice Department showed any signs of relenting on the Wounded Knee cases. It was as if the government needed desperately to prove that there were still "crooks" outside of Washington. Hurd was doubtful that he could still obtain a guilty verdict on any of the charges, but a deadlocked jury would allow him to try the case again; a second trial, which would be likely to occur out of the limelight of public scrutiny, could still result in convictions of the two AIM leaders.

Hurd no doubt realized what many inside AIM and the defense committee were already coming to grips with: despite their successes, their energy and resources could not hold out forever. More than one study of the longevity of social movements has documented the difficulty of keeping up the interest of both the participants and benefactors willing to contribute prestige and money, over the long term.[1] Movements that must spend increasing time defending themselves in court and in the media will often fail over time.[2] While the Banks/Means trial played to the spotlight in Saint Paul, the other Wounded Knee defendants and those charged in the Custer protest were being tried in South Dakota and Nebraska with little media attention. What was problematic for AIM and its defense committee in September 1974 was not just the waning attention of the media, but the increasing difficulty of recruiting lawyers and raising money. No matter how successful WKLDOC had been, legally or politically, in or outside the courtroom, the government still showed no signs of giving up.

In Lincoln the wheels of justice were grinding much faster than in Saint Paul, with acquittals and dismissals coming almost weekly. By mid-August, in the 120 nonleadership cases there had been sixteen dismissals, five acquittals, and one plea of no contest.[3] One newspaper report counted twenty-seven acquittals or dismissals in the month that followed. Normally content to try cases to the judge, the prosecution began requesting a jury, hoping that Nebraskans might convict where Judge Urbom would not.[4] The defendants faced the same basic charges that Banks and Means did, minus the conspiracy counts. Many had been arrested attempting to enter Wounded Knee with supplies, sometimes including ammunition, actions that translated into interfering with law enforcement officials in the performance of their lawful duties. Along with the normal problems of proof and getting witnesses to testify, the government was having difficulty demonstrating that certain acts constituted interference or that the operations of officials were legal under the provisions of the federal anti-riot statute, the same difficulty that prosecutors had encountered in Saint Paul.[5]

Newspapers had carried reports that the government was considering dismissing the remaining pending charges under the riot statute; these reports were quickly followed by others denying that any dismissals were forthcoming and announcing that the grand jury might be reconvened to consider new indictments. In court, U.S. Attorney Clayton denied telling reporters there would be more dismissals, saying that the government could not control what appeared in the press. From his new home in Florida, Joe Beeler continued his pursuit of volunteer defense attorneys from the NACDL and elsewhere. He counseled his former colleagues in Lincoln to keep the pressure on with mountains of paperwork, hoping that eventually the government would wear down.[6] The poor financial situation in Lincoln worsened when the Department of Agriculture cut off the food stamps that defense committee workers had been receiving, ruling that their communal living situation made them ineligible. AIM National Chairman John Trudell charged that the government, unable to win in the courts, was attempting to starve the defense into submission. Newspapers reported that local residents were helping out with donations of food.[7]

The only convictions to date had come in the state trials involving the charges arising from the protest in Custer. The Custer trials, which had been moved from Sioux Falls to Pierre, were just one reminder that the federal government was not the only adversary AIM faced. In South Dakota conflicts with state and local officials had not lessened since Wounded Knee, and pressure on activists who were organizing on reservations and trying to keep the tourist boycott in the news seemed to be coming from everywhere. In a letter to President Ford, Governor Richard Kniep complained of lawlessness on the reservations and the need for state law enforcement jurisdiction over those areas. Tribal councils from two reservations protested the letter.[8] Meanwhile, the former Assistant State Attorney General, William Janklow, opened his campaign for Attorney General, promising to make the past lack of forceful prosecution of AIM, whose members he referred to as "punks," a major issue in the race.[9]

At times it seemed to those struggling in South Dakota that Saint Paul was a long way from where the action was. The derailing of the government's case with cross-examination or the hearing on wiretaps and the discrediting of Louis Moves Camp, many argued, had been successful, but it had all gone on too long. The defense still hoped that a victory in Saint Paul would convince the Justice Department to dismiss the rest of the cases, but so far there had been only a fleeting indication that such a move was under consideration. AIM's central focus, the place where most of its mental attention, money, and volunteer resources went, was Saint Paul. This was also where the government's attention was, but it had more resources to spread around. The symbolism of that trial was powerful for both sides, and within AIM many still believed that it was of primary importance to win acquittals for their two most widely known leaders.

*   *   *

"What law have I broken?" Sitting Bull had asked a century before. It was a question that echoed throughout much of the trial in Saint Paul, from the opening statements to the defense's case in chief. As Hurd opened the government's summation, he would begin providing his own answers to that question. Over the next two days, eight lawyers competed for the attention and sympathy of the jury and the rest of the audience in the crowded courtroom. Everyone had something to say about the particulars of the evidence presented—who had allegedly said or done what and when, what testimony was credible and what was not. But it was Hurd and Kunstler, the two lawyers who had been the focus of much scrutiny and criticism in and outside of the courtroom, who perhaps came closest to addressing the questions that were at the philosophical and political heart of the case. In their summations each attempted to explain what it meant to live under a system of laws and what citizens could or could not do to redress grievances, to bring about change. In the end their closing remarks would say something about how these men viewed the world around them, what for them mattered most in achieving a just and humane society.

The Assistant U.S. Attorney began by thanking the jurors for their attentiveness throughout the long trial and reminding them of their pledge to follow the law, regardless of whether they agreed with it, and to base their verdict solely on the evidence that had been presented to them and nothing else.[10] Then, emphasizing the point he had tried to make for eight months, Hurd conveyed to the jury what he believed was the essence of the case: "This case, believe it or not, is a criminal case, and the issue in a criminal case is the guilt or innocence of these defendants."[11] Banks and Means were responsible for the crimes committed at Wounded Knee, Hurd told the jury, because those crimes were the "foreseeable consequences" of the actions and speeches of both defendants.

Hurd acknowledged that there were wrongs to be addressed concerning Indians, but, he insisted, that did not justify violations of the law: "Our system, our court, has spoken in this regard, and has come down and said no, you cannot commit crimes to right past wrongs or to bring about some sort of ultimate good." The question before the jury, Hurd said, was not whether the U.S. government had violated the 1868 Treaty, or whether the Indian Reorganization Act should have been passed by Congress, or even whether conditions on Pine Ridge were as they should be. Evidence of these things was allowed, Hurd told the jurors, to give them an understanding of why the defendants acted as they did, but the issue they must decide is whether the acts of the defendants constituted crimes: "Political reasons, religious beliefs, moral convictions, adherence to a higher law, personal advancement and financial gain are well recognized motives for human conduct ... [but] the law does not recognize religious or moral convictions or some higher law as justification for the commission of a crime no matter how noble that motive may be."[12]

Hurd then went on to discuss the conspiracy charge, recounting the testimony of several witnesses concerning the speeches, the looting of the trading post, the taking of churches and homes, the building of bunkers and roadblocks, and the demands made to the government; all these, he said, clearly demonstrated an agreement to violate the law and overt acts willfully committed by the defendants and their co-conspirators in furtherance of that agreement. The evidence, particularly their own statements, said Hurd, showed "that the defendants not only were members of the conspiracy, they were leaders of the conspiracy," regardless of how high their motives: "You cannot terrorize innocent people, you cannot steal from innocent people, you cannot seize communities, you cannot interfere with the orderly process of this country, because you think that you have a legitimate complaint. That's anarchy, ladies and gentlemen."[13]

"The theory that the end justifies the means is as old as history," Hurd went on, "but every civilized country has rejected it." The case is not the United States versus the Indians, he said, it is the United States versus Russell Means and Dennis Banks, adding that it was a case that fundamentally said "that under the laws of this nation you cannot commit crimes." Attempting to emphasize the point, Hurd uttered a phrase that would come back to haunt him: "I don't care, and I submit to you it doesn't make any difference if conditions on the Pine Ridge Indian Reservation are good or bad ... I don't care if the 1868 Treaty was violated or not violated." In our society, he added, there are "methods and means of redress."[14] Finally, Hurd told the jurors that they had two choices: to follow the instructions of the court concerning the law, or to forget about giving the defendants a fair trial, and forget about the innocent who had suffered, the property that was taken, and the lives that were lost. "I submit to you," he concluded, "that you really don't have two choices."[15]

Following Hurd's lead, Gienapp also told the jurors that the law did not permit them "to be governed by sympathy, prejudice, or public opinion." Both the public and the accused, he said, "expect that you will carefully and impartially consider all the evidence in the case, all of the law as stated by the court and reach a just verdict regardless of the consequences."[16] Gienapp then recounted the testimony that he said proved the defendants took "firearms, ammunition, food, and other items" from the trading post or "aided and abetted" persons who did. Though the prosecutors claimed the evidence showed that Banks and Means themselves had committed theft and had been seen in possession of stolen items, that evidence was in fact slim. Instead, it was the principle of aiding and abetting that the prosecution was relying on to win convictions—that, in Hurd's words, "a person or persons, who counsels, commands, induces, procures the commission of offenses are just as guilty as if they did it themselves." The stress was on what the defendants had said, with prosecutors arguing that the defendants had directed the thefts. Gienapp recalled for the jury Banks's comments to Mrs. Gildersleeve with respect to supplies taken from the trading post: "We needed it and we took it." The evidence clearly demonstrated, Gienapp told the jury, "that the defendants aided in that larceny, that they counselled in that larceny, that they commanded, that they induced that larceny, and that they procured that larceny."[17]

Then Gienapp, followed by Kaplan and Hurd, turned to a discussion of the assaults on FBI agents Joanne Pierce and Curtis Fitzgerald and Marshal Lloyd Grimm. Again, they emphasized testimony that tended to show that the defendants aided and abetted the assault, or were co-conspirators with someone who committed the assault. The prosecutors recounted testimony concerning meetings prior to the exchanges of gunfire, details of the incidents, and statements made by the defendants before and after. In each case, they reminded the jurors, the defendants need not have directly participated in the assaults to be found guilty.[18] Emphasizing the point, Hurd told the jurors that if you order people to construct bunkers and roadblocks, if you arm them and instruct them to fire those arms, and if you inform the government that it either has to assent to certain demands or risk violence, then, said the prosecutor, "what you do is procure people to commit assaults." If by actions and speech one knowingly puts into effect "the chain of circumstances which logically lead to those assaults," he argued, you cannot escape responsibility by claiming you were someplace else when the assaults occurred. Then, tying aiding and abetting to conspiracy, Hurd demonstrated the dangers of these concepts for any political defendant on trial: "If somebody does something in furtherance of a conspiracy, even if you don't know about it, even if there is no way for you to foresee that it would happen, if they do it in furtherance of the conspiracy while you are a member of the conspiracy, you are guilty, because you can be held for the overt act."[19]

After the noon recess, defense attorneys Tilsen, Leventhal, and Hall each took a turn before the jury. As the defense had done through much of the trial, each attorney had something to say concerning government misconduct, with respect to either Indian policy or the current trial. Tilsen and Hall went over different principles of law, such as specific intent, presumption of innocence, and the right of self-defense, contrasting the crime of taking groceries with the force of the government response. Leventhal discussed the 1868 Treaty and attempted to turn Hurd's "I don't care" phrase back on him, telling the jurors that those words had always been the government's response to injustices and poverty on Indian reservations. Using another of Hurd's phrases, Tilsen said that the whole trial was the "foreseeable consequence" of the white man's treatment of Indians throughout history. The only thing the government had proved, Tilsen said, was that there was agreement to go to Wounded Knee; what happened afterward was totally apart from what was intended. All three of the defense attorneys noted that the prosecution had not even mentioned Louis Moves Camp in their summations.[20]

The next day, September 11, while demonstrators marched outside carrying signs that read, "Nixon Is the Real Criminal, Free Banks and Means," the second day of closing arguments began. Emotions ran high on both sides; first Kunstler and then Hurd had tears in their eyes as they finished their individual statements.[21] At 9:00 A.M., Lane began the day with an attack on Hurd's claim that the law did not recognize political and religious beliefs. If that were true, he said, then if Washington, Jefferson, Martin Luther King, or Jesus Christ were the defendants, such considerations would still have to be set aside.[22] Nichol cut him off when he made a reference to Ford's pardon of Nixon, but Lane quickly moved on to his own attack on Hurd's "I don't care" statements. Cataloging the poor conditions on the Pine Ridge Reservation, including the alleged assaults and harassment by the "goon squad," he pointed out that the statement "I don't care" came from one of the men who was charged with upholding the law on the reservation. These are the same people, Lane said, who told Louie Moves Camp not to worry: "It's the arrogance of power by the white power structure."[23]

Why weren't others charged with conspiracy? Lane asked, pointing to William Leavitt, the rancher who had talked to Hurd about dropping dynamite on Wounded Knee. With respect to Moves Camp, he called putting that witness on the stand a "desperate" act and charged that the FBI had told him what to say: "It was just a desperate end of a case without any evidence . . . there's no relying upon Louie Moves Camp any more."[24] Lane also attacked the testimony of Joseph Trimbach, at first calling the latter John, which led to the following exchange:

NICHOL: I thought it was Joe.

LANE: I think you're right, I don't know him that well.

NICHOL: He's not a close friend of mine either.

LANE: I appreciate that, Your Honor. I think Mr. Hurd is disassociated with him also; is that correct?

HURD: He's not a personal friend of mine either.[25]

Recounting Trimbach's appearances in court, Lane charged that the FBI agent had committed perjury during his testimony in the wiretap hearing. Then, regarding the protest itself, he said that it was the government's response that turned it into a seventy-one-day siege in which people were injured and killed.[26] Reminding the jury of Watergate, he suggested that U.S. leaders could learn from Indian people "who lived in greater order and contentment with themselves and within nature before we arrived." He called the case against the defendants part of the continuing war against Indian people: "Like the rest of the war it is founded upon deceit, corruption, and speculation, and it's compounded by racism in this court-room." Finally, he told the jurors that they stood between the defendants and the "tyranny of their oppressors," and he asked them to return Banks and Means to their homes where they could continue to work for their people.[27]

Kunstler, the last defense attorney to address the jury, began by telling them that they were "privileged to have sat in on history." He called the jury "the last word in a historical process," adding that they were part of something they could tell their children and grandchildren about. "I ask you to forgive us all our trespasses," said Kunstler, acknowledging that "hard things" had been said in the course of the trial and that the court-room was not a place for peace and quiet, "particularly when social issues of great magnitude are in progress." It was, said the New York attorney, a case that would have far-reaching effects: "While it won't bring in the millennium, it may be part of a process of bringing us a new day in this country, a new understanding."[28]

Kunstler then moved on to discuss the charges of stealing from the trading post, contending that no direct evidence supported them: "Try to think of anybody who said, 'I saw Russell or Dennis steal,' " he challenged the jurors. Then, recounting the testimony of various witnesses concerning the treatment of the "hostages," he argued that what evidence did exist was circumstantial and was countered by evidence that showed no one had been harmed and that Banks had even helped one person retrieve her clock. Comparing the Indian movement to the early labor movement, Kunstler cited a number of labor actions, including the sit-down strikes during a lockout at the Flint, Michigan, auto plants in 1933.[29] Returning to the theft charges, he said that the only direct evidence linking Banks and Means to the charges had come from two witnesses who were not credible, Moves Camp and Hussman. The larceny charges, Kunstler said, were symbolic of the whole case: "If you can reduce a social movement to a question of whether its leaders are thieves, then I guess you can discredit a social movement."[30]

Conspiracy, Kunstler told jurors, was "the law that has always been used against all sorts of movements." Calling it a "nebulous and dangerous doctrine," he argued that it permitted hearsay evidence that allowed a jury to reason backwards to find a conspiracy. Yes, admitted Kunstler, there had been discussions about doing something on Pine Ridge; but he said that there was no evidence of an agreement to steal from the trading post, or to shoot at FBI agents: "The theory of conspiracy is that if you find these things were done, there must have been an agreement to do it. It takes all the heart out of a social upheaval."[31]

Kunstler conceded that merchandise was taken from the trading post but asked, "Where is there a word of proof in this record anywhere that you can find that Russell or Dennis said, do it, or that it was planned?" There was a "social catechism" in the first few days and items were taken, but some, like the clock and the artifacts, were also returned, he said. Echoing his colleagues, Kunstler called the testimony of Moves Camp a "tragic and sad event," accusing the prosecutors of not checking out their witness's story because they didn't want to. The evidence at the end of the trial finally demonstrated who the conspirators were, said Kunstler: "They were the old men of the tribe." Likening the meeting of the traditional leaders to the pre–Revolutionary War meetings in Boston, he recalled Gladys Bissonette's statement that Means had no choice but to go to Wounded Knee.[32]

Hurd, said Kunstler, will say this is not a political trial; but it is political, he insisted, adding that it had not lasted for months just because of some larceny and assault charges. Again he compared Wounded Knee to the American Revolution, stating that the action was a "last resort" for a people with no place else to go: "What really else was there to wait for, the next election so more babies could die in the hospital?" Kunstler acknowledged that Wounded Knee was not a revolution, but it was, he said, "an attempt to secure some reason for remaining alive." That is what's at stake in the courtroom, he told jurors, urging them to recall all the testimony, because upon their recollection "may depend a social movement that is gathering strength and attempting to change 400 years of neglect and deprivation and destruction." He then recounted the episodes of "government misconduct" during the trial: altered or missing documents, illegal monitoring, Moves Camp's testimony, and the FBI agents listening at the courtroom door.[33]

As he neared the end of his summation, Kunstler paid homage to people he called the rebels throughout history—rebels, he said, among whom Banks and Means would take their place:

> Every word said by the prosecution against these two men and the people they stand for has been said about everyone down the long range of history. Everyone has been so condemned who stands up. It is difficult, it is dangerous, it causes death, as it has been in this case, to two young Indians, but it is the way the world changes. Those who never speak never bring about change. Those who never act continue the same dreary path. Those who follow are those who go down in chains eventually, and all of us with them.[34]

"You have a role in that," Kunstler told the jury, "you have a role to judge whether these men are felons and should be sent to jail." Then, linking the treatment of Indians to the treatment of black slaves, he added, "There is a fighting chance for something decent in this world and it will not come by sending these men to prison."[35] Kunstler then read the last stanza of the poem "American Names" by Stephen Vincent Benet, which had been called to his attention the night before by the Minnesota writer and longtime activist Meridel LeSueur:

> I shall not rest quiet in Montparnasse.
> I shall not die easy in Winchelsea.
> You may bury my body in Sussex grass.
> You may bury my tongue at Champmedy.
> I shall not be there. I shall rise and pass.
> Bury my heart at Wounded Knee.[36]

"It's time each and every one of us understood we have a stake in this," Kunstler told the jurors. To close, he quoted from a statement read by Father Daniel Berrigan during his trial for the destruction of draft files: "These men are in your hands, take good care of them, they are my brothers." Reportedly both Kunstler and one juror had to fight back tears as the summation ended.[37]

At 2:00 P.M. Hurd stood for one final attempt to persuade the jury that the issue before them was the commission of crimes. Rising to the challenge and drama of Kunstler's closing in what one paper described as a "fiery two hour rebuttal," Hurd began by accusing the defense of not addressing the evidence that was set forth, but rather asking the jury to acquit regardless of that evidence. However, he reminded the jurors, their duty was to follow the law as set out by the court.[38] This is still a criminal case, said Hurd, but, because of the arguments of the defense counsel, "I feel compelled to deal with other matters." Acknowledging that there were reasons for Wounded Knee, that there were conditions that needed changing, Hurd said: "That is the reason why people do things. That does not justify it or excuse it." Then, throwing back at the defense the constant mention of the phrase he had used in the opening of his summation, Hurd repeated: "I don't care if they were right or wrong in wanting to bring about these changes, the law does not permit and cannot permit, in a free society, resorting to violence, theft, assaults, terrorism."[39]

Hurd then questioned the analogies to other movements, arguing that you cannot equate breaking into houses with a sit-in or equate a "bunch of hoodlums" with a labor movement.[40] He also challenged the contention that the defendants represented all Indians. They did not represent the Indians whose homes they broke into, whose property they stole, and they did not represent the Indians who elected and supported their tribal government, said Hurd, as he recounted the testimony of Oglalas who disavowed AIM: "They represent themselves and their supporters and the few, the few American Indians who are willing to use violent acts of crime to bring about what they consider to be desirable changes."[41]

Hurd reminded the jurors that even if they agreed with the defense that the conspiracy law was a bad law, they were bound by their oath to abide by it. As for the attacks on himself and the government, he accused the defense of trying to convince the jurors that he was a "heartless beast" to get their minds off the evidence and the law.[42] He countered the charges concerning Moves Camp's testimony, saying that there was no evidence that the FBI had told him what to say, that if anyone had destroyed Louie Moves Camp it was AIM, and that the evidence was such that the prosecutors did not need to rely on his testimony to prove their case. He also reminded them of the testimony of Ellen Moves Camp and her insistence that she never saw guns at Wounded Knee. Hurd also argued that the allegations of eavesdropping were not relevant to the jury's decision; rather, they should remember Agent Trimbach's testimony about the meetings with the defendants concerning their demands—testimony, he contended, that was corroborated by other evidence.[43]

Perhaps Hurd's strongest point was made when he reminded the jurors of all the things that Banks and Means had said they would prove and never did. He recalled that Means had called Father Manhart a liar but offered no proof; that the defendants had questioned Mrs. Gildersleeve about something she said on television but failed to produce the tape; that they suggested that a rancher was bringing liquor onto the reservation, but failed to prove it. They had also questioned Mrs. Hussman about carrying a gun at a roadblock and a BIA policeman about his alleged drinking on duty—all things, said Hurd, that the defense said they would prove, but never did.[44] Then reminding jurors once again that intent, not motive, is the key, Hurd said that the activities and speeches of the defendants demonstrated "criminal intent." To convict someone of conspiracy, he also reminded the jurors, there need not be an express agreement, and the names of all the actors need not be known. The evidence is clear, argued Hurd, that there was a plan to seize the village and to defend it until the demands were met, and that certain acts flowed from that plan.[45]

Finally, after reviewing the evidence on the assault charges one more time, he turned to Kunstler's comments that the trial was a historical moment, acknowledging that perhaps it was:

> Maybe the world is waiting to hear whether or not in our country today you can commit crimes of violence against people who are innocent, against Indians who are innocent and get away with it on the theory that there is some kind of philosophical dispute, and we are doing it for noble purposes, and so we are going to forget to cry. Well, if it's a historical moment, then to find these defendants not guilty would be a tragedy and if the world is looking on to endorse that type of action, it would be a tragedy.[46]

If the issue was respect for people's vision as the defense argued, Hurd asked, why did the evidence in the case demonstrate a complete disrespect for other people's vision, for the orderly processes of law and the ballot box? "Where was the respect for the Indians who did not share Mr. Banks' and Mr. Means' visions as to what type of government they ought to live under, or what type of religion they ought to practice, or how ought they to wear their hair? Where is the respect of those people's visions?"[47]

In closing, Hurd acknowledged that defendants had rights and that finding someone guilty could be a difficult decision for a jury, but he reminded them that he and the other prosecutors represented society and its laws, and that society too had rights that must be upheld. People had a right to be safe in their homes at night, argued Hurd, to have their possessions kept safe, and to be free from harm. To find these defendants not guilty, he continued, would undermine the rights of all people. "I don't know how a prosecutor could look yourself in the face after what occurred at Wounded Knee," said Hurd, "and say we are not going to prosecute it." Saying that he would probably never again "try a case where there is such an issue as to whether or not we really do what we believe," Hurd thanked the jurors for their attention during the long trial and took his seat.[48]

The next morning Judge Nichol told the jury that regardless of their opinions, it was their duty "to follow the law as stated in the instructions of the Court, and to apply the rules of law so given to the facts as you find them from the evidence in the case." The law, he said, did not permit jurors "to be governed by sympathy, prejudice, or public opinion." Nichol had reviewed 150 possible instructions, 108 submitted by the defense and 28 by the prosecution. The rest were the judge's, who later told reporters, "I think we eliminated as many as we considered."[49] Important for the defendants was the instruction that the jury could consider whether the means for redressing grievances under the 1868 Treaty had been blocked.[50] But as Nichol began to delineate the specifics of the 82 points of law, the wide leeway that had been granted the defense in what could be presented from the witness stand seemed to disappear into a tangle of rules and limitations concerning what evidence counted most and under what circumstances.

Nichol gave the usual admonishments concerning the presumption of innocence, and noted that the indictments and the statements of counsel were not evidence. He also cautioned jurors that the defendants' First Amendment right of free speech was protected, and that a jury may not convict if the evidence of a charged crime is limited to the First Amendment activities of the defendants, unless the speech "expressly advocates immediate illegal acts of violence."[51] As for the 1868 Treaty, Nichol said, it was the law of the land and as such was "properly applied to the consideration of whether conduct is or is not criminal." He also noted that treaties were to be interpreted from the point of view of the Indians who signed them and called attention to the provisions of the 1868 Treaty regarding law enforcement on the reservations. But, said Nichol, evidence of violations of the Treaty could only be considered for the purpose of determining motive, not as defenses to the crimes charged.[52]

Motive, said the judge, was not a defense to the charge of conspiracy "unless such motive related to the specific intent required for such crime."

Motive is what prompts a person to act, said Nichol, while intent refers to "the state of mind with which the act is done." As the prosecution had hoped, Nichol added that good motive alone was not a defense for a crime: "Even if you believe that the defendants have been motivated by the highest moral principles, and they may have been sincerely and passionately inspired, such motives do not confer immunity from prosecution or conviction for the violation of a valid law."[53] The judge also reviewed "direct" and "indirect" evidence and cautioned the jury not to consider evidence that he had struck from the record. Nichol then defined "reasonable doubt" as doubt based upon "reason and common sense—the kind of doubt that would make a reasonable person hesitate to act." Proof beyond a reasonable doubt, he said, must be proof "of such a convincing character that you would be willing to rely and act upon it unhesitatingly in the most important decisions of your own affairs."[54]

From there Nichol moved to the law concerning the specific charges against Banks and Means. For a conspiracy to have occurred, he told the jurors, the agreement need not be express; it is only necessary that it was knowingly formed, with an intent to violate the law, and that acts were done in furtherance of the plan, even if done without the knowledge of all the conspirators.[55] The larceny and assault, he went on, required "specific intent," which the government must prove by showing that the defendants "knowingly did an act which the law forbids, purposely intending by that act to violate the law," and that the act was done "willfully" and "knowingly," and not by mistake or accident.[56] To convict someone of larceny, Nichol continued, four essential elements must be proved: that the defendants or someone they "aided and abetted" took and carried away property from the trading post, that the property was worth over $100, that there was intent to deprive the owner of benefit of ownership, and that the acts were done willfully, knowingly, and unlawfully.[57]

Nichol then defined assault as any willful attempt to inflict injury upon a person coupled with the present ability to do it, and with any intentional display of force that would give the victim reason to fear or expect immediate harm. For a conviction, he continued, five essential elements needed to be proved: that the defendants or someone aided and abetted by them, or someone in the furtherance of a conspiracy, forcibly assaulted an officer while in the performance of official duties; that a dangerous weapon was used in the commission of the assault; that the act was done willfully; that the act was done knowingly; and that the act was done unlawfully. But, said Nichol, if a person was not the original aggressor and had reasonable ground to believe that he or someone else was in danger, then the act of

self-defense was a defense to the charge of assault.[58] Finally he emphasized a key point that the prosecution was relying on, that a person may
be found guilty of a crime if he or she "aids, abets, counsels, commands,
induces, or procures its commission." The act of the aider and abettor,
Nichol went on, must be willful and something which at least encourages
another to commit an unlawful act.[59]

In closing, he reminded the jurors that they were "the sole judges of the
credibility of witnesses and the weight their testimony deserves." He counseled them to consider each witness and all of the evidence carefully, and
he told them that they should not hold against the defendants their decision not to take the stand.[60] He explained that the verdict must be agreed
to by each individual juror and that although they should be open to a
change of mind in the course of deliberations, no one should surrender
his or her "honest convictions" solely because of the opinion of the other
jurors. Finally, after explaining the mechanics of the jury form and holding
a conference with the attorneys, Nichol released the four alternate jurors,
telling them that they had the right to talk to the attorneys and reporters,
as well as the right to refuse to do so.[61]

At 12:45 P.M. on Thursday, September 12, eight months after they had
made their first appearance as prospective jurors, the remaining twelve
men and women left the courtroom to begin their deliberations.[62] At the
same time reporters and defense committee members headed straight for
the four alternates. All learned very quickly that three of the four would
have voted for acquittal on all charges, with the fourth still undecided.
Said Elaine Grono, a resident of Saint Paul, "I felt the evidence didn't sustain any conviction."[63] After talking with reporters, the three women who
had said they would acquit, Joyce Selander, Linda Lacher, and Grono,
returned to the courtroom where they visited with the defendants and
their attorneys. The fourth alternate, Patrick Augusta, left the courthouse
immediately after he was excused.[64]

Newspapers were full of quotations from the alternates and photographs
of them talking with the defendants. Grono said that she had not joined
AIM, "but I'd probably demonstrate if they ask me." She also said she was
thinking of going to Wounded Knee to see the site of the protest for herself. All three said that the emotional closing arguments had left them confused. Lacher wondered out loud how such a decision could be made by
anyone, asking, "Do you cut off your heart and deal only with the head,
or use both or what?" They also praised the prosecution and defense attor-

neys, but had harsh words for the FBI. "The FBI came out as a very shoddy operation," Selander was quoted as saying, "there seems to be a lot of FBI agents who don't have very good memories." Said Lacher: "I hate to think of our government doing that kind of thing, because I love my country."[65]

The defendants, who had already expressed confidence in the jury, were elated. "It looks great, absolutely magnificent for us now," said Banks. Looking back on the moment, Tilsen said, "We now knew we had wiped them."[66] Hurd, however, was still holding out some hope, at least publicly, telling one reporter that there was a fifty-fifty chance of a conviction and that he would consider a hung jury a victory at this point.[67]

On the closing arguments, papers generally pointed out the contrasting styles and approaches to the case, often concentrating on Hurd's call for upholding the law and Kunstler's analogies to other struggles in history. Several articles noted that Hurd's "I don't care" phrase had been used against him and that there had been accusations concerning Moves Camp's testimony.[68] Most seemed caught up in the drama, noting the tears on the part of lawyers, jurors, and people in the audience. The *New York Times* even put it in its headline: "Kunstler in Tears, Gives 2 Indians' Case to Jurors."[69]

The effectiveness of attorneys in any criminal trial is difficult to assess. To the audience, particularly those who witness the proceedings through the media, lawyers often seem to be the dominant force in a trial. In high-profile political cases, analyzing the skill of opening and closing statements, cross- and direct examination, witness sequencing, objections, and other diversionary legal maneuvers may be almost impossible. In such trials the role of a defense attorney may not be limited to the traditional goal of winning an acquittal, and his or her reputation and presence may far exceed that of the prosecutor, if not that of an equally well-known defendant. As the trial of Banks and Means demonstrated, political trials are often filled with oratorical flourishes and dramatic legal maneuvering, but their lasting impact may be uncertain.

In *Reconstructing Reality in the Courtroom,* Lance Bennett and Martha Feldman argue that the impact of lawyers "lies in their connections to key structural elements of the stories in a case." In political trials the audience outside is as important as the one in the courtroom, and how these groups view the proceedings or interpret the stories being told may be different. As Bennett and Feldman note, what may be central for the media or the public may be a "peripheral factor" in the jury's perception of a case.

Viewed from the outside, the defense attorney may outwit, out-talk and otherwise outmaneuver the prosecutor and still lose the case.[70] Kunstler and his colleagues may have outmaneuvered the prosecution throughout most of the trial, but during closing arguments the credibility of Hurd's interpretation may, in the eyes of some observers, have equaled that of his more famous rival.

After eight months both men had become intertwined with the conflicting narratives that had unfolded in and outside the courtroom. Had Hurd's calls for law and order tied him to Richard Nixon or to the prosecutors who relentlessly pursued the Watergate investigation? Did Kunstler's passion for the defendants' cause, including the analogies he drew to other movements for change, link him and his clients to the American Revolution, or to the radicalism of the sixties that many people were trying to forget along with Watergate? All three alternate jurors said that they had been confused by the emotional closing arguments. The conflicting societal values presented by each side seemed irreconcilable. For the moment, it was unclear which story of law and social change had convinced the hearts and minds of the many audiences—Hurd's invoking of orderly processes and the right to be safe in one's home, or Kunstler's counsel that social struggle is often difficult and dangerous, and may even cause death, but is "the way the world changes."

Over the remainder of the day the jury sent out a series of questions and requests for Judge Nichol: a request for the transcript, which was denied; a request for the definition of "purloin," to which Nichol responded with, "to steal, to commit larceny or theft"; and, during the evening, a request for the testimony of undercover agents Stephenson and Keel, which was withdrawn when jurors learned that the testimony totaled several hundred pages. Finally the jury asked whether a permit was needed to carry guns in South Dakota, but Nichol deferred answering until the next day.[71] After eight hours of deliberation the jurors adjourned for the night, retiring to their rooms in the Saint Paul Hotel.

Rumors were already circulating that disagreements had begun to strain some of the friendships that had formed during the long trial. One reporter said that jurors were heard shouting at each other by people outside the jury room. Each juror had been affected in some way by the long trial, and as they began to discuss the case for the first time, different reactions to the experience began to surface. One juror reportedly had even watched her daughter get sprayed with Mace in the courtroom disturbance that occurred during the cross-examination of Louie Moves Camp.[72]

On Friday morning, September 13, the second day of deliberations, juror Therese Cherrier complained of being ill upon arriving at the courthouse after breakfast. Examined by her physician during the morning, she was hospitalized, reportedly for emotional strain and anxiety. At first Cherrier was expected to return, but doubts arose when it was reported that she was suffering from partial paralysis on her left side and also had a history of high blood pressure. Nichol sent the rest of the jury back to their hotel and called in the attorneys for what would be the first in a series of meetings to review possible alternatives. Legally the case could proceed with eleven jurors if both sides consented. The judge could also order a mistrial, which could result in a second trial; or dismiss the case, a decision that could be appealed by the government; or acquit the defendants, a decision that was not appealable.

The defense was eager to proceed with eleven jurors, but Hurd, first claiming that the missing juror was probably pro-prosecution and then noting the sentiments of the alternates, said that he doubted he would consent, but that he would consult with the Justice Department. Reports were circulating that the three women alternates had been seen having drinks with Means and several reporters and that two of them were also seen dining with the defendant and Marlon Brando, who was making his second appearance at the trial. Kunstler told the press that he would prefer deliberations to go on with eleven jurors, but that the defense as a whole had not made a decision yet. Hurd said he thought a mistrial might be the most appropriate outcome, adding that a second trial would be much shorter because the government would call fewer witnesses, and because there would be no need for special hearings on the legal matters.[73]

Hearing about Hurd's statements to the press, Nichol spoke to him privately, hoping that he could convince Hurd to agree to a verdict from eleven jurors. He told the U.S. Attorney that his clerk had overheard the jury foreman announce the results of two preliminary votes on which jurors were split on the theft charges against each defendant. Giving such information to one of the attorneys was forbidden under court rules, but Nichol hoped that the near-even split on Means would convince Hurd that a conviction was still possible. "I was trying to save the trial," commented Nichol when the conversation was revealed in January. The numbers, however—seven to five for acquittal on Means and eleven to one for acquittal on Banks—only served to reinforce what Hurd already suspected, that the government was in trouble with the current jury.[74]

By late Friday, the defense was moving ahead on a motion that could bring the trial to a favorable conclusion for the defendants and prevent a retrial.[75] On Saturday, in Judge Nichol's apartment, defense attorneys presented a motion for acquittal based on prosecutorial misconduct during the trial and the illegal use of the military in a domestic operation at Wounded Knee. The defense accused Assistant U.S. Attorney Hurd of violating professional and ethical standards by knowingly putting on the stand a witness he had reason to believe would commit perjury. The witness, of course, was Louis Moves Camp, and the particular testimony was his statement regarding his presence during certain events at Wounded Knee. The motion charged that Hurd knew Moves Camp was in California during the time he was claiming to be at Wounded Knee. The testimony of government witness Alexander David Richards was also noted, testimony contradicted by an FBI document that had been revealed only after he had left the stand. Further, the motion continued, Hurd violated professional and ethical moral standards by refusing to consent to an eleven-member jury verdict, putting conviction over justice as a goal.[76]

The defense also charged that federal officials had attempted to cover up the military involvement in the operation and raised "profound and serious questions about the integrity of Federal Court of Appeals Judge Joseph Sneed." Sneed, an assistant attorney general at the time of Wounded Knee, had testified during the trial that it was not a military operation. The motion also said that Sneed had held discussions with the Defense Department about possible plans to take the village by force. Testimony and documentary evidence, the motion argued, revealed that the Pentagon had provided for the direct involvement of two colonels, $300,000 worth of equipment and supplies, and a system of supply for the forces engaged in the operation. The defense asked for an acquittal over a mistrial "in the interest of justice, in furtherance of due process of law and to preserve the integrity of the court and the judicial process." In a new trial, the motion noted, the jury would not get to witness the many serious mistakes that had been made by the prosecution and the FBI in the present trial.[77]

Meanwhile, the status of the hospitalized juror remained in limbo. A neurologist who had examined Mrs. Cherrier on Friday afternoon reported to Nichol on Saturday that there was a one in three chance that she would be able to resume deliberations on Monday. The press also reported that Hurd did have doubts about Moves Camp and had asked the FBI to submit him to a lie detector test, but that FBI Area Director Trimbach had refused.[78] Hurd told reporters, however, that the defense motion was based on "false innuendos" and was an attempt to force him into accepting a verdict from the eleven remaining jurors: "I take it as a threat to blackmail me so I would be concerned about the personal implications rather than what is best for my client. I resent the improper attempt to blackmail me or pressure me into accepting an eleven person jury."[79]

Going through the prosecutor's mind were the possible outcomes of a second trial, one that would involve fewer charges, would have a different judge, and would not have certain legal battles, discovery problems, and surprises like Louis Moves Camp. Hurd even speculated to the press about where a new trial might be held, mentioning Bismarck, North Dakota, and Sioux City, Iowa.[80] The statements came amid reports that the alternate jurors were guessing that the split on the jury was probably eight to four for acquittal. But the decision, Hurd said, would be based on what he saw as his "responsibility to see that the United States government gets a fair trial." Then, recalling some of Judge Nichol's rulings in the case, he added: "I don't think we've gotten a fair shake in this trial."[81] As the weekend came to an end, everything seemed to be on hold, waiting for news of Mrs. Cherrier.

JUDGE NICHOL'S DECISION
AND ITS AFTERMATH

I guess this has been a bad year for justice.
JUDGE FRED NICHOL, SEPTEMBER 1974

B Y MONDAY MORNING, September 16, it was clear that juror Therese Cherrier would not be able to resume deliberations. Hurd told Judge Nichol that because of the personal attacks made against him in the defense motion, he would let the Justice Department make the final decision on whether to proceed with eleven jurors. Hurd had told reporters on Sunday that there was reason to believe that there would be a hung jury, but when asked by Justice Department officials what he thought the jury would do, he replied that they would probably acquit: "I still thought we had an outside chance of getting a conviction on maybe one or two counts, but no more than that and only an outside chance. I thought that was because we had not received a fair trial. I thought that if we retried it . . . we had an excellent chance of obtaining a conviction."[1]

Hurd also said that he did not believe Nichol would dismiss the case, but rather would declare a mistrial. Officials in Washington told reporters that the decision was based on recommendations from the prosecutors in the case and that several in the department were involved, but they refused to comment on how high up the discussions went, except to say that Harry Peterson, Chief of the Criminal Division, had been involved.[2] Nichol received the negative reply from the government about 2:00 P.M. on September 16 and wasted little time in finalizing his decision. By then he described himself as "very angry" about the whole situation, but more important, he was convinced that the jury would have acquitted the defendants.[3] As tension in the jury room mounted, one juror pulled out a roll of masking tape, stuck it to his chair, and passed it to the person next to him; when a marshal finally came to call them into the courtroom, the tape encircled the room.[4]

At 3:00 P.M., almost eight and a half months after the trial had begun, Nichol announced to a packed courtroom that he was dismissing the remaining counts against the defendants. He had "importuned" counsel on both sides to accept a verdict from the remaining eleven jurors, but, said Nichol, he was "powerless to do anything more than ask or suggest or highly recommend." He termed it "almost incredible" that after an eight and a half month trial involving the lives of so many, "it cannot be agreed upon that this case could proceed to verdict."[5] Although he acknowledged that the prosecution was within its rights to refuse to proceed, Nichol asserted that as a representative of the government the U.S. Attorney's role was not just to win his case, but to see that justice was done: "In my opinion, the Department of Justice should have sought justice in this case by permitting this case to go to verdict, rather than to in effect deny that justice because they refuse to accept the unanimous verdict of eleven jurors, good and true."[6] Referring to his ruling on the dismissal motion early in the trial, Nichol said, "I think it's only fair to say . . . I am now over the brink."[7] Quickly silencing the applause from the audience, he compared his decision to Judge Matthew Byrne's in the Ellsberg case, which he noted had not been appealed. Nichol said he had studied Byrne's reasons carefully at the close of the wiretap hearing before deciding not to dismiss the case, but now, he said, four "very serious matters" had made him decide differently: the failure of the prosecution to turn over the FBI statement that contradicted David Richards's testimony; the Louie Moves Camp matter, which he termed the "most serious misconduct"; the question of military involvement at the protest; and the government's refusal to allow the case to go forward.

On the Richards matter, he admitted that he could not "be so bold" as to say he thought Hurd deliberately withheld the statement, but, said Nichol, he had to know about it, and if he didn't, "he was very, very negligent." It was negligence to such a degree as to constitute misconduct, said Nichol. As for Moves Camp, he said it was "probably the most bizarre incident in the trial." Nichol also said that his earlier statements concerning the deterioration of the FBI were "clearly justified by the manner in which the FBI has operated in this trial."[8]

Remarking, "I don't think Mr. Hurd is going to like this," he leveled harsh criticism at the lead prosecutor: "Mr. Hurd deceived the Court up here at the bench in connection with the Moves Camp incident in Wisconsin. It hurts me deeply. It's going to take me a long time to forget it."[9] To that extent, "I think the prosecutor in this case was guilty of misconduct," the judge said. "I guess this has been a bad year for justice," lamented Nichol, "a bad year for justice."[10] After recounting the rest of the Moves Camp affair, Nichol questioned the FBI's claim that it had checked out their witness's story: "I don't know what their checking was. A lot of it, I know, must have taken place in bars over there in Wisconsin." Terming the incident "incredible," he said he hadn't known the FBI was "stooping so low" that they would give a prospective witness the "royal treatment" that Moves Camp had received. Although he admitted he couldn't say that the FBI had actually quashed the prosecution in Wisconsin, Nichol made it clear that he believed they had attempted to influence the decision. "But it's hard for me to believe," he continued, "that the FBI, which I have revered for many years, has fallen to that low an estate." Then, referring to Trimbach's refusal of the U.S. Attorney's request to give Moves Camp a lie detector test, he asked, "Since when does the head of the FBI start telling the prosecution that they can't have a lie detector test if they want to?"[11]

While the Assistant U.S. Attorney sat staring at the desk with his head in his hands, Nichol said that there was nothing to prevent the prosecutor from verifying when Moves Camp was in California. Hurd's errors, said Nichol, were errors of judgment that could have been avoided, adding: "I'm rather ashamed that our government was not represented better in the trial of this case."[12] Finally, after explaining his reasons for believing that there was no doubt that the military was involved at Wounded Knee and thus in violation of U.S. law, Nichol formally granted the motion for dismissal.[13] When he had finished, he thanked the jurors for their service and told them that they could choose whether or not to talk with the press and the attorneys about the case: "Let me thank you very much for what has been a very long trial. It's been boring through a lot of it. Some of you may have had a little trouble keeping awake, but there have been moments when you didn't have to worry about being bored. Some of those moments I've regretted very much. Nevertheless, I guess I've done my share of coming in and telling you, when I felt I was wrong, I would say so."[14] Saying that he would be glad to get back home and that he hoped he never had to go through "another one like this," Nichol discharged the bonds on the defendants, dismissed the jury, and left the courthouse to visit Mrs. Cherrier at the hospital.[15] An hour after he had called court back into session, the trial was over.[16]

There was a sigh of relief from the audience, followed by a some brief applause as Banks and Means embraced their attorneys and reporters rushed in to interview them. Television reports and front page stories the next morning focused on Nichol's criticism of federal officials and the various reactions to the decision. One reporter described it as a "harsh—almost bitter—one hour denunciation of the FBI, the Justice Department and the prosecutors."[17] Asked for his reaction, Hurd told reporters, "I still have a great deal of respect for Judge Nichol as an individual, but he is wrong, very wrong in this case."[18] The prosecutor had reportedly followed Nichol out of the courtroom, attempting to discuss the decision, but the judge would not respond to him. U.S. Attorney Clayton also called the decision a mistake and joined Hurd in saying that he would urge the Justice Department to appeal it.[19]

"One of the problems Hurd faced was that the government indicted Russell and Dennis first and then set out to get the evidence," said Tilsen, commenting on the prosecution's dismay over the decision.[20] For the defendants and the legal team, the reaction to the decision was "euphoric."[21] Banks told reporters that he would be lying if he said he wasn't "apprehensive" throughout the trial, but added that Nichol had "hit the nail on the head" in his decision. Banks also commented on the value of the trial for the Indian cause: "Of course Russell and I were at Wounded Knee. Everybody knew that. But what did they know about Indian treaty rights, human rights, until now?"[22] He quickly added, however, that the decision did not mean that the struggle for Indian rights was over: "We can't be claiming victory until all injustices are corrected."[23] Noting the big investment the U.S. government had in the case, defense attorney Kunstler and others praised Nichol for his courage. "If this isn't a clear warning that someone must begin the cleansing process in America," said Kunstler, "then I don't know what a clear warning is."[24]

Defense attorney Hall characterized Nichol as "one who genuinely worries about the fact that as a judge, he has tremendous power over people and events." Said a Sioux Falls attorney, "Occasionally federal judges think their appointment came from God; Fred knows his came from the President."[25] Even Means, who had clashed with Nichol throughout the trial, praised the decision: "At least there is one federal judge with enough guts to say Indians do have rights and the right to live their own lives."[26] Complimented from one side and condemned from the other, Nichol spoke of his criticism of the government's conduct during the trial: "I think that distrust of all government, to a degree is a healthy thing."[27]

The jurors were also talking to reporters, some commenting that they were satisfied with Nichol's decision, others that they were stunned. Five jurors said that they believed there was not enough evidence to convict on any of the charges, while a sixth said she would have voted to acquit on the conspiracy charges, but she was not sure on the others. Another juror noted that the first vote taken on the conspiracy charges was eight to three in favor of acquittal, with one undecided, and unanimous for acquittal on a second vote taken later. On the theft charges, an early vote was reportedly eleven to one for acquittal on Banks and eight to four for acquittal on Means. Three said they believed it would have been impossible to reach a decision on the assault charges.[28]

Two jurors, including the foreman, refused to talk with reporters, and three others could not be located. Meanwhile, Nichol told reporters after a visit at the hospital with Therese Cherrier that she had told him that he had done the right thing and that no agreement would have been possible on the assault charges. Another juror told reporters that Cherrier had argued for acquittal from the beginning.[29]

In the days that followed, the press provided its own analysis of the eight-month trial. Several papers, including the *New York Times,* pointed to the strategy of putting the government on the defensive as being key in the trial. A *Times* editorial on September 21 called on the Attorney General to take a close look at the FBI and its use of agents provocateurs, saying that the Wounded Knee trial was not an isolated case but "part of a dangerous pattern in American law enforcement." It was time, the editorial went on, for FBI Director Kelley, the Department of Justice, and the Senate Judiciary Committee to do what was necessary to turn the FBI into what it was "cracked up to be—a highly professional, non-ideological, law enforcement agency . . . It is incumbent on the Government to require that the Federal Bureau of Investigation, too, live by the rule of law."[30]

In a similar vein, the *Christian Science Monitor* called for the government to "clean up its act" in the wake of the Ellsberg and Wounded Knee decisions.[31] But in the *Saint Paul Pioneer Press,* under the headline, "Wounded Knee Trial: Nichol Couldn't Hack It," reporter J. C. Wolfe called the trial "one of the more incredible chapters in the history of American jurisprudence." Citing what he called Nichol's "amazing stance" and "casual manner," he criticized the judge for allowing too much time for evidentiary hearings, jury selection, and cross-examination, and for giving too much leeway to the defendants and their attorneys. Means, in Wolfe's words, "did as he damned well pleased through most of the trial," while Kunstler and Lane played Nichol like "masterful musicians." The judge's decision to let the defendants cross-examine witnesses, wrote Wolfe, was a "virtual surrender of judicial authority."[32]

Other papers gave the proceedings mixed reviews. The *Minneapolis Tribune* noted that the trial had quickly become a political forum that ultimately lent weight to the defendants' contentions "that the government cannot be trusted in dealings with tribal people." The editorial said that Nichol's decision was the right one because the government's attorneys had been "repeatedly caught in failures to observe the rules of its own judicial system."[33] The *Sioux Falls Argus Leader* criticized both the "government's mishandling of the Indian problem since frontier days" and the "legal niceties" of a cumbersome judicial system. Calling for more constraints on defendants and attorneys and an overall speedier process, the editorial said, "The government must act to cope with this problem before crime engulfs America."[34]

Also in South Dakota, Congressman James Abnor, a frequent critic of AIM, expressed astonishment at Nichol's decision: "After witnessing the personal injury, damage and destruction caused to property during the occupation, it is hard to believe that all the charges should be dismissed against the alleged leaders without a jury decision." Abnor went on to level criticism at the federal judicial system: "Our judicial system was established to protect the people, and I personally feel we have just witnessed one of the fallacies in the system, a fallacy our forefathers tried desperately to protect all Americans against."[35]

Melvin Grarreau, a member of the Cheyenne River Sioux Tribal Council, called the decision "the greatest day the Indian has known since the Little Big Horn."[36] On the Rosebud Reservation, Tribal Chairman Robert Burnette also praised the decision: "My contention was that the grounds existed all along for dismissal."[37] Pine Ridge Tribal Chairman Dick Wilson, however, called the acquittal "ridiculous" and "a total breakdown of the judicial system," and he warned that "AIM will have no victory dances and celebrations" on the reservation: "Because of the climate set by President Ford's pardon of Richard Nixon, there's been a breakdown of the judicial system. If we want law and order we will have to take it into our own hands."[38] Wilson said that he expected another Wounded Knee–like protest and warned that if it happened he would not wait for the government to act: "I won't fool around with the government again . . . I won't screw around with the BIA police either . . . If it happens again we'll be able to take care of it ourselves." He also quipped that Nichol "must have joined AIM."[39] BIA officials, however, said they did not expect trouble. Superintendent Al Trimble told reporters that although many on the reservation opposed AIM, there was considerable "latent sympathy" for the group because it articulated the views of many Indians who believed they were not receiving fair treatment from the federal government. Interviews with Wounded Knee residents echoed Trimble's comments, with one person noting that poverty and unkept government promises were still the central issues on the reservation. Agnes Gildersleeve, a key witness for the prosecution, said that she was surprised by Nichol's decision, but would make no further comment.[40]

AIM supporters announced plans for a celebration in Means's hometown of Porcupine. Wilson, who had declared martial law on the reservation, said he would prevent it. Despite the threats, Means promised to attend: "It's my home, why shouldn't I go there?" As South Dakota braced for another confrontation and state newspapers tracked the unfolding story on page one, Means was indicted for assaults on two BIA police officers in the Mission Country Club altercation in June. But the AIM leader still joined with about 800 others from on and off the reservation to celebrate the Saint Paul victory. The event took place under heavy security, but without incident. Afterward Wilson turned his wrath toward local BIA officials, demanding the removal of Superintendent Trimble.[41]

At the same time, the former prosecutor of the Custer cases, William Janklow, was keeping his promise to make AIM an issue in the South Dakota race for attorney general. Using campaign advertisements that boasted, "He's the only one who ever stopped AIM in court," Janklow charged that the current attorney general had prevented vigorous prosecution of AIM radicals. AIM's public criticism of the former legal aid attorney turned prosecutor only helped to boost his campaign. In November, Janklow won by a landslide—98,500 to 51,400—with a 71 percent turnout.[42]

The day after the decision in Saint Paul, the first draft resister seeking amnesty under President Ford's new plan surrendered himself in California, and Attorney General William Saxbe announced that all imprisoned draft resisters from the Vietnam War would be freed.[43] But almost in the same breath, Saxbe ordered a study of recent political trials to discover why the government kept losing. A spokesperson for the Attorney General said, "If you look back on the last four, five, or six years, the government record in those kinds of cases in terms of winning and losing is not so good."[44]

Two days later the Justice Department announced that Hurd and Gienapp had been named two of the outstanding Assistant U.S. Attorneys in the nation, citing their "superior performance" in the handling of the case against Banks and Means. When asked about the criticism leveled against him, Hurd said, "I sleep well at night; my ego is intact. Nobody likes criticism but I'm willing to accept it." Banks still likens the award to "handing medals of honor to Custer's soldiers," a reference to the medals received by the 7th Cavalry after the massacre at Wounded Knee in 1890.[45]

In a statement released immediately after Nichol's decision, WKLDOC tried to focus attention on the remaining cases, saying that unless the government was forced to stop further prosecutions, the victories in Saint Paul and elsewhere would be hollow ones: "We understand that the purpose of these trials is to break the spirit of the American Indian Movement by tying up its leaders and supporters in court and forcing us to spend huge amounts of money, time and talent to keep our people out of jail, instead of building an organization that can work effectively for the Indian people."[46] A week later Kunstler carried a similar message to Canada, speaking to audiences at the University of Winnipeg and the University of Manitoba. The purpose of the prosecution, said Kunstler, was to destroy the movement and scare the silent majority. AIM, he said, had lost much of its force as a result of the time spent defending its membership in the courts: "In the United States, there is a wearisome repetition in the indictments of nuns, priests, panthers, yippies and radicals for conspiracy. The system wins even when they manage to defeat the courtroom proceedings."[47]

In Saint Paul, ten of the sixteen jurors and alternates wrote to Attorney General Saxbe, asking him to dismiss the remaining Wounded Knee charges: "We wish you to know we would not have voted to convict either of the two defendants on any of the charges and we would not have voted to convict because each of us concluded that there was not enough evidence to do so. In our view a government that cannot in an eight-month trial present enough evidence against the two leaders of the Wounded Knee siege to secure a conviction on any count should for moral and ethical reasons drop the criminal charges against all the other Indian people and their supporters."[48] The letter went on to say that since the leaders were not guilty of any crimes, those that followed them should not continue to be prosecuted: "It is in the spirit of reconciliation and redemption that we urge you to respect this gesture and join with us and other Americans in an effort to bind up the wounds that have been caused by this our longest and perhaps least honorable war."[49]

Mark Lane told the press that four of the jurors had not been contacted, and that two others had considered signing but had not done so. The idea, he said, came out of a conversation between himself and three jurors the night of Nichol's decision. Calling themselves "Jurors and Others for Reconciliation," the group had set up an office in Saint Paul and started to hold regular meetings and organize speaking engagements.[50] Not all the former jurors agreed, however. John Kilbride, the jury foreman, who reportedly had been the most adamant for conviction, told a reporter in September that one had to admire the defendants for acting on their beliefs, but that their actions were wrong.[51]

At the time the letter was written, 35 of the original 124 nonconspiracy cases had either been dismissed or resulted in verdicts of acquittal. There had been no convictions. The only word on dismissals, however, came from the U.S. Attorney's office in Minnesota, which announced that it was dropping charges against Richard Carlson for sending an anti-AIM pamphlet to the Saint Paul jurors because Carlson had thought that they would not receive the mailings until after the trial.[52] Judge Bogue also dismissed Means's suit seeking to overturn the Pine Ridge tribal election, saying that the law did not require an election to be free of error, and that the plaintiffs had not exhausted all the remedies available to them in the tribal courts.[53]

In mid-October the government finally won a case in Lincoln, Nebraska, when four people were convicted of conspiracy to "obstruct, impede, and interfere" with U.S. Marshals in the performance of their duties.[54] WKLDOC publicly attacked the verdict, accusing the government of using perjured testimony and engaging in other misconduct to gain the convictions. The press statement noted that four people had been acquitted for the same acts in a previous trial. Within the defense committee, the ruling caused dissension over how to proceed, with some legal workers and defendants feeling betrayed by Warren Urbom, the judge they had come to trust. Despite the counsel of Beeler and other veteran committee members, several defendants awaiting trial said that they now wanted their cases to go before a jury.[55]

Meanwhile, AIM continued the campaign for dismissals, while doing fund-raising for the defense and trying to keep other Indian rights issues alive around the country.[56] Clyde Bellecourt called for churches to relinquish their land holdings on reservations, and AIM asked the federal government to return Fort Robinson in Nebraska to the Sioux for an Indian educational center, rather than continue its use as a "tourist trap."[57] Means, Lane, and juror Joyce Selander appeared on NBC's *Today Show* to talk about the cases and were followed a few weeks later by William Janklow, who had demanded equal time to tell the "truth" about AIM.[58] Marlon Brando, who had just announced his intention to make a movie about Wounded Knee, spoke at a rally in Pierre, South Dakota, in support of Sara Bad Heart Bull; she had been sentenced to a year in jail for her role in the Custer demonstration, which had been called to protest the murder of her son.[59] In Topeka, Kansas, supporters held a rally attended by Russell and Ted Means and Vernon Bellecourt. In December, however, AIM leaders were denied a request to address the Democrats' mini-convention in Kansas City and settled for a private meeting with Senator Edward Kennedy.[60]

As the debates over the Wounded Knee prosecutions continued, the House of Representatives remained divided on the issue of compensation for the Black Hills. Opponents argued that it set a dangerous precedent and opened the federal government to other such claims. The Senate had approved a $104 million payment to the Sioux after the favorable ruling from the Indian Claims Commission. At the same time, there were warnings of a growing crisis in Indian health services on reservations, especially among the Sioux. The report noted that health care was one of the guarantees in the 1868 Treaty.[61]

By mid-November there still had been no response from Attorney General Saxbe to the letter from the Saint Paul jurors. Justice Department officials met with five of the jurors in Washington but refused to discuss the remaining cases, saying only that they would report on the meeting to Saxbe. Former juror Maureen Coonan told reporters that the delegation had received the "runaround," adding that the officials had answered questions the way FBI agents had on the stand in Saint Paul.[62]

A month later the Justice Department filed a brief in the Eighth Circuit Court of Appeals, challenging Nichol's decision. The 127-page document, signed by Assistant Attorney General Henry Peterson, argued that the dismissal had been based on "unsupported allegations" and served "no purpose beneficial either to the administration of justice or the public." Even if prosecutors had committed errors, Peterson contended, the charges should be reinstated: "Dismissal of an indictment is a harsh remedy, a consequence of which is the guilty may go free because the prosecution has erred."[63] The Justice Department was also appealing two of Judge Urbom's acquittals in order to challenge his ruling, similar to Nichol's, that the presence of the military at Wounded Knee had been unlawful.[64]

The struggle for Indian rights that had begun on the Pine Ridge Indian Reservation and then shifted to the courts in the spring of 1973 was still in the courts as 1974 came to an end, nineteen months later. Forty cases had been brought into court, with only five resulting in convictions.[65] In Lincoln, an agreement had been reached to consolidate several of the non-conspiracy cases into a single hearing to determine whether the 1868 Treaty still affected law enforcement on the reservation. If successful in convincing Judge Urbom that the Treaty barred federal jurisdiction for the crimes alleged at Wounded Knee, the defense would win dismissals on a number of cases.[66]

John Throne, a California lawyer who had been at Wounded Knee, and Larry Leventhal, a member of the Saint Paul defense team, had gathered together a number of experts and volumes of documentation for the hearing. Fifty witnesses, including authors, historians, anthropologists, and descendants of signers of the Treaty, spoke about what the Treaty meant to the Indians who had signed it.[67] Among the witnesses was Russell Means, who declared, "I only went into Wounded Knee because of the treaty." Historians told the court that oral interpretations were important and should be recognized legally because the Sioux had no written language. As in Saint Paul, the defense argued that the signers believed that they had retained jurisdiction to deal with crimes on the reservation.[68]

The government presented its own version of the historical record, bringing to the stand a University of South Dakota professor who testified that the Sioux had originally pushed other Indians out of the area when they arrived from the east. He admitted, however, that the Treaty did give the Sioux the option of criminal jurisdiction over the reservation.[69] But the government argued that Indian tribes were now "sovereign dependent nations," and that laws superseding sections of the Treaty had been upheld in the courts, making Congress the venue to resolve current claims.[70]

Judge Urbom announced his decision in mid-January. "The conclusion that Indian tribes do not have complete sovereignty is irresistible," he said, concluding (as Judge Nichol had earlier) that the 1868 Treaty did not preclude federal jurisdiction for certain crimes committed on reservations. The Major Crimes Act together with legislation giving the federal court jurisdiction over offenses enumerated in it, said Urbom, "is explicit legislation which overcomes the Treaty of 1868 regarding criminal jurisdiction and is a valid and constitutional law." The judge did note what he termed a history of duplicity in U.S.-Indian relations, calling it an "ugly history" and one that "white Americans may retch at the recollection of."[71] But Urbom questioned what the remedy was to be and who was to decide, adding that recognizing what was wrong did not necessarily determine what is right:

Relations with Indian tribes are given exclusively to the executive and legislative branches. Perhaps it should be otherwise, but it is not. When and if the people amend the Constitution to put limits on the executive and legislative branches in their affairs with Indian tribes, the federal courts will uphold those limits, but in the meantime the courts cannot create limits. In short, a judge must hold government to the standards of the nation's conscience once declared, but he cannot create the conscience or declare the standards.[72]

Remedies must be sought from the executive and legislative branches and not the courts, said Urbom, agreeing with the government's argument. The defendants, he said, were "addressing the wrong forum for gaining relief in their sovereignty grievances."[73] In 1976 a three-judge panel of the Eighth Circuit Court of Appeals said that they saw no purpose in attempting to improve on Urbom's "thoughtful opinion" and adopted it as their own for the purpose of considering appeals on several Wounded Knee convictions.[74]

WKLDOC lawyers thought that they had received a fair hearing on the Treaty and admitted that their argument was a long shot to begin with.[75] Still, it was a setback for the treaty rights struggle and left the defense committee with more cases to be tried. Having exhausted the resources of both the NLG and the NACDL, legal workers scoured the country for volunteer attorneys.[76] It was little consolation when the U.S. Civil Rights Commission announced that an investigation of the previous year's tribal election on Pine Ridge indicated widespread irregularities, including fraud. Stating that almost one-third of the votes cast were found to be improper, the report urged a new election. Wilson had defeated Means 1,714 to 1,514.[77]

With the treaty decision the government had finally won a major legal battle to go with its first convictions near the end of 1974. Apparently learning some lessons in Saint Paul and elsewhere, prosecutors seemed to be narrowing their focus; in February, they asked Federal District Judge Bogue, who had taken over the cases from Urbom, to dismiss fifty indictments. "We are not bailing out of the Wounded Knee situation," the special prosecutor cautioned, citing time, costs, and the unlikelihood of convictions as reasons for the request. The fifty dismissals left fewer than twenty cases to be tried.[78]

In Gresham, Wisconsin, however, the seizure of the Alexian Brothers Abbey by Menominee Indians threatened to start the process all over again. The protest, which was intended to dramatize land claims, was supported by AIM and covered by reporters, who compared it to the siege on Pine Ridge two years before. Yet despite the presence of the national media and the arrival of AIM leaders to help with negotiations, the protest failed to galvanize the Indian community and the other supporters as Wounded Knee had. There would be no massive prosecution and defense effort and no star-studded trials to come.[79]

Still, as winter gave way to spring in 1975, it did seem as if recent history was repeating itself. There was news of an armed takeover of a building on Navajo land in New Mexico by a group attempting to dramatize poor health and economic conditions.[80] Russell Means was charged with the murder of a man in a bar near the Pine Ridge Reservation. Despite the victim's recorded statement shortly before dying that Means was not the one who had shot him, the AIM leader spent six weeks in jail until Marlon Brando finally posted bond.[81] Though Means would eventually be acquitted, the process consumed more time and money.

In May, Attorney General Janklow lived up to his tough talk and ordered a tear gas attack to end a takeover of a Yankton Sioux Reservation industrial plant by armed Indians in Wagner, South Dakota. Editorials in three South Dakota papers praised Janklow's decisive handling of the situation.[82]

The Justice Department finally announced that a federal grand jury would begin a probe of the violence on Pine Ridge. The week before, several WKLDOC volunteers reported having been beaten by "goon squad" members under direct orders from Wilson. The next month Wilson announced the formation of a new anti-AIM group, the "Indian Restoration Committee." In July the Tribal Chairman wrote a letter to the *New York Times* charging that the problems on Pine Ridge were brought on by outsiders. The government blamed the situation on the dispute between Means and Wilson, but the tribal chairman's hold on power was rooted in the decades-old conflicts between "mixed bloods" who congregated around the BIA and tribal offices in the town of Pine Ridge, and the traditional "full bloods" who lived in the outlying areas of the reservation.[83]

A report in the *Times* said that two years after Wounded Knee, conditions on Pine Ridge were worse than before. The Justice Department laid the blame on the 1973 protest for creating a "climate of hate." But the article also noted that it was full-blooded Oglalas, many of them opposed to Wilson, who tended to be arrested most often by the BIA police and that the only indictments issued by the new grand jury were against AIM supporters. It pointed out that some of the existing problems were those that OSCRO and AIM had originally complained about, such as the unemployment rate, which reached 70 percent during the winter, and the inexpensive leases of land granted to white ranchers. There was little evidence, said the report, of the $25 million a year the government was spending on the reservation.[84]

President Ford's response to the situation was to request $10.9 million for "expansion and improvement" of law enforcement on reservations. Congress also announced the establishment of the American Indian Policy Review Commission, but the recommendations made by its mostly Indian staff and membership were largely ignored. Stories such as AIM's participation in the establishment of a new Cultural Learning Center for Indians in Rapid City and a resolution of sovereignty based on the 1868 Treaty issued by the Oglala traditional chiefs on Pine Ridge remained local news.[85]

What did make national news in the spring was the revelation of something that WKLDOC and AIM had long suspected—that they had been infiltrated by an FBI informant during the Saint Paul trial. Douglas Durham, the administrator for AIM in WKLDOC in Saint Paul, appeared at press conferences in Chicago and Minneapolis to relate how he had infiltrated the AIM chapter in Des Moines, from there traveling to South Dakota and eventually Saint Paul. Durham said he was paid $1,000 a month for his efforts.[86]

Upon hearing the press reports Judge Nichol initially accused Hurd of holding back information during the trial, but later laid the blame on the FBI: "I do think it's true that the FBI withheld stuff from the government and that I've been blaming the prosecution for some matters they were innocent of."[87] Durham's name had been on the membership list that WKLDOC had submitted to the government pursuant to Nichol's order pertaining to informants. Hurd had maintained that FBI files "contained no material which could arguably be considered as evidence of an invasion of the defense legal camp." Both Hurd and Durham insisted that the informant had not provided the FBI with any information on the defense, even though he was privy to numerous conversations concerning the Saint Paul trial.[88]

In 1956 the FBI had initiated a program called COINTELPRO to infiltrate, gather intelligence on, and disrupt the activities of the Communist Party. In the 1960s and early 1970s this activity expanded to groups in the student antiwar and black nationalist movements, and even the more moderate civil rights groups. According to a 1967 memo, its purpose was to "expose, disrupt, misdirect, discredit, or otherwise neutralize" these groups and "their leadership, spokesman, membership, and supporters, and to counter the propensity for violence and civil disorder."[89] The operation was officially terminated in 1971 after documents relating to the program were taken from an FBI regional office and released to the press. But reports of incidents like the one involving Durham indicated that the continued harassment of radical groups, including AIM, had not ended with the demise of COINTELPRO.

The incident that tied all this to Watergate and lent credence to the calls for congressional probes was the break-in at the office of Daniel Ellsberg's psychiatrist, an operation by the White House "plumbers" to find incriminating materials on the former government employee who had released the Pentagon Papers to the press. By 1975 both houses of Congress were investigating government intelligence agencies, including the Senate Select Committee on Intelligence headed by Frank Church, which uncovered a long history of abuses by the FBI and the CIA. Documents acquired later by several researchers through the Freedom of Information Act support the complaints of AIM and other groups concerning infiltration and harassment after 1971.[90]

The revelations and investigations, however, came too late for many groups who had been subjected to a combination of criminal prosecutions and extralegal activities by law enforcement agencies. As had happened with the Black Panther Party and other groups who went outside established channels of political redress, Stephen Cornell observes in *The Return of the Native*, Indian activists were characterized as "renegades, urban hoodlums, criminals, youthful adventurers, and the like." And as Cornell also notes, "Harassment and infiltration exacerbated factional divisions within some groups and fostered crippling internal suspicions." By 1975 AIM had become increasingly wary of its own membership, and open debate over future plans and recruitment of new members had all but ceased.[91]

On April 16, the Eighth Circuit Court of Appeals announced that it would let stand Nichol's dismissal in Saint Paul. In a unanimous fifteen-page opinion, a three-judge panel ruled that the government had no right to appeal the dismissal, saying that whether Nichol's decision was correct "is not the question before the court." A retrial, said the panel, would constitute double jeopardy. Citing the "substantial expenditures of public funds" in a trial that produced "no definitive results," the court also expressed concern for the "tactics and procedures" used by both sides and the possible "erosion of public confidence in the effective administration of justice."[92]

Two days later the Justice Department released the results of the study ordered by Saxbe on political trials.[93] The study concluded that the goal of defense attorneys "appears to be to make the case untriable, by orchestrating the activities of the defendants, spectators, and themselves to constitute a purposeful interference with the orderly processes of trial." Tactics pointed to were excessive motions and objections, accusations of judicial bias, disrespectful behavior toward the court, and disregard of court rulings. The report singled out lawyers in the National Lawyers Guild and at the Center for Constitutional Rights in New York City. However, the central problem for the government, according to the report, was not the tactics of defense attorneys, but rather the attitudes of jurors. Juries, the study said, were too willing to be convinced of government misconduct and to believe that certain prosecutions were politically motivated: "A substantial portion of the American people seem willing to believe that the government, at least since the birth of the 'credibility gap' in the 1960's, will itself engage in misconduct in order to insure that the misconduct of others will be punished."[94]

The report blamed the media for magnifying controversies during trials and also pointed to the new jury selection process that allowed the defense to "inquire extensively into the political and social attitudes" of prospective jurors. The report also commented that no attempt was made to ascertain "the truth or falsity" of allegations of prosecutorial misconduct made in the Wounded Knee cases or in any of the other cases that were reviewed. It did concede that the use of investigative techniques such as electronic surveillance and undercover informants constituted "extensive intrusions into the daily lives of the investigated individuals" and were probably "feared by a significant segment of the populace." The report concluded, however, that judges must maintain control of the courtroom, using the power of contempt or having defendants removed, and further suggested that more attention should be given to the judicial appointment process and that stricter controls be placed on appearances by out of state attorneys.[95]

Meanwhile the legal battles continued. Midway through jury selection in the trial of five people charged in the Sioux Falls courthouse riot the year before, Judge Richard Braithwaite dismissed the charges, saying that it was impossible to select an impartial jury. The judge blamed the media for contributing to the tension and prejudice. A few days later the *Rapid City Journal* criticized the dismissal, arguing that the situation was partly the judge's fault for barring the public and the media from viewing jury selection.[96] In Iowa, where the nonleadership cases were now being tried, surveys conducted by the defense questioned whether fair trials were possible in that state. Judge Bogue's response was to move the remaining trials back to South Dakota.[97]

On June 2, in Cedar Rapids, Iowa, the trial of three of the original Wounded Knee "conspiracy" defendants, Carter Camp, Stan Holder, and Leonard Crow Dog, moved into jury selection. The prosecution had argued that the case should be heard in South Dakota, while the defense had pushed for a return to Saint Paul or another major city outside of South Dakota.[98] The relatively short trial would provide a stark contrast with its counterpart in Saint Paul. Though some of the participants were the same—Hurd and Gienapp for the prosecution and Tilsen for the defense—gone were the luminary lawyers Kunstler and Lane, the well-known defendants, and the large defense team that supported them. Tilsen was joined by attorneys Joe Beeler, who had coordinated the nonleadership cases, and Frances Schreiberg, who had helped coordinate recruitment within the NLG and worked on pretrial motions throughout 1973. In addition to the lawyers, one law student was on hand to assist during the trial.[99]

Two people from WKLDOC had arrived early to attempt to organize local support, but unlike Saint Paul there was no base of political supporters from which to build. Gone too were the masses of national and regional reporters. The defense tried to generate some pretrial publicity, but received little outside of Iowa. The *Cedar Rapids Gazette* provided coverage of rallies, and carried photographs and biographical sketches of the defendants and a summary of the events at Wounded Knee. An editorial said that although it did not endorse AIM's "goals and tactics," it welcomed them as "road weary itinerants bearing an awesome emotional load."[100] At a news conference, Tilsen called the continued prosecution "malicious" and part of an effort to destroy AIM. The indictments, he said, "are based on improper motives, lack of evidence, and were brought for the purpose of harassment." Headquartered at the People's Unitarian Church and bringing people into camp sites at a city park, AIM received some community support and held a demonstration for the opening day of the trial. But the crowds that had gathered in Saint Paul would not be duplicated.[101]

Perhaps the most important absence in Cedar Rapids was that of Judge Nichol. The U.S. Attorney had filed a motion requesting that Nichol remove himself from the trial because of "personal bias or prejudice" against the government. The motion pointed to what it termed Nichol's respect for the defendants and sympathy for what they stood for and cited his participation in a standing ovation for Kunstler at a Saint Paul luncheon and his criticism of the FBI. Nichol rejected the accusations but removed himself from the case anyway, commenting that "the court reluctantly believes that the affidavits accepted as true could lead a reasonable person to believe that bias or prejudice is present."[102]

The trial was now before U.S. District Judge Edward J. McManus, of the Northern District of Iowa. Known as a "no-nonsense" judge, McManus had disposed of all the pretrial motions during three days in May. During the hearing Hurd and Joseph Trimbach again took the stand to answer charges of government misconduct, including the new revelations of FBI informants within the defense committee. Hurd testified that the only information received from informers was that related to possible violence by AIM. He also argued that even if he had received information concerning the defense in Saint Paul, it was not relevant to the present case. Trimbach testified that at the time he denied the existence of informants inside the defense committee, he did not know that Durham was working for the Bureau. FBI agent Raymond Williams testified that he had approximately fifty contacts with Durham during the Saint Paul trial, but that he did not know of Trimbach's courtroom denials until well after they had taken place.[103]

To back up its claim of misuse of the judicial process, the defense presented figures showing that only 7 percent of the 153 Wounded Knee cases brought into court had resulted in convictions. They also put forward testimony concerning the nonprosecution of Wilson's "goon squad." Tilsen argued that "the overriding consideration in these cases is political," while Hurd maintained that there was no misconduct, despite the defense tactic of always trying to put the government on trial. Noting that the allegations were "serious," McManus took the dismissal motions under advisement, but later denied them.[104]

For jury selection, McManus allowed only a few of the numerous questions on prejudice requested by the defense and asked by Judge Nichol in Saint Paul. The whole process took less than a day and resulted in a panel of four women and eight men. Only one prospective juror was excused for cause.[105] Jay Schulman complained to the press that McManus had not allowed enough time to question the panel sufficiently regarding their views on Indians, but the newspaper noted that selection took a whole day longer than was usual for the judge.[106] Defendant Holder charged that jury selection was held in a "kangaroo-like atmosphere" and called McManus a "hurry up judge" who had made it impossible for the defendants to receive a fair trial.[107]

For the trial, the prosecution had narrowed its case to the point where one could hardly call it a conspiracy trial anymore.[108] All three defendants were charged with aiding and abetting the capture and robbery of the postal inspectors who had been detained for several hours when they tried to enter Wounded Knee on March 11. After barely two days of testimony from only three witnesses, interrupted once for a hearing on a motion to suppress evidence, the prosecution rested its case on June 4, three days after jury selection had begun. The government again presented the photographs of the inspectors lined up under armed guard and testimony placing all three defendants at the scene, including statements that Holder had identified himself to the inspectors, that Camp had explained the conditions of their release, and that Crow Dog had lectured them for forty-five minutes on the "evils of the white man." McManus had also placed strict limits on cross-examination, ruling against questions on treaty rights and conditions on the reservation.[109]

Even more surprising than the brevity of the government's case was the total lack of one for the defense. The next morning before a half-empty courtroom, Tilsen announced that the defense rested without calling a single witness to the stand. Though there had been disagreement the night before, Camp told reporters that the decision was unanimous among the three defendants: "We put on no evidence because the government had nothing for us to rebut."[110] During closing arguments the defense stressed the misstatements and identification problems on the part of government witnesses, while the prosecution argued that all three defendants had played a role in the incident. Instructions were given to the jury by McManus, and they retired to begin deliberations at 1:00 P.M. Two hours later they returned with their verdict: guilty on all counts.[111]

"Wounded Knee Three Guilty; 'No Surprise,' " read the headline in the *Cedar Rapids Gazette* the next day.[112] Confident throughout, Hurd expressed satisfaction afterward: "Even before the verdict, I felt I could go away from this case with a good taste because I felt it was a fair trial. I think justice was done."[113] Camp called McManus a "fascist" and promised demonstrations for the city in July. Holder criticized the makeup of the jury: "We are three Indians tried in an all white court by an all white jury; this proves Indians cannot receive justice."[114] He also charged the people of Cedar Rapids with harboring a "deep seated racism" behind a "liberal facade." Tilsen too blamed the decision on the racism of the all white jury, noting that two hours was not enough time to consider the evidence seriously.[115] An editorial in the *Gazette*, however, called the trial "fair" and a "model of jurisprudence," noting that the case against the defendants was "singularly uncomplicated," and that both sides had adopted "low-key strategies."[116] Calling Judge McManus "Fast Eddie," the *Minneapolis Tribune* contrasted the proceedings with the Saint Paul trial.[117]

In four days the U.S. government had won its first and only convictions against any of the individuals who had been singled out as leaders of the

Wounded Knee takeover. Tilsen believed that, considering the number of charges and years in prison that the conspiracy defendants faced under the original indictments, the conviction could still be considered a victory for the defense.[118] Prosecutors, however, pointed to the case as an example of how a criminal trial should be conducted.[119] After the verdict they announced that they were dropping additional charges against Camp and those against the remaining co-conspirator, Clyde Bellecourt. A motion for a new trial, alleging jury bias, insufficient evidence, and various other due process errors, was denied.[120] July would come and go without the large demonstrations that Holder and Camp had promised. Instead, in August, calling the protest at Wounded Knee an "armed insurrection" which went "beyond the non-violent approach to social injustice," McManus sentenced Crow Dog to three years on one count and eight years on the other, to run concurrently, then suspended the sentence and placed him on probation for five years. Camp and Holder failed to appear for sentencing and had their bonds revoked and warrants issued for their arrest.[121]

By summer it must have looked to AIM as if the frustration and disappointment of 1975 would never end. Newspapers commenting on the poor attendance at the AIM convention in New Mexico claimed that the organization was dead. Amid heavy security, Dennis Banks went on trial in South Dakota for his role in the Custer riot, represented by a court-appointed attorney. On June 26, a gun battle on Pine Ridge left two FBI agents and one Native American dead. The case would eventually result in the conviction of Leonard Peltier and would become a new cause for AIM and its supporters. In separate incidents, Russell Means was shot by a BIA policeman and assaulted by a group of anti-AIM men. Means said that he had been arrested thirteen times in the past twenty-five months, had bonds totaling $130,000, and was facing eight trials. There were also reports of bombings at the Mount Rushmore Visitors Center and the BIA office in Alameda, California. Before the summer was over, John Trudell had been charged with assault in Nevada, and Crow Dog had been arrested for an alleged assault on the Rosebud Reservation.[122]

In July 1975, the U.S. Commission on Civil Rights issued the first of two reports to the Attorney General criticizing the conduct of the FBI on Pine Ridge following the deaths of two of its agents. The reports also noted that there had been numerous murders and assaults, which, according to many Pine Ridge residents, had not been satisfactorily investigated or explained. With the exception of the well-known activist Anna Mae Aquash, most of the deaths had not been publicized outside of South Dakota.[123] As the numbers rose—by one count there were more than fifty violent deaths from June 1973 to May 1976—charges and countercharges as to who was responsible flew back and forth between AIM and WKLDOC on one side and Wilson and the Justice Department on the other. While journalists and others who investigated the situation were divided on the question, the government remained reluctant to criticize anyone other than those identified as AIM supporters.[124]

The only indictments handed down against Wilson and his supporters had come in May, for the alleged assaults committed against WKLDOC volunteers on Pine Ridge in February. The columnist Jack Anderson claimed that the indictments came only after prodding by him, a charge that U.S. Attorney Clayton denied.[125] In September the U.S. Court of Appeals announced that it was upholding the dismissal of a civil suit against six FBI agents for false arrest of people trying to bring food into Wounded Knee in 1973, contending that the agents had been acting in good faith despite the technicalities of the federal anti-riot statute.[126] In October an explosion damaged the BIA office in Pine Ridge, as the battles on the reservation continued through the fall, and FBI agents and U.S. Marshals maintained a presence on the reservation.[127]

By the end of the year WKLDOC had dwindled down to a handful of people coordinating what remained of the Custer and Wounded Knee–related cases and, later, the defense of those arrested for the murder of the two FBI agents in June.[128] Dennis Banks had been convicted of rioting and assault for his part in the Custer protest. Facing fifteen years in a South Dakota prison, he went underground, eventually receiving asylum from California Governor Jerry Brown.[129] Russell Means had been sentenced to thirty days for petty assault while being acquitted of aggravated assault in the altercation at the country club in Mission and then found guilty of rioting for his part in the Sioux Falls courthouse altercation in 1974. Dick Wilson was found not guilty of assaulting two WKLDOC volunteer lawyers on Pine Ridge in February. He continued as Tribal Chairman for another year before being defeated in a bid for a third term.[130]

On March 31, as the North Vietnamese army overran South Vietnam, President Ford's "earned reentry program" for fugitive draft resisters and military deserters came to an end, less than one year after it had been announced. Only 6 percent of the 350,000 eligible men had applied for the program, and fewer than half of those would complete the two years of alternative service required to earn an undesirable or clemency discharge. Many contrasted the terms of the President's plan with his unconditional pardon of Nixon. Just as many, perhaps, believed that any "amnesty" for war resisters and deserters was unforgivable.[131] Yet Ford had persisted, and President Jimmy Carter announced yet another plan for pardoning resisters the day after his inauguration in 1977.

Even by the end of 1975, few in Washington and even fewer in South Dakota seemed willing to offer AIM any amnesty. In the end, perhaps there was little difference between official Washington's response to draft resisters and its response to Indian protesters. The "amnesty" or pardons that had been offered to resisters had been couched in terms like "mercy" and "clemency." During the 1976 presidential campaign Carter told veterans' groups that offering a pardon meant offering forgiveness for acts that were wrong.[132] The rewriting of the history of the Vietnam War and the surrounding period had begun even before the fall of Saigon in the spring of 1975. As those who had protested and resisted America's intervention in Southeast Asia read how it was they who had caused the deaths of over 50,000 Americans, they entered another war, one over the ownership of history, a war in which Native Americans had been involved since the European invasion.

In 1865, when the Civil War came to an end, few confederate officials spent any time in prison, and only one was hanged for war crimes. Within a relatively short period of time, many were once again holding public office. The treatment of those who rebelled against the union in 1860, causing a war that took half a million lives, stood in stark contrast to the treatment of the Dakota Indians who had also rebelled against the union in 1862, causing a war that took fewer than a thousand lives. The Dakota who awaited trial before a military court were not to be considered prisoners of war, said General Henry Sibley, "but rather as outlaws and villains."[133] On December 26, a few days before President Lincoln's Emancipation Proclamation was to take effect, thirty-eight Dakota were hanged in Mankato. The remaining 1,300 who had been imprisoned were banished from Minnesota. The stories of these two uprisings are rarely told together, and one is rarely told at all.

In December 1975, the Pentagon released documents that supported the defense contention that Wounded Knee had been a military operation, including a memo stating that the protest had posed no threat to the nation, but rather was "a source of irritation if not embarrassment to the Administration in general and the Department of Justice in particular."[134] A *New York Times* story reported on the "spectacular successes" of Indian tribes who "without much fanfare" were "using the system" to assert treaty rights through litigation and lobbying and contrasted those efforts with the "militant" protest tactics of AIM, which the article said played only a "minor" role in the Indian rights struggle.[135] A week later, in response to a bill before the U.S. Senate to compensate the heirs of the victims of Wounded Knee 1890, the U.S. Army announced that, contrary to current accounts, army documents showed that the deaths of more than 150 Sioux constituted not a massacre but rather a "spontaneous battle," during which "both sides got carried away." Both Vernon Bellecourt and author Vine Deloria denounced the report.[136]

Both inside and outside of the courtroom, the government and the media repeatedly sought to separate the leadership of AIM from what they viewed as more moderate forces in the Indian community. Now the links between protest and legal reform in the Indian movement were being severed, just as some had tried to do with the civil rights struggle. Earlier in the year, representatives of twenty-four Indian tribes from seven western states had told federal officials that they were not interested in participating in the upcoming bicentennial celebration. Indians are "fighting day-to-day just to survive," said Jerry Flute, Chairman of the Sisseton-Wahpeton Sioux Tribal Council in South Dakota: "Just to make it through one more day alive—and we just are not very interested in celebrating anything."[137]

10
RETELLING STORIES
OF HISTORY AND POWER

What law have I broken? Is it wrong for me to love my own? Is it wicked for me because my skin is red? Because I am Lakota, because I was born where my father died, because I would die for my people and my country?

TATANKA-IYOTANKA (SITTING BULL)

L ITTLE BY LITTLE an image was built up of an enemy of society who can equally well be a revolutionary or a murderer," writes Foucault, "since all revolutionaries do sometimes kill."[1] On the last day of 1975, a South Dakota judge, saying "you and society are at odds," sentenced Russell Means to four years in prison for his conviction in the Sioux Falls courthouse riot in 1974.[2] At the same time his former co-defendant, Dennis Banks, convicted on the charge of riot for his part in the protest at Custer, was out on bail in California, awaiting extradition proceedings that could return him to South Dakota for sentencing.

More than a year after the two AIM leaders' charges for crimes committed at Wounded Knee had been dismissed, the law had answered the question posed by the media at the start of their trial in Saint Paul; Banks and Means had gone from "modern day Sitting Bulls" to "common criminals." What most of the media chose to ignore was that in the history of Indian resistance there had been little difference between the two characterizations. In the 1880s after his surrender, Sitting Bull traveled with Buffalo Bill's Wild West Show as the "Conqueror of Custer," on display as a living relic of the "Indian wars" that were already being rewritten in the media and popular culture. But in 1890 the aging Lakota leader died resisting arrest because U.S. officials feared he might rekindle the armed resistance of his people if he were allowed to meet with the leaders of the Ghost Dance movement.

What the state is afraid of, writes Jacques Derrida, is "fundamental, founding violence, that is, violence able to justify, to legitimate, . . . or to transform the relations of law ('legal conditions'), and so to present itself as having a right to law."[3] In the late 1960s and early 1970s, it must have seemed as if revolutionaries were everywhere; even the children of the upper classes were rebelling on college campuses across the country. If the Indian resurgence seemed more frightening than the free speech movement or even the Vietnam antiwar movement, it may have been because Indian resistance had always challenged something fundamental in American society.

Throughout history, the assertion of any vocal presence by Indians challenged a whole nation's interpretation of its glorious past. From the beginning U.S.-Indian relations were dominated by the question of land, and the treaties that were negotiated still provide Indian tribes with a "distinct legal standing" and bargaining power even in the late twentieth century.[4] But while the challenges today are often made through traditional legal channels, the contest is still between distinctly different systems, in one of which the importance placed on the land is often spiritual as well as economic.

Following John Locke's assertion that "the great and chief end" of men in forming a government was the "preservation of their property," the framers of the Constitution devised a governmental structure that protected unequal property holdings and insulated both property and inequality from democratic and legal transformation.[5] The superiority of this law over the customs of the "fierce savages" who occupied the continent before the coming of the Europeans was legitimized by the Supreme Court early on. "To leave them in possession of their country," wrote Chief Justice John Marshall in 1823, "was to leave the country a wilderness."[6] Throughout the nineteenth century the shifting law of property continually justified the encroachments into Indian territory, despite treaties to the contrary, and this law was eventually imposed on the Lakota and other tribes with the establishment of the reservation and allotment systems. In the eyes of Indian reformers, the "civilizing influences" of property ownership were the Indians' only hope for survival into the twentieth century.[7]

What made the Ghost Dance dangerous in 1890 was what made Wounded Knee dangerous in 1973: both events challenged the intended dominance of the nation's values and institutions by stepping outside those institutions, including the established channels of redress under American constitutionalism. Legal claims for the return of land taken a century earlier were frightening enough, but AIM and others used the treaties to justify direct action, from Alcatraz to Pine Ridge to the BIA offices in Washington. "You had the guns, you had the ammunition, you had the food, we needed it and we took it," Dennis Banks reportedly told a Wounded Knee trading post employee in 1973. Indians who challenged U.S. authority in 1890 and in 1973 all committed crimes, but just as the Ghost Dance could have been regarded as an act of religious freedom as well as an exercise of sovereignty, so too could the 1973 occupation of reservation land have been considered, in the words of a Justice Department report, "a forceful exercise of Indian self-determination on Indian territory."

Exercises of self-determination, however, challenge rules, rules that define social and economic relations of society and confer authority on dominant social interests. As Alan Hunt observes, the ideology of the rule of law reinforces and celebrates a social unity and cohesion that do not exist in actuality by representing certain political and social relations as natural and universal.[8] The sudden resurgence of Native American activism that erupted in the late sixties "had the potential to undercut more than a century of settled expectations and redistribute power in a material way."[9] Those challenged expectations had defined who Indians were, how and where they lived—or, to be more precise, how and where they no longer lived.

When Sitting Bull asked what laws he had broken, the answer from U.S. authorities could have been given in a single word: "Ours." From the establishment of the Constitution of 1787 to the challenge to U.S. authority issued at Wounded Knee in 1973, Indians did not make the policies that governed their lives. "We are not free. We do not make choices," said National Indian Youth Council president Clyde Warrior in 1967. "Our choices are made for us; we are the poor."[10]

In 1973, government prosecutors who sought to enforce the law took it as they found it—from the simple charge of crimes against property to the elaborate conspiracy counts—recorded in legislative acts and judicial opinions. That both whites and Indians were "victims" of the takeover reinforced the contention that the rules were being enforced equally.[11] Such equality in the protection of property, however, hid fundamental cultural differences and regarded the property relations between Indians and the government as if they had never been in conflict.[12] What the law did not reflect was that the small plots of land held by individuals at

Wounded Knee had derived from the imposition of the allotment system, which had stripped away the Oglalas' "natural rights" to hold their land according to their laws and traditions, and sought to rob them of their cultural identity as well.[13]

Once they had been forced into court, the task of the protesters turned criminal defendants was to direct the focus of the proceedings toward the history and political issues that directly challenged the validity of the law as applied to Native Americans and the authority of anyone other than Indians to govern Indian conduct. Reflecting back on the conflicting legal and political agendas, even former U.S. Attorney Clayton conceded that the defense had succeeded in its efforts: "They wanted to make it a political case as part of their defense and we tried to keep the treaty issue out and treat it as common law crimes, and I think they succeeded in their view better than we succeeded in our view."[14]

What success WKLDOC and its clients had, however, came as the result of a tremendous organized effort and a certain amount of luck. The factors that proved helpful at different points—juries, judges, defense attorneys, and even the media—all necessitated a struggle for the defendants. And when it was over, a Justice Department study of political trials singled out each of those factors as having failed to live up to its "proper" role in the proceedings.

Moving the central trial to Saint Paul, a city with a strong liberal and even radical political history, and one that was a considerable distance from the conflict at Wounded Knee, was certainly a factor. Whether, as the Justice Department argued in its study, Minnesota jurors were susceptible to being convinced that the government could be guilty of misconduct is not clear, but according to press interviews the majority of the jurors seemed to be leaning toward the defense by the time Nichol dismissed the charges. In addition, the Twin Cities provided legal and political activists, both white and Indian, who rallied to the cause.

Judges were also an issue in the cases. When Judge Nichol dismissed the case against Banks and Means in the fall of 1974, he added to the victories that had already been won by the defense before Judge Urbom. Urbom's acquittals saved many defendants from being tried by South Dakota juries, yet the government reserved its criticism for the judge who presided over the only trial where the media was regularly in attendance. The prosecutors believe that Nichol's natural openness made him susceptible to being used, and that his fear of being accused of being another Judge Hoffman caused him to bend over backwards to accommodate the defense and ultimately to lose control of the trial.[15] On the other side, the defense praises his courage, and both Banks and Kunstler refer to Nichol as a barometer of the case, leaning toward the government in the beginning and becoming strongly critical of it by the end.[16] For his part, Nichol denies that the defense's courtroom tactics intimidated him, but the Justice Department's review pointed to judges as the key to controlling political cases and suggested that it might consider "pressing Congress to revise the present methods of selection of judges."[17]

Attorneys also played a major role, not just in Saint Paul, where Kunstler and Lane received their share of the publicity, but also in less publicized trials, where lawyers from the NLG and NACDL, backed by legal workers and law students, were also successful in navigating their clients' stories through and around the rules of the courtroom. The Justice Department report complained about the ability of certain attorneys to try cases to the general public and urged judges to exercise more control over their activities. Even Chief Justice Warren Burger attacked what he termed "disruptive" lawyers in a 1973 speech, cautioning that their proper role was as "society's peace makers, problem solvers and stabilizers." Kunstler responded by asserting that "the existence of an independent bar [was] directly related to the continuance and expansion of our most fundamental rights and liberties."[18]

What was effective in Saint Paul and elsewhere was not courtroom disruption, but the ability of the defense to put constant pressure on the prosecution and at the same time present a narrative to which judges, juries, and the public were receptive. Throughout the proceedings, prosecutors were forced to defend either government misdeeds toward Native Americans or the FBI's mishandling of evidence, topics which too easily fit into the headlines emanating from Washington. The daily news stories on Watergate provided the right context for the attacks, and the Justice Department commented that juries were "composed of people willing to be convinced of government misconduct."[19] David Gienapp laments: "We were in the middle of Watergate and everybody was seeing a conspiracy under every stone."[20]

As Watergate unraveled, many in the Nixon administration blamed the media for the public's willingness to believe the worst about their elected officials. It was an attitude that carried over to the losses in political trials. The government criticized the media for providing "an additional extensive audience" for such trials and helping to rally support among people with no prior affiliation to radical causes. Prosecutors felt that the media attention devoted to the defendants and their political issues distracted from the courtroom testimony.[21]

From the televised Kennedy/Nixon debates to the coverage of the Vietnam War protests, the media had begun to play an increasingly pivotal role in shaping the public's views of political and social relations. The American people were becoming dependent on media images to shape their attitudes and assumptions about the political and cultural changes taking place around them. As Stanley Kutler notes in *The Wars of Watergate*, Nixon's presidency paralleled this rising importance of the media, and the administration continually sought to "manipulate and tame" its coverage of politics. In Kutler's words, "the media had become an essential component in the task of governance in the late-twentieth century America."[22]

As government increasingly used the media to promote its agenda, so too did those challenging it. Social movements became increasingly reliant on the press to bring attention to their causes.[23] In 1973, even the Justice Department agreed that AIM and the activists on Pine Ridge had scored a publicity coup with the protest at Wounded Knee.[24] A year later in Saint Paul, AIM and WKLDOC used the high-profile trial of Banks and Means to again make substantive points about history and current conditions on reservations and in cities throughout the country. "We wanted the courtroom packed," says Banks, and the capacity crowds helped to keep up the interest and enthusiasm that supplied much-needed volunteers and money, and kept some involved in the Indian movement long after the trials had ended.[25]

The publicity, however, came at a price, as it had for other political movements that surged onto the floodlit stage of national attention during the 1960s. "In the ratings game," writes Stuart Ewen, "the news—out of economic necessity—must be transformed into a drama, a thriller, entertainment."[26] The high-profile occupations of Alcatraz and Wounded Knee provided the kind of flamboyance and drama that easily attracted national media attention, and during the trials that followed, too often it was only when the drama of courtroom confrontations matched the armed standoff on the plains that the story moved to the front pages and the nightly network news programs.

Like Sitting Bull, vocal or militant Native Americans had always been easily marginalized in the press and popular culture, alternately portrayed as sideshow attractions and dangerous enemies. The confrontation between protesters and federal officials at Wounded Knee conjured up too many Hollywood images of Indian warriors versus the U.S. cavalry to be resisted. Indians, as Robert Berkhofer notes in *The White Man's Indian*, are real enough, but they are also an invention or stereotype in the white imagination. "For most Whites throughout the past five centuries," writes Berkhofer, "the Indian of imagination and ideology has been as real, perhaps more real, than the Native American of actual existence and contact." In paintings, photographs, novels, movies, and finally television, Indians have served as art and entertainment for generations.[27]

In the political and social upheaval of the 1960s, however, Indians were not the only group marginalized by images developed in the popular press. By the end of Wounded Knee, the Indian movement's experience reflected not just its own history, but also the experiences of other political and cultural movements that had attempted to capitalize on national media attention to promote their goals. By the late sixties the antiwar movement, for instance, had gained momentum with the help of the media, but the attention had also turned many of its leaders into celebrities and its issues into slogans and headlines.[28]

The highly publicized takeovers of the BIA headquarters and Wounded Knee bestowed celebrity status on some AIM leaders that had as much to do with white expectations as with Indian actions. Women in AIM watched as the image of the warrior took center stage in front of the cameras, and they recognized both the risks and the necessity of what was happening.[29] From the Panthers to the PLO, the white media's fascination with the image of the Third World warrior could serve both the movement and the male egos that led it. Militant actions and rhetoric brought the cameras and microphones to people and voices that were otherwise ignored, but the image-making publicity could also separate leaders from their constituencies and reduce the movement to an interesting curiosity or a dangerous conspiracy. "We got lost in our own manhood," says John Trudell; "we became men who became leaders and then we started protecting our political leader image, our political leader identity, which became more important than the overall needs of the community."[30]

As the Saint Paul trial opened, the press devoted space and air time to describing the physical characteristics and the dress of both the defendants. The equally famous male criminal lawyers, skilled at verbal battles and identified with radical causes, fit the bill perfectly as advocates for such towering figures as Means and Banks. Press descriptions of courtroom conflicts often meshed the images of Indian warriors with those of Vietnam antiwar militants, and fit right into media coverage of violence or potential violence on reservations and college campuses. The witnesses and issues of both sides received coverage, but just as often it was what these dynamic, articulate men did or said that was the main story of the trial.

When the first eruption between Kunstler and Nichol drove most of the defendants' opening statements off the front pages, the most frequently quoted part of the two speeches was Means's discussion of newfound Indian manhood on the reservation. The coverage of closing arguments was also treated as drama and had as much to do with contrasting styles as with substance. Through it all women legal workers and defendants were instrumental in holding WKLDOC together outside Saint Paul and contributed substantially to the cases in every location. Women in AIM and OSCRO continued to organize on Pine Ridge; women elders participated in the treaty hearing in Lincoln; and occasionally, women such as Madonna Gilbert or Gladys Bissonette would get the attention of the press in a news conference or on the witness stand. Yet the names still associated with the Wounded Knee trials are the names of the male defendants, attorneys, and judge in the Saint Paul trial.

Even the successful attack on government misconduct which eventually tied itself to the intrigues in Washington may have helped to overshadow the more substantive issues. Watergate, which dominated the front pages and served as the context for the charges of misconduct in Saint Paul, was also a battle of men. Gladys Bissonette stood out on the stand in Saint Paul for the same reasons Barbara Jordan stood out in the impeachment hearings in the House of Representatives. There was a different tone and quality to what both women had to say in the midst of proceedings that were dominated by men. After the Saint Paul trial ended and the postmortems had been exhausted, substantive issues such as treaty rights or the reorganization of the BIA had to compete with all the other stories of social conditions that get scant attention. Another arrest of Means was just as likely to get coverage as a new account of the hungry on Pine Ridge. The press had drifted away until the takeover of an abbey in Wisconsin and the deaths of two FBI agents on Pine Ridge in 1975 put Indians back on the front pages and in the nightly news.

Still, in the end, the words and phrases that articulated Indian existence, Indian dissent, had been heard. Often the message was muted or distorted, reduced to the one-liners we now call sound bites, but more information from the perspective of the witnesses, those living the experience, was available to a larger number of people than at any previous time in history. The broken treaties, the conditions on Pine Ridge and other reservations, all the constant reminders of one of the saddest chapters in American history, had forced their way onto the national agenda over a longer period of time than ever before.

Small substantive changes after Wounded Knee and the trials that followed could also be seen. Congress authorized compensation for the Black Hills, and the government allocated more money to the Pine Ridge Reservation for schools, housing, and an Indian-run radio station. Reservation residents also won greater control over the BIA police. The BIA Superintendent for Pine Ridge was transferred, an audit was performed on the tribal books, and the Justice Department convened a grand jury to investigate violence on the reservation and filed a brief questioning the recent tribal election.

South Dakota Senator James Abourezk credited Wounded Knee with helping to bring the issue of Indian-government relations into the public arena and noted that it was getting easier to win congressional funding for Indian programs. In 1975 Congress passed the Indian Self-Determination and Educational Assistance Act, and in 1977 the Interior Department established the post of assistant secretary of the interior for Indian affairs and named an Indian to be its first occupant.[31]

On Pine Ridge, the basic issues of treaty rights and extreme poverty still remain, but there have been changes, according to Ted Means, who still lives on the reservation.[32] AIM may have ceased to function as a national organization for the most part, but many activists who have stayed involved in local Indian struggles continue to think of themselves as part of an ongoing movement. They see Wounded Knee as helping to instill a positive self-consciousness in Indians that is still evident in struggles today, whether today's participants give AIM credit or not.[33] Most observers note an awareness of culture, tradition, treaty rights, and sovereignty on the part of Native Americans that did not exist prior to 1960.[34] Across the country, lobbying and litigation increased as more tribes sought enforcement of old treaties guaranteeing boundaries, fishing and hunting rights, and protection of natural resources. "We put out a bumper sticker, 'AIM for Sovereignty.' Most of our people didn't even know what the word meant," said Vernon Bellecourt: "Now they know."[35]

The multicultural struggle that WKLDOC organized is also significant. Like "freedom summer" in the midst of the civil rights movement, the defense constituted a genuine interracial political effort that lasted for several years and helped inspire a continuing multiracial treaty rights effort and the birth of the Native American Solidarity Committee and Committee on Native American Struggles of the National Lawyers Guild. During the 1980s, on Pine Ridge and elsewhere, Indians and whites began to recognize a commonality on issues concerning land use and the environment.[36]

As much as it was rooted in Indian history, the story of the Native American resurgence and its confrontation with the U.S. government is a part of the story of 1960s political activism. Few movements that emerged during that time had survived in one unified piece by 1975. As the country moved toward the election of Ronald Reagan, people looked for ways to forget, to rewrite the stories of the civil rights struggle, Vietnam, and Watergate. The tide of public opinion turned, not against Indians, but against all the messengers who were blamed for the recent painful past. Despite the defeat in Vietnam and the fall of Nixon, the left's general critique of society had not captured the hearts and minds of many Americans. Even AIM's highly visible victory in Saint Paul came by a judge's ruling on the law— or rather, violations of the law that were tied to a corrupt administration and not necessarily the institutions of government.[37]

What was perhaps most striking about the times is also what is most striking about the official reaction to the Indian resurgence and AIM in particular: the unrelenting government desire to quash dissent from wherever and whomever it came. Whether it was nonviolent civil rights organizers or militant black power advocates, radical students or Catholic priests who opposed the war, the government spied on, harassed, maligned, subverted, and jailed virtually anyone who questioned its policies and the motives behind them. Before the era had passed, AIM had drawn as much attention as anyone. Few political organizations can boast of going up against the White House, Congress, the FBI, the U.S. Marshals, the Pentagon, the BIA, the Justice Department, the U.S Attorney's office, the 82nd Airborne, and various state and local law enforcement and prosecutorial branches, all within a period of less than ten years.

From May 1973 through the end of 1975, AIM and its supporters battled to defend the people charged with committing crimes at Wounded Knee, Custer, and elsewhere. Forced to travel to raise money and publicize the trials, AIM members were constantly on the road, away from the reservation or other home bases, becoming more disconnected from their constituencies. They were also increasingly wary of the constant infiltration and surveillance. By the mid-1970s, suspicion and fear affected AIM's ability to openly debate and discuss plans for the future and recruit new members. The cost of the trials and the continued battles with law enforcement agencies had drained all potential donors, leaving the organization without the resources to initiate new campaigns and continue the struggle.[38] Ultimately the defense work, no matter how many victories or how much favorable publicity there had been, had taken its toll.

Many critics of the government's reaction to Wounded Knee still believe that the legal and extralegal campaign waged against the movement was unrelenting precisely because of the depth and credibility of AIM's critique of Indian-government relations. In an article published in the fall of 1976, Ken Tilsen noted that of the original 185 indictments, all but two had been disposed of. There were fifteen convictions, eleven for felonies, six of which were pending before the Court of Appeals, while four others were being appealed to the Supreme Court. Tilsen pointed out that the conviction rate for indictments disposed of in the U.S. District Courts within the Eighth Circuit was 78.2 percent, compared with the 7.7 percent conviction rate for the Wounded Knee cases. The statistics, Tilsen argued, raised serious questions about the validity of the prosecutions.[39]

There was also the Justice Department report on Wounded Knee, which admitted that the seizure of the BIA building on Pine Ridge could have been considered a "forceful exercise of Indian self-determination on Indian territory." A national poll taken during the siege showed a nation in sympathy with the protesters inside the small village. Yet the government began filing charges before it was over, and later, despite continued courtroom losses, kept on prosecuting.

Under existing laws, prosecutors could rightfully claim that they had no choice but to prosecute. Win or lose in court, the government's belief was that the prosecutions sent a message to AIM and others who committed crimes to further a political agenda:

> I think to some extent the prosecutions accomplished as much by getting dismissed or an acquittal as they would have had there been a conviction. Because I think Russell Means and Dennis Banks realized even if you get off, sitting nine months in a courtroom isn't what they want to do, and that's what potentially would happen if they did this again. If you look historically, there was the Custer courtroom situation, there were the courthouse riots in Sioux Falls, there was the Wounded Knee situation, all in 72, 73, 74—this hasn't occurred since then.[40]

Further, the prosecutors note that charging certain participants with felony conspiracy is a standard prosecutorial decision aimed at identifying those who are the most culpable because they encouraged others to commit crimes. "If the Wounded Knee takeover had ended and there had been no prosecution of leadership," argues Hurd, "the leadership would have caused another incident someplace else."[41] Colonel Volney Warner, the Pentagon's liaison at Wounded Knee, expressed similar sentiments: "AIM's most militant leaders and followers (over 300) are under indictment, in jail or warrants are out for their arrest, but the government can win even if no one goes to prison."[42]

Does all this give credence to the claim that the prosecutions were politically motivated? Words uttered in defense of the prosecution of a criminal conspiracy may easily be viewed by some as an expression of intent to quash a political movement. Others, like Pine Ridge Tribal Chairman Dick Wilson, continued to assert that the government had not done enough.[43]

Arguing about the intent or motives of particular officials, however, perhaps deflects a more damning criticism of the prosecutions and the legal and political institutions that generated them. What is deeply disturbing about the prosecution of a small group of Native Americans, who out of frustration and anger with government policies did break laws, is that their prosecution need not have started with evil intent or proceeded with violations of the rules of procedure. As William Kunstler so eloquently pointed out in his closing argument, the prosecution for crimes may be lawful and still take the heart out of a social movement. Surely the American revolutionaries were "guilty" of theft or destruction of property under English law, just as AIM activists were guilty under U.S. law. Stealing tea and tossing it in Boston Harbor certainly constitutes taking something and depriving the owner of its use, one of the crimes with which Wounded Knee defendants were charged. The law, as Foucault points out, must be able to turn revolutionaries into criminals to maintain order in society.

It is true that the rule of law, particularly as enforced by judges like Nichol and Urbom, offered the Wounded Knee defendants some protection from excessive government abuse. But the defendants and their attorneys, including those who give credit to Nichol and Urbom, quickly point out that without their well-organized and very public campaign around the trials, the rules might not have provided protection or allowed alternative voices to be heard in the courtroom.[44]

The Justice Department, the FBI, and the prosecutors could all have played by the rules, as they claim they did, and still have charged protesters with crimes under the law. For the prosecution to have its desired effect, there need not have been lost evidence, illegal military involvement, telephone eavesdropping, FBI cover-ups, or even a Louie Moves Camp. Any massive but lawful prosecution of the crimes that admittedly were committed at Wounded Knee could have tied AIM up in court long enough to quell its effectiveness as a national organization. "Courtrooms are used to dissipate political energy," says John Trudell; "those who get dragged into the courtroom must look at it as a way of promoting their program, of educating people, but if you're not careful it can dissipate your political energy, your momentum."[45]

Debates over the rule of law too often seem to focus on whether the law went astray. Yet a body of law designed to protect property and political power need not stray very far in its application, if at all, to discredit and destroy those who seek to voice alternatives to the assumptions that underlie the prevailing social order. Few, if any, who have even come remotely close to having an audience for such change have escaped the courtroom. Minimum protection of rules and procedures may be the best that any society can offer. That, however, is not necessarily reason for testimonials and accolades. It *is* a basis for recognizing that, given the state of the state, the courtroom will continue to be a potential forum for political debate, and rightly so.

"Why resurrect it all now. From the past. History, the old wound," asks Theresa Hak Kyung Cha. "To name it now so as not to repeat history in oblivion. To extract each fragment by each fragment from the word from the image another word another image the reply that will not repeat history in oblivion."[46] As philosophers who ponder the horror of the Holocaust remind us, the memory of history, the names of those who experienced it, who demanded and were denied justice, are always being erased, eliminated from the written record.[47] The struggle for history is the struggle for political power, for documentation of the silenced voices. "In the culture of forgetfulness," writes bell hooks, "memory alone has no meaning."[48] The very act of telling one's story, voicing an alternative to the official historical record, may become an expression of dissent capable of challenging the structures of legal and political power legitimized by that record.[49]

The modern-day resurgence of native peoples that reached beyond the North American continent continues into the 1990s, challenging the historical narrative that was considered complete a century ago and that is still invoked as precedent for law and policy decisions.[50] In 1978, the U.S. Supreme Court used an 1834 report of the Commissioner of Indian Affairs to support the proposition that Indian tribes were "without laws" or any traditional rules of governance relevant to the issue of tribal sovereignty, allowing the Court to substitute its own interpretation for that of the Suquamish tribe with respect to the latter's nineteenth-century treaty with the U.S. government.[51] In the 1980s the idea that Indians will finally disappear into American society again held sway, resulting in significant cuts in federal assistance to Native Americans that affected jobs, human services, and incomes on every reservation. Recent attempts to implement old treaty rights have been opposed as granting special privileges, while at the same time names of athletic teams are defended as designations honoring native peoples.[52]

When the old narratives are questioned, when the old myths replayed in classrooms and stadiums, legislatures and courthouses are challenged, where should the writers be? Historians concerned with the past, David William Cohen argues, must confront "the ways that popular and official constructions of the past, as well as political suppressions of historical knowledge, shape and deform the processes of knowledge production and the general knowledge of the past in the world."[53] Those who search for stability and continuity in political developments, past and present, will find it.[54] But the belief that history is an uninterrupted progression toward justice may be dislodged by introducing the testimony of the survivors, the voices that may finally find the words and phrases to describe the harm that has been done.[55]

Like the sudden, startling transgressions of saxophonist John Coltrane, where the music is redefined in a place outside the established melody, the slow, orderly progression of liberal ideals was blasted out of its continuum in the 1960s by the unexpected, explosive violence of Watts, Stonewall, and Chicago.[56] The first wave of activists had taken the principles of American democracy out of the history books and turned them into a critique of the institutions that they legitimized. But by 1970 the textbooks were being burned, and history was being written in the countereducationals conducted in Black Panther breakfast programs, feminist consciousness-raising groups, and AIM survival schools, and transformed into the disconcerting terms of *Soul on Ice, Sisterhood Is Powerful,* and *Custer Died for Your Sins.*

This is perhaps the kind of history that Foucault urged historians to write, the events that become "the reversal of a relationship of forces, the usurpation of power, the appropriation of a vocabulary turned against those who once used it . . . the entry of a masked 'other.' " Effective history, he contended, introduces discontinuity and deprives us of the reassuring stability of life and nature, and in the end, "will uproot its traditional foundations and relentlessly disrupt its pretended continuity."[57]

Indians had waged a cultural, political, and legal struggle of resistance, above and below ground, for centuries. In the late 1960s that resistance exploded into the open once again, and with it, the past came hurtling into the present. Writers and other commentators scurried to translate the unfolding events into terms easily understood by themselves and the mass American audience. Much of what was written, however, only added to the myths and prejudices of the already established record, further separating a people from their past and the contemporary activists from the events they helped to shape.

"History" must do more than legitimize the old narratives. Historical writing must unfold consciously in the present, but it must also challenge what is "known" by the contemporary audience. However impossible, writing must attempt to scrape away at the layers of interpretation that keep us disconnected from the lived experience of those who have come before us, from the possibilities intended by the historical actor. In seeking to revive the extinguished or marginalized conversation, writing recreates the possibility of new action. Writing thus undoes writing, as Blanchot counsels: "Invisibly, writing is called upon to undo the discourse in which, however unhappy we believe ourselves to be, we who have it at our disposal remain comfortably installed. From this point of view writing is the greatest violence, for it transgresses the law, every law, and also its own."[58]

In the winter of 1890, at the top of a hill near Wounded Knee Creek, the frozen dead were thrown into a mass grave. In the years that followed, the imposition of laws intent on eradicating Lakota culture sought to silence the ghosts of the men and women who had attempted one last act of defiance. But in 1973, those with memories came back to reoccupy the land, bringing with them new voices: "We're ghost dancing again," said a young Oglala warrior returned from the city. As before, word reached Washington that wild Indians were dancing in the snow, and again the soldiers came. But this time the witnesses could not be silenced, the ghosts would be heard, the rules would bend under the weight of history, and an old treaty would find its way into a court of law, where Tatanka-Iyotanka's question would be asked again and again: "What law have I broken?"

NOTES

INTRODUCTION

1. Stephen Cornell, *The Return of the Native: American Indian Political Resurgence* (New York: Oxford University Press, 1988), pp. 187–218.
2. Vine Deloria, Jr., *Behind the Trail of Broken Treaties: An Indian Declaration of Independence* (Austin: University of Texas Press, 1985), p. 23.
3. Studies of the effect of surveillance on movements other than AIM include Kenneth O'Reilly, *Racial Matters: The FBI's Secret File on Black America, 1960–1972* (New York: The Free Press, 1989); Ward Churchill and Jim Vander Wall, *Agents Of Repression: The FBI's Secret War Against the Black Panther Party and the American Indian Movement* (Boston: South End Press, 1988); Michal R. Belknap, *Cold War Political Justice: The Smith Act, The Communist Party and American Civil Liberties* (Westport, Conn.: Greenwood Press, 1978), who discusses the effect of the prosecutions and undercover agents on the Communist Party in chapter 7; Paul Chevigny, *Cops and Rebels: A Study Of Provocation* (New York: Pantheon, 1972); David G. Bromley and Anson D. Shupe, "Repression and the Decline of Social Movements: The Case of the New Religions," in *Social Movements in the Sixties and Seventies,* ed. Jo Freeman (New York: Longman, 1983), pp. 345–347; Doug McAdam, "The Decline of the Civil Rights Movement," in Freeman, *Social Movements,* pp. 298–319; Anthony Oberschall, "The Decline of the 1960s Social Movements," in *Research in Social Movements, Conflicts and Change* (Greenwich, Conn.: JAI Press, 1978), pp. 257–289.
4. Jean-François Lyotard, *The Differend: Phrases in Dispute,* trans. Georges Van Den Abbeele (Minneapolis: University of Minnesota Press, 1988), pp. 8–13.

5. Peter Nabokov, ed., *Native American Testimony: A Chronicle Of Indian-White Relations from Prophecy to the Present, 1492–1992* (New York: Penguin Books, 1991), pp. 129–133.

6. Deloria, *Behind the Trail of Broken Treaties*, p. ix.

7. Lyotard, *The Differend*, pp. 8–10. See also Jonathan Boyarin, "Europe's Indian, America's Jew: Modiano and Vizenor," in *American Indian Persistence and Resurgence*, ed. Karl Kroeber (Durham: Duke University Press, 1994), pp. 198–223. Boyarin discusses the tendency of Germans and Americans to eulogize the other's victim, which he argues encourages "amnesia" about the domination closer to home.

8. Maurice Blanchot, *The Writing of the Disaster*, trans. Ann Smock (Lincoln: University of Nebraska Press, 1986), p. 143.

9. Other writings on the trials include Peter Matthiessen, *In the Spirit of Crazy Horse* (New York: Viking Press, 1991), chap. 4; Roland Dewing, *Wounded Knee, The Meaning and Significance of the Second Incident* (New York: Irvington, 1985), chap. 7; Ken Tilsen, "Fair and Equal Justice: The FBI, Wounded Knee and Politics," *Quaere* (September 1976): 1–9, which relates the FBI influence on the prosecution; Ron Christenson, *Political Trials: Gordian Knots in the Law* (New Brunswick: Transaction, 1989), chap. 8, pp. 197–227.

10. Quoted in Nabokov, *Native American Testimony*, p. 179.

11. Quoted in Robert Anderson et al., eds., *Voices from Wounded Knee, 1973* (Rooseveltown, N.Y.: Akwesasne Notes, 1974), p. 89.

12. As Kristin Bumiller argues with respect to the testimony of rape victims, their own accounts of their experience can give authority to excluded voices: "But their perceptions of social reality, and our ability to reflect upon and understand their reality, are bounded by their capacity to express themselves in language." Bumiller, "Fallen Angels: The Representation of Violence Against women in Legal Culture," *International Journal of the Sociology of Law* 18 (1990): 132.

13. John R. Wunder, " 'Doesn't Anyone Speak Injun in This Courtroom?': New Perspectives in Native American Legal History," in *Reviews in American History* 4 (1977): 469.

14. Gerald Torres and Kathryn Milun, "Translating *Yonnondio* by Precedent and Evidence: The Mashpee Indian Case," *Duke Law Journal* (September 1990): 625–659. For a book-length study of the Mashpee case see Jack Campisi, *The Mashpee Indians: Tribe on Trial* (Syracuse: Syracuse University Press, 1991).

15. "What is at stake in a literature, in a philosophy, in a politics perhaps," argues Lyotard, "is to bear witness to differends by finding idioms for them." Lyotard, *The Differend*, p. 13. On writing legal history see William Forbath, Hendrik Hartog, and Martha Minow, "Introduction: Legal History Symposium," *Wisconsin Law Review* (1985): 759–766.

16. Steven Barkan, *Protesters on Trial: Criminal Justice in the Southern Civil Rights and Vietnam Antiwar Movements* (New Brunswick: Rutgers University Press, 1985); see, for instance, his discussion of the trial of Benjamin Spock, pp. 98–101, and of pro se defendants, pp. 117–118. See also David Sternberg, "The New Radical Criminal Trials: A Step Toward a Class-for-Itself in the American Proletariat," *Science and Society* 36 (Fall 1972): 274–301, who sees the links between

defendants and the audience as key when the defense seeks to confront the legal system during the course of the trial.

17. This is Bumiller's argument in her study of the New Bedford rape trial ("Fallen Angels," pp. 125–126, 139–140). Rape victims, as Bumiller points out, are constrained by the prosecutor's task of proving the accused rapist's guilt and thus may not have any of the agency that defendants in a political case have in influencing how their case is presented.

   In Robert Hariman's Introduction in *Popular Trials: Rhetoric, Mass Media, and the Law* (Tuscaloosa: University of Alabama Press, 1990), ed. Robert Hariman, pp. 1–16, he argues that popular trials (which he equates with political trials) should be recognized as a "genre of public discourse," providing a forum for advocacy and a means of persuasion. See also Hariman, "Performing the Laws: Popular Trials and Social Knowledge," in *Popular Trials*, pp. 17–30.

18. Steven Barkan argues that coverage of antiwar defendants was often sympathetic and that the defendants and their lawyers sought media publicity through "moral and political arguments." Barkan, *Protesters on Trial*, p. 94. See also John F. Bannan and Rosemary S. Bannan, *Law, Morality and Vietnam: The Peace Militants and the Courts* (Bloomington: Indiana University Press, 1974); Peter Schrag, *Test of Loyalty: Daniel Ellsberg and the Rituals of Secret Government* (New York: Simon and Schuster, 1975); and J. Justin Gustainis, "Crime as Rhetoric: The Trial of the Catonsville Nine," in *Popular Trials*, ed. Hariman, pp. 164–178, who argues that despite a strong political defense the defendants never were able to reach a wide audience with their political message.

19. *The Whole World Is Watching: Mass Media in the Making and Unmaking of the New Left* (Berkeley: University of California Press, 1980), p. 9.

20. Murray Edelman, *Constructing the Political Spectacle* (Chicago: University of Chicago Press, 1988), p. 1.

21. Guy Debord, *Society of the Spectacle* (Detroit: Black and Red, 1983), secs. 3 and 4.

22. Hall argues that minorities can define themselves on the margins but that they must compete in what he calls the "center" where meaning is shaped. The media, television, film, visual arts, photography, and the evening news, he asserts, all make that struggle easier, but he cautions that the closer any group moves to the center, the closer it comes to losing by being co-opted. Lecture by Stuart Hall given at the Silha Center for the Study of Media Ethics and Law at the University of Minnesota, Spring 1987.

23. Juliet Dee, "Constraints on Persuasion in the Chicago Seven Trial," in *Popular Trials*, ed. Hariman, pp. 86–113. See also Barkan, *Protesters on Trial*, pp. 102, 117, 140; David J. Danelski, "The Chicago Conspiracy Trial," in Theodore L. Becker, *Political Trials* (Indianapolis: Bobbs-Merrill, 1971), pp. 134–180; and James W. Ely, Jr., "The Chicago Conspiracy Case," in Michal R. Belknap, *American Political Trials* (Westport, Conn.: Greenwood Press, 1981), pp. 262–285.

24. Gitlin, *The Whole World Is Watching*, p. 3. Gitlin maintains that the narrower the movement's base, the greater is its commitment to specific society-wide goals; and the more it thinks of itself as being in a revolutionary situation, the more dependent it is on the mass media. This contradiction, he argues, put Students

for a Democratic Society (SDS) at war with itself, debating its own media-produced image. A similar point applied to the sixties movements in general is made by Anthony Oberschall in "The Decline of the 1960s Social Movements." See also Richard B. Kielbowicz and Clifford Scherer, "The Role of the Press in the Dynamics of Social Movements," in *Research in Social Movements, Conflicts and Change* (Greenwich, Conn.: JAI Press, 1986), vol. 9, pp. 71–86.

25. Lucie E. White, "Subordination, Rhetorical Survival Skills, and Sunday Shoes: Notes on the Hearing of Mrs. G," *Buffalo Law Review* 38 (1990): 48.

26. Foucault's comments with respect to discourses of sexual repression were aimed at sexual liberationists Wilhelm Reich and Herbert Marcuse, who believed that repression of sexual awareness and sexual activity supported militarist regimes and commodity capitalism. *The History of Sexuality: Volume I, An Introduction* (New York: Vintage Books, 1980), pp. 130–131. Bumiller makes the same point with respect to highly publicized rape trials in "Fallen Angels," p. 132.

27. Jean Genet, *Prisoner of Love*, trans. Barbara Bray (Hanover: Wesleyan University Press, 1992), p. 10.

28. Barkan demonstrates that coverage of civil rights demonstrations and the "police and civilian brutality" in the south was crucial in securing northern sympathy and putting pressure on Congress, but that the coverage usually "stopped at the courtroom door" where thousands of criminal proceedings took place with relatively little outside scrutiny. Barkan, *Protesters on Trial*, pp. 94–95.

29. See Mary Crow Dog, *Lakota Woman*, with Richard Erdoes (New York: Harper Perennial edition, 1991), pp. 65–69, 131–132. See also Marla N. Powers, *Oglala Women: Myth, Ritual and Reality* (Chicago: University of Chicago Press, 1986), pp. 141–160, 203–214; Rayna Green, "Native American Women," *SIGNS*, 6 (Winter 1980): 248–276; Nancy Shoemaker, Introduction for *Negotiators of Change: Historical Perspectives on Native American Women* (New York: Routledge, 1995), pp. 2–13.

30. Carol Smart terms courtroom discourse "phallogocentric," arguing that trials test the truth of testimony according to set rules of argument and logic that replicate masculine aggressive verbosity and machismo. Doing law and being identified as masculine, she argues, are congruent. *Feminism and the Power of Law* (London and New York: Routledge, 1989), pp. 86–87.

31. Women in AIM, even those considered to be in leadership, generally played less prominent roles in the organization, as did women, especially the non-lawyers, who worked on the trials for the defense. Their experiences derived from their history as Indian women, but were also similar to those of women in the civil rights movement and the new left. On the latter see Alice Echols, *Daring to Be Bad: Radical Feminism in America, 1967–1975* (Minneapolis: University of Minnesota Press, 1989), chaps. 1–3; Sara Evans, *Personal Politics: The Roots of Women's Liberation in the Civil Rights Movement and the New Left* (New York: Random House, 1979); and on nonhierarchical leadership in the women's movement, see M. Helen Brown, "Organizing Activity in the Women's Movement: An Example of Distributed Leadership," *International Social Movement Research*, vol. 2, ed. Bert Klandermans (Greenwood, Conn.: JAI Press, 1989), pp. 225–240.

32. Without losing sight of the long history of Native American resistance from which it derives, the modern Indian movement must also be integrated into future narratives of the 1960s, a period of history, as Alice Echols argues, that needs to be more broadly defined and placed into the context of the postwar struggle for social justice. Alice Echols, " 'We Gotta Get Out of This Place': Notes Toward a Remapping of the Sixties," *Socialist Review* 22 (1992): 9–33.

33. Douglas Coupland, *Generation X: Tales for an Accelerated Culture* (New York: St. Martins Press, 1991), p. 151.

34. For a discussion of the Indian activists' difficulty in communicating even with their allies, see Deloria, *Behind the Trail of Broken Treaties,* pp. 2–4, 23–25.

35. See Karl Marx, "The Eighteenth Brumaire of Louis Bonaparte," first published in 1852 (a portion of which is quoted in the epigraph at the beginning of this chapter). Karl Marx and Frederick Engels, *Selected Works* (Moscow: Progress Publishers, 1973) vol. 1, pp. 389–487. I do not, however, agree with Marx that all of the symbols of the past need be rejected in order for a progressive movement to be successful, and I suspect that most people in the Indian movement, which has its cultural history at its core, would probably disagree also.

1. THE ROAD TO WOUNDED KNEE

1. Vine Deloria, *Behind the Trail of Broken Treaties: An Indian Declaration of Independence* (Austin: University of Texas Press, 1985), p. 251.

2. Donald Fixico, *Termination and Relocation: Federal Indian Policy, 1945–1960* (Albuquerque: University of New Mexico Press, 1992), p. x.

3. The seven bands of the Lakota or Teton Sioux were the Oglala, Brûlé, Miniconjou, Sans Arc, Two Kettles, Hunkpapa, and Sihaspa (Blackfeet). Richard White, "The Winning of the West: The Expansion of the Western Sioux in the Eighteenth and Nineteenth Centuries," *Journal of American History* 65 (1978): 321–323, 339–340.

4. Ibid., pp. 340–342; Robert M. Utley, *The Lance and the Shield: The Life and Times of Sitting Bull* (New York: Henry Holt, 1993), pp. 43–45, 71–75.

5. The "Treaty with the Sioux-Brule, Oglala, Miniconjou, Yanktonai, Hunkpapa, Blackfeet, Cuthead, Two Kettle, Sans Arcs, and Santee—and Arapaho," is reprinted in Edward Lazarus, *Black Hills, White Justice: The Sioux Nation versus the United states, 1775 to the Present* (New York: Harper Collins, 1991), pp. 433–439. For a discussion of the treaty and this period of Sioux history, see Lazarus, *Black Hills, White Justice,* pp. 45–53; Utley, *The Lance and the Shield,* pp. 82–84; and, focusing on Red Cloud, James C. Olson, *Red Cloud and the Sioux Problem* (Lincoln: University of Nebraska Press, 1975), chaps. 1–6.

6. Raymond J. DeMallie, "Lakota Belief and Ritual in the Nineteenth Century," in Raymond J. DeMallie and Douglas R. Parks, *Sioux Indian Religion* (Norman: University of Oklahoma Press, 1987), p. 32.

7. On the visit see Olson, *Red Cloud,* pp. 111–113; Red Cloud is quoted on p. 113.

8. Act, 16 Stat. 566, now codified as Title 25, U.S. Code, Sec. 71. The 1871 Resolution is discussed in John R. Wunder, *"Retained by the People": A History of American Indians and the Bill of Rights* (New York: Oxford University Press, 1994), pp. 29–31.

9. On the immediate events leading up to the battle at the Little Big Horn, see Utley, *The Lance and the Shield*, pp. 106–164; Olson, *Red Cloud*, pp. 214–222; Lazarus, *Black Hills, White Justice*, pp. 71–89. Greasy Grass was the stream the whites called the Little Big Horn.

10. Frances Paul Prucha, *The Great Father: The United States Government and the American Indians*, vol. 2 (Lincoln: University of Nebraska Press, 1984), pp. 632–633; Olson, *Red Cloud*, pp. 224–230.

11. Prucha, *The Great Father*, pp. 636–640.

12. Ibid., p. 640.

13. Secretary of the Interior John W. Noble to acting Commissioner of Indian Affairs R. V. Belt, July 1, 1889. Quoted in Olson, *Red Cloud*, p. 318.

14. Prucha, *The Great Father*, pp. 640, 726; Utley, *The Lance and the Shield*, p. 281.

15. Utley, *The Lance and the Shield*, pp. 281–287; William K. Powers, *Oglala Religion* (Lincoln: University of Nebraska Press, 1982), pp. 120–122; James Mooney, *The Ghost Dance Religion and the Sioux Outbreak of 1890* (Chicago: University of Chicago Press, 1965; originally published 1896), pp. 1–32.

16. Agent D. F. Royer, quoted in Olson, *Red Cloud*, p. 326.

17. On the events leading up to Wounded Knee, see Utley, *The Lance and the Shield*, pp. 281–307; Olson, *Red Cloud*, pp. 320–329; Mooney, *The Ghost Dance Religion*.

18. Utley, *The Lance and the Shield*, p. 312.

19. Fred Hoxie, *A Final Promise: The Campaign to Assimilate the Indians, 1880–1920* (New York: Cambridge University Press, 1989), p. 70.

20. Merrill Gates, a member of the Board of Indian Commissioners, quoted in Stephen Cornell, *The Return of the Native: American Indian Political Resurgence* (New York: Oxford University Press, 1988), p. 44.

21. On assimilation and allotment see Wunder, *Retained by the People*, pp. 31–39; Hoxie, *A Final Promise*, pp. 41–81, 147–187, 189–210; Cornell, *The Return of the Native*, pp. 40–50; and in general on the distribution of land, Kirke Kickingbird and Karen Ducheneaux, *One Hundred Million Acres* (New York: MacMillan, 1973).

22. Quoted in Frederick E. Hoxie, "From Prison to Homeland: The Cheyenne River Indian Reservation Before World War I," in *The Plains Indians of the Twentieth Century*, ed. Peter Iverson (Norman: University of Oklahoma Press, 1985), pp. 55–75, 57.

23. Prucha, *The Great Father*, pp. 694–700; Harvey Markowitz, "The Catholic Mission and the Sioux: A Crisis in the Early Paradigm," in *Sioux Indian Religion: Tradition and Innovation*, ed. Raymond J. DeMallie and Douglas R. Parks (Norman: University of Oklahoma Press, 1987), pp. 121–129; Powers, *Oglala Religion*, pp. 95–100, 113, 139–143; Thomas Biolsi, *Organizing the Lakota: The Political Economy of the New Deal on the Pine Ridge and Rosebud Reservations* (Tucson: University of Arizona Press, 1992), pp. 3–7.

24. Hoxie, *A Final Promise*, p. 15. It should be noted that on Pine Ridge and other Sioux reservations, the Catholic Church was a strong force in the process of Christianizing the Lakota. See Markowitz, "Catholic Mission and the Sioux," pp. 113–147; Powers, *Oglala Religion*, pp. 112–116.

25. Commissioner Thomas Morgan, quoted in Olson, *Red Cloud*, p. 335.

26. Frank Fools Crow, Oglala traditional chief, quoted in Thomas E. Mails, ed., *Fools Crow* (Garden City, New York: Doubleday, 1979), p. 113.

27. Hoxie, "From Prison to Homeland," p. 58; see also Deloria, *Behind the Trail of Broken Treaties*, p. 68.

28. By 1956 every claim but one had been lost. That year the Indian Claims Commission decided the one remaining claim, compensation for the loss of the Black Hills, ruling that the United States had paid the Sioux in full in 1877. On the beginnings of the Black Hills claim, see Lazarus, *Black Hills, White Justice*, chaps. 7–8; on Oglala cultural resistance see Powers, *Oglala Religion*, pp. 120–128.

   Biolsi argues that the Lakota basically acquiesced to the reservation system and the dominance of the OIA, primarily because of their continued dependence on government rations and the artificial economy provided by OIA programs. Biolsi, *Organizing the Lakota*, pp. 4, 183–184.

29. In addition, between 1936 and 1976, estimates of land taken by the government through eminent domain and other legislative action run as high as 1.8 million acres. Figures for national statistics are from Kickingbird and Ducheneaux, *One Hundred Million Acres*, pp. 30–32; see also Deloria, *Behind the Trail of Broken Treaties*, p. 68. For statistics on poverty and a discussion of the Meriam Report see Wunder, *Retained by the People*, pp. 62–63; other information for Pine Ridge can be found in Biolsi, *Organizing the Lakota*, pp. 3–4, 29.

30. Hoxie, *A Final Promise*, chap. 7.

31. Wunder, *Retained by the People*, pp. 64–66.

32. The name was changed to Bureau of Indian Affairs in the 1940s.

33. Wunder, *Retained by the People*, pp. 66–71; Biolsi, *Organizing the Lakota*, p. xviii; Vine Deloria, Jr., and Clifford M. Lytle, *American Indians, American Justice* (Austin: University of Texas Press, 1983), pp. 12–15; see also Prucha, *The Great Father*, pp. 940–992.

34. Wunder, *Retained by the People*, pp. 72–74.

35. Deloria and Lytle, *American Indians, American Justice*, p. 15; the statistics from Pine Ridge are in Lazarus, *Black Hills, White Justice*, p. 163.

36. Biolsi, *Organizing the Lakota*, pp. xx–xxi.

37. Ibid., pp. 184–185; Wunder, *Retained by the People*, pp. 76–77; Lazarus, *Black Hills, White Justice*, pp. 161–223; Deloria, *Behind the Trail of Broken Treaties*, p. 69.

38. Biolsi, *Organizing the Lakota*, pp. xx–xxi, 151–155. Biolsi argues that the dissent was directed primarily at the tribal governments rather than the OIA, because the traditionalists or old dealers were basically not separatists any more than the new dealers were. See pp. 183–184; note 5, p. 222.

39. Ibid., pp. 184–185.

40. Ibid., pp. 185–186; Cornell, *The Return of the Native*, pp. 87–105.

41. Frances Paul Prucha, *The Indians in American Society: From the Revolutionary War to the Present* (Berkeley: University of California Press, 1985), p. 70.

42. Fixico, *Termination and Relocation*, p. 183.

43. On termination and relocation in general see Fixico, *Termination and Relocation*. See also Wunder, *Retained by the People*, pp. 98–107; Tom Holm, "Fighting a White Man's War: The Extent and Legacy of American Indian Participation in

World War II," in Iverson, *Plains Indians*, pp. 149–168; Cornell, *The Return of the Native*, pp. 121–125, 129–148, 156–161; Nancy Shoemaker, "Urban Indians and Ethnic Choices: American Indian Organizations in Minneapolis, 1920–1950," *The Western Historical Quarterly* 19 (1988): 431–447.

44. On the ICC see Wunder, *Retained by the People*, pp. 89–93; Fixico, *Termination and Relocation*, pp. 26–31.

45. Prior to the establishment of the Indian Claims Commission, Indians seeking to sue over unjust taking of land had first to get the U.S. Congress to enact special legislation granting them permission to do so. Under the ICC, six hundred claims had been filed by 1951. See George S. Grossman, "Indians and the Law," in *New Directions in Indian History* (Norman: University of Oklahoma Press, 1992), p. 103. On the NCAI and other early activity, see Cornell, *The Return of the Native*, pp. 101–105, 118–123, 187–190.

46. Quoted in Cornell, *The Return of the Native*, p. 198.

47. Quoted in Peter Nabokov, ed., *Native American Testimony: A Chronicle of Indian-White Relations from Prophecy to the Present, 1492–1992* (New York: Penguin Books, 1992), p. 356.

48. The culmination of this attention was perhaps the Indian Bill of Rights passed in 1968. See Wunder, *Retained by the People*, pp. 121–141. As Vine Deloria and others have pointed out, the demand for tribal sovereignty could mean something very different from a demand for civil rights within U.S. society. See Deloria, *Behind the Trail of Broken Treaties*, pp. 2–4, 23–25; Fixico, *Termination and Relocation*, p. 199.

49. For a general discussion of AIM and the rise of Indian activism, see Cornell, *The Return of the Native*, pp. 132–148, 156–161, chap. 11; Nabokov, *Native American Testimony*, pp. 355–362; Peter Matthiessen, *In The Spirit of Crazy Horse* (New York: Viking, 1991), chap. 2; Deloria, *Behind the Trail of Broken Treaties*, chap. 2; Lazarus, *Black Hills, White Justice*, pp. 290–311; James S. Olson and Raymond Wilson, *Native Americans in the Twentieth Century* (Urbana: University of Illinois Press, 1984), chap. 7; Adam Fortunate Eagle, *Alcatraz! Alcatraz! The Indian Occupation of 1969–1971* (Berkeley: Heyday Books, 1992). Information also comes from interviews with Dennis Banks, April 3, 1989; Vernon Bellecourt, October 5, 1989; Ted Means, October 28, 1988; Lorelei DeCora Means, October 26, 1988; Madonna Gilbert Thunder Hawk, October 28, 1988; John Thomas, September 4, 1988; and John Trudell (who was at Alcatraz), January 23, 1989.

50. On AIM and urban activism see Matthiessen, *In the Spirit of Crazy Horse*, chap. 2; Shoemaker, "Urban Indians and Ethnic Choices," p. 431; Nabokov, *Native American Testimony*, pp. 355–362, 372–376; Cornell, *The Return of the Native*, pp. 189–199; AIM "Fact Sheet," Wounded Knee Legal Defense Offense Committee Records (hereafter cited as WKLDOC Records), Minnesota Historical Society (hereafter cited as MHS); also Ken Tilsen interview, February 24, 1991; Clyde Bellecourt interview, July 11, 1991.

51. Shoemaker, "Urban Indians and Ethnic Choices." On AIM and the Sun Dance see Beatrice Medicine, "Indian Women and the Renaissance of Traditional Religion," in DeMallie and Parks, *Sioux Indian Religion*, pp. 163–164.

52. Matthiessen, *In the Spirit of Crazy Horse*, pp. 60–61; Robert Anderson et al., eds., *Voices From Wounded Knee, 1973: In the Words of the Participants* (Rooseveltown,

N.Y.: Akwesasne Notes, 1974), p. 13; Deloria, *Behind the Trail of Broken Treaties,* pp. 45, 73.

53. The income figure is from Matthiessen, *In the Spirit of Crazy Horse,* p. 61; the unemployment figure is from Anderson et al., eds., *Voices,* p. 12; two defense committee members remember seeing figures as high as 70 percent for this period of time. Karen Northcott interview, September 9, 1989; Ken Tilsen interview, February 4, 1991. See also Powers, *Oglala Religion,* pp. 110–112; Anderson et al., eds., *Voices,* pp. 9–13; Matthiessen, *In the Spirit of Crazy Horse,* pp. 31, 65–66; Deloria, *Behind the Trail of Broken Treaties,* pp. 69–70; Fixico, *Termination and Relocation,* pp. 174–175; Olson and Wilson, *Native Americans,* pp. 185–186; Biolsi, *Organizing the Lakota,* pp. 182–185.

54. According to Matthiessen, Wilson's wife was the head of the Head Start Program, which was allegedly floundering as a result of her incompetence; Wilson's brother George ran the Water Works; his brother Jim was in charge of the Planning Commission at a salary of $25,000 plus other consulting fees; and his nephew was appointed to the position of Personnel Director of the Tribe. See *In the Spirit of Crazy Horse,* pp. 61–62. See also Anderson et al., eds., *Voices,* pp. 14–21; Deloria, *Behind the Trail of Broken Treaties,* pp. 70–72; Wunder, *Retained by the People,* p. 150.

55. On the Trail of Broken Treaties see Deloria, *Behind the Trail of Broken Treaties,* chap. 3; Matthiessen, *In the Spirit of Crazy Horse,* pp. 51–56. Information on the negotiations also comes from an interview with Leonard Garment and Bradley H. Patterson, July 6, 1992. Garment, a former law partner of Nixon's who was appointed Special Consultant to the President in 1969, approved the agreement with the demonstrators on behalf of the White House. By the end of the year he had become the White House official responsible for Indian policy. Patterson was his Executive Assistant and devoted a considerable amount of his time to helping Garment on Indian matters.

56. Quoted in Deloria, *Behind the Trail of Broken Treaties,* p. viii.

57. Ibid., p. ix.

58. See internal FBI Memorandum, entitled "The Use of Special Agents of the FBI in a Paramilitary Law Enforcement Operation in the Indian Country," dated April 24, 1975, p. 2, reprinted in Larry B. Leventhal, "Wounded Knee 1890, 1973 and Beyond, Course Materials," for the course "American Indians 5352" (taught at the University of Minnesota), pp. 230–235.

59. Matthiessen, *In the Spirit of Crazy Horse,* pp. 55–56. On the general topic of the FBI, COINTELPRO, the Black Panthers, and AIM, see also Ward Churchill and Jim Vander Wall, *Agents of Repression: The FBI's Secret Wars Against the Black Panther Party and the American Indian Movement* (Boston: South End Press, 1988), and Churchill and Vander Wall, *The COINTELPRO Papers: Documents from the FBI's Secret Wars Against Dissent in the United States* (Boston: South End Press, 1990). Many at the BIA protest did not want to leave, and some, like John Trudell who had been at Alcatraz, believed that the move was calculated to lure AIM out of the limelight of Washington and back to a remote Indian area such as Pine Ridge. Trudell interview; Vernon Bellecourt interview.

60. Two police cars and two buildings were set on fire. One, the abandoned Chamber of Commerce building next to the Court House, burned to the

ground. See Matthiessen, *In the Spirit of Crazy Horse*, pp. 63–64; Northcott interview. On Wilson and the events leading to Wounded Knee in general, see Matthiessen, *In the Spirit of Crazy Horse*, chap. 3; Deloria, *Behind the Trail of Broken Treaties*, chap. 4; Anderson et al., eds., *Voices*, pp. 14–32.

61. An earlier organization to fight corruption on the reservation was called the Inter-District Tribal Council. Anderson et al., eds., *Voices*, p. 16.

62. Ibid., p. 26; Matthiessen, *In the Spirit of Crazy Horse*, pp. 64–65. Despite the criticism of the BIA and the U.S. government, Biolsi argues that the dissent on Pine Ridge was rooted in the opposition to the IRA, but was not separatist and thus was directed primarily at the tribal government. He acknowledges that other scholars would disagree with this. Biolsi, *Organizing the Lakota*, pp. 182–186; 222, note 5.

63. Anderson et al., eds., *Voices*, pp. 14–19; Matthiessen, *In the Spirit of Crazy Horse*, pp. 62–64.

64. Excerpts from the U.S. Marshal's radio logs for February 14–22 and 25–27 are reprinted in Anderson et al., eds., *Voices*, pp. 24–32. See also ibid., pp. 22–24; Matthiessen, *In the Spirit of Crazy Horse*, pp. 64–65; William Clayton interview, September 8, 1988. Critical accounts of AIM and the takeover can be found in Harlington Wood, Jr., "Footnote to History: A Personal Account of a Segment of Wounded Knee 1973 Told for Lauren and Alex," *University of Illinois Law Review* 30 (1995): 30–92; Gerald Vizenor, "Dennis of Wounded Knee," *American Indian Quarterly* 7 (1983): 51–65; *Wounded Knee: A Personal Account by Stanley David Lyman*, ed. Floyd A. O'Neil, June K. Lyman, and Susan Mckay (Lincoln: University of Nebraska Press, 1991); and Roland Dewing, *Wounded Knee: The Meaning and Significance of the Second Incident* (New York: Irvington Publishers, 1985). Lyman's account also contains a good deal on government operations before and during the protest; see pp. xvi, xxiv–xxv, 4–6, 17–18, 37–38.

65. Ellen Moves Camp, quoted in Anderson et al., eds., *Voices*, p. 31. AIM and others would later give credit to Indian women for their work at Wounded Knee. Eighty-seven were charged with criminal offenses stemming from the protest. See defense committee pamphlet, "The Women Of Wounded Knee," WKLDOC Records, MHS; Matthiessen, *In the Spirit of Crazy Horse*, p. 66.

66. Participants reported counting fifty-four cars. Anderson et al., eds., *Voices*, pp. 31–32.

67. Ibid., pp. 34–35.

68. Ibid., p. 35.

69. Ibid., p. 36.

70. Ibid., p. 36; see also Matthiessen, *In the Spirit of Crazy Horse*, p. 67.

71. FBI internal memorandum, "The Use of Special Agents." See also *New York Times*, March 2, 1973, p. 1; March 3, 1973, pp. 1, 36; and March 5, 1973, p. 1. The South Dakota newspaper was the *Rapid City Journal*, cited in Lyman, *Wounded Knee 1973*, p. xxiii.

72. For some in the White House the chief purpose of having high-ranking army personnel on the scene was to make sure that law enforcement did not do anything that could provoke a more violent situation. These concerns were communicated to General Alexander Haig, the Army's Vice Chief of Staff. Information from Garment and Patterson interview.

73. The Marshal's log for February 27 read: "Do not let newspaper personnel into Wounded Knee area . . . No TV coverage of the Wounded Knee area . . . no photos of personnel"; quoted in Anderson et al., eds., *Voices,* p. 42; see also ibid., pp. 41–45, 67; Matthiessen, *In the Spirit of Crazy Horse,* pp. 68–70, 80.

74. Information on meetings comes from Garment and Patterson interview.

75. Matthiessen, *In the Spirit of Crazy Horse,* p. 72.

76. Wilson is quoted in Anderson et al., eds., *Voices,* p. 125. See also ibid.,
    pp. 125–129, 189–193; Matthiessen, *In the Spirit of Crazy Horse,* pp. 74–75.

77. Matthiessen, *In the Spirit of Crazy Horse,* p. 74. Some non-Indian VVAW people did come to Wounded Knee, but there is no record of members of the other listed groups being present. Some people from left-leaning political circles did make brief appearances, such as Angela Davis and Reverend Ralph Abernathy.

78. Anderson et al., eds., *Voices,* pp. 54–55.

79. Ibid., p. 114.

80. Ibid., p. 113.

81. On the petition see Anderson et al., eds., *Voices,* p. 113. In general, see ibid.,
    pp. 92–102; Matthiessen, *In the Spirit of Crazy Horse,* pp. 71–83; Vernon Belle-court interview. On negotiations and the stand-down see Matthiessen, *In the Spirit of Crazy Horse,* pp. 69–81; Anderson et al., eds., *Voices,* pp. 133–152, 224–244; Deloria, *Behind the Trail of Broken Treaties,* pp. 79–80. The government asserted that people inside Wounded Knee were low on food and water and that the press and many supporters had lost interest in the protest. See "Report Submitted to the U.S. Senate Interior Committee by the Department of Justice," pp. 45–47, reprinted in Leventhal, "Course Materials,"
    pp. 172–217.
        Frank Clearwater, an Apache from North Carolina, was wounded on April 17 and died in Rapid City on April 25. Buddy Lamont was killed on April 27. U.S. Marshal Lloyd Grimm was seriously wounded on March 26 and left paralyzed from the waist down.

82. *New York Times,* May 8, 1973, p. 1; *Minneapolis Tribune,* May 7, 1973, p. 1; *Rapid City Journal,* May 8, 1973, outstate edition, p. 1.

83. Lazarus, *Black Hills, White Justice,* pp. 308–311; Anderson et al., eds., *Voices,*
    pp. 240–244; Matthiessen, *In the Spirit of Crazy Horse,* pp. 81–82; Bob Lyman interview. At first the government was not going to let attorneys oversee the processing, but they forced their way in. Anderson et al., eds., *Voices,*
    p. 240; interview with Lorelei DeCora Means, October 26, 1988.

84. *New York Times,* May 7, 1973, p. 77. A copy of the agreement, dated April 5, 1973, is in Leventhal, "Course Materials," pp. 118–119.

85. Anderson et al., eds., *Voices,* p. 250.

86. *Minneapolis Tribune,* June 1, 1973, p. 1; *Sioux Falls Argus Leader,* June 2, 1973, p. 9; *Rapid City Journal,* June 13, 1973, p. 1; Anderson et al., eds., *Voices,*
    pp. 251–258.

87. Letter from Leonard Garment, dated May 29, 1973, reprinted in Leventhal, "Course Materials," pp. 134–138. See also *New York Times,* June 1, 1973, p. 38.

88. *Minneapolis Tribune,* June 17, 1973, sec. B, p. 9; *Rapid City Journal,* June 14, 1973, p. 1, and June 17, 1973, p. 1; and Anderson et al., eds., *Voices,* p. 260.

89. *New York Times,* June 17, 1973, p. 14.

90. Letter from Matthew King to Leonard Garment, dated June 9, 1973, reprinted in Leventhal, "Course Materials," pp. 139–145.
91. Nabokov, *Native American Testimony,* pp. 383–385; Deloria, *Behind the Trail of Broken Treaties,* p. 266; Olson and Wilson, *Native Americans,* p. 162; and interview with Garment and Patterson.
92. The Harris Survey, April 2, 1973. Copy in WKLDOC Records, MHS.
93. *New York Times,* May 13, 1973, p. 60, and sec. 4, p. 3; see also *Rapid City Journal,* May 11, 1973, p. 1; May 17, 1973, p. 3; and May 20, 1973, p. 3.
94. See editorials in *Saint Paul Pioneer Press,* May 11, 1973, p. 12; *Sioux Falls Argus Leader,* May 14, 1973, p. 4, and June 13, 1973, p. 4; and *Rapid City Journal,* May 9, 1973.
95. *Sioux Falls Argus Leader,* June 1, 1973, p. 16; *Rapid City Journal,* May 27, 1973, p. 23; May 29, 1973, p. 3.
96. *Rapid City Journal,* May 13, 1973, p. 3, and May 17, 1973, p. 3.
97. *Rapid City Journal,* May 21, 1973, p. 1, and May 25, 1973, p. 2.
98. *Rapid City Journal,* May 19, 1973, p. 3.
99. Cornell, *The Return of the Native,* p. 5.

2. THE BUILDUP TO THE TRIALS

1. Kenneth Tilsen interview, October 11, 1989. One of the people in jail that weekend was Bill Means; Bill Means interview, July 3, 1991.
2. *Agnes Lamont et al. vs. Alexander Haig et al.,* copy in WKLDOC Records, MHS, and *Eugene White Hawk, Chairman of the Wounded Knee District Comm. vs. Stanley Lyman, Superintendent of the Pine Ridge Indian Reservation, Rogers C. B. Morton, Secretary of the Interior, Harlington Wood, Justice Department,* copy in WKLDOC Records, MHS, and *Oglala Sioux Civil Rights Organization vs. Richard Wilson, et al.,* copy in WKLDOC Records, MHS. The last suit named as defendants, along with tribal president Wilson, various officials of the tribal government, the BIA police, and the Sheriff's Department. See also Anderson et al., eds., *Voices,* pp. 124, 184–185. While the siege was still in progress, some of the early legal work was being coordinated out of an office in Rapid City. Bill Means interview, July 3, 1991.
3. William Clayton interview, September 8, 1988.
4. Clayton interview; R. D. Hurd interview, September 7, 1988; David Gienapp interview, September 7, 1988.
5. Clayton interview.
6. Indicted were Russell Means, Dennis Banks, Clyde Bellecourt, Pedro Bissonette, and Carter Camp. Matthiessen, *In the Spirit of Crazy Horse,* p. 72; Clayton, Hurd, and Gienapp interviews.
7. A count-by-count list of charges can be found in WKLDOC Records, MHS. See also copy of indictment #CR 73-5035, U.S. v. Means, filed in U.S. District Court, Western District of South Dakota, March 20, 1973, in WKLDOC Records, MHS.
8. Crow Dog and Means in *Rapid City Journal,* May 11, 1973, p. 3; and again on Means, June 6, 1973, p. 2. On Banks, Banks interview and *Rapid City Journal,* June 7, 1973, p. 12, and June 27, 1973, p. 1; *New York Times,* June 27, 1973, p. 36.

9. Hurd interview.
10. Sign-up sheet in WKLDOC Records, MHS. NLG members had met prior to the weekend and arrived with an agenda that included discussing the specifics of the cases and staffing and communications needs. Cavise interview and notes from the meeting, in Cavise personal files.
11. Information from Banks interview; Joe Beeler and M. G. Beeler interview, May 6, 1989; Leonard Cavise interview, April 8, 1989; Robert Lyman interview, September 20, 1989. Kunstler was contacted by telephone on February 29, 1973. William Kunstler interview, December 13, 1988. Several of those present had been recruited by Beverly Axlerod, a California attorney who had represented the Black Panther Party. Tilsen interview.
12. Cavise interview and personal notes of the meeting in Cavise files; Tilsen and Lyman interviews.
13. Tilsen and Lyman interviews. Tilsen in his interview referred to Black Elk's "eloquence and humanity."
14. Cavise interview.
15. Tilsen and Lyman interviews. Lawyers like Kunstler, who were willing to work with a defense committee, were the exception among established lawyers, according to Tilsen. Tilsen interview, February 4, 1991.
16. Cavise and Tilsen interviews.
17. The name had actually been adopted by some lawyers inside Wounded Knee in mid-March; Cavise interview.
18. In 1950 a HUAC report labeled the Guild the "legal bulwark of the Communist Party." See "A History of the National Lawyers Guild, 1937–1987," National Lawyers Guild Foundation, 1987. Information on recruitment from Cavise and Lyman interviews.
19. Cavise interview. Copy of press release dated May 9, 1973, in Cavise files.
20. In August 1971, inmates in New York's maximum-security unit staged a silent protest, wearing black items on their clothing and refusing to eat lunch, in response to the death of Black Panther George Jackson inside San Quentin prison in San Francisco. In the days following the silent protest, tension mounted inside Attica as guards strictly enforced prison rules. A week later, declaring "We Are Men" and demanding to be treated with respect, inmates took over the prison. On the morning of the fourth day, Governor Nelson Rockefeller, after refusing to negotiate with the inmates, ordered guards and state police to retake the prison. Forty-three people, including ten hostages, were killed by police bullets. The Guild set up a mass defense effort in Buffalo to represent inmates targeted for prosecution after the takeover. See Peter N. Carroll, *It Seemed Like Nothing Happened: The Tragedy and Promise of America in the 1970s* (New York: Holt, Rinehart and Winston, 1984), pp. 52–53; "A History of the National Lawyers Guild," p. 48.
21. People from Chicago, one of the largest Guild chapters, were encouraged to volunteer for either project. Cavise and Lyman interviews. Notes of the meetings taken by Cavise and a report of the meetings to WKLDOC written by Fran Schreiberg, dated June 25, 1973, are in Cavise files.
22. DeCora Means, Cavise, and Tilsen interviews.
23. Tilsen interview.

24. Joe Beeler had received some Playboy Foundation money for his original trip to Wounded Knee during the siege. Joe Beeler and Tilsen interviews.
25. Tilsen, Cavise, Lyman, and Joe and M. G. Beeler interviews.
26. Tilsen, Cavise, DeCora Means, and Joe Beeler interviews.
27. Lyman, Cavise, and Joe Beeler interviews; Cavise letter in Cavise files. By fall the committee had a ten-page questionnaire to send out to prospective volunteers, asking for past addresses and references. This was followed by an interview in person or by telephone. Katherine James interview, June 12, 1989.
28. Banks, Cavise, Lyman, Gilbert Thunder Hawk, Joe and M. G. Beeler, Lyman, and Tilsen interviews.
29. Joe Beeler and Lyman interviews; letter from Len Cavise to author, February 11, 1991; letter from "Coalition for Better Government" to William Clayton requesting an investigation of alleged harassment dated May 14, 1973, copy in Cavise files.
30. Banks, Ted Means, John Thomas, Gilbert Thunder Hawk, and DeCora Means interviews.
31. Banks interview.
32. Tilsen, James, Gilbert Thunder Hawk, Cavise, Lyman, and Northcott interviews.
33. Cavise and Joe Beeler interviews.
34. Cavise, Tilsen, and Joe Beeler interviews. Two legal workers were asked to leave the committee by collective decision in mid-summer but only did so when the lawyer they were working under also left. An attempt by one lawyer to have another lawyer removed was stalled by heated committee discussions. Cavise and Cohoes interviews.
35. Gilbert Thunder Hawk, Ted Means, and DeCora Means interviews.
36. Ted Means and DeCora Means interviews.
37. Ted Means, Gilbert Thunder Hawk, and Banks interviews, and Vernon Bellecourt interview, October 5, 1989.
38. Letter from Fran Schreiberg to Len Cavise, dated July 1, 1973, copy in Cavise files. In the summer of 1973, law students were recruited by the Seattle NLG chapter to go to Denver, but only a couple of law students made it to South Dakota; the vast majority of those on the committee were either legal workers or lawyers. During the summer of 1974, things changed when the NLG organized a "law student summer project" to help with the defense. Cohoes interview; memo on the NLG "Summer Project," dated July 26, 1973, from the Seattle NLG chapter, copy in Cavise files.
39. Quote is from Cavise letter to author. By September figures showed that almost half of the money that had been raised, $34,897 of $75,440, had gone to pay bail for the defendants; *Minneapolis Tribune*, September 3, 1973, p. 1.
40. Joe and M. G. Beeler, Cavise, Tilsen, Cohoes, Means, and Lyman interviews. Permission to use the county law library was granted and then rescinded, pending payment of a membership in the county bar.
41. Indian law expert John Throne left the committee, saying that he could not work in that "atmosphere." Throne, however, continued to work on treaty issues (appearing in court on behalf of the defense in 1974) and to recruit other lawyers for the defense. See letter from Throne to the committee, dated April

19, 1973, in WKLDOC Records, MHS. Beverly Axlerod left the committee in early summer, tiring of the fighting between attorneys. She, too, continued to recruit other lawyers and advised on the defense. Tilsen interview.

42. Ted Means interview; also Northcott, Thomas, James, Joe and M. G. Beeler, Lyman, and Gilbert Thunder Hawk interviews.

43. Cavise, Northcott, and Cohoes interviews.

44. Gilbert Thunder Hawk, DeCora Means, M. G. Beeler, Joe Beeler, Cavise, and Ted Means interviews.

45. Cavise, Gilbert Thunder Hawk, DeCora Means, and Banks interviews, on Means and AIM; Beelers and Lyman interviews, on Means and the committee.

46. Ted Means, DeCora Means, and Gilbert Thunder Hawk interviews.

47. Ted Means interview.

48. Joe and M. G. Beeler, Cavise, Northcott, James, Cohoes, Thomas, Lyman, and Joan Scully interviews.

49. Both Gilbert Thunder Hawk and DeCora Means admit that they were exceptions within AIM at that time, referring to themselves as the "second string leadership." Gilbert Thunder Hawk and DeCora Means interviews.

50. Mary Crow Dog, *Lakota Woman,* with Richard Erdoes (New York: Harper Perennial, 1991), p. 131.

51. Rayna Green, "Native American Women," in *SIGNS: A Journal of Women in Culture and Society* 6 (1980): 248–267, 264. See also the section entitled "Activist Women" in Marla N. Powers, *Oglala Women* (Chicago: University of Chicago Press, 1988), pp. 149–154; Shoemaker, "Introduction," in *Negotiators of Change: Historical Perspectives On Native American Women* (New York: Routledge, 1995), pp. 11–13. As Sara Evans points out, the women's movement's emphasis on "women" as a group in the early 1970s often assumed a white, middle-class norm, which "obscured differences *among* women along lines of race, class and ethnicity." Sara M. Evans, *Born for Liberty: A History of Women in America* (New York: Free Press, 1989), p. 293.

52. Joe and M. G. Beeler, Northcott, James, DeCora Means, Gilbert Thunder Hawk, Thomas, and Tilsen interviews, and Rachel Tilsen interview, July 12, 1991. Ken Tilsen remembers being confronted early on when he completely rewrote some pleadings a woman lawyer had worked on for several days without a word of discussion. Says Tilsen, "I discovered I was a sexist, arrogant pig who had no respect for her work." For Tilsen, the episode was a "learning experience" that forced him to make adjustments from a law practice where he ran the show.

53. Bellecourt was later arrested and charged with violating the federal anti-riot law for a speech he gave in Colorado urging students to take supplies to Wounded Knee. Students with supplies had been arrested in Wyoming and Nebraska on their way to Wounded Knee. Bellecourt interview; *Minneapolis Tribune,* July 23, 1973, p. 2B; *Sioux Falls Argus Leader,* August 5, 1973, p. 2.

54. Bellecourt, Banks, Gilbert Thunder Hawk interviews, and Bill Means interview, July 3, 1991.

55. *Rapid City Journal,* July 24, 1973, p. 10. See also *New York Times,* July 29, 1973, p. 29; Bellecourt interview, and *New York Times,* July 23, 1973, p. 17; *Sioux Falls Argus Leader,* July 23, 1973, p. 12.

56. Cavise and James interviews. One promotion offered copies of Dee Brown's *Bury My Heart at Wounded Knee* in exchange for a donation. See also fundraising letter signed by Dick Gregory and Noam Chomsky, dated June 1, 1973, copy in Cavise files; and copies of various newsletters and press releases in WKLDOC Records, MHS.

57. DeCora Means and Ted Means interviews. Sometimes just locating a witness or client was a difficult enough task. Rachel Tilsen and Bill Means interviews; see also copy of "Clients" newsletter, dated October 1973, in Cavise files.

58. According to Joe Beeler, when the telegram from WKLDOC arrived, NACDL members were sitting around some "plush watering hole" trying to compose a tongue-in-cheek letter to the current Attorney General, praising him on his "liberal views" on pretrial discovery. The letter was in reference to the decision to allow Spiro Agnew's attorneys (prior to his indictment) to look at the Justice Department's entire investigative file; NACDL lawyers suggested that this procedure be adopted across the board for all federal criminal defendants. Joe Beeler interview.

59. See letters from Heeney to WKLDOC dated 10/3/73 and from Heeney "To All Members of the Wounded Knee Committee of the NACDL," dated October 3, 1973. Copies of both letters, and numerous others by Heeney reporting on the situation in 1973 and 1974, are in WKLDOC Records, MHS. Joe Beeler notes that many in the NACDL point to the Wounded Knee defense work as a catalyst for converting the organization from a "private lawyers' club" that liked to gather at major resorts and exchange war stories, into a group that is involved in criminal justice reform. Heeney became a hero within the NACDL, turning the presidency into a position of leadership and activism requiring a significant time commitment. The NACDL now has well over 5,000 members, a professional staff, and an office in Washington, D.C. Joe Beeler interview.

60. Lyman and Joe Beeler interview.

61. Tilsen, Cohoes, and James interviews.

62. *Sioux Falls Argus Leader,* October 26, 1973, p. 2; *Saint Paul Pioneer Press,* October 26, 1973, p. 39.

63. Clayton interview.

64. Judge Fred Nichol interview; *Sioux Falls Argus Leader,* October 26, 1973, p. 2. Before his death, Pedro Bissonette was the sixth conspiracy defendant in this group. Nichol had severed Banks and Means from the others, setting their cases for trial in January. The defense had argued that the indictments, pretrial matters, and evidence to be presented were identical, that it was impossible to hold concurrent trials, and that jury selection in a later trial would be prejudiced by the outcome of the first; the decision was challenged unsuccessfully by the defense in the Circuit Court of Appeals. See "Status Report" of the cases, dated August 19, 1973, in Cavise files; "Summary of pre-trial motions" in Leventhal, "Course Materials," pp. 256–258. Neither side was completely happy, since the U.S. Attorney had hoped to try Banks and Means individually; see *Rapid City Journal,* August 8, 1973, p. 23; *New York Times,* August 8, 1973, p. 34.

65. *Minneapolis Tribune,* October 26, 1973, p. 2; *Sioux Falls Argus Leader,* November 24, 1973, p. 1.

66. *Sioux Falls Argus Leader,* October 11, 1973, p. 1; see also a summary of pretrial motions in Leventhal, "Course Materials," pp. 256–258. Nichol did grant a government request for specific notification of what items the defense planned to introduce.

67. Nichol also denied a prosecution motion to exclude any mention of the 1868 Treaty; Leventhal, "Course Materials," pp. 257–258; *Sioux Falls Argus Leader,* October 26, 1973, p. 2; *Saint Paul Pioneer Press,* October 26, 1973, p. 39.

68. Oliphant was a passenger in a plane that had dropped supplies into Wounded Knee. Coverage of the hearings can be found in *Sioux Falls Argus Leader,* November 26, 1973, p. 2; November 28, 1973, p. 2; *Rapid City Journal,* November 28, 1973, p. 2; November 30, 1973, p. 1; *Saint Paul Pioneer Press,* November 28, 1973, p. 13.

69. Nichol also denied motions to dismiss based on lack of government jurisdiction under the Treaty of 1868 and the absence of Indians on the indicting federal grand juries. *Rapid City Journal,* November 30, 1973, p. 1; Cavise letter to author.

70. Banks and Tilsen interviews; *Rapid City Journal,* November 30, 1973, p. 1.

71. *Sioux Falls Argus Leader,* October 10, 1973, p. 7; *Rapid City Journal,* October 6, 1973, p. 1.

72. See copies of Bogue's order dated September 27, 1973, the letter dated November 19, 1973, and the signed waivers in WKLDOC Records, MHS. Bogue had set out five possible conflicts resulting from joint representation: guilt by association, the possible need for different defenses, the possibility that one tactic may help one defendant and hurt another, that an offer of immunity may be impeded, and that attorneys may owe allegiance to an organization or cause and that the individual defendant could be sacrificed for that organization or cause. The committee letter pointed out that the defendants could choose their own lawyers, but that unity was the key to a successful defense.

    In a related matter in the Custer cases, State Judge Joseph Bottum finally relented on his requirement that all the defendants have South Dakota counsel, after negotiations with the ACLU. *Sioux Falls Argus Leader,* October 12, 1973, p. 11.

73. In October Bogue wrote to Tilsen and Roubideaux complaining of "unexplained absences or lack of preparation" on the part of committee attorneys, demonstrating "an extremely cavalier attitude toward this Court." Some volunteer attorneys apparently had not followed through on their assignments, but the defense also claimed that Bogue was rushing through pretrial hearings without giving attorneys adequate time to prepare. Several attorneys responded to the Judge's letter, including Tilsen, and someone was designated to act as committee docket clerk and receive service. See letter from Judge Bogue, dated October 24, 1973, and letter from Tilsen to Bogue, dated November 11, 1973, copies in WKLDOC Records, MHS; Joe Beeler interview. The defense motion to disqualify Bogue was denied in September and later upheld by the Eighth Circuit Court of Appeals. *Sioux Falls Argus Leader,* September 1, 1973, p. 1.

74. *Sioux Falls Argus Leader,* October 18, 1973, p. 14.

75. The agent charged was Morris Pierson, and the victim of the alleged assault was Carolyn Mugar, a legal worker from Boston. *Rapid City Journal*, August 10, 1973, p. 2; August 11, 1973, p. 2; *New York Times*, August 8, 1973, p. 15; *Minneapolis Tribune*, September 3, 1973, p. 1; and *Sioux Falls Argus Leader*, August 8, 1973, p. 9; August 10, 1973, p. 7. On the meeting with the county see shorthand notes of the discussion taken by Len Cavise, Cavise files.

76. *Rapid City Journal*, September 1, 1973, p. 3.

77. *Rapid City Journal*, August 15, 1973, p. 2; *Sioux Falls Argus Leader*, August 14, p. 18.

78. Joe Beeler and Lyman interviews; information on leaflet, Ted Means interview.

79. *Minneapolis Tribune*, August 31, 1973, p. 1; September 3, 1973, p. 1; *Rapid City Journal*, September 1, 1973, p. 2.

80. *Rapid City Journal*, September 1, 1973, p. 2. Beeler told reporters that the unusually low rent the committee was paying for its new offices in downtown Rapid City made him suspicious of phone taps. The press also noted that a reporter for the *Rapid City Journal* became convinced that his phone had been tapped during Wounded Knee, when the FBI started asking him questions about confidential conversations. *Minneapolis Tribune*, September 3, 1973, p. 1; *New York Times*, August 9, 1973, p. 18.

81. Trimbach speech in *Sioux Falls Argus Leader*, September 19, 1973, p. 2; *Minneapolis Tribune*, September 19, 1973, p. 10.

82. On the investigative committee see *Sioux Falls Argus Leader*, October 18, 1973, p. 19; *Rapid City Journal*, October 17, 1973, p. 3. On the denial of the injunction for harassment see *Sioux Falls Argus Leader*, September 29, 1973, p. 4; *Rapid City Journal*, September 29, 1973, p. 3.

83. *New York Times*, August 14, 1973, p. 16.

84. *Sioux Falls Argus Leader*, December 29, 1973, p. 5.

85. Gilbert Thunder Hawk and Ted Means interviews.

86. See copy of pamphlet in WKLDOC Records, MHS; see also *Sioux Falls Argus Leader*, August 2, 1973, p. 8; *Rapid City Journal*, August 7, 1973, p. 1; on the Sun Dance, see *Sioux Falls Argus Leader*, August 5, 1973, p. 2, and August 6, 1973, p. 6. The Sun Dance was originally scheduled to be held near Custer, at the site of the "Crazy Horse Monument" being carved out of the side of a cliff in the Black Hills by sculptor and landowner Korczak Ziolkowski. Ziolkowski withdrew permission for use of his land under pressure from local and state officials, who feared another incident involving AIM. The governor's office denied putting pressure on the sculptor, but acknowledged that it had advised him on the matter. *Sioux Falls Argus Leader*, July 29, 1973, p. 2; *Rapid City Journal*, July 26, 1973, pp. 1, 3; and July 27, 1973, p. 1.

87. Banks interview.

88. Reports on the shooting can be found in *New York Times*, August 28, 1973, p. 23; *Minneapolis Tribune*, August 28, 1973, p. 1; *Rapid City Journal*, August 28, 1973, p. 4; *Sioux Falls Argus Leader*, August 28, 1973, p. 1; committee response in Cavise letter to author and Lyman interview. Camp was a student activist at UCLA, and had worked with Cesar Chavez and the United Farm Workers on the grape boycott. Biographical material in Cavise files.

89. *Rapid City Journal,* August 29, 1973, p. 1, and September 6, 1973, p. 1; *Minneapolis Tribune,* August 29, 1973, p. 1, August 30, 1973, p. 1, sec. B, and September 2, 1973, p. 1; *Saint Paul Pioneer Press,* August 28, 1973, p. 4; *Sioux Falls Argus Leader,* August 28, 1973, p. 16.

90. *Rapid City Journal,* September 9, 1973, p. 2; *New York Times,* September 13, 1973, p. 13; *Sioux Falls Argus Leader,* September 9, 1973, p. 1.

91. Three weeks later Russell Means accused the senator of having advocated ending the siege at Wounded Knee by any means necessary. *New York Times,* September 1, 1973, p. 22.

92. *Minneapolis Tribune,* October 19, 1973, p. 1, October 20, 1973, p. 7B, October 22, 1973, p. 2B, and October 23, 1973, p. 13; *Rapid City Journal,* October 19, 1973, p. 1; *Sioux Falls Argus Leader,* October 19, 1973, p. 5; *Saint Paul Pioneer Press,* October 22, 1973, p. 11, October 23, 1973, p. 14, and October 24, 1973, p. 9.

93. On the shooting of BIA officers see *New York Times,* October 23, 1973, p. 8; *Rapid City Journal,* October 23, 1973, p. 1; *Sioux Falls Argus Leader,* October 22, 1973, p. 1. For coverage of the funeral, see *Minneapolis Tribune,* October 24, 1973, p. 1, sec. B. Federal District Judge Fred Nichol issued an order that allowed AIM members to attend the funeral, over the strenuous objections of the U.S. Attorney's office and despite his own personal reservations. Banks, however, decided not to challenge the tribal court order in an effort to diffuse the threats of force coming from Wilson and stayed just off the reservation. *Sioux Falls Argus Leader,* October 23, 1973, p. 1; *Rapid City Journal,* October 24, 1973, p. 1.

94. Clayton and Banks in *Rapid City Journal,* October 19, 1973, p. 1, and October 20, 1973, p. 1; on Bissonette's importance, Banks and James interviews. The government claimed he was shot once with a shotgun, while WKLDOC claimed it was several times at close range. *Minneapolis Tribune,* October 20, 1973, p. 7, sec. B; *Rapid City Journal,* October 19, 1973, p. 1. Part of the controversy arose from the removal of the body to Scotsbluff, Nebraska, for an autopsy, without the knowledge of the Bissonette family or its lawyers. *Rapid City Journal,* October 21, 1973, p. 2.

95. *New York Times,* September 1, 1973, p. 22; *Sioux Falls Argus Leader,* September 7, 1973, p. 6.

96. Drug arrests in *Minneapolis Tribune,* September 25, 1973, p. 13; *Sioux Falls Argus Leader,* September 26, 1973, p. 33. Bellecourt in *Minneapolis Tribune,* October 20, 1973, p. 7B; Banks in *Sioux Falls Argus Leader,* October 10, 1973, p. 24. Also, in mid-October an independent audit of Pine Ridge Tribal finances, requested by the BIA, revealed inefficiency and sloppiness, but no "misuse of funds," undercutting one of the claims of the dissidents on the reservation; *Sioux Falls Argus Leader,* October 10, 1973, p. 4; *Rapid City Journal,* October 13, 1973, p. 3. A summary of the report is contained in Leventhal, "Course Materials," pp. 219–224.

97. *Minneapolis Tribune,* September 26, 1973, p. 22C, and September 27, 1973, p. 1; *Saint Paul Pioneer Press,* September 26, 1973, p. 22. See also coverage of a Means speech in West Virginia, *Sioux Falls Argus Leader,* September 21, 1973, p. 2, and a Banks speech in Iowa, *Rapid City Journal,* August 24, 1973, p. 2.

98. Coverage on hearings conducted on Pine Ridge by a senate subcommittee on "Nutrition and Human Needs," *Rapid City Journal,* August 30, 1973, p. 1; on poverty among Native Americans, *New York Times,* June 17, 1973, p. 14; on McLaughlin, *Sioux Falls Argus Leader,* November 21, 1973, p. 4, December 2, 1973, p. 2, and December 15, 1973, p. 4; *Rapid City Journal,* November 20, 1973, p. 3, December 5, 1973, p. 3, and December 6, 1973, p. 2; conditions on Pine Ridge in *Rapid City Journal,* November 20, 1973, p. 3; Means's campaign, *Rapid City Journal,* September 2, 1973, p. 9; AIM's call for meetings with the National Tribal Chairman's Association and the National Congress of American Indians, *New York Times,* November 1, 1973, p. 12.

99. *New York Times,* November 11, 1973, p. 2, sec. 4; a similar story in a Saint Paul paper focused on the violence connected to AIM, highlighting the shootings of Bellecourt and Bissonette, *Saint Paul Pioneer Press,* October 29, 1973, p. 5; other criticism of AIM in *Minneapolis Tribune,* September 6, 1973, p. 1B, and September 13, 1973, p. 1B.

100. *Minneapolis Tribune,* November 10, 1973, p. 8B.

101. *New York Times,* October 23, 1973, p. 8; October 24, 1973, p. 13. Earlier Indian groups had charged thirty-two federal agencies with discrimination in a complaint filed with the newly created Indian Rights Unit of the Justice Department. Comments on the Navajo in *New York Times,* August 30, 1973, p. 54; October 10, 1973, p. 29.

102. Michel Foucault, "The Dangerous Individual," in *Politics, Philosophy, Culture: Interviews and Other Writings, 1977–1984,* ed. Lawrence D. Kritzman, trans. Alain Baudot and Jane Couchman (New York: Routledge, 1988), pp. 123–151; the quote is on p. 142.

103. *Sioux Falls Argus Leader,* October 11, 1973, p. 16. Information on speaking engagements in general is in Banks and Bellecourt interviews.

104. *Rapid City Journal,* November 28, 1973, p. 2; *Saint Paul Pioneer Press,* November 28, 1973, p. 13.

105. *Rapid City Journal,* November 30, 1973, p. 1; Hurd's comments on ordinary crimes in *New York Times,* September 23, 1973, p. 32.

106. Banks interview; Kunstler, *Sioux Falls Argus Leader,* December 10, 1973, p. 4; Roubideaux, *Rapid City Journal,* December 11, 1973, p. 2.

107. Laura Hengehold, "An Immodest Proposal: Foucault, Historization and the 'Second Rape,' " *Hypatia: A Journal of Feminist Philosophy* 9 (1994): 98.

108. Lucie E. White, "Subordination, Rhetorical Skills, and Sunday Shoes: Notes on the Hearing of Mrs. G.," *Buffalo Law Review* 38 (1990): 1–58; the quote is on p. 9.

109. The case was *Montoya v. United States,* 180 U.S. 261 (1901), which defined "tribe" as "a body of Indians of the same or similar race, united in community under one leadership or government, and inhabiting a particular though sometimes ill-defined territory." The quote is on p. 266. The dismissal of the Mashpee claim was upheld by the Court of Appeals: *Mashpee v. New Seabury Corp.,* 592 F.2d 575 (1st Cir.), cert. denied, 444 U.S. 866 (1979).

110. Gerald Torres and Kathryn Milun, "Translating *Yonnondio* by Precedent and Evidence: The Mashpee Indian Case," *Duke Law Journal* 4 (1990): 628–636.

111. As Kristin Bumiller argues in her studies of rape cases, highly publicized trials

become symbols that project certain messages "through language and legal form about identity and social relationships in a struggle between the agonistic world views of the defense and the prosecution." Kristin Bumiller, "Fallen Angels: The Representation of Violence Against Women in Legal Culture," *International Journal of the Sociology of Law* 18 (1990): 126–127.

112. In 1973 there were approximately 843,000 Native Americans in the United States, or one-half of 1 percent of the population; figures in *New York Times,* November 11, 1973, p. 2, sec. IV.

3. THE SAINT PAUL TRIAL BEGINS

1. The Ojibway are also known as the Chippewa, which was the name used on treaties and the one still used for legal purposes in Minnesota. The Ojibway were divided onto five reservations in the northern third of the state and successfully resisted further consolidation. In 1889 the Nelson Act applied the allotment provisions of the Dawes Act to Minnesota reservations and for state jurisdiction in some matters. The Ojibway reservation of Red Lake was excluded from the Nelson Act and remains under tribal control. For a general overview of Minnesota Indians see Elizabeth Ebbott and Judith Rosenblatt, *Indians in Minnesota* (Minneapolis: University of Minnesota Press, 1985).

2. In its aftermath all but a few Dakota were forced to leave the state and settle in South Dakota. For an excellent study of the Dakota trials see Carol Chomsky, "The United States-Dakota War Trials: A Study in Military Injustice," *Stanford Law Review* 43 (1990): 13–95.

3. Frederick E. Hoxie, *A Final Promise: The Campaign to Assimilate the Indians, 1880–1920* (New York: Cambridge University Press, 1989), p. 233.

4. Diane Wiley interview, March 29, 1990. Information also from Scully and Cohoes interviews; press reports in *Saint Paul Pioneer Press,* January 10, 1974, p. 3.

5. See Affidavit by Jay Schulman, dated January 24, 1974; see also letter from Diane Wiley dated May 1974, summarizing the findings; both documents in Cavise files. Further analysis concluded that potential jurors in South Dakota were twice as likely as those of the Third Division of Minnesota to disapprove of the tactics used by Indians at Wounded Knee, three times as likely to put the blame on Indians for what happened at Wounded Knee, and 35 percent more likely to state that their sympathies were with the federal government; Affidavit of Jay Schulman, signed February 13, 1974, in WKLDOC Records, MHS.

6. Today such jury studies are less focused on biases and profiles, and include studies of how people understand specific arguments and how they react to witnesses, certain types of documents, and the attorneys themselves. See The National Jury Project's *Jurywork: Systematic Techniques* (New York: Clark Boardman, 1994).

7. *Saint Paul Pioneer Press,* January 10, 1974, p. 3.

8. WKLDOC had split in two, setting up offices in Saint Paul and Sioux Falls, and AIM had closed all its field offices to consolidate its resources in the Twin Cities. Tilsen, Wiley, Joe and M. G. Beeler, Cohoes, James, Leventhal, and Hall interviews.

9. Hurd and Gienapp interviews.
10. *New York Times,* January 8, 1974, p. 11; January 9, 1974, p. 18; *Saint Paul Pioneer Press,* January 7, 1974, p. 27.
11. The defense had proposed a team concept to Nichol, but the judge insisted on designated attorneys for each defendant. Roubideaux would play a limited role and eventually left Saint Paul altogether, citing the obligations of family and his private practice back in South Dakota. Later he would handle some of the other Wounded Knee–related cases; Banks interview. Originally Lane was to take responsibility for the Custer cases, but decided to join the defense team in Saint Paul instead. Tilsen, Gallant, and Cohoes interviews.
12. Kunstler quoted in *Rapid City Journal,* January 9, 1974, p. 2; rally coverage in *Minneapolis Tribune,* January 8, 1974, p. 1.
13. *Minneapolis Tribune,* January 8, 1974, p. 1.
14. See reports in *Minneapolis Tribune,* January 8, 1974, p. 1; *Saint Paul Pioneer Press,* January 23, 1974, p. 2.
15. See reports in *New York Times,* January 8, 1974, p. 11, January 9, 1974, p. 18, and January 12, 1974, p. 30; *Saint Paul Pioneer Press,* January 8, 1974, pp. 1, 4.
16. Quoted in *Minneapolis Tribune,* January 9, 1974, p. 1; see also *Saint Paul Pioneer Press,* January 8, 1974, p. 1.
17. Clayton quoted in *Minneapolis Tribune,* January 6, 1974, p. 1; Hurd quoted in *Saint Paul Pioneer Press,* January 9, 1974, p. 11.
18. See copies of the press packet in WKLDOC Records, MHS.
19. *Rapid City Journal,* January 25, 1974, p. 3; *Minneapolis Tribune,* February 4, 1974, pp. 1, 5; see also *Saint Paul Pioneer Press,* January 9, 1974, p. 20; *Sioux Falls Argus Leader,* January 20, 1974, p. 1.
20. Nichol interview. On the treaty rulings, information also from Hall and Leventhal interviews. The motion to dismiss was based on defense contentions that the defendants could not get a fair trial because of harassment of witnesses and defense committee members. Nichol also ordered that both prosecution and defense witnesses be sequestered while their respective cases were being put on, that the attorneys submit to a metal-detection search along with everyone else entering the courthouse, and that a courtroom seating plan agreed to by both sides be approved. Internal memo for defense committee summarizing the hearing, written by Len Cavise; Cavise files.
21. *New York Times,* January 15, 1974, p. 13; *Minneapolis Tribune,* January 10, 1974, p. 1.
22. See criticism of the decision in *Minneapolis Tribune,* January 14, 1974, p. 8, January 15, 1974, p. 2B, and January 19, 1974, p. 8; on the appeals court decision, see *Minneapolis Tribune,* February 26, 1974, p. 7B.
23. *Saint Paul Pioneer Press,* January 11, 1974, p. 20; *Minneapolis Tribune,* January 9, 1974, pp. 1, 9, and December 28, 1973, p. 4C; see also memo on security in Cavise files.
24. *Transcript of the United States v. Dennis Banks* #CR 73-5034 and 73-5062, *Transcript of the United States v. Russell Means,* #CR 73-5035 and 73-5063, U.S. District Court, District of South Dakota (hereafter cited as *Transcript*), copy in WKLDOC Records, MHS, vol. 11, pp. 2028–2046, 2227–2237. Press coverage on the security debate in *Minneapolis Tribune,* January 9, 1974, p. 9, and Jan-

uary 24, 1974, p. 1B; *Saint Paul Pioneer Press,* January 8, 1974, p. 1, January 24, 1974, p. 1, and January 25, 1974, p. 4; *Rapid City Journal,* January 10, 1974, p. 2, and January 25, 1974, p. 6.

25. *Transcript,* vol. 11, pp. 2033–2036.

26. The defense filed seventeen pretrial motions in 1973 and thirteen more between January 7 and February 11, 1974. See internal defense memo, January 22, 1974, prepared by Len Cavise, Cavise files. One local paper, however, summed it all up as the "ponderous motions" of the defense, "countered by brief prosecution rebuttals." *Saint Paul Pioneer Press,* January 10, 1974, p. 1.

27. Means quoted in *Rapid City Journal,* January 12, 1974, p. 16. The defense also claimed that the rural population was overrepresented and that professionals were underrepresented. Pointing out that only ninety-five members of the panel were professionals, defense attorneys said that their survey and the census put the percentage of professionals at 17.6 percent and 22 percent respectively and noted that doctors, nurses, teachers, and ministers were all excused on request. Prosecutors had also expressed concerns about excusing people who held positions of responsibility because of the possible length of the trial, saying it was not clear which side was prejudiced more. *Transcript,* vol. 11, pp. 1998–2002; Gienapp interview. Of the 7,500 prospective jurors, every four names, numbering 1,875, were put into a box and then 200 names were drawn and called for the panel.

28. *Transcript,* vol. 1, pp. 3–19.

29. Copies of the government submission, dated December 17, 1973, and the defense submission, "Voir Dire Questions Requested by Defendants," undated, are in Larry Leventhal, "Wounded Knee: 1890, 1973 and Beyond, Course Materials," American Indians 5352, University of Minnesota, pp. 259–275.

30. *Minneapolis Tribune,* January 8, 1974, pp. 1, 9.

31. Wiley interview.

32. Jury selection in the transcript runs from pp. 21–2757, with breaks for other matters at various points.

33. *Transcript,* vol. 3, pp. 1998–2002. See also Ron Christenson, *Political Trials: Gordian Knots in the Law* (New Brunswick, N.J.: Transaction Publishers, 1989), pp. 261–264, for a summary of the jury selection in the case.

34. Seven were dismissed directly by the judge, eleven after challenges by the defense, and two after challenges by the prosecution. *Transcript,* vol. 16, p. 2906; vol. 3, p. 429; see also vol. 10, p. 1888; vol. 6, p. 933; and Christenson, *Political Trials,* pp. 261–267.

35. *Transcript,* vol. 4, p. 527.

36. See for instance *Transcript,* vol. 5, p. 798, and vol. 8, pp. 1438, 1758.

37. *Saint Paul Pioneer Press,* January 21, 1974, p. 13.

38. *Transcript,* vol. 3, pp. 353–367; see also Christenson, *Political Trials,* pp. 264–265.

39. Hurd interview.

40. Comment from Hurd interview. Information on the defense from Larry Leventhal interview, November 15, 1989; Doug Hall interview, October 10, 1989; and Tilsen, Kunstler, and Wiley interviews. Tilsen called the whole process "incredibly valuable," while Kunstler remained skeptical about the system: "I

come from the old school where instincts govern, but I go along with it," he said, calling it "good politics." Kunstler also credited Phillip Deere's ability to read how white people reacted to Indians as well as some of the background gathered by the jury study volunteers.

41. The examinations of the twelve jurors finally seated appear in the *Transcript* as follows: Therese M. Cherrier, vol. 3, pp. 85–524; Robert H. Christensen, vol. 4, pp. 527–581; Maureen A. Coonan, vols. 6 and 7, pp. 1131–1182; James L. Putnam, vol. 9, pp. 1542–1548; Susan C. Overas, vol. 9, pp. 1599–1641; Nancy L. Claeson, vol. 9, pp. 1646–1679; John J. Kilbride, vol. 11, pp. 2073–2117; Fran Jeanne Aiken, vol. 12, pp. 2118–2133, 2158–2189; Richard Garcia, vol. 13, pp. 2387–2417; Theola May DuBois, vol. 14, pp. 2604–2633; Katherine A. Valo, vol. 14, pp. 2646–2700; Geraldine L. Nelson, vol. 15, pp. 2757–2797. The selection of the alternates is contained in *Transcript*, vol. 16, pp. 2816–3667.

See also *Minneapolis Tribune*, January 30, 1974, p. 1; January 31, 1974, p. 1B; February 6, 1974, p. 6; February 11, 1974, p. 1B; *Rapid City Journal*, January 28, 1974, p. 1; *Saint Paul Pioneer Press*, January 30, 1974, p. 19; January 31, 1974, pp. 19, 25; February 6, 1974, p. 5. On the alternate who was part Indian, see *Saint Paul Pioneer Press*, February 1, 1974, p. 13; *Rapid City Journal*, February 2, 1974, p. 18.

42. Each defendant had ten strikes, for a total of twenty, to six for the prosecution. The prosecution protested strenuously at the time and continued to complain that the decision left them at a distinct disadvantage. *Transcript*, vol. 12, pp. 2154–2155; Gienapp and Hurd interviews.

43. Tilsen, Leventhal, Hall, and Kunstler interviews; Means quoted in *Sioux Falls Argus Leader*, January 31, 1974, p. 7.

44. Banks quoted in *Sioux Falls Argus Leader*, January 31, 1974, p. 7.

45. "Minutes of Coalition Meeting," AIM Center, January 20, 1974, 7:30 P.M., prepared by Paula Giese; copy in Cavise files.

46. *New York Times*, January 21, 1974, p. 10; *Minneapolis Tribune*, January 24, 1974, p. 1B; *Sioux Falls Argus Leader*, January 22, 1974, p. 5; January 23, 1974, p. 1.

47. Press coverage of the campaign in the *New York Times*, January 24, 1974, p. 25; *Sioux Falls Argus Leader*, January 13, 1974, p. 1; coverage of the vote and the reaction in *Saint Paul Pioneer Press*, January 24, 1974, p. 1; *Sioux Falls Argus Leader*, January 24, 1974, p. 4. The *Rapid City Journal* and *Sioux Falls Argus Leader* covered the campaign almost daily in January and February.

48. Tilsen interview.

49. *Minneapolis Tribune*, January 10, 1974, p. 2.

50. A copy of the motion and affidavit are in WKLDOC Records, MHS.

51. A copy of *AIM v. Nixon* filed in the District of South Dakota is in WKLDOC Records, MHS. The suit, which also sought monetary damages, was dismissed in January 1975.

52. *Transcript*, vol. 4, pp. 582–589; vol. 5, pp. 773–785.

53. Quoted in *Saint Paul Pioneer Press*, January 12, 1974, p. 3; see also *New York Times*, January 15, 1974, p. 13; *Minneapolis Tribune*, January 12, 1974, p. 8B, and January 15, 1974, p. 2B. Mark Lane also accused U.S. Marshals of trying

to intimidate people at a a WKLDOC fund-raising event held in Crystal, a suburb of Minneapolis, but Nichol quickly denied a motion to investigate the matter and it, too, was largely ignored in the press. *Transcript,* vol. 20, pp. 3760–3870.

54. Kunstler also had a lengthy interview with the *Rapid City Journal,* February 3, 1974, p. 1. Coverage of Press Club speech in *Saint Paul Pioneer Press,* January 22, 1974, p. 29.

55. *Minneapolis Tribune,* January 20, 1974, p. 11.

56. *Minneapolis Tribune,* January 20, 1974, p. 1. Kunstler also got to air his views in an interview with a reporter from the *Rapid City Journal,* February, 3, 1974, p. 1.

57. *Transcript,* vol. 13, p. 2489. Kunstler was to attend a hearing before the New York State Bar professional responsibility committee, which was proceeding against him even though the contempt citations from the trial in question were still on appeal. *Minneapolis Tribune,* January 26, 1974, p. 4; *Saint Paul Pioneer Press,* January 26, 1974, p. 13.

58. *Minneapolis Tribune,* January 23, 1974, p. 2B; January 26, 1974, p. 4. Kunstler believes that the appearances and support of black leaders throughout the trial helped heal some historical distrust of African Americans on the part of Indian people. William Kunstler interview.

59. *Minneapolis Tribune,* January 26, 1974, pp. 1, 4; *Saint Paul Pioneer Press,* January 26, 1974, pp. 13, 18. Brando reportedly had given people inside Wounded Knee a check for $25,000. *Rapid City Journal,* January 28, 1974, p. 6. A few weeks later the *Minneapolis Tribune* carried a feature story on the actor and his views on Indians. *Minneapolis Tribune,* February 16, 1974, p. 1D.

60. Hurd interview.

61. By January 1974, most of Garment's time was taken up by the Watergate investigation. The letter was actually prepared by his executive assistant, Bradley Patterson, who had been involved in Indian matters on behalf of his boss from the beginning. Garment and Patterson interview.

62. The summary is from a copy of Garment's four-page letter to Fools Crow, written on White House stationery, plus attachment, dated January 8, 1974. Copy in Leventhal, "Course Materials," pp. 147–171.

63. *Minneapolis Tribune,* January 11, 1974, p. 1; *Saint Paul Pioneer Press,* January 11, 1974, p. 13. Defense complaints to Nichol, *Transcript,* vol. 4, p. 589.

64. *Minneapolis Tribune,* January 30, 1974, p. 8; *Saint Paul Pioneer Press,* January 30, 1974, p. 3.

65. Testimony of Margaret Jenner, *Transcript,* vol. 6, pp. 3179–3183, 3672–3860. Press coverage in *Minneapolis Tribune,* February 2, 1974, p. 7B; February 12, 1974, p. 3B; *Saint Paul Pioneer Press,* February 2, 1974, p. 9; February 12, 1974, p. 27.

66. William H. Chafe, *The Unfinished Journey: America Since World War II* (New York: Oxford University Press, 1986), p. 429.

67. Todd Gitlin, *The Whole World Is Watching: Mass Media and the Making and Unmaking of the New Left* (Berkeley: University of California Press, 1980), pp. 286, 283–287.

68. Ibid., p. 271.

69. *New York Times,* February 8, 1974, p. 36; February 9, 1974, p. 23.
70. *Minneapolis Tribune,* February 3, 1974, p. 1B.
71. *Sioux Falls Argus Leader,* February 4, 1974, p. 4.
72. *New York Times,* February 9, 1974, p. 23.
73. On Means's reaction to the vote, see *Saint Paul Pioneer Press,* February 9, 1974, p. 9; *Rapid City Journal,* February 11, 1974, p. 3; *Sioux Falls Argus Leader,* February 10, 1974, p. 10. On Ted Means see *Rapid City Journal,* January 31, 1974, p. 2; February 3, 1974, p. 4.
74. *Minneapolis Tribune,* February 8, 1974, p. 1; on Wilson's earlier comments, see *Rapid City Journal,* February 1, 1974, p. 2.
75. *Rapid City Journal,* February 9, 1974, p. 3.
76. *Minneapolis Tribune,* February 10, 1974, p. 1; *Saint Paul Pioneer Press,* February 9, 1974, p. 9; *Rapid City Journal,* February 9, 1974, pp. 1–3. Some did note that four Means supporters were elected to the Tribal Council, along with four others who identified themselves as anti-Wilson, leaving twelve others as possible Wilson supporters; see *Minneapolis Tribune,* February 10, 1974, p. 1.
77. W. Lance Bennett and Martha S. Feldman, *Reconstructing Reality in the Courtroom: Justice and Judgement in American Culture* (New Brunswick, N.J.: Rutgers University Press, 1984), pp. 150–154.

4. THE OPENING STATEMENTS

1. See for instance Steven Lubet, *Modern Trial Advocacy: Analysis and Practice* (Notre Dame, Ind.: National Institute for Trial Advocacy, 1993), pp. 335–384.
2. Ibid., p. 337.
3. *Transcript,* vol. 21, pp. 3863–3870. Banks credits Means with the original idea to give opening statements. Banks interview.
4. Lubet, *Modern Trial Advocacy,* pp. 337–338.
5. *Transcript,* vol. 21, pp. 3878–3882. The statutes involved were as follows: theft from the trading post, 18 USC 1153, 661, South Dakota Compiled laws, 22-32-9; assault, 18 USC 1111, 1114; obstruction, 18 USC 231(a)(3); Molotov cocktails, 18 USC 5861(d), 5871; theft of automobile, 18 USC 1153 and 661.
6. *Transcript,* vol. 21, p. 3883.
7. *Transcript,* vol. 21, pp. 3883–3887.
8. *Transcript,* vol. 21, pp. 3887–3889.
9. Statute, 18 USC 111, 1114; *Transcript,* vol. 21, pp. 3889–3890.
10. *Transcript,* vol. 21, pp. 3889–3898.
11. *Transcript,* vol. 21, pp. 3898–3899.
12. *Transcript,* vol. 21, pp. 3899–3906.
13. *Transcript,* vol. 21, p. 3906. The transcript incorrectly reads, "Hau mi tok pi." The guess at what the words probably were and the translation come from the Lakota Studies Department of Sinte Gleske University in Mission, South Dakota.
14. *Transcript,* vol. 21, pp. 3908–3911.
15. *Transcript,* vol. 21, p. 3912.
16. *Transcript,* vol. 21, p. 3914.
17. *Transcript,* vol. 21, pp. 3914–3916.

18. *Transcript,* vol. 21, pp. 3919–3920.
19. *Transcript,* vol. 21, p. 3922; see also pp. 3920–3922.
20. *Transcript,* vol. 21, pp. 3923–3928, 3930–3934.
21. *Transcript,* vol. 21, p. 3929; see also pp. 3928–3934.
22. *Transcript,* vol. 21, p. 3936; see also pp. 3934–3936.
23. *Transcript,* vol. 21, p. 3936.
24. *Transcript,* vol. 21, p. 3938.
25. *Transcript,* vol. 21, p. 3940.
26. *Transcript,* vol. 21, p. 3941.
27. *Transcript,* vol. 21, p. 3943.
28. *Transcript,* vol. 21, pp. 3943–3947; the newspaper story is in *Sioux Falls Argus Leader,* January 8, 1974, p. 1.
29. *Transcript,* vol. 21, pp. 3947–3950.
30. *Transcript,* vol. 21, pp. 3955–3956; see also pp. 3950–3956.
31. *Transcript,* vol. 21, p. 3956.
32. *Transcript,* vol. 21, p. 3959.
33. *Transcript,* vol. 21, pp. 3958–3961; Nichol's quote in *Minneapolis Tribune,* February 13, 1974, p. 4.
34. *Transcript,* vol. 21, pp. 3962–3963; Nichol's press statements in *Minneapolis Tribune,* February 13, 1974, pp. 1, 4.
35. Quoted in *Transcript,* vol. 21, p. 3968; see generally pp. 3963–3968.
36. *Transcript,* vol. 21, p. 3968.
37. *Transcript,* vol. 21, pp. 3968–3972.
38. *Transcript,* vol. 21, pp. 3968–3975.
39. *Transcript,* vol. 21, pp. 3976–3977.
40. *Transcript,* vol. 21, p. 3977.
41. Mary Crow Dog, *Lakota Woman,* with Richard Erdoes (New York: Harper Perennial, 1990), pp. 65–66.
42. Ibid., pp. 65–67; see also William K. Powers, *Oglala Religion* (Lincoln: University of Nebraska Press, 1982), pp. 63–64; Beatrice Medicine, "Indian Women and the Renaissance of Traditional Religion," in *Sioux Indian Religion: Tradition and Innovation,* ed. Raymond J. DeMallie and Douglas R. Parks (Norman: University of Oklahoma Press, 1987), pp. 159–171.
43. Rayna Green, "Native American Women," in *SIGNS: Journal of Women in Culture and Society* 6 (1980): 264–267.
44. Päivi H. Hoikkala, "Mothers and Community Builders: Salt River Pima and Maricopa Women in Community Action," in Nancy Shoemaker, *Negotiators of Change: Historical Perspectives on Native American Women* (New York: Routledge, 1995), pp. 213–234; Marla N. Powers, *Oglala Women: Myth, Ritual, and Reality* (Chicago: University of Chicago Press, 1986), pp. 145–154.
45. As Nancy Shoemaker notes, historical narratives usually depict Indian women as either the overworked "squaw" or the sexually desirable Indian "princess." Shoemaker, "Introduction," in *Negotiators of Change,* p. 3.
46. When Banks had finished, Judge Nichol himself immediately redirected the jury's attention to the removal of Kunstler and Lane, reminding them that it was the duty of attorneys on both sides to make objections, even to the judge's rulings, and adding that while it is also the duty of the judge to

admonish an attorney who he believes "is not in keeping with proper courtroom procedure," the jurors should "draw no inference whatever against the
client" because of any admonition. *Transcript,* vol. 21, pp. 3977–3978.

47. *Minneapolis Tribune,* February 13, 1974, p. 1; *Saint Paul Pioneer Press,* February
13, 1974, pp. 1, 2; *New York Times,* February 13, 1974, p. 14. The headline in
the *Rapid City Journal* read "Attorneys Ordered Removed from Court," February 14, 1974, p. 22. The *Sioux Falls Argus Leader* headline read, "Flare Up
Causes Kunstler, 2 Others to Be Ousted by Nichol at AIM Trial," February 13,
1974, p. 17.

48. *Sioux Falls Argus Leader,* January 9, 1974, p. 1; January 12, p. 7; see also *Rapid
City Journal,* January 14, 1974, p. 13.

49. *New York Times,* January 8, 1974, p. 11; January 9, 1974, p. 18; January 12,
1974, p. 30; *Saint Paul Pioneer Press,* January 9, 1974, pp. 1, 4.

50. The pamphlet, entitled "The Opening Statements of Russell Means and Dennis
Banks, February 12, 1974," included a reprint of the 1868 Treaty. Copy in
Northcott files. The local newspaper story is in *Minneapolis Tribune,* February
18, 1974, p. 1B.

5. THE GOVERNMENT'S CASE GETS DERAILED

1. See *U.S. v. Hutchinson,* 488 F.2d 484, and *Glasser v. U.S.,* 315 U.S. 60.

2. Hurd and Gienapp were assisted by Earl Kaplan, who reported to the Justice
Department on the progress of the case, and another Justice Department
attorney, who helped with the logistics of making sure that witnesses were in
court ready to testify when their time came. The prosecutors were using office
space provided by the Saint Paul U.S. Attorney's office in the courthouse, but
had brought along two secretaries from their office in Sioux Falls. The FBI
remained in charge of the documentary evidence and had assigned an agent
to act as a liaison with the prosecution team. The U.S. Attorneys maintained
throughout that the case was theirs to try, with little direction coming from
the Justice Department. Gienapp, Hurd, and Clayton interviews.

3. Gienapp, Hurd, and Clayton interviews.

4. Any time the 1868 Treaty could be brought in on cross-examination, the
defense would seize the opportunity. Banks, Tilsen, Leventhal, Hall, and Gallant interviews. Privately Tilsen was skeptical about the treaty defense, while
Banks believed it was central to the case. See also a memorandum on defense
strategy for cross-examination, no author listed, and another memorandum on
defense strategy by Tim Lund, both dated January 19, 1974, in WKLDOC
Records, MHS.

5. Copies of the summaries were also sent to the Sioux Falls office. As well as
exchanging summaries, witness statements, motions, and other legal research,
the two offices were also in regular telephone contact. Joe and M. G. Beeler,
Tilsen, Gallant, Cohoes, and Cavise interviews; see also copies of letters
between WKLDOC offices, notes of Evidence Collective meetings, legal memo-
randums, listings of collective members and duties, correspondence, and the
original witness and document files, in WKLDOC Records, MHS.

To enable them to keep track of all the witnesses over the coming weeks,

Nichol ruled that jurors could take notes for their own use. *Transcript*, vol. 21, p. 3989; the judge also ruled that no witnesses could be in the courtroom while other witnesses for their side of the case were testifying. *Transcript*, vol. 21, p. 3979.

6. Nelson direct examination, *Transcript*, vol. 21, pp. 4021–4050. (Hereafter direct and cross-examination will be referred to as "direct" and "cross.")

7. Cross, *Transcript*, vol. 21, pp. 4050–4094; also, Leventhal interview. Press coverage in *Minneapolis Tribune*, February, 14, 1974, pp. 1, 2.

8. The Clerk of Courts for the reservation had been brought to testify about the court order that requested the presence of U.S. Marshals on the reservation. Direct, *Transcript*, vol. 21, pp. 4094–4148; cross, pp. 4151–4200.

9. Several newspapers explained that such examination was part of the defense strategy in the case. *Minneapolis Tribune*, February 14, 1974, pp. 1, 2; the headline in the Times read, "Sioux Land Loss Is Cited at Trial," *New York Times*, February 14, 1974, p. 15; *Rapid City Journal*, February 19, 1974, p. 6. Another paper, however, characterized testimony as already having "slowed to a crawl." *Saint Paul Pioneer Press*, February 14, 1974, p. 21.

The defense also challenged a tribal court order which allegedly requested the U.S. Marshals to enter the reservation in February 1973, casting doubt on the charges involving obstruction of officers which hinged on their being involved in the "lawful performance" of their duties and giving credence to their case for treaty violations. The prosecution argued that it was unlawful to shoot at a law enforcement officer if he was in good faith trying to serve an illegal arrest warrant, and thus still protected by law. See testimony of Ivy Goings, Clerk of Tribal Court, *Transcript*, vol. 21, pp. 4094–4200.

10. The FBI agent was one of two who had tried to infiltrate AIM in Rapid City just prior to Wounded Knee; both gave similar testimony about seeing weapons and hearing statements about plans for a takeover. On cross-examination, defense attorneys pointed out inconsistencies between the agents' testimony and their written reports, their "lies" to AIM people about who they were, and their lack of knowledge of Indian traditions and the Oglala Sioux. See testimony of Stanley Keel and Charles Stephenson, who were both part Indian: Keel's direct testimony in *Transcript*, vol. 21, pp. 4201–4244; cross, *Transcript*, vol. 23, pp. 4244–4398, vol. 24, pp. 4423–4494; cross of Stephenson, vol. 25, pp. 4640–4725, vol. 26, pp. 4730–4853. For press coverage noting the tactics of the defense on cross-examination see *Minneapolis Tribune*, February 15, 1974, p. 1B; also *Sioux Falls Argus Leader*, February 22, 1974, p. 3; *Rapid City Journal*, February 23, 1974, p. 9.

11. Direct, *Transcript*, vol. 24, pp. 4409–4423.

12. Direct, *Transcript*, vol. 26, pp. 4877–4905.

13. See cross, *Transcript*, vol. 27, pp. 5004–5012, 5029–5041; entire cross, vol. 27, pp. 4938–5058.

14. *Transcript*, vol. 27, pp. 5121–5127; entire cross, pp. 5092–5127; direct, pp. 5067–5076.

15. Direct testimony, *Transcript*, vol. 28, pp. 5142–5167; cross, vol. 28, pp. 5169–5185, 5204–5206.

16. *Transcript*, vol. 28, pp. 5256–5262, 5297–5299, 5356–5362, and vol. 29,

pp. 5422–5441. Press reports in *Saint Paul Pioneer Press,* February 27, 1974, p. 32; *Minneapolis Tribune,* February 27, 1974, p. 1B; Nichol's comment to reporters in *Minneapolis Tribune,* February 28, 1974, p. 4B.

17. Witness James Propotnick, direct, *Transcript,* vol. 29, pp. 5459–5467; cross, pp. 5467–5488.

18. Testimony of Jere Brennan, a BIA child welfare worker: direct, *Transcript,* vol. 29, pp. 5543–5554, cross, pp. 5554–5605, and vol. 30, pp. 5609–5611, 5611–5623.

19. *Transcript,* vol. 30, pp. 5725–5795.

20. Questions to Thomas concerning the "goon squad" were ruled beyond the scope of cross; *Transcript,* vol. 30, pp. 5799–5808; vol. 31, pp. 5826–5903.

21. Direct, *Transcript,* vol. 31, pp. 5903–5939; vol. 32, pp. 5943–5983; cross, vol. 32, pp. 6051–6118.

22. *Minneapolis Tribune,* March 5, 1974, p. 4B. The *Rapid City Journal* headline was "Priest Says He Was Taken Prisoner, Tied by AIM Members in His Church," March 4, 1974, p. 2.

23. *Transcript,* vol. 33, pp. 6282–6361.

24. *Transcript,* vol. 34, p. 6430.

25. The petition was read to the jury in *Transcript,* vol. 33, p. 6271; the rest of the debate over the document is in vol. 33, pp. 6270–6272, 6282–6334, 6340–6361, 6420–6449, 6465–6637.

26. *Transcript,* vol. 35, pp. 6731–6732; see also vol. 35, pp. 6685–6686, 6696–6731; and generally, cross, vol. 36, pp. 6757–6833; re-direct, pp. 6833–6856, 6874–6887; re-cross, pp. 6887–6922.

27. *Transcript,* vol. 34, pp. 6403–6420.

28. Enlow's quote is in *Minneapolis Tribune,* March 7, 1974, p. 1B. The agreement on the search of the files is in *Transcript,* vol. 36, pp. 6859–6874. The judge's quotes to the press are in *Minneapolis Tribune,* March 7, 1974, p. 1B; *Saint Paul Pioneer Press,* March 7, 1974, p. 21; and the reports on Nichol's meeting with Enlow are in *Minneapolis Tribune,* March 6, 1974, p. 1B; March 7, 1974, p. 1B; *Saint Paul Pioneer Press,* March 6, 1974, p. 15; March 7, 1974, p. 21; March 8, 1974, p. 39; *Rapid City Journal,* March 11, 1974, p. 2.

29. *Minneapolis Tribune,* March 10, 1974, p. 7B; March 10, 1974, p. 1.

30. The *Tribune* story was headlined "U.S. Is Facing Sanctions in Wounded Knee Trial," *Minneapolis Tribune,* March 12, 1974, p. 1B; see also *Sioux Falls Argus Leader,* March 12, 1974, p. 4; March 13, 1974, p. 4; *Rapid City Journal,* March 11, 1974, p. 6; March 12, 1974, p. 2; March 14, 1974, p. 12; March 18, 1974, p. 2.

31. *Minneapolis Tribune,* March 13, 1974, p. 7B.

32. Direct, *Transcript,* vol. 36, pp. 6994–7021, 7033–7055; cross, vol. 39, pp. 7021–7033, 7055–7056.

33. *Sioux Falls Argus Leader,* March 9, 1974, p. 4; see also *Saint Paul Pioneer Press,* March 9, 1974, p. 11.

34. Cross-examination of Irene Jumping Bull in *Transcript,* vol. 37, pp. 7106–7107. For other testimony and cross, see: Jumping Bull, vol. 37, pp. 7059–7092, cross, pp. 7093–7115, 7115–7127; John Provost, direct, pp. 7128–7145, cross, pp. 7145–7172; Reuben Mesteth, direct, vol. 37, pp. 7172–7188, cross, pp. 7188–7231, 7231–7234.

35. See testimony of Serena Hall, direct, *Transcript*, vol. 38, pp. 7290–7304, and Harry Weston, direct, vol. 37, pp. 7304–7316; and Rufus C. Williams, direct, *Transcript*, vol. 39, pp. 7319–7328, and cross, pp. 7328–7329, where only one question was asked.

36. Direct testimony of FBI Agent Stephen Travis, *Transcript*, vol. 39, pp. 7319–7328; FBI Agent Lawrence Dick, vol. 39, pp. 7411–7419; and U.S. Marshal James Propotnick, vol. 39, pp. 7463–7474.

37. See cross-examination of the three witnesses: Travis, *Transcript*, vol. 39, pp. 7336–7408; Dick, pp. 7419–7460; Propotnick, pp. 7474–7502, 7539–7641.

38. On the FBI and Indian history see *Transcript*, vol. 39, pp. 7422–7423, 7450–7460; on snipers, p. 7460; on military equipment, pp. 7474–7501, 7539–7550, 7620–7635.

39. For Means's comments see *Transcript*, vol. 39, pp. 7501–7502; for Hurd and Nichol the next day, vol. 40, pp. 7520–7538.

40. Leavitt direct, *Transcript*, vol. 40, pp. 7671–7675; cross, vol. 40, pp. 7675–7734; vol. 41, pp. 7741–7770.

41. *Transcript*, vol. 41, pp. 7816–7868.

42. *Transcript*, vol. 41, p. 7795. The description of Means is from *Minneapolis Tribune*, March 16, 1974, p. 14C.

43. Questioning of Leavitt, *Transcript*, vol. 41, pp. 7869–7877; Hurd's testimony, vol. 41, pp. 7877–7898. Most of the press noted the dispute over Hurd's laughter, the reprimand of Means, and the testimony of Hurd, while one paper characterized the cross-examination of Leavitt as going "far afield." On Hurd's laugh, see *Minneapolis Tribune*, March 14, 1974, p. 6; *Rapid City Journal*, March 14, 1974, p. 1; *Sioux Falls Argus Leader*, March 14, 1974, p. 1; *Saint Paul Pioneer Press*, March 14, 1974, p. 23. On Hurd's testimony, see *Minneapolis Tribune*, March 16, 1974, pp. 1B, 14C; *Sioux Falls Argus Leader*, March 15, 1974, p. 4; *Saint Paul Pioneer Press*, March 16, 1974, p.15.

44. *Minneapolis Tribune*, March 14, 1974, p. 1; March 15, 1974, p. 1B; *Saint Paul Pioneer Press*, March 12, 1974, p. 12; March 13, 1974, p. 13.

45. *Transcript*, vol. 39, p. 7524. The defense also claimed that the FBI had attempted to intimidate a key witness, but Hurd insisted that they had only tried to interview him; when he refused, they left him alone. *Transcript*, vol. 40, pp. 7906–7920.

46. See copies of Sioux Falls and Saint Paul WKLDOC newsletters for February, March, April, and May 1974, and a copy of Paula Giese's review of the issues in the trial entitled "Wounded Knee: the Trials Begin," put out by Saint Paul WKLDOC; all in Cavise files. A copy of a booklet, "Wounded Knee 1890, 1973," which provides historical background on the Oglala, AIM, and an overview of the trials and background on some of the defendants and lawyers is in Northcott files. The WKLDOC Records, MHS, contain Saint Paul trial newsletters for February, April, and May 1974; assorted leaflets and pamphlets on women defendants, Wounded Knee 1890, the 1868 Treaty, AIM's goals and history, the opening statements of Banks and Means, background on defense lawyers, Means's Pine Ridge Campaign, announcements of fund-raising events, transcripts of radio ads; mailing lists for press contacts and others consisting of hundreds of names and addresses; copies of client newslet-

ters; and Saint Paul Committee lists entitled "Wounded Knee Communications Committee," "Personal Job Descriptions," and "Staff and Organization Duties." On the speakers' bureau and fund-raising, see Gilbert Thunder Hawk, Vernon Bellecourt, and Banks interviews. According to Bellecourt and Banks the money was to be split among the speaker, WKLDOC, and AIM. Banks noted that speakers would get part of the money because for many it was their only means of support, adding that several of the AIM people also had families at the time. Banks and Bellecourt interviews.

47. Tilsen calls Kunstler's sense of what the press would pick up on "as good as anyone's." Information taken from interviews with Tilsen, Kunstler, Gallant, Leventhal, and Northcott. Comments on the prosecution are from Hurd interview.

48. *Saint Paul Pioneer Press,* February 24, 1974, sec. 9, p. 1; February 25, 1974, p. 8; February 28, 1974, p. 21; March 2, 1974, p. 8; *Minneapolis Tribune,* February 28, 1974, p. 1B; see also Saint Paul WKLDOC Newsletter dated February 16, 1974, in Cavise files.

49. On the anniversary ceremony, see *Saint Paul Pioneer Press,* February 28, 1974, p. 21; *Sioux Falls Argus Leader,* February 28, 1974, p. 23; *Rapid City Journal,* March 1, 1974, p. 1; on communications with Pine Ridge, see Gilbert Thunder Hawk, DeCora Means, Ted Means, and Banks interviews. A copy of the petition for *Means et al., v. Wilson et al.,* filed on March 25, 1974 (civil action 74-5010), is in WKLDOC Records, MHS. Joining Means in the suit were Gladys Bissonette, Severt Young Bear, Marvin Ghost Bear, and Eugene White Hawk. Along with Wilson the suit listed as defendants various tribal and BIA officials, and the Department of Justice. The complaint alleged a denial of rights under federal civil rights laws, including Title 28, Chapter 15, section 1302 (1), (2), (8), of the U.S. Code, the Indian Civil Rights Act. A copy of the official challenge made to the tribal authorities along with supporting affidavits is also in WKLDOC Records, MHS.

50. *Rapid City Journal,* February 24, 1974, pp. 1, 2, 3; February 25, 1974, p. 1; *Sioux Falls Argus Leader,* February 27, 1974, p. 2. For Abnor's request for aid for Wounded Knee residents, see *Sioux Falls Argus Leader,* February 28, 1974, p. 3; *Rapid City Journal,* March 1, 1974, p. 28.

51. *Rapid City Journal,* March 4, 1974, p. 1; *Sioux Falls Argus Leader,* February 20, 1974, p. 6.

52. On congressional legislation, see *New York Times,* April 2, 1974, p. 27; Abourezk statements in *Sioux Falls Argus Leader,* February 27, 1974, p. 4; *Rapid City Journal,* March 1, 1974, p. 14. In Denver the regional office of the U.S. Commission on Civil Rights announced an investigation into allegations of irregularities and fraud during the Pine Ridge tribal election. *Rapid City Journal,* March 11, 1974, p. 5. The report on Indian education is in *New York Times,* April 7, 1974, p. 10.

53. For McGovern's speech at Macalester College in Saint Paul, see *Saint Paul Pioneer Press,* March 11, 1974, p. 15.

54. *Minneapolis Tribune,* February 15, 1974, p. 5; February 21, 1974, p. 12; *Saint Paul Pioneer Press,* February 16, 1974, p. 20; February 21, 1974, p. 5; *Sioux Falls Argus Leader,* February 21, 1974, p. 4.

55. *Sioux Falls Argus Leader,* February 20, 1974, p. 6; on Bellecourt's denial see *Minneapolis Tribune,* February 20, 1974, p. 4; February 21, 1974, p. 5; *Saint Paul Pioneer Press,* February 21, 1974, p. 5; March 5, 1974, p. 5.

56. Direct, *Transcript,* vol. 42, pp. 7915–8011; cross, pp. 7968–7990, re-direct, pp. 7990–7996.

57. See testimony of Myron Ellwein, *Transcript,* vol. 42, pp. 8018–8038; Phyllis Fast Wolf, vol. 42, pp. 8039–8091. On conversations concerning eavesdropping with Kent Frizell, who was an Assistant Attorney General from the Department of Justice in March of 1973, now Solicitor for the Department of the Interior, see *Transcript,* vol. 43, pp. 8150–8258; on phone conversations see Kunstler, vol. 44, pp. 8426–8444; William Mattheson, a lawyer with Black Hills Legal Services, vol. 43, pp. 8303–8328; Ramon Roubideaux, vol. 44, pp. 8400–8403, vol. 46, pp. 8827–8845, cross, pp. 8845–8866; Larry Leventhal, vol. 46, pp. 8879–8887, cross, pp. 8887–8889; Ken Tilsen, vol. 46, pp. 8890–8964, cross, pp. 8965–9000; Clyde Bellecourt, vol. 50, pp. 9936–9943, cross, vol. 52, pp. 10273–10297. On cross-examination Bellecourt admitted that he knew that telephones on the reservation were party lines.

58. Memo from Gerald Bertineau, Jr., discussed in *Transcript,* vol. 43, pp. 8251–8253. The stipulation by Hurd on March 3 had admitted to three informants. Tilsen pointed out that news of a fourth informant had already been revealed in testimony in Sioux Falls the week before. *Transcript,* vol. 44, pp. 8346–8349.

59. The equipment consisted of cords, jacks, batteries, a recorder, and a headset. Testimony of Myron Ellwein, plant supervisor of Bison State Telephone on Pine Ridge, in *Transcript,* vol. 43, pp. 8352–8399, 8410–8418.

60. *Transcript,* vol. 45, p. 8661.

61. *Transcript,* vol. 45, p. 8717.

62. Trimbach's testimony is in *Transcript,* vol. 44, pp. 8460–8527, vol. 45, pp. 8531–8775, vol. 46, pp. 8776–8812, cross, pp. 8812–8826. Press coverage in *Minneapolis Tribune,* March 21, 1974, p. 16B; March 22, 1974, p. 5B; *Saint Paul Pioneer Press,* March 21, 1974, p. 11; March 22, 1974, p. 11; March 23, 1974, p. 23.

63. *Rapid City Journal,* March 21, 1974, p. 2; see also *Saint Paul Pioneer Press,* March 20, 1974, p. 11.

64. See copy of letter signed by Joseph Beeler on behalf of WKLDOC in WKLDOC Records, MHS.

65. *Minneapolis Tribune,* March 22, 1974, p. 5B; March 25, 1974, pp. 1, 6–7; *Saint Paul Pioneer Press,* March 19, 1974, p. 10; *Rapid City Journal,* March 23, 1974, p. 1.

66. *Saint Paul Pioneer Press,* March 19, 1974, p. 32; see also *Minneapolis Tribune,* March 19, 1974, pp. 1, 11; March 20, 1974, pp. 1B, 2B; *Sioux Falls Argus Leader,* March 18, 1974, p. 8; March 19, 1974, p. 4; March 20, 1974, p. 10; March 21, 1974, p. 4.

67. *Minneapolis Tribune,* March 27, 1974, p. 5B.

68. Ibid. Kunstler gave a similar speech in Saint Cloud, Minnesota; see *Sioux Falls Argus Leader,* March 28, 1974, p. 16.

69. *Transcript,* vol. 46, p. 8954.

70. *Transcript,* vol. 46, pp. 8890–9000; vol. 47, pp. 9024–9110.

71. *Transcript,* vol. 47, pp. 9132–9143.

72. See testimony of U.S. Marshal Tommy Hudson, *Transcript,* vol. 47, pp. 9143–9155, cross, pp. 9155–9204; B. G. McDaniel, pp. 9204–9213, cross, pp. 9214–9229; FBI Agents Gerald Bertinot, vol. 48, pp. 9292–9304, cross, pp. 9304–9363; Kelly Hemmert, pp. 9364–9372, 9374–9408; Susan Malone, pp. 9409–9450, cross, pp. 9450–9466; Herbert Hoxie, vol. 49, pp. 9476–9489, 9489–9559; Howard McPherson, vol. 49, pp. 9660–9706, cross, vol. 50, pp. 9757–9787, who said that the equipment bought at Radio Shack was for radio hookups.

73. *Transcript,* vol. 49, pp. 9711–9723, 9286–9288.

74. Hall quote in *Transcript,* vol. 50, p. 9739.

75. *Transcript,* vol. 50, pp. 9746–9752.

76. *Transcript,* vol. 51, pp. 9950–9953; news reports on Hurd, *Minneapolis Tribune,* March 28, 1974, p. 1; on Saxbe, *Minneapolis Tribune,* March 29, 1974, p. 1; Nichol's quote in *Transcript,* vol. 51, p. 9952.

77. The defense had turned over a list of defense committee members to be checked against a list of informants, with the caveat that it not be turned over to the FBI; *Transcript,* vol. 49, pp. 9559–9576. Press coverage in *Minneapolis Tribune,* March 26, 1974, p. 7B; March 27, 1974, p. 5B; March 30, 1974, p. 6B; April 3, 1974, pp. 1B, 2B; *Saint Paul Pioneer Press,* March 26, 1974, p. 4; March 27, 1974, p. 4; March 28, 1974, p. 9; *Rapid City Journal,* March 25, 1974, p. 2; March 26, 1974, p. 3; March 28, 1974, p. 5; March 30, 1974, p. 5; April 1, 1974, p. 3.

78. *Saint Paul Pioneer Press,* March 28, 1974, p. 8.

79. See testimony of FBI agent Thomas Parker, *Transcript,* vol. 51, pp. 10000–10040, cross, pp. 10040–10126; vol. 52, pp. 10179–10247, 10247–10269; Hurd in *Transcript,* vol. 52, pp. 10130–10173.

80. Clayton in *Transcript,* vol. 52, pp. 10299–10300. Kunstler pointed out that under USC Title 18, sec. 2516, a U.S. Attorney cannot authorize a wiretap anyway. Hurd in *Transcript,* vol. 53, pp. 10325–10511, 10512–10528; Enlow in vol. 53, pp. 10563–10573, cross, pp. 10573–10583, vol. 54, pp. 10595–10665.

81. *Minneapolis Tribune,* April 4, 1974, p. 1B. Even the *Pioneer Press,* which had just published the supportive editorial, admitted that Trimbach had not made a good witness: *Saint Paul Pioneer Press,* April 4, 1974, p. 17.

82. Direct, *Transcript,* vol. 54, pp. 10667–10675; cross, pp. 10676–10780. Hurd said that he had seen FBI agents cutting documents for telecopying during Wounded Knee, suggesting a possible reason for the cutting and stapling: *Transcript,* vol. 54, pp. 10780–10783.

83. Martin Rudd, a Radio Shack manager in Rapid City, in *Transcript,* vol. 54, pp. 10795–10822. Joseph Pourier: direct, vol. 54, pp. 10822–10837; cross, pp. 10837–10848, vol. 55, pp. 10858–10872.

84. On Trimbach's testimony see *Minneapolis Tribune,* April 5, 1974, pp. 1B, 2B; April 6, 1974, p. 14C; *Saint Paul Pioneer Press,* April 6, 1974, p. 1; *Rapid City Journal,* April 8, 1974, p. 2; on the letter see *Minneapolis Tribune,* April 7, 1974, pp. 1, 8; *Saint Paul Pioneer Press,* April 8, 1974, p. 17.

85. *Transcript,* vol. 58, pp. 11560–11627. Press coverage in *Minneapolis Tribune,* April 10, 1974, p. 1; *Saint Paul Pioneer Press,* April 12, 1974, p. 17.

86. In addition to the Peterson affidavit, government rebuttal witnesses included U.S. Marshal Tommy Thompson, who said he never had a key to the phone office and never discussed monitoring with the FBI, in *Transcript*, vol. 55, pp. 10886–10893, cross, pp. 10893–10925. See also Denzil Staple, U.S. Marshal who backed up Thompson's testimony, on pp. 10926–10934, cross, pp. 10934–10966; FBI agent Thomas Parker, who said Pourier was never disallowed access to his office and that he knew of no monitoring during Wounded Knee, pp. 10966–10972, cross, pp. 10972–11048; and Lawrence D. Billis, another U.S. Marshal who corroborated Thompson's testimony, vol. 56, pp. 11079–11107.

87. Belcher in *Transcript*, vol. 56, pp. 11139–11271; Moore in vol. 57, pp. 11315–11428, cross, pp. 11428–11434, 11434–11452; Nichol's questions of Moore in vol. 57, pp. 11422–11458.

88. Felt testimony, *Transcript*, vol. 57, pp. 11465–11534, vol. 58, pp. 11560–11627, 11627–11647, cross, pp. 11650–11664; questions from Nichol, pp. 11657–11661; subpoena issued, vol. 57, pp. 11541–11543; testimony of Jim Mone, the AP photographer, is in *Transcript*, vol. 59, pp. 11679–11710, 11710–11746. Banks later accused the AP of working with the government to suppress coverage of first the protest and then the trial. The AP denied the charges but fired the photographer who had given information to the Bureau. *Rapid City Journal*, April 15, 1974, p. 12; April 17, 1974, p. 2; *Minneapolis Tribune*, April 15, 1974, p. 9B; April 16, 1974, p. 1B; April 20, 1974, p. 6; *New York Times*, April 17, 1974, p. 17; *Saint Paul Pioneer Press*, April 20, 1974, p. 2. The AP said that Mone had violated its longstanding policy that reporters should not become participants. Mone replied that he had only told the FBI what would come out in the papers. The *Pioneer Press* published an editorial condemning the firing of Mone, saying that it was every citizen's responsibility to respond to questioning by the government. *Saint Paul Pioneer Press*, April 18, 1974, p. 7.

89. Hurd in *Transcript*, vol. 59, pp. 11747–11777. Press coverage, *Minneapolis Tribune*, April 12, 1974, p. 1B; April 17, 1974, p. 1; *Rapid City Journal*, April 10, 1974, p. 3; April 12, 1974, p. 5.

90. *Transcript*, vol. 60, pp. 11854–11875; the last quote is on pp. 11886–11887.

91. *Transcript*, vol. 60, pp. 11895–11896.

92. Final quote is in *Transcript*, vol. 60, pp. 11895–11896; see also pp. 11851–11852; the reading of the decision is in vol. 60, pp. 11851–11891. Nichol's memorandum opinion was filed on April 30, 1970, and appears in 374 Fed. Supp. 321; the final warning is on pp. 335–336. A copy of the Memorandum in Support of the Motion to Suppress and copies of exhibits, including the request signed by Trimbach and the Felt memos, are in WKLDOC Records, MHS.

93. Quote from *Minneapolis Tribune*, April 18, 1974, p. 1; see also *New York Times*, April 18, 1974, p. 22; *Saint Paul Pioneer Press*, April 18, 1974, pp. 1, 2C; *Rapid City Journal*, April 18, 1974, p. 1; April 19, 1974, p. 1.

94. Clayton quoted in *Saint Paul Pioneer Press*, April 18, 1974, p. 2. Gienapp still terms the motion "ludicrous" and as having "no substance," and Hurd expresses similar views when questioned on the matter. Hurd also contends

that they did their best to comply with the discovery orders, blaming the lapses on the massive amount of documentation—a problem, he acknowledges, that was never solved, adding, "I wouldn't stand here today and say that we ever did turn over everything that we were supposed to turn over." Hurd also does not believe that the FBI withheld anything from the prosecution. Hurd and Gienapp interviews.

95. Kunstler quoted in *Saint Paul Pioneer Press*, April 18, 1974, p. 2, and *Rapid City Journal*, April 19, 1974, p. 1; defendants in *Pioneer Press* and *Sioux Falls Argus Leader*, April 18, 1974, p. 1.

96. *Rapid City Journal*, March 29, 1974, p. 4.

97. Black Hills claim, *Minneapolis Tribune*, March 21, 1974, p. 5; Senate hearing, *Rapid City Journal*, March 29, 1974, p. 10; Billings meeting, *Rapid City Journal*, March 29, 1974, p. 18.

98. *Transcript*, vol. 59, pp. 11830–11839.

99. *Minneapolis Tribune*, April 1, 1974, p. 12. Kelley had spoken at Harvard and the University of Kansas.

100. See, for instance, *Minneapolis Tribune*, February 16, 1974, p. 1.

101. *New York Times*, April 7, 1974, p. 41; see also *Sioux Falls Argus Leader*, April 18, 1974, p. 1; *Saint Paul Pioneer Press*, April 18, 1974, p. 2C.

102. Means quoted in *Rapid City Journal*, April 14, 1974, p. 21; see also Lane and Banks speech, *Minneapolis Tribune*, April 6, 1974, p. 7; Banks at Augsburg College in Minneapolis stressing treaty rights, *Saint Paul Pioneer Press*, April 23, 1974, p. 3.

6. MONTH FIVE AND COUNTING

1. *Rapid City Journal*, April 28, 1974, p. 26.

2. *Sioux Falls Argus Leader*, April 25, 1974, p. 1. The dispute was over the number of preemptory challenges. Northcott interview.

3. *New York Times*, May 1, 1974, p. 18; May 4, 1974, p. 9; *Minneapolis Tribune*, April 26, 1974, p. 11B; April 27, 1974, p. 9B; *Saint Paul Pioneer Press*, May 1, 1974, p. 3; May 2, 1974, p. 1; *Sioux Falls Argus Leader*, April 26, 1974, pp. 1, 5; *Rapid City Journal*, April 26, 1974, p. 2; April 27, 1974, p. 1.

4. *Rapid City Journal*, April 27, 1974, p. 1.

5. On Sioux Falls, see *Sioux Falls Argus Leader*, April 30, 1974, p. 4; May 1, 1974, p. 1; May 2, 1974, p. 2; *Minneapolis Tribune*, May 1, 1974, p. 1; May 2, 1974, p. 1B; May 3, 1974, p. 2B; Northcott interview. Nichol's ruling on the motion in *Transcript*, vol. 62, p. 12126. WKLDOC and AIM members who were in the courtroom still claim that the police charged in without warning and started hitting people. Bellecourt, Northcott, and Ted Means interviews.

6. *Transcript*, vol. 61, pp. 12029–12030.

7. *Transcript*, vol. 61, pp. 12031–12033; Nichol's explanation to the jury on the misconduct hearing is in vol. 61, pp. 11903–11911.

8. Some papers did note that Nichol also reprimanded the defense for wasting time with cross-examination. See reports in *Saint Paul Pioneer Press*, May 2, 1974, p. 1; *Minneapolis Tribune*, May 2, 1974, p. 1B; *Sioux Falls Argus Leader*, May 2, 1974, p. 6; *Rapid City Journal*, May 2, 1974, p. 17.

9. *Transcript,* vol. 62, pp. 12112–12134.

10. Adrienne Fritze, direct, *Transcript,* vol. 61, pp. 11914–11932, 11954–11959; cross, pp. 11959–11968, 11968–11990; Mrs. Fritze, vol. 61, direct, pp. 11991–12019, cross, pp. 12019–12020, 12036–12076; Mr. Fritze, vol. 61, pp. 12076–12087, vol. 62, pp. 12135–12297; cross, vol. 62, pp. 12198–12256, 12324–12400; re-direct, pp. 12430–12447, cross, pp. 12448–12477, 12478–12491. Press coverage in *Minneapolis Tribune,* May 2, 1974, p. 1B; May 3, 1974, p. 1B; May 4, 1974, p. 10B; *Saint Paul Pioneer Press,* May 4, 1974, p. 13; *Rapid City Journal,* May 6, 1974, p. 2.

11. *Transcript,* vol. 62, pp. 12092–12107; Nichol signed the subpoena on p. 12188. Press coverage in *New York Times,* May 4, 1974, p. 9; *Minneapolis Tribune,* May 3, 1974, p. 1B; May 4, 1974, p. 10B; *Saint Paul Pioneer Press,* May 3, 1974, p. 17; *Sioux Falls Argus Leader,* May 3, 1974, p. 9. Documents released in May again suggested that the White House tapes might contain conversations regarding Wounded Knee. One was a May 21, 1973, letter from President Nixon to Harlington Wood, the Pentagon's representative during the siege, and the other was a Justice Department memo to Senator Henry Jackson dated March 22, 1973, regarding the occupation. The press noted that the March 22 memo was written the day after one of the key conversations between the President and John Dean. The memo listed three presidential assistants—Leonard Garment, Kenneth Cole, and Brad Patterson—as being kept informed about the situation in South Dakota. *Minneapolis Tribune,* May 14, 1974, p. 7B.

12. South Dakota papers provided regular coverage of both sets of cases: *Sioux Falls Argus Leader,* February 20, 1974, p. 4; February 22, 1974, p. 1; February 27, 1974, p. 2; March 1, 1974, p. 7; March 7, 1974, p. 6; March 5, 1974, p. 1; March 8, 1974, p. 3; March 10, 1974, p. 2; March 13, 1974, p. 4; March 15, 1974, p. 2; March 27, 1974, p. 2; April 9, 1974, p. 1; April 15, 1974, p. 1; April 16, 1974, p. 1.

13. Attitudes expressed in opinion surveys conducted in late 1973 contrasted sharply with the findings in Minnesota. Only 9.5 percent said that they sympathized with the Indians who occupied Wounded Knee, compared with 50.4 percent in the Saint Paul area; 55.5 percent felt that the Indians should be punished for the takeover, compared with 21.5 percent in Saint Paul. See copies of two affidavits by Jay Schulman, dated February 13, 1974, and a copy of a memo signed by jury project worker Diane Wiley, dated May 1974, in WKLDOC Records, MHS.

John Thomas from Oklahoma was the AIM liaison on the Sioux Falls committee and had the responsibility of negotiating with the city. Information on the contrasts between Sioux Falls and Saint Paul comes from Gallant, Northcott, Gilbert Thunder Hawk, Cohoes, Joe and M. G. Beeler interviews, and John Thomas interview, September 4, 1989.

14. "Armed camp" comment from Northcott interview; other background from M. G. Beeler, Thomas, and James interviews. Press coverage in *Minneapolis Tribune,* May 3, 1974, p. 1; May 4, 1974, pp. 1, 10B; *Sioux Falls Argus Leader,* May 2, 1974, p. 1; May 3, 1974, p. 6; *Rapid City Journal,* May 2, 1974, p. 1.

15. Editorial in *Rapid City Journal,* May 3, 1974, p. 4; bar president's statement in *Rapid City Journal,* May 6, 1974, p. 1.

16. *Rapid City Journal,* May 9, 1974, p. 1; see also *Minneapolis Tribune,* May 7, 1974, p. 2B.

17. *Rapid City Journal,* May 9, 1974, p. 12.

18. Kneip in *Sioux Falls Argus Leader,* May 8, 1974, p. 1; *Rapid City Journal,* May 8, 1974, p. 1; AIM statement in *Rapid City Journal,* May 9, 1974, pp. 1, 2. Gilbert also complained about the *Rapid City Journal*'s coverage of the events in Sioux Falls.

19. *Rapid City Journal,* May 11, 1974, p. 1; *Sioux Falls Argus Leader,* May 4, 1974, pp. 1, 2, 4; May 5, 1974, p. 1; May 7, 1974, p. 1; May 8, 1974, pp. 1, 2. The statistics presented on prosecutions since 1972 showed 5,000 misdemeanors, including 100 Indians, and 525 felonies, including only 17 Indians. *Sioux Falls Argus Leader,* May 9, 1974, p. 1.

20. On moving the trials, see *Sioux Falls Argus Leader,* May 9, 1974, p. 1; editorial in *Sioux Falls Argus Leader,* May 13, 1974, p. 4; other Custer aftermath in *Sioux Falls Argus Leader,* May 9, 1974, pp. 2, 6; May 12, 1974, p. 4; May 13, 1974, p. 1; May 14, 1974, p. 1; and *Rapid City Journal,* May 10, 1974, p. 2.

21. *Rapid City Journal,* May 15, 1974, p. 1; May 16, 1974, p. 1; *Minneapolis Tribune,* May 14, 1974, p. 1B; May 15, 1974, p. 3; *Sioux Falls Argus Leader,* May 16, 1974, p. 1; information also from Northcott interview.

22. The transcript for the pretrial hearings in *United States v. Madonna Mae Gilbert, Lorelei Decora, and Tonia Ackerman* begins as vols. 1–7, pp. 1–625, of *U.S. v. Vaughn Dix Baker* and then continues as *Gilbert et al.,* vols. 8–17, pp. 643–1877, copies in WKLDOC Records, MHS. The waiver of trial by jury for the three is in *Gilbert et al., Transcript,* vol. 18, pp. 1858–1872. Other information comes from DeCora Means, Gilbert Thunder Hawk, and Joe Beeler interviews.

23. Krieger and Shellow were assisted by attorneys Joe Beeler, John Thorne, and John Connolly and legal workers Katherine James and Lynn Mitchell. Information from Decora Means, Gilbert Thunder Hawk, Joe and M. G. Beeler, and James interviews.

24. Clayton interview.

25. Czywczynski's testimony is in *Gilbert et al., Transcript,* vol. 22, pp. 2488–2643; vol. 23, pp. 2645–2889. Other testimony is in vols. 24–27, pp. 2890–3400. Information also comes from DeCora Means and Gilbert Thunder Hawk interviews. Press coverage is in *Sioux Falls Argus Leader,* May 15, 1974, p. 1; May 21, 1974, p. 1.

26. Gilbert Thunder Hawk, DeCora Means, James, and Northcott interviews. Press coverage in *Sioux Falls Argus Leader,* May 18, 1974, p. 1.

27. Direct, *Transcript,* vol. 64, pp. 12494–12546; cross, vol. 64, pp. 12546–12617, vol. 65, pp. 12621–12633, 12633–12670; re-direct, pp. 12671–12697.

28. *Rapid City Journal,* May 9, 1974, p. 2; *Saint Paul Pioneer Press,* May 8, 1974, p. 1.

29. Direct, *Transcript,* vol. 65, pp. 12705–12771.

30. *Transcript,* vol. 65, pp. 12805, 12839.

31. *Transcript,* vol. 65, pp. 12807–12838; cross, vol. 65, pp. 12771–12833, 12833–12854, vol. 66, pp. 12858–12961; on redirect Hurd questioned her again about items that were taken from her home and never returned, vol. 66, pp. 12961–12973. Press coverage on Gildersleeve in *Minneapolis Tribune,*

May 8, 1974, pp. 1, 4; May 9, 1974, p. 2B; *Saint Paul Pioneer Press*, May 8, 1974, p. 1.

32. *Transcript*, vol. 67, pp. 13080–13090.

33. On cross-examination the agent was questioned about various details, including trading post finances, treaty provisions, and an alleged government plan to assault the village, most of which was excluded. John Frazier, direct, *Transcript*, vol. 66, pp. 12998–13015; cross, pp. 13015–13047, 13047–13074.

34. *Transcript*, vol. 67, p. 13127.

35. *Transcript*, vol. 67, pp. 13127–13165. Press coverage in *Minneapolis Tribune*, May 15, 1974, p. 1; *Saint Paul Pioneer Press*, May 15, 1974, p. 1; *Sioux Falls Argus Leader*, May 15, 1974, p. 16; *Rapid City Journal*, May 16, 1974, p. 1. Hall dissented from the decision to walk out but told Nichol that he would abide by the decision of his client. Hall and Gallant interviews.

36. *Transcript*, vol. 68, pp. 13168–13176. The agreement was that when a defendant conducted cross-examination, his attorney could not do so, and that he must abide by the same rules that attorneys were subject to. Nichol also said that he reserved the right to reverse his ruling if it became "troublesome," pp. 13176–13184. The judge had denied a motion to let Banks and Means act as co-counsel at the beginning of the trial. Kunstler and Leventhal interviews.

37. According to Tilsen, the defendants would often ask about making a certain statement or protest in court, and he took the position that his role as their attorney was to tell them what would probably happen and then leave the decision up to them; Tilsen interview.

38. Tilsen, Kunstler, Leventhal, and Gienapp interviews. Tilsen attributes the adage on juries and defendants to Clarence Darrow.

39. Direct, *Transcript*, vol. 68, pp. 13265–13280; cross, pp. 13280–13302, 13302–13316; see also Amelia Clark cross, vol. 68, pp. 13179–13234, 13234–13242. Means's shirt described in *Sioux Falls Argus Leader*, May 16, 1974, p. 7.

40. *Transcript*, vol. 68, pp. 13316–13336. Press coverage in *Minneapolis Tribune*, May 16, 1974, p. 12B; *Saint Paul Pioneer Press*, May 15, 1974, p. 20; *Rapid City Journal*, May 17, 1974, p. 1.

41. *Transcript*, vol. 68, pp. 13341–13370.

42. Direct, *Transcript*, vol. 69, pp. 13415–13473. The defense had brought out that Richards had been arrested the same day he gave a statement to the FBI, cross, pp. 13473–13489; revelation of the missing statement is on pp. 13515–13542.

43. *Transcript*, vol. 69, p. 13523. Banks credits Means with the idea of putting pressure on Hurd and characterizing him as a buffoon. Banks interview. Nichol's explanation to jury is in vol. 70, pp. 13544–13559.

44. *Minneapolis Tribune*, May 17, 1974, p. 1B. The *Saint Paul Pioneer Press* said that Hurd tried to explain, but ended up admitting the mistake was his fault: May 17, 1974, p. 25; see also *Sioux Falls Argus Leader*, May 17, 1974, p. 3; *Rapid City Journal*, May 18, 1974, p. 2.

45. Leventhal, Tilsen, and Banks interviews. On the continued publicity campaign see "Trial Newsletters" for May 6, 1974, a flyer announcing a May 24 rally at the courthouse, an AIM press release on travel in South Dakota, and press

packets and guidelines for dealing with the media in Lincoln, in WKLDOC Records, MHS.

46. *Rapid City Journal,* May 21, 1974, p. 1; *Minneapolis Tribune,* May 22, 1974, p. 9B; *Saint Paul Pioneer Press,* May 23, 1974, p. 10. See also court exchanges between Kunstler and Nichol, in *Transcript,* vol. 71, p. 13661, and between Nichol and Means, pp. 13855–13857.

47. *Transcript,* vol. 75, pp. 14183–14188.

48. *Transcript,* vol. 75, pp. 14250–14253.

49. *Transcript,* vol. 65, p. 14256.

50. The whole of Means's cross is in *Transcript,* vol. 65, pp. 14246–14318; Banks's cross on pp. 14189–14246. For descriptions see *Minneapolis Tribune,* May 29, 1974, p. 1; *Saint Paul Pioneer Press,* May 29, 1974, p. 8; *Sioux Falls Argus Leader,* May 29, 1974, p. 8; *Rapid City Journal,* May 30, 1974, p. 19. Kunstler called the cross-examination by both defendants "marvelous." Kunstler interview.

51. Dr. Thomas M. Foley, assigned to Ellsworth Air Force Base, Rapid City, South Dakota: direct, *Transcript,* vol. 88, pp. 16666–16676, cross, pp. 16676–16687, 16698–16731, 16734–16737.

52. *Saint Paul Pioneer Press,* May 29, 1974, p. 8; *Sioux Falls Argus Leader,* May 29, 1974, p. 8; *Rapid City Journal,* May 30, 1974, p. 19; *Minneapolis Tribune,* May 29, 1974, p. 1; May 31, 1974, p. 14. *Transcript,* vol. 75, pp. 14296–14297.

53. Arguments on the motion for judgment of acquittal for defendants Gilbert Thunder Hawk, DeCora Means, and Ackerman are in *Decora Means et al., Transcript,* vol. 28, pp. 3401–3469, and vol. 29, pp. 3470–3553. Urbom's decision is in vol. 29, pp. 3554–3567; copy in WKLDOC Records, MHS. The government, he ruled, had not proved that the defendants had knowledge of the stolen property; a key factor was that they did not have a key for the trunk in the car when stopped. This was the same car and contraband that Nichol had just ruled on in Saint Paul. Other information comes from Gilbert Thunder Hawk and DeCora Means interviews. DeCora Means said later of Urbom's reaction to the testimony: "This Judge was getting shocked every day just in our trial and he had to be reading what was happening in St. Paul." For press coverage of the verdict see *Minneapolis Tribune,* May 29, 1974, p. 10; *Rapid City Journal,* May 30, 1974, p. 1; *Sioux Falls Argus Leader,* May 29, 1974, p. 1. The *Argus Leader* was referring to the case as the " 'Lesser' Wounded Knee trial."

54. The exchanges of compliments are in *Transcript,* vol. 29, pp. 3568–3571; see also Warren K. Urbom, "You Can Bury My Heart at Wounded Knee," *International Society of Barristers Quarterly* 17 (April 1982): 259–266; Albert J. Krieger, "Wounded Knee: The Defense Story," *Criminal Defense* 1 (February 1975): 4–8; and Joe Beeler and James interviews. Some in WKLDOC expressed concern about the small numbers of Native Americans in Lincoln (one-half of one percent of the population), making it unlikely that any Indians would be called for a jury panel; see *Sioux Falls Argus Leader,* April 18, 1974, p. 1.

55. Joe Beeler and James interviews. See also *Minneapolis Tribune,* May 30, 1974, p. 1B; *Sioux Falls Argus Leader,* May 30, 1974, p. 16; *Rapid City Journal,* May 31, 1974, p. 2.

56. Clayton's teletype quoted in Ken Tilsen, "Fair and Equal Justice: The FBI, Wounded and Politics," in *Quaere,* September 1976, pp. 1–9, 7.

57. Discussions about plea bargain in interviews with Joe Beeler, Tilsen, and James; opposition by John Trudell and others in *Sioux Falls Argus Leader,* June 1, 1974, p. 8; *Minneapolis Tribune,* June 12, 1974, p. 5C.
58. On finances, *Saint Paul Pioneer Press,* May 31, 1974, p. 39; the Custer trials, *Sioux Falls Argus Leader,* June 1, 1974, p. 1; June 4, 1974, p. 2; June 5, 1974, p. 2; *Rapid City Journal,* June 1, 1974, p. 2; June 4, 1974, p. 3; coverage of AIM conference, *Sioux Falls Argus Leader,* May 26, 1974, p. 1; May 27, 1974, p. 7; *Rapid City Journal,* May 26, 1974, p. 32.
59. The U.S. Attorney said he would investigate the matter; *Minneapolis Tribune,* May 31, 1974, p. 2B; *Saint Paul Pioneer Press,* May 31, 1974, p. 8.
60. Kenneth A. Jacobson, FBI agent, direct, *Transcript,* vol. 75, pp. 14320–14333, cross, pp. 14333–14369, 14369–14383, vol. 76, pp. 14383–14405; Gerald J. Bertinot, Jr., FBI agent, direct, vol. 76, pp. 14413–14441, cross, pp. 14441–14473, 14473–14512, vol. 76, pp. 14542–14566; William W. Willis, FBI agent, vol. 76, pp. 14512–14542; Mark R. Fritshel, FBI agent, vol. 77, pp. 14606–14630, cross, pp. 14630–14666; Kenneth W. Nimmick, FBI agent, vol. 77, pp. 14641–14687; Raymond L. Lesage, FBI agent, vol. 77, pp. 14693–14695; John Lelleck, U.S. Marshal, vol. 77, pp. 14697–14704, cross, pp. 14705–14741, 14742–14781; Vernard Grimes, FBI agent, vol. 77, pp. 14789–14803, cross, pp. 14807–14836, 14836–14886.
61. Means in *Transcript,* vol. 78, pp. 14846–14849. Press comments in *Minneapolis Tribune,* June 5, 1974, p. 1B; *Saint Paul Pioneer Press,* June 5, 1974, p. 14; *Sioux Falls Argus Leader,* June 5, 1974, p. 16; *Rapid City Journal,* June 5, 1974, p. 1. Tilsen says that he criticized Kunstler at times for not arguing more with Means and Banks about how they dealt with the judge. He adds that Means believed that anyone who grew up in South Dakota was a racist, but that he (Tilsen) felt that Nichol was struggling with that racism and was trying to be sympathetic to Indian people. Tilsen interview. Nichol also had an exchange with Lane over the scope of cross-examination the day before, and one paper reported him once again at the "boiling point." *Saint Paul Pioneer Press,* June 4, 1974, p. 5.
62. *Rapid City Journal,* June 1, 1974, p. 2.
63. *Transcript,* vol. 76, pp. 14589–14593; vol. 77, pp. 14598–14606. Press coverage in *Minneapolis Tribune,* May 30, 1974, p. 1B; *Saint Paul Pioneer Press,* May 30, 1974, p. 22.
64. Pierce's testimony on being fired at is in *Transcript,* vol. 78, pp. 14933–14944, cross, pp. 14844–14963, 14968–14993, 14993–15042. See also *Minneapolis Tribune,* June 6, 1974, pp. 1B, 2B.
65. Kunstler interview.
66. Leventhal and Hall interviews.
67. Hurd, Gienapp, and Nichol interviews. Nichol says that Kunstler was trying to do to him what he did to Judge Julius Hoffman, "to get my goat," to get him "to overreact." But Nichol was quick to add: "On the other hand, he was a good lawyer." Of Hall, with whom he spoke privately on occasion, Nichol says, "I liked him very much, though he still wears his hair in a pony tail." Nichol interview. Tilsen describes the dynamic between Kunstler and Nichol as a love-hate relationship—that both men liked each other, but that Kunstler

knew just how far to push the judge. Tilsen interview. Information also from Hall, Gallant, and Cohoes interviews; *Minneapolis Tribune*, May 16, 1974, p. 1.

68. Nichol also acknowledges that he regarded Banks and Means differently; Banks, he says, was "easier to get along with." Nichol interview. Tilsen thinks that Nichol was concerned about appearing racist, but also notes that Means "would never concede Nichol anything." Tilsen interview. Kunstler thought that Nichol's racism came through at times, that he regarded Means as an "uppity Indian" and Banks as more "benign"; Kunstler interview. Information on the judge's mail from Nichol interview and *Sioux Falls Argus Leader*, May 15, 1974, p. 16.

69. Erwin Latshaw, Denby, South Dakota, direct, *Transcript*, vol. 79, pp. 15052–15059, cross by Means, pp. 15059–15100; Louis Palmer Hansen, Pine Ridge, South Dakota, vol. 79, pp. 15104–15158, vol. 80, pp. 15341–15370, vol. 81, pp. 15390–15406, 15406–15460, re-direct, pp. 15460–15472; Trimbach, vol. 80, pp. 15172–15182, cross, pp. 15182–15232, 15232–15250, 15322–15337. The press picked up on the direct but said little about the cross: *Minneapolis Tribune*, June 7, 1974, p. 1B; *Saint Paul Pioneer Press*, June 7, 1974, p. 9. Raymond Froelich, a Montana detective in the Sheriff's Department, testified that the U-Haul van at Wounded Knee was reported stolen in Montana; vol. 81, pp. 15472–15491.

70. Graham direct, *Transcript*, vol. 81, pp. 15521–15580; Jack Eugene Hanson, direct, vol. 83, pp. 15702–15724.

71. Graham cross, *Transcript*, vol. 83, pp. 15580–15590, vol. 83, pp. 15615–15666, 15666–15702; Ben Mahoney, deputy U.S. Marshal, direct, vol. 87, pp. 16359–16371; Bruce Jacob, deputy U.S. Marshal, direct, vol. 87, pp. 16582–16585; Alyce Merrill, Postmaster for Pine Ridge, on the interrupted mail delivery, direct, vol. 87, pp. 16591–16613, cross, pp. 16634–16655; Hanson cross, vol. 83, pp. 15725–15756, 15756–15771, re-direct, pp. 15771–15777, re-cross, pp. 15777–15784. See also *Minneapolis Tribune*, June 8, 1974, p. 10A; *Saint Paul Pioneer Press*, June 8, 1974, p. 7; Cohoes interview, in which he spoke of the defense team's concern for the charges.

72. Direct, *Transcript*, vol. 83, pp. 15785–15799. See also direct of Curtis Fitzgerald, vol. 86, pp. 16233–16243; cross of McGee, vol. 83, pp. 15799–15832, vol. 85, pp. 16054–16090, 16090–16168; cross of Fitzgerald, pp. 16243–16310, 16310–16331; James J. Caverly, FBI agent who took photographs of the injured Fitzgerald, direct, vol. 86, pp. 16194–16219, cross, pp. 16219–16224; Daniel C. Dotson, Deputy U.S. Marshal, vol. 87, pp. 16504–16509, cross, pp. 16509–16572. One witness did put Banks in the U-Haul van, but not at the time of the shooting: Richard Siedschlaw, South Dakota highway patrol, vol. 87, pp. 16373–16447. Press coverage in *Minneapolis Tribune*, June 18, 1974, p. 1B; *Saint Paul Pioneer Press*, June 18, 1974, p. 7.

73. Quote from *Saint Paul Pioneer Press*, June 20, 1974, p. 17; see also *New York Times*, June 18, 1974, p. 15.

74. *Minneapolis Tribune*, July 9, 1974, p. 6C; *Saint Paul Pioneer Press*, July 9, 1974, p. 18; *Rapid City Journal*, July 10, 1974, p. 9.

75. *Transcript*, vol. 86, pp. 16206–16210; see also *Minneapolis Tribune*, June 21, 1974, p. 5B; *New York Times*, June 18, 1974, p. 15.

76. Quote in *Transcript,* vol. 84, p. 16022; direct, *Transcript,* vol. 84, pp. 15833–15842, cross, pp. 15842–16050. Press coverage in *Minneapolis Tribune,* June 19, 1974, pp. 1B, 5B; *Saint Paul Pioneer Press,* June 19, 1974, p. 12. Leonard Garment concurs with respect to Nixon's lack of involvement in Wounded Knee decisions; Garment interview.

77. The judge was referring to Harlington Wood and Wayne Colburn. *Transcript,* vol. 84, p. 15899.

78. Hearing discussed in *Transcript,* vol. 87, pp. 16354–16358; press reports in *Sioux Falls Argus Leader,* June 23, 1974, p. 1; June 26, 1974, p. 6; June 27, 1974, p. 2; June 28, 1974, pp. 2, 9; *Minneapolis Tribune,* June 24, 1974, p. 9B; June 26, 1974, p. 10; June 29, 1974, p. 15; July 4, 1974, p. 2B; *Saint Paul Pioneer Press,* June 30, 1974, p. 16; July 3, 1974, p. 3; July 4, 1974, p. 5; *Rapid City Journal,* June 25, 1974, p. 1; June 26, 1974, p. 1; June 27, 1974, p. 2; July 1, 1974, p. 1.

79. Mayor's commission: *Minneapolis Tribune,* June 6, 1974, p. 1B; June 7, 1974, p. 1B; school: *Saint Paul Pioneer Press,* June 15, 1974, p. 33.

80. *Minneapolis Tribune,* June 9, 1974, p. 10A; June 10, 1974, p. 2B; *Saint Paul Pioneer Press,* June 10, 1974, p. 13; June 12, 1974, p. 35; June 17, 1974, p. 16; *Sioux Falls Argus Leader,* June 10, 1974, p. 5; June 12, 1974, p. 5; June 3, 1974, p. 12; *Rapid City Journal,* June 10, 1974, p. 3; June 11, 1974, p. 1; June 14 1974, p. 1; June 15, 1974, p. 1. There was further evidence of how easily violence attached itself to AIM when it had to explain to the press that a shooting that occurred thirty miles from the conference was unconnected with the event; *Sioux Falls Argus Leader,* June 9, 1974, p. 1; *Saint Paul Pioneer Press,* June 9, 1974, p. 3. There was also an AIM meeting in Wisconsin in May; *Saint Paul Pioneer Press,* May 9, 1974, p. 44; May 25, 1974, p. 18; May 26, 1974, p. 11, sec. 3; May 27, 1974, p. 3; *Sioux Falls Argus Leader,* May 26, 1974, pp. 1, 2; May 27, 1974, p. 7. The defense committee also put out a pamphlet on the conference, "Sioux Nation Treaty Conference," June 1974, copy in WKLDOC Records, MHS. On the caravan to Aberdeen, see *Sioux Falls Argus Leader,* June 17, 1974, p. 6; the Washington trip: *Saint Paul Pioneer Press,* June 20, 1974, p. 39; June 23, 1974, p. 10; *Rapid City Journal,* June 23, 1974, p. 3; tourism in South Dakota: *Sioux Falls Argus Leader,* June 22, 1974, p. 2; *Rapid City Journal,* June 13, 1974, p. 1.

81. *Sioux Falls Argus Leader,* June 20, 1974, p. 1; June 21, 1974, p. 2; *Rapid City Journal,* June 22, 1974, p. 1.

82. *Sioux Falls Argus Leader,* June 21, 1974, p. 18; *Rapid City Journal,* June 26, 1974, p. 2. The press had carried statements by AIM and WKLDOC member John Thomas and AIM leader John Trudell expressing opposition to the agreement; *Sioux Falls Argus Leader,* June 1, 1974, p. 8.

83. See Tilsen, "Fair and Equal Justice," pp. 7–9; interviews with Beeler and Tilsen; see also Krieger, "Wounded Knee: The Defense Story," who writes that he received a letter from a Justice Department official stating that the Department had been informed by U.S. Attorney Clayton that the defense had withdrawn its offer, p. 8.

84. On Custer, see *Sioux Falls Argus Leader,* June 22, 1974, p. 1; on the Lincoln trial, see *Rapid City Journal,* June 26, 1974, p. 2; July 3, 1974, p. 17; July 5,

1974, p. 14. The case was that of Gregorio Jaramillo and Michael Eugene Sturdevant, who were charged with attempting to bring ammunition and weapons into Wounded Knee. Information on WKLDOC from Joe Beeler, James, and Northcott interviews. Citing personal reasons, Ramon Roubideaux stepped down as chief counsel for AIM. Newspapers that had just reported his contempt citation a few weeks earlier referred to him as a well-respected trial lawyer. *Sioux Falls Argus Leader,* June 22, 1974, p. 6; *Rapid City Journal,* June 22, 1974, p. 2.

85. Means quote: *Sioux Falls Argus Leader,* June 28, 1974, p. 1. On finances, see "Trial Newsletter" dated April 4, 1974, in WKLDOC Records, MHS.

86. *Transcript,* vol. 89, pp. 17690–17805. Press coverage in *Minneapolis Tribune,* July 10, 1974, p. 1B; *Saint Paul Pioneer Press,* July 11, 1974, p. 9; *Sioux Falls Argus Leader,* July 11, 1974, p. 6; *Minneapolis Tribune,* July 12, 1974, p. 2B.

87. Tilsen interview.

88. *Transcript,* vol. 90, p. 16879; the entire cross-examination is on pp. 16854–16908, 16909–16942; vol. 90, pp. 16812–16854. The coverage noted points from both direct and cross-examinations. *Minneapolis Tribune,* July 12, 1974, p. 2B; *Saint Paul Pioneer Press,* July 12, 1974, p. 15.

89. *Transcript,* vol. 91, pp. 17163–17205. Press coverage in *Minneapolis Tribune,* July 13, 1974, p. 8B; *Saint Paul Pioneer Press,* July 13, 1974, p. 9; *Sioux Falls Argus Leader,* July 13, 1974, p. 4; *Rapid City Journal,* July 15, 1974, p. 1. Clayton denied press reports that the move to revoke Means's bond came on orders from the Justice Department because of pressure from South Dakota congressional representatives; he insisted that he had made the decision. *Minneapolis Tribune,* July 11, 1974, p. 1.

90. *Saint Paul Pioneer Press,* July 16, 1974, p. 4.

91. *Saint Paul Pioneer Press,* July 25, 1974, p. 6.

92. *Saint Paul Pioneer Press,* July 27, 1974, p. 4. In April, Kunstler and Banks had traveled to Washington to hold a press conference because they said the national media were not covering the trial. *Saint Paul Pioneer Press,* April 3, 1974, p. 7.

93. Granville Slack, Deputy U.S. Marshal, *Transcript,* vol. 89, pp. 16771–16783; David Waldron, Deputy U.S. Marshal, vol. 91, pp. 17098–17115; John Lelleck, Deputy U.S. Marshal, vol. 92, pp. 17265–17271; Eugene H. Trottier, Criminal Investigator, Department of Interior, vol. 92, pp. 17300–17310; Melvin C. Jenson, FBI agent who introduced photographs of the area, vol. 92, pp. 17352–17406; Paul J. Hayes, Deputy U.S. Marshal, vol. 93, pp. 17415–17420.

94. *Transcript,* vol. 93, pp. 17511–17564.

95. Press coverage in *Minneapolis Tribune,* July 18, 1974, p. 12B; *Saint Paul Pioneer Press,* July 18, 1974, p. 4; *Sioux Falls Argus Leader,* July 18, 1974, p. 3.

96. Hurd's press statements in *Minneapolis Tribune,* July 19, 1974, p. 1B; Lane in *Transcript,* vol. 94, p. 17738.

97. *Transcript,* vol. 94, pp. 17564–17738, 17746–17754; vol. 95, pp. 17785–17822, 17827–17898.

98. *Minneapolis Tribune,* July 20, 1974, pp. 1, 14C.

99. *Sioux Falls Argus Leader,* July 20, 1974, p. 1; *Rapid City Journal,* July 22, 1974, p. 1; criticism of Lane in *Saint Paul Pioneer Press,* July 20, p. 1; Lane's press

statement in *Sioux Falls Argus Leader*, July 20, 1974, p. 1. Three days later, one newspaper interpreted the defense's abbreviated cross-examination of trading post co-owner Czywczynski as an attempt to go easy on the judge. Tilsen read into the record the testimony from Sioux Falls during which Czywczynski had repeatedly invoked the Fifth Amendment in response to questions about his finances. The prosecution came under fire from Nichol for not having the trading post records available, as Czywczynski again testified about the value of the merchandise allegedly taken. *Transcript*, vol. 96, pp. 18014–18035, 18037–18056; direct, vol. 96, pp. 18008–18014. Press coverage in *Minneapolis Tribune*, July 23, 1974, p. 2B; *Sioux Falls Argus Leader*, July 23, 1974, p. 15; *Rapid City Journal*, July 24, 1974, p. 2.

100. Grimm direct, *Transcript*, vol. 97, pp. 18084–18089.

101. For the cross of the other marshals, see: Slack, vol. 90, pp. 16989–17017, vol. 91, pp. 17023–17058, 17058–17096; Waldron, vol. 91, pp. 17115–17159, vol. 92, pp. 17208–17234, 17234–17242; Lelleck, vol. 92, pp. 17271–17399; Trottier, vol. 92, pp. 17310–17352; Hayes cross, vol. 93, pp. 17421–17472, 17472–17505. Press coverage which noted both direct and cross in *Minneapolis Tribune*, July 17, 1974, p. 10B; *Saint Paul Pioneer Press*, July 17, 1974, p. 3.

102. *Transcript*, vol. 97, pp. 18089–18105; the press summarized both parts of the testimony, most with accompanying photographs of Grimm being pushed along by one of his fellow marshals. See, for instance, *Minneapolis Tribune*, July 24, 1974, p. 2B; *Saint Paul Pioneer Press*, July 23, 1974, p. 4. The defense's view of the situation is from Kunstler interview.

103. See testimony of Stephen Ramey, FBI agent, *Transcript*, vol. 95, pp. 17899–17911; Frederich S. Hillman, FBI agent, vol. 95, pp. 17916–17928; Ronni L. Jaco, FBI agent, vol. 95, pp. 17949–17952; Melvin DeGraw, FBI agent, vol. 95, pp. 17982–17987; James Propotnick, vol. 97, pp. 18108–18121. The defense challenged the photographs for a number of reasons and kept a few of them out. Vol. 97, pp. 18132–18140; vol. 98, pp. 18171–18172; vol. 98, pp. 18148–18153, 18159–18170. The dates for the films are: ABC, March 1, 5–11, 1973; CBS, February 28, March 1–12, 14, 18, 25, and April 5, 9, 1973. Judge Nichol told the jury not to pay attention to the newscaster or reporters, but only to what was said by participants, as well as what they saw.

104. The prosecution rested: *Transcript*, vol. 98, p. 18180. Hurd's statement in *Sioux Falls Argus Leader*, July 25, 1974, p. 16; Means's statement: *Rapid City Journal*, July 25, 1974, p. 2; other stories in *Minneapolis Tribune*, July 25, 1974, p. 1B; July 28, 1974, p. 1; *Saint Paul Pioneer Press*, July 24, 1974, p. 13; *Rapid City Journal*, July 25, 1974, p. 2; July 26, 1974, p. 2.

105. *Saint Paul Pioneer Press*, July 25, 1974, p. 6; *Minneapolis Tribune*, July 25, 1974, p. 1; July 28, 1974, p. 1.

106. On convictions: *Sioux Falls Argus Leader*, July 30, 1974, p. 1; one defendant received 1 to 5 years and the other two received 5 to 7. On the opinion survey, see affidavit signed by Jay Schulman, dated July 7, 1974, in WKLDOC Records, MHS, 31.M.3.9B. On Means, see *Minneapolis Tribune*, August 1, 1974, p. 1B; July 31, 1974, p. 12; *Sioux Falls Argus Leader*, August 1, 1974, p. 28; *Rapid City Journal*, August 1, 1974, pp. 1, 2.

107. *Rapid City Journal*, August 6, 1974, p. 2.

108. The summary of Nichol's decision is from his memorandum opinion, reported as *U.S. v. Banks, U.S. v. Means,* 383 F. Supp. 368 (Dist. S. D., W. D., 1974); his decision in the transcript on everything except the posse comitatus motion is in vol. 99, pp. 18188–18203.

109. The quote is from chap. 1, sec. 1, of the Treaty. A copy of the defendant's motion for acquittal is in WKLDOC Records, MHS.

110. *Choate v. Trapp,* 224 U.S. 665 (1912), pp. 670–671, quoted in Nichol's opinion on p. 371. The Major Crimes Act is in 18 USC 1153. The legislation giving the federal courts jurisdiction over offenses charged under the Major Crimes Act is in 19 USC 3242.

111. The co-conspirators who were yet to be tried were Crow Dog, Clyde Belle-court, Holder, and Camp. The conspiracy count was Count IX, based on 18 USC, sec. 371.

112. Opinion, pp. 372–373. See 18 USC, secs. 1153, 661; and South Dakota Criminal Laws, sec. 22-32-9. South Dakota law required larceny "or any felony" accompanying the breaking in, but the indictment only alleged larceny; larceny generally being defined as a taking by "fraud or stealth," with stealth being synonymous with secrecy.

113. Opinion, pp. 373–374; the Molotov cocktails considered illegal firearms were in Count VII, see 26 USC, sec. 5861(d); on the automobile theft, Count VIII, see 18 USC secs. 1153, 661.

114. The statute read in part: "Whoever, except in cases and under circumstances expressly authorized by the Constitution or Act of Congress, willfully uses any part of the Army or the Air Force as a posse comitatus or otherwise to exercise the laws shall be fined not more than $10,000 or imprisoned not more than two years, or both." See 18 USC, sec. 1385; quoted by Nichol on p. 374 of his opinion; on the presidential proclamation exception, see 10 USC, secs. 331, 332, 333. Judge Urbom's opinion is in *U.S. v. Jarmillo,* 380 F. Supp. 1375 (1974).

115. *Transcript,* vol. 99, pp. 18204–18232. Tilsen had received all the material from the office in Lincoln and consulted with several NLG lawyers who were in the Twin Cities for a conference while the hearing was going on. Tilsen interview.

116. *Transcript,* vol. 100, p. 18316.

117. See testimony of Ronald M. Gleszer, formerly the Major General in charge of supply for the Army: direct, *Transcript,* vol. 100, pp. 18484–18499, vol. 101, pp. 18525–18574; cross, vol. 101, pp. 18574–18582, re-direct, pp. 18582–18594; Jack Potter, Colonel U.S. Army retired, was observer and logistics coordinator for the 6th Army and in charge of supplies for Wounded Knee: direct, vol. 101, pp. 18615–18677, cross, pp. 18677–18681, re-direct, pp. 18681–18683.

118. Warner testimony: direct, *Transcript,* vol. 99, pp. 18240–18292, vol. 100, pp. 18296–18381, 18283–18476, and re-direct, pp. 18476–18484. A Justice Department report maintained that the military involvement had been discussed but decided against for three reasons: (1) it would substantially increase the risk of loss of life; (2) the full prestige of the United States government would be committed to what was primarily a dispute between rival tribal factions; and (3) the use of army troops against the Indians might be misinter-

preted by the press and some citizens. See "Jackson Committee Report On Wounded Knee," submitted to the U.S. Senate Interior Committee by the U.S. Department of Justice, p. 10, undated copy in Cavise files.

119. Opinion, pp. 374–377; this applied to Counts III, X, and XI. See 18 USC, secs. 111, 1114. Nichol's ruling is in *Transcript*, vol. 101, pp. 18683–18690. The judge explained his decision to the jury in vol. 102, pp. 18696–18699. Both Hurd and Gienapp still believe that the ruling was wrong on this point. Hurd and Gienapp interviews.

Newspaper coverage discussed the military issue and the other rulings, with some particularly noting that prosecution errors had resulted in certain elements of the larceny charges not being presented. *Minneapolis Tribune*, August 8, 1974, p. 1B; August 9, 1974, p. 14B; August 10, 1974, p. 14C; *Saint Paul Pioneer Press*, August 8, 1974, p. 21; August 9, 1974, p. 19; August 10, 1974, p. 7; *Rapid City Journal*, August 9, 1974, p. 7; August 13, 1974, p. 12.

120. Gallant, Leventhal, and Tilsen interviews; in-court discussions in *Transcript*, vol. 101, pp. 18517–18521; press coverage in *Minneapolis Tribune*, August 9, 1974, p. 1; August 10, 1974, pp. 1, 14C; August 12, 1974, p. 2B; *Saint Paul Pioneer Press*, August 13, 1974, p. 8; *Sioux Falls Argus Leader*, August 7, 1974, p. 32, August 8, 1974, p. 17, August 10, 1974, p. 4; *Rapid City Journal*, August 13, 1974, p. 12.

121. Banks interview.

122. Kunstler, Tilsen, Banks, Leventhal, Hall, Cohoes, and Gallant interviews.

123. Rachel Tilsen, Northcott, James, and Gallant interviews.

124. Quote from Gallant interview; information also from Northcott and James interviews. Law students were recruited by the NLG to work in South Dakota or Nebraska, or to conduct legal research in Denver or in their home cities; this helped but still did not address the need for trial lawyers.

125. Comparisons with Saint Paul from interviews with Thomas, Gallant, Northcott, James, DeCora Means, Ted Means, Gilbert Thunder Hawk, Cohoes, and Joe and M. G. Beeler; see also lists of Saint Paul subcommittees in WKLDOC Records, MHS.

126. See also notes on the NLG meeting, minutes of the WKLDOC meeting in Saint Paul, August 14, 1974, and letters from 1974 to various law schools from the "Indian Summer Law Student Project" organized by the Oregon Chapter of the NLG, in WKLDOC Records, MHS. Information also from Joe and M. G. Beeler, Northcott, Gallant, and James interviews.

7. THE DEFENSE CASE AND THE GOVERNMENT'S REBUTTAL

1. Vine Deloria, *Custer Died for Your Sins* (New York: Macmillan, 1969; paperback edition, New York: Avon Books, 1970); Dee Brown, *Bury My Heart at Wounded Knee* (New York: Holt, Rinehart and Winston, 1970; paperback edition, New York: Bantam Books, 1972).

2. Stephen Cornell, *Return of the Native: American Indian Political Resurgence* (New York: Oxford University Press, 1988), p. 173.

3. *Transcript*, vol. 102, pp. 18703–18729.

4. *Transcript,* vol. 102, pp. 18724–18725.

5. *Transcript,* vol. 182, pp. 18731–18734, 18752–18753, 18807.

6. The treaty discussion up to Banks's "thank you" is in *Transcript,* vol. 102, pp. 18757–18774.

7. *Transcript,* vol. 102, p. 18792.

8. *Transcript,* vol. 102, p. 18800; this section of Deloria's direct in vol. 102, pp. 18775–18807.

9. *Transcript,* vol. 102, pp. 18707–18708.

10. Cross-examination in *Transcript,* vol. 102, pp. 18807–18813; Nichol's comment in vol. 102, p. 18814.

11. *Transcript,* vol. 102, pp. 18820–18825.

12. *Transcript,* vol. 102, p. 18837.

13. *Transcript,* vol. 102, pp. 18833–18834, 18842–18843, 18846–18847.

14. *Transcript,* vol. 102, p. 18840.

15. *Transcript,* vol. 102, p. 18845.

16. *Transcript,* vol. 102, pp. 18850–18864.

17. *Transcript,* vol. 102, p. 18866.

18. Cross, *Transcript,* vol. 102, pp. 18864–18874; the rest of Brown's direct is in vol. 102, pp. 18815–18864.

19. *Transcript,* vol. 102, pp. 18892–18893.

20. *Transcript,* vol. 102, pp. 18893–18900.

21. *Transcript,* vol. 103, pp. 18917–19020. Some in the media were paying more attention to the renewed discussions of the White House tapes. Before Kills Enemy took the stand, Nichol had signed an order directing federal officials to hold on to tapes that might contain discussions of the events at Wounded Knee. *Minneapolis Tribune,* August 15, 1974, p. 1B; August 16, 1974, p. 1B; August 17, 1974, p. 1.

22. *Transcript,* vol. 103, pp. 19021–19050.

23. Banks, Cohoes, Leventhal, and Hall interviews.

24. Quote in *Transcript,* vol. 104, p. 19184; on the chiefs, see vol. 103, pp. 19095–19101.

25. *Transcript,* vol. 103, p. 19175.

26. *Transcript,* vol. 103, p. 19176; description of scene in *Minneapolis Tribune,* August 17, 1974, p. 1.

27. *Transcript,* vol. 104, pp. 19109–19114.

28. *Transcript,* vol. 104, p. 19138; the last part of the answer was struck as not responsive to the question.

29. Direct, *Transcript,* vol. 104, pp. 19122–19169.

30. *Transcript,* vol. 104, pp. 19184–19185.

31. *Transcript,* vol. 104, p. 19185; Bissonette's direct in full: vol. 103, pp. 19050–19106, vol. 104, pp. 19109–19187.

32. Banks, Gallant, and Cohoes interviews. Putting together her testimony was a collective effort; though Lane handled the direct examination, he received input on how to approach it from others, particularly Tilsen.

33. *Transcript,* vol. 104, pp. 19199–19200.

34. *Transcript,* vol. 104, pp. 19200–19223.

35. *Transcript,* vol. 104, p. 19233.

36. *Transcript,* vol. 104, pp. 19234–19241, 19262–19270.

37. *Transcript,* vol. 104, p. 19276.

38. *New York Times,* August 17, 1974, p. 50; *Minneapolis Tribune,* August 17, 1974, pp. 1, 4; the *Saint Paul Pioneer Press* gave some space to Hurd's cross-examination but still had several paragraphs on Bissonette's direct examination, including several quotes, August 16, 1974, p. 13; August 17, 1974, p. 1; *Rapid City Journal,* August 17, 1974, p. 2; *Sioux Falls Argus Leader,* August 15, 1974, p. 29; August 17, 1974, p. 10.

39. Lane's quote in *Minneapolis Tribune,* August 17, 1974, p. 4; *Sioux Falls Argus Leader,* August 17, 1974, p. 10; on the decision to rest: Tilsen, Kunstler, and Banks interviews.

40. Kunstler and Hurd quoted in *Sioux Falls Argus Leader,* August 17, 1974, p. 10; on the decision not to put the defendants on: Kunstler, Tilsen, Banks, Hall, Leventhal, Gallant, and Cohoes interviews.

41. W. Lance Bennett and Martha S. Feldman, *Reconstructing Reality in the Courtroom: Justice and Judgement in American Culture* (New Brunswick: Rutgers University Press, 1984), pp. 3–6.

42. Ibid., p. 157.

43. bell hooks, *Black Looks: Race and Representation* (Boston: South End Press, 1992), p. 193.

44. Press coverage in *Minneapolis Tribune,* August 14, 1974, p. 1B; *Saint Paul Pioneer Press,* August 14, 1974, p. 22; *Rapid City Journal,* August 15, 1974, p. 17; August 16, 1974, p. 2; *Sioux Falls Argus Leader,* August 10, 1974, p. 4.

45. *Saint Paul Pioneer Press,* August 17, 1974, p. 1; see also *Rapid City Journal,* August 17, 1974, p. 6.

46. Quote from Kunstler interview; information also from Banks, Gallant, Tilsen, and Leventhal interviews.

47. On the resolution, see press release dated August 15, 1974, in Cavise files; on Banks, see *Minneapolis Tribune,* August 18, 1974, p. 18; August 19, 1974, p. 5B; *Rapid City Journal,* August 17, 1974, p. 28.

48. *New York Times,* August 19, 1974, p. 1; reported also in *Rapid City Journal,* August 19, 1974, p. 3.

49. *Minneapolis Tribune,* August 21, 1974, p. 1B.

50. Direct, *Transcript,* vol. 105, pp. 19314–19413, vol. 106, pp. 19417–19428.

51. Press reports in *Saint Paul Pioneer Press,* August 22, 1974, pp. 1, 2; *Minneapolis Tribune,* August 22, 1974, pp. 1, 11; *Rapid City Journal,* August 23, 1974, p. 2; August 24, 1974, p. 2.

52. Leventhal and Gallant interviews.

53. *Transcript,* vol. 106, pp. 19445, 19449, 19464–19465.

54. *Transcript,* vol. 106, p. 19473.

55. *Transcript,* vol. 106, p. 19474. The defense team still maintains that it did not prearrange Moves Camp's disruption; Banks, Kunstler, Tilsen, and Gallant interviews. Tilsen says that Nichol knew that Moves Camp had been staying at Tilsen's house, which is why he suspected that the defense lawyers had instigated her outburst. Tilsen, second interview, February 1991.

56. The suggestion for the meeting came from Mary Hall, a professor of clinical psychology at the University of Minnesota and wife of defense attorney Doug

Hall. She told Judge Nichol and later the press that she had been sitting next to Ellen Moves Camp while her son testified and that Moves Camp became increasingly upset, trembling at times, trying to control herself before she finally rose and headed toward her son. It was Mary Hall who had suggested to Nichol that he meet with Mrs. Moves Camp, taking up the role of mediator that her husband had been playing throughout the trial. *Minneapolis Tribune,* August 23, 1974, p. 9.

57. Nichol in *Minneapolis Tribune,* August 23, 1974, pp. 1, 9; *Saint Paul Pioneer Press,* August 23, 1974, pp. 1, 2; Moves Camp quoted in *Minneapolis Tribune,* August 23, 1974, p. 9.

58. Direct, *Transcript,* vol. 106, pp. 19476–19490.

59. *Transcript,* vol. 106, pp. 19506–19508.

60. *Transcript,* vol. 106, pp. 19509–19515.

61. *Minneapolis Tribune,* August 24, 1974, p. 1; see also *Saint Paul Pioneer Press,* August 24, 1974, p. 1; *Minneapolis Tribune,* August 23, 1974, p. 9, for coverage on Moves Camp's first day.

62. *Transcript,* vol. 107, p. 19631; see also pp. 19518–19631.

63. *Transcript,* vol. 107, pp. 19698–19718. The sequence of events and of who said what is not totally clear from the transcript; part of this account comes from Tilsen interview.

64. *Saint Paul Pioneer Press,* August 24, 1974, p. 1; *Minneapolis Tribune,* August 24, 1974, pp. 1, 9; *New York Times,* August 24, 1974, p. 1; *Sioux Falls Argus Leader,* August 24, 1974, p. 1; August 25, 1974, p. 1; August 26, 1974, p. 1. For two days in the *Rapid City Journal* the focus was on the defense attorneys, with little on Moves Camp's testimony: *Rapid City Journal,* August 25, 1974, p. 1; August 26, 1974, p. 9, with the headline, "AIM Lawyers Pursue Confrontational Tactics."

65. Leventhal interview.

66. Tilsen says that the two New York attorneys who were both friends of Kunstler were particularly angry with him for getting himself thrown in jail. Tilsen himself thought that the whole episode was unnecessary. "It wasn't needed," said Tilsen, adding, "Nichol had no choice but to do what he did." Tilsen interview. Nichol's thoughts from Nichol interview.

67. *Minneapolis Tribune,* August 25, 1974, p. 1; *New York Times,* August 25, 1974, p. 20; *Saint Paul Pioneer Press,* August 25, 1974, p. 1; *Sioux Falls Argus Leader,* August 25, 1974, p. 1; *Rapid City Journal,* August 27, 1974, p. 1; on Kunstler and jail see *Sioux Falls Argus Leader,* August 26, 1974, p. 1.

68. *Transcript,* vol. 108, pp. 19721–19723.

69. *Transcript,* vol. 108, pp. 19725–19847.

70. *Transcript,* vol. 108, pp. 19848–19925, vol. 109, pp. 19930–20043.

71. *Transcript,* vol. 109, pp. 20044–20055.

72. *Transcript,* vol. 109, pp. 20060–20066.

73. The *Pioneer Press* referred to it as a full day of "minutiae"; *Saint Paul Pioneer Press,* August 27, 1974, p. 6. See also *Minneapolis Tribune,* August 27, 1974, p. 1B; August 28, 1974, p. 2B; *Sioux Falls Argus Leader,* August 27, 1974, p. 16.

74. Quoted in *Minneapolis Tribune,* August 28, 1974, p. 2B.

75. *Minneapolis Tribune,* August 28, 1974, p. 2B; *Saint Paul Pioneer Press,* August 28, 1974, p. 3; *Sioux Falls Argus Leader,* August 28, 1974, p. 10.

76. *Minneapolis Tribune,* August 28, 1974, p. 2B.

77. Tilsen, Leventhal, and Gallant interviews.

78. Tilsen interview.

79. Hurd interview. Regarding the comments on the Soviet Union being present, Hurd says that while Moves Camp may not have got it quite right, AIM was soliciting help from the Soviet Union and other Eastern European countries, so that it was not so far-fetched to consider that the Soviet Union, for their own propaganda purposes, might have made contact with people inside Wounded Knee. Gienapp, who had little to do with Moves Camp's testimony, believes that he should have been called as a rebuttal witness.

80. *Minneapolis Tribune,* August 29, 1974, p. 2B.

81. *Transcript,* vol. 110, pp. 20098–20126; cross, pp. 20127–20136.

82. Direct, *Transcript,* vol. 110, pp. 20159–20164; cross, vol. 110, pp. 20164–20254. Newspapers commented that Ellen Moves Camp had not helped her cause. See *Minneapolis Tribune,* August 29, 1974, p. 2B; *Saint Paul Pioneer Press,* August 29, 1974, p. 19; *Rapid City Journal,* August 29, 1974, p. 3; August 30, 1974, p. 6.

83. See testimony of Ted Hughett, brought in from California, *Transcript,* vol. 111, pp. 20460–20476; Julie Rencountre, a relative, vol. 112, pp. 20577–20578; Alex Rencountre, vol. 112, pp. 20577–20585.

84. Frizzell's affidavit stated that to the best of his knowledge, by March 27, 1973, Banks had been outside of Wounded Knee for several days; vol. 114, pp. 20989–20998. Tilsen in *Transcript,* vol. 110, pp. 20255–20296.

85. Headlines from the *Sioux Falls Argus Leader,* August 30, 1974, p. 1; *Rapid City Journal,* August 31, 1974, p. 2; see also *Minneapolis Tribune,* August 30, 1974, p. 2B; *Saint Paul Pioneer Press,* August 30, 1974, p. 36.

86. Northcott and Tilsen interviews.

87. *Minneapolis Tribune,* August 30, 1974, p. 2B; August 31, 1974, p. 1; *Saint Paul Pioneer Press,* August 31, 1974, p. 13.

88. *Transcript,* vol. 110, pp. 20137–20152; vol. 112, pp. 20587–20592.

89. *Transcript,* vol. 112, pp. 20633–20638.

90. *Minneapolis Tribune,* August 31, 1974, p. 2B; *Saint Paul Pioneer Press,* August 31, 1974, p. 13; *Rapid City Journal,* September 3, 1974, p. 3; Kunstler and Cohoes interviews.

91. Williams, direct, *Transcript,* vol. 112, pp. 20597–20660.

92. Williams, cross, *Transcript,* vol. 112, pp. 20660–20695.

93. Robert W. Lindsay was the district attorney for Pierce County, Wisconsin, which includes River Falls, the town in which the rape was to have occurred; see *Transcript,* vol. 113, pp. 20734–20764. Lindsay's comments about the four people who alleged they had seen Moves Camp and the woman having sex came during cross-examination by Hurd, vol. 113, pp. 20764–20769.

94. Testimony of Sergeant Carlisle W. Shrank, River Falls Police Department, *Transcript,* vol. 113, pp. 20793–20838, 20855–20872, cross, pp. 20873–20880; discussion of Chief Perry Anderson, vol. 113, pp. 20840–20848.

95. *Minneapolis Tribune,* August 31, 1974, p. 1; September 4, 1974, p. 1B; see also *Sioux Falls Argus Leader,* August 31, 1974, p. 4; September 5, 1974, p. 5. Nichol still maintains that Hurd lied to him about his knowledge of the alleged rape, while Hurd maintains that he did not bring the matter to the judge's attention, not in an attempt to cover it up but because he did not believe and still does not believe it was relevant to Moves Camp's testimony. Nichol and Hurd interviews. Gienapp also contends that the episode in Wisconsin should not have been admissible. Gienapp interview.

96. Direct, *Transcript,* vol. 113, pp. 20849–20854, 20885–20896, vol. 114, pp. 20901–20936; cross, vol. 114, pp. 20937–20941. Hurd then took the stand to corroborate what Price had said. *Transcript,* vol. 114, pp. 20948–20953. See also testimony of John Tescher, who was with Moves Camp at the bar in Wisconsin, vol. 114, pp. 20953–20970. Lane denied an allegation by Wisconsin officials that he identified himself as working for the government when investigating the rape allegations; vol. 114, pp. 20970–20989.

97. Testimony of George Gap, direct, *Transcript,* vol. 114, pp. 21004–21026. On cross-examination Hurd produced a document prepared by Means that listed Red Cloud as a traditional chief, but the witness still insisted he was not; vol. 114, pp. 21028–21040. The defense claimed that Charlie Red Cloud was considered the hereditary chief descendant from Red Cloud, and that the wrong name was put on the list; p. 21040. Testimony of Gaylene Roach Moves Camp: *Transcript,* vol. 114, pp. 21041–21053; on cross-examination she admitted that she had little contact with her husband recently and did not know about his feelings for Banks and Means, cross, vol. 114, pp. 21059–21068.

 Hurd's testimony in *Transcript,* vol. 114, pp. 21076–21093. On September 9, Hurd read a stipulation agreed to by both sides that stated that Moves Camp had received $1,990.50, consisting of witness fees, per diem under the government witness security program, relocation expenses, and a one-way airplane ticket. *Transcript,* vol. 115, pp. 21109–21114.

 Press coverage in *Minneapolis Tribune,* September 5, 1974, p. 1; *Saint Paul Pioneer Press,* September 4, 1974, pp. 15, 23; September 5, 1974, p. 21; *Rapid City Journal,* September 3, 1974, p. 3; September 4, 1974, p. 25; September 5, 1974, p. 22; September 7, 1974, p. 2.

98. *Minneapolis Tribune,* September 5, 1974, p. 1; September 6, 1974, p. 2B; *New York Times,* September 5, 1974, p. 18; *Saint Paul Pioneer Press,* September 6, 1974, p. 13; September 9, 1974, p. 20; *Sioux Falls Argus Leader,* September 6, 1974, p. 14.

8. THE CLOSING ARGUMENTS

1. See, for instance, John D. McCarthy and Mayer N. Zald, "Resource Mobilization and Social Movements: A Partial Theory," *American Journal of Sociology* 82 (May 1977): 1212–1241; and Bert Klandermans, "Mobilization and Participation: Social Psychological Expansions of Resource Mobilization Theory," *American Sociological Review* 49 (October 1984): 583–600.

2. See Michal R. Belknap, *Cold War Political Justice: The Smith Act, the CIA, and*

American Civil Liberties (New York: Greenwood Press, 1978), who discusses the effect of the prosecutions and undercover agents on the Communist Party in chap. 7; Paul Chevigny, *Cops and Rebels: A Study Of Provocation* (New York: Pantheon, 1972); David G. Bromley and Anson D. Shupe, "Repression and the Decline of Social Movements: The Case of the New Religions," in *Social Movements of the Sixties and Seventies,* ed. Jo Freeman (New York: Longman, 1983), pp. 335–347; Doug McAdam, "The Decline of the Civil Rights Movement," in *Social Movements,* ed. Freeman, pp. 298–319; Anthony Oberschall, "The Decline of the 1960s Social Movements," in *Research in Social Movements, Conflicts and Change* (Greenwich, Conn.: JAI Press, 1978), pp. 257–289.

3. *New York Times,* August 15, 1974, p. 34; *Sioux Falls Argus Leader,* August 15, 1974, p. 1; *Minneapolis Tribune,* August 21, 1974, p. 2B; *Saint Paul Pioneer Press,* August 24, 1974, p. 18.

4. The figure twenty-seven is from the *New York Times,* September 13, 1974, p. 15; on the prosecution and juries see *Sioux Falls Argus Leader,* September 18, 1974, p. 3C.

5. Urbom acquitted four defendants in one case, citing insufficient evidence. Two witnesses had refused to testify, one reportedly because he was afraid of AIM, and the other invoking the Fifth Amendment when called to the stand. *Minneapolis Tribune,* September 13, 1974, p. 5; *Sioux Falls Argus Leader,* September 12, 1974, p. 19.

6. Announcements by prosecution: *Sioux Falls Argus Leader,* August 24, 1974, p. 5; August 30, 1974, p. 3; Clayton in *Sioux Falls Argus Leader,* August 27, 1974, p. 16; Joe Beeler interview.

7. *Saint Paul Pioneer Press,* August 31, 1974, p. 2.

8. Kniep in *Sioux Falls Argus Leader,* August 24, 1974, p. 10; response, *Rapid City Journal,* August 26, 1974, p. 1.

9. *Rapid City Journal,* August 15, 1974, p. 2.

10. *Transcript,* vol. 116, pp. 21123–21127.

11. *Transcript,* vol. 116, p. 21128.

12. *Transcript,* vol. 116, p. 21135; see also pp. 21128–21134.

13. *Transcript,* vol. 116, p. 21181; and generally, pp. 21136–21189.

14. *Transcript,* vol. 116, pp. 21190–21191.

15. *Transcript,* vol. 116, p. 21192.

16. *Transcript,* vol. 116, p. 21194.

17. Quote in *Transcript,* vol. 116, p. 21214; see generally pp. 21195–21214.

18. *Transcript,* vol. 116, pp. 21220–21253.

19. *Transcript,* vol 116, pp. 21253–21257.

20. See generally *Transcript,* vol. 116, pp. 21259–21354.

21. *Minneapolis Tribune,* September 12, 1974, p. 2B.

22. *Transcript,* vol. 117, pp. 21359–21360.

23. *Transcript,* vol. 117, pp. 21367–21375.

24. *Transcript,* vol. 117, pp. 21376–21391; see also pp. 21304–21305.

25. *Transcript,* vol. 117, pp. 21393–21394.

26. *Transcript,* vol. 117, pp. 21394–21395, 21401–21402.

27. *Transcript,* vol. 117, pp. 21407–21410.

28. *Transcript,* vol. 117, pp. 21412–21413.

29. *Transcript*, vol. 117, pp. 21414–21422.

30. *Transcript*, vol. 117, pp. 21422–21424.

31. Quote in *Transcript*, vol. 117, p. 21434; generally, pp. 21424–21433.

32. Theft: *Transcript*, vol. 117, pp. 21433–21436; Moves Camp, pp. 21438–21443; elders, pp. 21443–21445.

33. *Transcript*, vol.117, pp. 21446–21454, 21457–21462.

34. *Transcript*, vol. 117, p. 21465.

35. *Transcript*, vol. 117, p. 21470.

36. *Transcript*, vol. 117, p. 21471. The night before, while trying to figure out how to end his summation, Kunstler paid a visit to the activist and writer Meridel Le Sueur (who is also Rachel Tilsen's mother), who advised him to read Benet's poem. Kunstler related the story in a speech at Concordia College on March 3, 1990.

37. *Transcript*, vol. 117, pp. 21471–21475. The description is from *Minneapolis Tribune*, September 12, 1974, p. 2B; Cohoes interview.

38. *Transcript*, vol. 117, pp. 21476–21477.

39. *Transcript*, vol. 117, pp. 21482–21483.

40. *Transcript*, vol. 117, pp. 21478–21483, 21489.

41. Quote in *Transcript*, vol. 117, p. 21487; generally, pp. 21483–21488.

42. *Transcript*, vol. 117, pp. 21493, 21495.

43. Moves Camp: *Transcript*, vol. 117, pp. 21497–21503; on Trimbach, see p. 21507.

44. *Transcript*, vol. 117, pp. 21512–21527.

45. *Transcript*, vol. 117, pp. 21534–21536, 21538–21543, 21551–21559.

46. *Transcript*, vol. 117, pp. 21559–21560; on assaults, pp. 21544–21551; recounting events, pp. 21551–21559.

47. *Transcript*, vol. 117, pp. 21564–21565.

48. *Transcript*, vol. 117, pp. 21565–21567.

49. *Transcript*, vol. 118, p. 21577; comments to press, *Rapid City Journal*, September 11, 1974, p. 2.

50. Leventhal interview. Nichol said that he felt the treaty was a mitigating factor; Nichol interview.

51. *Transcript*, vol. 118, pp. 21579–21588, 21603–21604.

52. *Transcript*, vol. 118, pp. 21604–21607.

53. Quote in *Transcript*, vol. 118, pp. 21607–21609.

54. Evidence: *Transcript*, vol. 118, pp. 21609–21611; reasonable doubt, pp. 21611–21612.

55. *Transcript*, vol. 118, pp. 21612–21621; he also outlined the substantive crimes the defendants were charged with conspiring to commit, pp. 21621–21627.

56. *Transcript*, vol. 118, pp. 21627–21629.

57. *Transcript*, vol. 118, pp. 21629–21634.

58. *Transcript*, vol. 118, pp. 21634–21642.

59. *Transcript*, vol. 118, pp. 21643–21648.

60. *Transcript*, vol. 118, pp. 21648–21654.

61. *Transcript*, vol. 118, pp. 21655–21661. In chambers during the recess, the prosecution expressed satisfaction with the instructions and declined to record any objections. The defense, however, registered several objections, suggesting

either modification or elimination of a number of the instructions, all of which were noted for the record and denied by the judge. *Transcript*, vol. 118, pp. 21662–21694.

62. *Transcript*, vol. 118, pp. 21696–21701.

63. Quoted in *Sioux Falls Argus Leader*, September 13, 1974, p. 1.

64. *Minneapolis Tribune*, September 13, 1974, p. 1; *New York Times*, September 13, 1974, p. 15; *Sioux Falls Argus Leader*, September 13, 1974, p. 1; *Saint Paul Pioneer Press*, September 13, 1974, p. 1.

65. Reporters, noting that Marlon Brando was making his second appearance at the trial, were told by the alternates that the appearance of celebrities at the trial had no influence on them. Quotes in *Minneapolis Tribune*, September 13, 1974, pp. 1, 5.

66. Banks quoted in *Sioux Falls Argus Leader*, September 13, 1974, p. 1; *Rapid City Journal*, September 4, 1974, p. 2; Tilsen's comment from Tilsen interview. Information on defense reaction to alternates also comes from Kunstler and Cohoes interviews.

67. *New York Times*, September 13, 1974, p. 15.

68. Some also mentioned other legal points, as well as Lane's discussion of conditions on Pine Ridge. *Minneapolis Tribune*, September 11, 1974, p. 2B; September 12, 1974, pp. 1B, 2B; *Saint Paul Pioneer Press*, September 11, 1974, p. 19; September 12, 1974, pp. 1, 2; *Sioux Falls Argus Leader*, September 11, 1974, p. 15; September 12, 1974, p. 27.

69. *New York Times*, September 12, 1974, p. 79.

70. W. Lance Bennett and Martha S. Feldman, *Reconstructing Reality in the Courtroom: Justice and Judgement in American Crime* (New Brunswick: Rutgers University Press, 1984), pp. 150–154.

71. *Transcript*, vol. 118, pp. 21707, 21709, 21714–21716, 21716–21718.

72. *Minneapolis Tribune*, September 13, 1974, p. 1; October 1, 1974, p. 15; *New York Times*, September 13, 1974, p. 15.

73. *Minneapolis Tribune*, September 14, 1974, pp. 1, 4; *New York Times*, September 14, 1974, p. 15; *Saint Paul Pioneer Press*, September 14, 1974, p. 1; *Sioux Falls Argus Leader*, September 14, 1974, p. 1.

74. *Minneapolis Tribune*, January 8, 1975, p. 1B. The conversation was revealed in the government's appellate brief filed with the Eighth Circuit; in response to questions from reporters, Hall and Tilsen said they knew nothing of the votes or Nichol's conversation with Hurd at the time.

75. Gallant interview.

76. *New York Times*, September 16, 1974, p. 23.

77. *Minneapolis Tribune*, September 15, 1974, pp. 1, 8; *New York Times*, September 16, 1974, p. 23; *Sioux Falls Argus Leader*, September 15, 1974, p. 1.

78. *Minneapolis Tribune*, September 15, 1974, p. 15.

79. *Minneapolis Tribune*, September 16, 1974, p. 1.

80. The speculation on the possibilities of a new trial came from Hurd and Gienapp interviews; Hurd's speculations on a new site are in *Saint Paul Pioneer Press*, September 15, 1974, p. 1.

81. Hurd also denied allegations that he knew that Moves Camp had been in California, saying that he did not ask the FBI to interview Jay West because he

did not want to be accused of tampering with a defense witness. *Saint Paul Pioneer Press*, September 16, 1974, p. 21; *Minneapolis Tribune*, September 16, 1974, p. 8; see also *New York Times*, September 15, 1974, p. 28; *Sioux Falls Argus Leader*, September 16, 1974, p. 1.

9. JUDGE NICHOL'S DECISION AND ITS AFTERMATH

1. Both Hurd and Clayton still maintain the decision was a correct one. Hurd and Clayton interviews.
2. Hurd interview; for reasons to reporters, see *Minneapolis Tribune*, September 17, 1974, p. 8.
3. Nichol interview.
4. *Minneapolis Tribune*, October 1, 1974, p. 15.
5. *Transcript*, vol. 119, pp. 21723–21724.
6. *Transcript*, vol. 119, pp. 21722–21729; on the duty of the prosecution, Nichol quoted language of Justice Sutherland in *Berger v. U.S.*, 295 U.S. 78, p. 88; he also referred to the ABA Standards for Prosecution in criminal cases.
7. *Transcript*, vol. 119, p. 21731.
8. On Richards, see *Transcript*, vol. 119, pp. 21744–21746; on Moves Camp, p. 21746. The cases cited by Nichol to support his decision to treat the matter as a motion for dismissal were *U.S. v. Coplon*, 185 F.2d. 629 (1950), *U.S. v. Apex Distributing*, 270 F.2d. 747 (1959), and *U.S. v. Heath*, 260 F.2d. 623 (1958). *Transcript*, vol. 119, p. 21743.
9. *Transcript*, vol. 119, p. 21747.
10. *Transcript*, vol. 119, pp. 21747–21748.
11. On the FBI see *Transcript*, vol. 114, pp. 21746–21754.
12. *Transcript*, vol. 119, pp. 21754–21755; description of Hurd in *Minneapolis Tribune*, September 17, 1974, p. 9.
13. On the military Nichol cited *Laird v. Tatum*, cited in *U.S. v. Walden*, 490 F.2d. 372, p. 375 (1974); *Transcript*, vol. 119, pp. 21755–21758; final comments, pp. 21758–21759.
14. *Transcript*, vol. 119, p. 21759.
15. *Transcript*, vol. 119, pp. 21759–21765.
16. *Sioux Falls Argus Leader*, September 20, 1974, p. 1. The AP story put the trial costs at $100,000 for witness expenses; $87,000 for copies of the transcript, six copies at $4 per page (three to the defense, two to the government, one to the judge, and one to the clerk); $37,000 in jury costs, including room and board; $20,000 to $25,000 for defense attorneys and estimates of prorated salaries for prosecutors, marshals, and the judge. See also *Minneapolis Tribune*, September 14, 1974, p. 4; *New York Times*, September 18, 1974, p. 44; *Rapid City Journal*, September 20, 1974, p. 16.
17. Quote in *Minneapolis Tribune*, September 17, 1974, p. 1; see also *New York Times*, September 17, 1974, pp. 1, 12; *Saint Paul Pioneer Press*, September 17, 1974, pp. 1, 2; *Rapid City Journal*, September 18, 1974, p. 2.
18. Quoted in *Minneapolis Tribune*, September 17, 1974, p. 9; Hurd expressed similar sentiments in his interview.
19. Hurd's actions are described in the *New York Times*, September 18, 1974, p. 44;

his comment is from Hurd interview. Clayton's comments in *Sioux Falls Argus Leader,* September 17, 1974, p. 4; *Rapid City Journal,* September 18, 1974, p. 1.

20. *New York Times,* September 18, 1974, p. 44.
21. Quote from Gallant interview; reactions also from Cohoes interview.
22. *Saint Paul Pioneer Press,* September 17, 1974, p. 2.
23. *Rapid City Journal,* September 18, 1974, p. 2.
24. *Sioux Falls Argus Leader,* September 17, 1974, p. 1. Ten years later Kunstler still praised Nichol for his decision. Kunstler interview.
25. *Sioux Falls Argus Leader,* September 18, 1974, p. 1B; see also *Rapid City Journal,* September 19, 1974, p. 2.
26. *Rapid City Journal,* September 30, 1974, p. 1.
27. Labeling himself a political liberal, Nichol also remarked that the difference between a liberal and a conservative was that "the liberal is more interested in human rights, whereas the conservative is more interested in the status quo and hanging on to what he's got." *Sioux Falls Argus Leader,* September 18, 1974, p. 1B.
28. *Minneapolis Tribune,* September 17, 1974, p. 1. Nelson was the juror reached by phone; Garcia gave the count on the theft vote; Garcia and Aiken made the comments on the assault charges.
29. *Sioux Falls Argus Leader,* September 18, 1974, p. 4C. The foreman, John Kilbride, and Theola May DuBois refused to talk to reporters; Boeke and Claeson could not be reached; the juror quoted on Cherrier's views was James Putnam. See also *Minneapolis Tribune,* September 17, 1974, p. 10; *New York Times,* September 18, 1974, p. 44; *Saint Paul Pioneer Press,* September 17, 1974, p. 1; *Rapid City Journal,* September 18, 1974, pp. 1, 38. The *Argus Leader* noted that the defendants' victory celebration was held in a "plush hotel room," in "stark contrast" to Wounded Knee; *Sioux Falls Argus Leader,* September 17, 1974, p. 1; see also *Rapid City Journal,* September 18, 1974, p. 1.
30. *New York Times,* September 21, 1974, p. 28; see also *New York Times,* September 18, 1974, p. 44.
31. Reprinted in *Rapid City Journal,* October 7, 1974, p. 3.
32. *Saint Paul Pioneer Press,* October 6, 1974, p. 2.
33. *Minneapolis Tribune,* September 18, 1974, p. 6.
34. *Sioux Falls Argus Leader,* September 19, 1974, p. 4.
35. *Sioux Falls Argus Leader,* September 18, 1974, p. 3C.
36. *Sioux Falls Argus Leader,* September 18, 1974, p. 1.
37. *Sioux Falls Argus Leader,* September 17, 1974, p. 2.
38. *Saint Paul Pioneer Press,* September 17, 1974, p. 2; see also *Minneapolis Tribune,* September 17, 1974, p. 9.
39. *Sioux Falls Argus Leader,* September 17, 1974, pp. 1, 2; *Rapid City Journal,* September 18, 1974, p. 1.
40. BIA officials in *Rapid City Journal,* September 18, 1974, p. 36; *Rapid City Journal,* September 18, 1974, p. 1; *Sioux Falls Argus Leader,* September 17, 1974, p. 4; residents in *Sioux Falls Argus Leader,* September 18, 1974, p. 5; *Rapid City Journal,* September 18, 1974, p. 36; Gildersleeve in *Sioux Falls Argus Leader,* September 17, 1974, p. 4.
41. *Sioux Falls Argus Leader,* September 27, 1974, p. 1; September 28, 1974, p. 1;

September 29, 1974, p. 1; September 30, 1974, p. 1; *Minneapolis Tribune*, September 23, 1974, p. 8B; September 27, 1974, p. 8B; September 30, 1974, p. 10C; *New York Times*, September 29, 1974, p. 4; *Rapid City Journal*, September 24, 1974, p. 2; September 27, 1974, p. 1; September 28, 1974, p. 1; September 29, 1974, p. 1; September 30, 1974, p. 1; October 1, 1974, p. 2. On Means see *New York Times*, September 20, 1974, p. 22; *Sioux Falls Argus Leader*, September 19, 1974, p. 1. AIM in Custer: *Saint Paul Pioneer Press*, October 26, 1974, p. 21; October 30, 1974, p. 24; shooting on Pine Ridge: *New York Times*, October 13, 1974, p. 51; reports of tension: *Saint Paul Pioneer Press*, October 29, 1974, p. 3; Tribal Council vote to oust Trimble: *Sioux Falls Argus Leader*, November 24, 1974, p. 2.

42. Election results in *Sioux Falls Argus Leader*, November 6, 1974, p. 1; on the race, see issues dated October 30, 1974, p. 1; October 4, 1974, p. 1; October 9, 1974, p. 1. During the campaign, Banks alleged that Janklow had raped a 15-year-old girl in January 1967. Janklow called the allegations "slanderous" and an attempt by AIM to divert attention from its legal problems. He later sued Banks and others for libel. One of the suits, brought against Peter Matthiessen for using the account in his book *In the Spirit of Crazy Horse*, was eventually dismissed. *Sioux Falls Argus Leader*, October 22, 1974, p. 10; October 29, 1974, p. 9; October 30, 1974, p. 1; November 9, 1974, p. 1; *Rapid City Journal*, October 30, 1974, p. 1; October 19, 1974, pp. 3, 4; see also Roland Dewing, *Wounded Knee: The Meaning and Significance of the Second Event* (New York: Irvington Publishers, 1985), pp. 296–297. Dewing notes that there were a number of investigations, but that no charges were ever filed in the matter.

43. *Minneapolis Tribune*, September 18, 1974, p. 1.

44. The study was reportedly ordered before Nichol's decision, and someone from the Justice Department had been sent to Saint Paul to observe the proceedings. *New York Times*, September 18, 1974, p. 44.

45. *New York Times*, September 20, 1974, p. 22; Hurd quote in *Sioux Falls Argus Leader*, September 19, 1974, p. 1; Banks's comments from Banks interview.

46. *Sioux Falls Argus Leader*, September 19, 1974, p. 20.

47. *Sioux Falls Argus Leader*, September 28, 1974, p. 10.

48. *Minneapolis Tribune*, September 25, 1974, p. 1.

49. Ibid., p. 1; see also *New York Times*, September 26, 1974, p. 55. The letter was signed by jurors Therese Cherrier, Maureen Coonan, Geraldine Nelson, Susan Overas, Katherine Valo, Richard Garcia, and Fran Aiken, and alternates Joyce Selander, Linda Lacher, and Elaine Grono.

50. *Minneapolis Tribune*, October 1, 1974, pp. 1, 2; *New York Times*, November 13, 1974, p. 44. Tilsen credits Lane with organizing the effort.

51. *Minneapolis Tribune*, October 1, 1974, p. 1.

52. *Minneapolis Tribune*, September 26, 1974, p. 2B; March 11, 1974, p. 1B.

53. *Means v. Wilson*, 383 F. Supp. 378 (Dist. S.D., 1974). The Court of Appeals reversed the decision in part in 1975, saying that there was a claim against some of the defendants and that the action could be maintained under the Indian Civil Rights Act; 522 F.2d. 833 (8th Cir. Ct. App., 1975). Press coverage on Bogue's decision in *Rapid City Journal*, September 25, 1974, p. 1.

54. *Sioux Falls Argus Leader*, October 18, 1974, p. 1; the four accused of conspiracy

to interfere with police officers were Mark Fleury, Colin Weslaw, Reginald Dodge, and Larry Johns.

55. WKLDOC statement in *Rapid City Journal,* October 21, 1974, p. 2.; information on WKLDOC from Joe Beeler and James interviews. Beeler remembers telling people that they could not expect Urbom to acquit everyone, maintaining that he was still a "terribly fair fact finder." The next case tried to a jury was an acquittal, to the relief of WKLDOC members, who were afraid of Nebraska juries. Beeler interview.

56. *Sioux Falls Argus Leader,* November 25, 1974, p. 5; *Minneapolis Tribune,* November 25, 1974, p. 8B; Banks and Means with Marlon Brando at a benefit for Indian economic development, *Minneapolis Tribune,* November 28, 1974, p. 14B; campaign for prison rights in South Dakota, *Sioux Falls Argus Leader,* December 1, 1974, p. 9. See also letters on finances and fund-raising dated October 11, 1974, and December 11, 1974; copies of minutes of meetings of the Bay Area WKLDOC Support Committee of the Bay Area NLG chapter, for October 3, October 23, November 29, and December 16, all 1974, discussing fund-raising for Lincoln; a news release put out by the Lincoln office of WKLDOC dated December 16, 1974, on the treaty hearing, which included a copy of the 1868 Treaty and its history and current relevance. All documents in Cavise files. Various letters recruiting lawyers for 1974, including letters between Ken Tilsen and Norton Tooby and Phyllis Girourd, two California attorneys, dated December 11 and December 23, 1974, and a copy of a letter from Joe Beeler to the Playboy Foundation are in WKLDOC Records, MHS.

57. On Bellecourt see *Minneapolis Tribune,* December 2, 1974, p. 1B; *Saint Paul Pioneer Press,* December 2, 1974, p. 28; on Fort Robinson see *Sioux Falls Argus Leader,* September 21, 1974, p. 12.

58. *Sioux Falls Argus Leader,* December 11, 1974, p. 1; *Rapid City Journal,* October 26, 1974, p. 6; December 12, 1974, p. 1; see also Dewing, *Wounded Knee,* p. 298.

59. On the Wounded Knee movie see *New York Times,* September 29, 1974, p. 54; on the demonstration, *Sioux Falls Argus Leader,* November 2, 1974, p. 1; *Rapid City Journal,* November 4, 1974, p. 1.

60. Topeka rally in *Rapid City Journal,* December 10, 1974, p. 27; on the Kansas City meeting, see *Saint Paul Pioneer Press,* December 8, 1974, p. 15, sec. 3; *Sioux Falls Argus Leader,* December 8, 1974, p. 2.

61. The original figure on the Black Hills was $17.5 million, but interest since 1877 brought the figure to $104 million; *Sioux Falls Argus Leader,* September 26, 1974, p. 1; *Rapid City Journal,* September 27, 1974, p. 1; October 9, 1974, p. 1. On health and education proposals, see *Rapid City Journal,* October 6, 1974, pp. 2, 3.

62. *Sioux Falls Argus Leader,* November 13, 1974, p. 9.

63. *Minneapolis Tribune,* December 17, 1974, p. 8B; *Saint Paul Pioneer Press,* December 19, 1974, p. 38; *Sioux Falls Argus Leader,* December 19, 1974, p. 1.

64. *New York Times,* October 10, 1974, p. 31; *Rapid City Journal,* October 11, 1974, p. 2; *Minneapolis Tribune,* October 10, 1974, p. 2B.

65. *New York Times,* December 29, 1974, p. 29. Nine more cases were dismissed near the end of December; *Sioux Falls Argus Leader,* December 25, 1974, p. 12.

66. Information on the treaty hearing from Leventhal interview. Press coverage in *Minneapolis Tribune,* December 16, 1974, p. 14B; *Saint Paul Pioneer Press,* December 17, 1974, p. 22; *Rapid City Journal,* December 18, 1974, p. 2. The government voluntarily dropped nine more cases while the hearing was in progress. See *Sioux Falls Argus Leader,* December 25, 1974, p. 2. Information on Urbom and Bogue in *Sioux Falls Argus Leader,* December 7, 1974, p. 17.

67. Leventhal interview; see also press releases and witness lists contained in WKLDOC Records, MHS.

68. Means quoted in *Saint Paul Pioneer Press,* December 28, 1974, p. 13; historian in *Rapid City Journal,* December 23, 1974, p. 2; other press coverage in *Rapid City Journal,* December 26, 1974, p. 2; December 29, 1974, p. 2; December 30, 1974, p. 7.

69. *Rapid City Journal,* January 2, 1975, p. 1.

70. *New York Times,* December 29, 1974, p. 24; January 1, 1975, p. 22; see also *Sioux Falls Argus Leader,* December 18, 1974, p. 18; December 20, 1974, p. 7; December 21, 1974, p. 3; December 22, 1974, p. 2; December 29, 1974, p. 2; December 31, 1974, p. 3; *Rapid City Journal,* January 4, 1975, p. 2.

71. The Major Crimes Act is in 18 USC 1153; the jurisdictional section is sec. 3242; its constitutionality was upheld by the Supreme Court in *U.S. v. Kagama,* 118 U.S. 375 (1886). Urbom's opinion is reported as *U.S. v. Consolidated Wounded Knee Cases,* 389 F. Supp. 235; his discussion of history is on pp. 238–239.

72. *U.S. v. Consolidated,* p. 239.

73. Ibid.

74. The court threw out four convictions on other grounds and upheld two others in this consolidated appeal reported as *U.S. v. Reginald Dodge; U.S. v. Bernard Escamilla; U.S. v. Allen Cooper;* and *U.S. v. Mark Fleury, Colin Wesaw, and Larry Johns.* A petition for re-hearing in front of the entire Court of Appeals on the treaty issue alone was denied: 538 F.2d. 770 (8th Cir. Ct. App., Opinion Withdrawn, April 26, 1976, New Opinion, July 15, 1976).

75. Leventhal and James interviews. The *Sioux Falls Argus Leader* (with stories on December 15, 16, 18, 20, 21, 22, 25, and 29, 1974) and the *Rapid City Journal* had provided almost daily coverage of the hearings. The story rated four paragraphs in the *Minneapolis Tribune,* January 1, 1975, p. 2B, plus coverage of the announcement of Urbom's decision, January 8, 1975, p. 1B. The *Saint Paul Pioneer Press* had one story that gave most attention to the testimony of Russell Means: *Saint Paul Pioneer Press,* December 28, 1974, p. 13. See also *New York Times,* January 18, 1975, p. 4.

76. Cohoes and Northcott interviews. Letters trying to recruit lawyers, promising payment of $25.00 a day in court under the Criminal Justice Act, can be found in WKLDOC Records, MHS, 31.M.3.9B; see also copies of letters between Len Cavise and Fran Schreiberg, both members of WKLDOC, discussing recruitment with the NLG, dated February 6, 1975, February 14, 1975, and March 24, 1975, in Cavise files.

77. The commission said that it could not prove whether or not the irregularities were intentional. *New York Times,* January 18, 1975, p. 14; January 13, 1975, p. 20; *Rapid City Journal,* January 8, 1975, p. 1.

78. *Minneapolis Tribune*, February 5, 1975, p. 1B; March 8, 1975, p. 4; *Saint Paul Pioneer Press*, February 5, 1975, p. 4. Apparently still at war with WKLDOC, Bogue insisted on reviewing each case.

79. *New York Times*, January 2, 1975, p. 15; January 3, 1975, p. 44; January 5, 1975, p. 34; January 6, 1975, p. 30; January 8, 1975, p. 14; January 9, 1975, p. 16; January 12, 1975, p. 55; January 15, 1975, p. 46; January 19, 1975, p. 26. Agreement ending the siege: *New York Times*, February 3, 1975, p. 28; February 4, 1975, p. 17; *Minneapolis Tribune*, February 3, 1975, p. 1; February 4, 1975, p. 1. Thirty-nine people were charged with trespass and disorderly conduct, with only five charged with felonies of armed robbery, burglary, and false imprisonment; *New York Times*, February 5, 1975, p. 20.

80. *New York Times*, February 25, 1975, p. 42; March 4, 1975, p. 27.

81. Richard Marshall was convicted for the shooting. Tilsen, second interview, February 4, 1991; documents in WKLDOC Records, MHS; press coverage in *New York Times*, March 8, 1975, p. 25; *Minneapolis Tribune*, March 11, 1975, p. 1B; March 12, 1975, p. 6: *Saint Paul Pioneer Press*, March 4, 1975, p. 1; March 12, 1975, p. 11.

82. *Rapid City Journal*, May 5, 1975, p. 1; for a sample of the editorials, see *Rapid City Journal*, May 12, 1975, p. 4.

83. *Minneapolis Tribune*, March 13, 1975, p. 7. On April 3 fifteen indictments were handed down by the grand jury; *Minneapolis Tribune*, April 5, 1975, p. 14. The WKLDOC volunteers who were attacked by the "goon squad" were Roger Finzel, Eda Gordon, Martha Copelman, William Rossmore, and Katherine James. James interview. On reservation murders, see *New York Times*, March 28, 1975, p. 22; Wilson's anti-AIM group, *New York Times*, April 6, 1975, p. 39; Wilson's letter, *New York Times*, July 16, 1975, p. 36. In September the *Saint Paul Pioneer Press* did a four-part series on violence and economic conditions on Pine Ridge from September 2 to September 5, 1975. WKLDOC lawyers also filed a civil suit on behalf of several Indians for violation of civil rights by the U.S. government for the illegal use of the military during Wounded Knee; *Saint Paul Pioneer Press*, March 1, 1975, p. 2. See also Peter Matthiessen, *In the Spirit of Crazy Horse* (New York: Viking, 1991), chaps. 5–6, on Pine Ridge during the post–Wounded Knee period.

84. *New York Times*, April 22, 1975, p. 1.

85. Law enforcement request in *New York Times*, April 25, 1975, p. 5; AIM story in *Rapid City Journal*, May 5, 1975, p. 3; on the AIPRC see Stephen Cornell, *The Return of the Native: American Indian Political Resurgence* (New York: Oxford University Press, 1988), p. 203; on the Treaty resolution see Matthiessen, *In the Spirit of Crazy Horse*, pp. 144–145.

86. *New York Times*, March 13, 1975, p. 31; *Minneapolis Tribune*, March 13, 1975, p. 1; March 14, 1975, p. 1. According to Tilsen, information on Durham had been turned over to the defense by a U.S. Attorney during proceedings in a Wounded Knee–related case in Phoenix, Arizona. Tilsen, second interview, February 4, 1991. Vernon Bellecourt, Banks, and others finally confronted the informant on his activities. Bellecourt interview.

Two other informants, Harry and Jill Schafer, surfaced during the trials. He had been inside Wounded Knee from March 23 to May 2, and she had worked in the communications office in Rapid City from March 31 to April 10, 1973. The Eighth Circuit Court of Appeals ruled in 1976 that there was no evidence that the Schafers were privy to defense meetings any of the time they were on the scene. *U.S. v. Leonard Crow Dog*, 532 F.2d. 1182 (8th Cir. Ct. App., 1976). The court further ruled that Durham's presence in Saint Paul did not connect with any of the nonleadership cases, nor the cases of Leonard Crow Dog, Stan Holder, and Carter Camp (the situation was moot with respect to Banks and Means), pp. 1196–1198.

87. *Minneapolis Tribune*, April 5, 1975, p. 3; *New York Times*, March 14, 1975, p. 77; April 5, 1975, p. 16.

88. Hurd said in his interview that Durham turned over nothing on the defense. Copies of defense committee letters to lawyers and defendants concerning Durham and the Schafers are in WKLDOC Records, MHS; see also *New York Times*, April 5, 1975, p. 16.

89. FBI Memorandum: "Counterintelligence Program Black Nationalist-Hate Groups," August 25, 1967; excerpted in Brian Glick, *War at Home: Covert Action Against U.S. Activists and What We Can Do About It* (Boston: South End Press, 1989), p. 77.

90. According to the *New York Times*, March 23, 1975, p. 37, actions against AIM included diversion of funds from South Dakota and delaying of food shipments into Wounded Knee until after the siege had ended. See also Tilsen, "Fair and Equal Justice," pp. 7–8; Glick, *War at Home*, pp. 22–23; Ward Churchill and Jim Vander Wall, *The COINTELPRO Papers: Documents from the FBI's Secret Wars Against Dissent in the United States* (Boston: South End Press, 1990), pp. 231–302; Stanley I. Kutler, *The Wars of Watergate: The Last Crisis of Richard Nixon* (New York: Norton, 1992), on the "Huston Plan," pp. 96–101; Kenneth O'Reilly, *Racial Matters: The FBI's Secret File on Black America, 1960–1972* (New York: The Free Press, 1991), on the Black Panther Party, chaps. 8–10; Dewing, *Wounded Knee*, on Durham and Jill and Harry Schafer, pp. 307–309; Kenneth Stern, *Loud Hawk: The United States versus the American Indian Movement* (Norman: University of Oklahoma Press, 1994), pp. 174–175; Samuel Walker, *In Defense of American Liberties: A History of the ACLU* (New York: Oxford University Press, 1990), on the Church Committee and reform, pp. 295–296; and Matthiessen, *In the Spirit of Crazy Horse*, pp. 120–126. In October 1989, the NLG settled a twelve-year-old lawsuit against the FBI for political spying and disruption conducted up to 1977; some of the activities about which the FBI admitted wrongdoing and agreed not to use the information collected related to the Wounded Knee defense. *Guild Notes*, November/December, 1989.

91. Cornell, *The Return of the Native*, pp. 202–203. Information on AIM from Thomas, Trudell, Ted Means, Lorelei Decora Means, Gilbert Thunder Hawk, Vernon Bellecourt, and Banks interviews. At least one internal FBI document, if authentic, seems to support the contention that this is what the Bureau intended: "Predication for Investigation of Members and Supporters of AIM," June 1976, excerpted in Ward Churchill and Jim Vander Wall, *The COIN-TELPRO Papers*, p. 300.

92. The decision in the appeal is in 513 F.2d. 1329 (8th Cir. Ct. App., 1975). Press coverage in *New York Times*, April 17, 1975, p. 34; *Minneapolis Tribune*, April 17,

1975, pp. 1, 8; *Saint Paul Pioneer Press*, April 17, 1975, p. 1. During oral arguments in March, one justice had reportedly commented that Hurd had been "pretty sloppy" in failing to investigate Moves Camp's story; *Minneapolis Tribune*, March 12, 1975, p. 17.

93. Department of Justice, "Disruption in the Courtroom and the Publicly Controversial Defendant," 10 pages, undated copy in Cavise files; hereafter cited as Justice Department Report.

94. Justice Department Report, p. 2.

95. Ibid., pp. 2–7. The report did say that the FBI was conducting a further investigation into the problems of the Saint Paul trial; p. 7. Press coverage on the report in *New York Times*, April 19, 1975, p. 15; *Saint Paul Pioneer Press*, April 19, 1975, p. 4.

96. Dismissal: *Rapid City Journal*, May 7, 1975, p. 2; *Minneapolis Tribune*, May 6, 1975, p. 8B; editorial: *Rapid City Journal*, May 9, 1975, p. 4.

97. In Council Bluffs 400 prospective jurors were questioned, with 60 percent regarding AIM as troublemakers. The total Indian population in Iowa in 1975 was approximately 5,000. See jury survey in WKLDOC Records, MHS. Press coverage in *Cedar Rapids Gazette*, March 7, 1975, p. 15; May 27, 1975, p. 4; July 13, 1975, p. 20B; *Rapid City Journal*, May 26, 1975, p. 1. Bogue had insisted from the beginning that the defendants could get a fair trial in South Dakota.

98. Federal District Court, Cedar Rapids Division, Northern Division of Iowa. The case numbers are 75-18, 75-19, and 75-20. The Justice Department's report credits Holder with being able to help enforce cease-fires during the siege and noted that he was trusted enough to be released from jail and returned to Wounded Knee to try to get stalled negotiations going again in mid-April; "Jackson Committee Report on Wounded Knee," submitted to the U.S. Senate Interior Committee by the Department of Justice, undated copy in Cavise files; information on change of venue from Joe Beeler interview; also *Cedar Rapids Gazette*, April 16, 1975, p. 3.

99. Cohoes interview.

100. *Cedar Rapids Gazette*, June 1, 1975, pp. 6, 18; June 2, 1975, p. 1; June 3, 1975, p. 17.

101. Quotes in *Saint Paul Pioneer Press*, May 27, 1975, p. 17; *Rapid City Journal*, May 29, 1975, p. 25; second Tilsen quote in *Cedar Rapids Gazette*, May 26, 1975, p. 3. Copies of WKLDOC publicity in WKLDOC Records, MHS; other background on the effort to organize in Cedar Rapids comes from Gallant interview. The other advance person was Rachel Tilsen. Tilsen interview, February 4, 1991. Only about twenty-five spectators had shown up in court for pretrial hearings at the end of May. *Cedar Rapid Gazette*, May 27, 1975, p. 3; May 28, 1975, p. 2.

102. *Minneapolis Tribune*, March 4, 1975, p. 1; *Saint Paul Pioneer Press*, March 4, 1975, p. 1; *Minneapolis Star*, March 13, 1975, p. 140.

103. The transcript of the pretrial hearing is in three volumes, pp. 1–548, copy in WKLDOC Records, MHS; Trimbach's testimony is on pp. 49–124, Williams's on pp. 125–187, and Hurd's on pp. 226–287.

104. The arguments of the attorneys are in *Transcript*, vol. 3, pp. 508–545; Tilsen's discussion of the statistics is on pp. 527–529. See also *New York Times*, June 15,

1975, p. 60; *Cedar Rapids Gazette*, May 31, 1975, pp. 1, 3; *Cedar Rapids Gazette*, May 31, 1975, p. 3.

105. Jury selection is in *Transcript*, vol. 1, pp. 41–199, copy in WKLDOC Records, MHS. The judge asked general questions, and the attorneys were allowed to ask a few specific questions.

106. *Cedar Rapids Gazette*, June 3, 1975, p. 2; June 4, 1975, p. 1.

107. *Cedar Rapids Gazette*, June 4, 1975, p. 1.

108. Joe Beeler, Tilsen, Gienapp, and Hurd interviews; all said that the prosecution had learned something from Saint Paul.

109. The government's case did not go perfectly, however. Several witnesses had difficulty identifying one or more of the defendants or remembering what was said by whom. For the testimony of the government witnesses, see: Inspector Gene Graham, hearing on identification in vol. 2, pp. 237–287; testimony, pp. 290–402; Inspector Jack Hanson, hearing, vol. 3, pp. 408–450; testimony, pp. 480–501; Donald Schneider, testimony, vol. 3, pp. 501–565. Press coverage in *Minneapolis Tribune*, June 5, 1975, p. 7; *Cedar Rapids Gazette*, June 4, 1975, p. 1; *New York Times*, June 15, 1975, p. 60.

110. Camp quote in *Cedar Rapids Gazette*, June 5, 1975, p. 1. The press quoted Tilsen as saying: "Obviously we feel the government failed to prove its case"; but in fact Tilsen had argued the night before that the jury needed to hear the defendants tell their side of the story, including the politics of the Wounded Knee protest. Hurd called the announcement a "happy surprise." Quotes from Hurd and Tilsen in *Cedar Rapids Gazette*, June 5, 1975, p. 1; Tilsen's position on the defense from Tilsen interview.

111. *Transcript*, vol. 4: defense rests, p. 599; motions decided, pp. 600–610; closing arguments, pp. 617–679; verdict, p. 697.

112. *Cedar Rapids Gazette*, June 6, 1975, p. 1.

113. Ibid.

114. Ibid.

115. Holder and Camp comments in *Cedar Rapids Gazette*, June 9, 1975, p. 1; June 12, 1975, p. 1; Tilsen in *Rapid City Journal*, June 7, 1975, p. 2.

116. *Cedar Rapids Gazette*, June 15, 1975, p. 8.

117. Twin Cities papers had compiled their stories on the trial from the wire services. None of it made the front pages, though the *Minneapolis Tribune* did run an analysis piece a few days later noting that trial had ended "quickly and calmly," in contrast with its predecessor; *Minneapolis Tribune*, June 8, 1975, pp. 1, 7. For other coverage see *Minneapolis Tribune*, June 3, 1975, p. 2; June 5, 1975, p. 3B; June 6, 1975, p. 2B; the *Saint Paul Pioneer Press* had one article after the verdict on June 6, 1975, p. 18. In South Dakota the *Rapid City Journal* carried daily coverage from the AP with little comment: May 29, 1975, p. 25; June 4, 1975, p. 1; June 5, 1975, p. 2; June 6, 1975, p. 2; June 7, 1975, p. 2.

118. Tilsen interview.

119. Hurd asserted that McManus correctly restricted the trial to the issue of guilt and innocence on the charges; Hurd interview.

120. On the dismissal see *Minneapolis Tribune*, June 6, 1975, p. 2B; *Cedar Rapids Gazette*, June 11, 1975, p. 8D. Bellecourt was the one conspiracy defendant who was never tried. On the motion to dismiss see *Cedar Rapids Gazette*, June

27, 1975, p. 3. The defendants were facing a possible eighteen years in prison; their sentencing was delayed until August 5, pending a pre-sentencing report, while they remained free on their own recognizance. McManus denied the prosecution's request to set a $5,000 bond on each defendant. *Transcript,* vol. 4, pp. 697–705. Press coverage in *New York Times,* June 15, 1975, p. 60.

121. The sentencing for Crow Dog is in a separate volume dated August 5, 1975; McManus's comments are on p. 49. Copy in WKLDOC Records, MHS. Camp and Holder later received sentences similar to Crow Dog's. Coverage in *Cedar Rapids Gazette,* August 5, 1975, p. 1.

122. AIM meeting in *Minneapolis Tribune,* June 11, 1975, p. 2B; *Saint Paul Pioneer Press,* June 10, 1975, p. 7; June 13, 1975, p. 3; Banks trial in *New York Times,* June 17, 1975, p. 34; *Rapid City Journal,* May 21, 1975, p. 1; June 11, 1975, p. 1; coverage of the gun battle in *New York Times,* June 27, 1975, pp. 1, 6; June 28, 1975, pp. 1, 12; June 29, 1975, pp. 1, 34. Four people were indicted in November—Peltier, Robert Eugene Robideau, Darrelle Dean Butler, and James Theodore Eagle—but only Peltier was convicted; *New York Times,* November 25, 1975, p. 16. Means was ordered to stand trial on the murder charge in the Scenic barroom shooting, *New York Times,* May 15, 1975, p. 15. In what Kunstler called an assassination attempt and the BIA called an accident, Means was shot in the stomach in an altercation with a BIA policeman on the Standing Rock Indian Reservation in North Dakota; see *New York Times,* June 9, 1975, p. 45; June 10, 1975, p. 42; *Saint Paul Pioneer Press,* June 9, 1975, p. 17; *Rapid City Journal,* June 13, 1975, p. 1. Means was later acquitted of assault on the charges. A month later he was assaulted while riding in a car on the reservation; *New York Times,* July 30, 1975, p. 6. For the number of Means's arrests, see *Cedar Rapids Gazette,* August 14, 1975, p. 19; bombings, *New York Times,* June 28, 1975, p. 12; Trudell arrest, *Cedar Rapids Gazette,* July 18, 1975, p. 1; Crow Dog, *Cedar Rapids Gazette,* September 6, 1975, p. 3. Crow Dog would eventually serve a short sentence for violation of his parole.

123. A second report by the Civil Rights Commission issued in March 1976 raised questions concerning the deaths of Aquash and Brian DeSersa, also active with AIM. Kenneth Tilsen, "Fair and Equal Justice," pp. 7–8.

124. The figure on the number of deaths, 61 to 69, is credited to a list compiled by WKLDOC and cited in Churchill and Vander Wall, *The COINTELPRO Papers,* p. 249, pp. 263–273, and p. 388, note 78; the authors place most of the blame on Wilson's supporters and the FBI. For a counter-view see Dewing, *Wounded Knee,* chap. 8; see also Matthiessen, *In the Spirit of Crazy Horse,* chaps. 5–9; Stern, *Loud Hawk,* pp. 93–98, 175–176, 337–340.

125. *Rapid City Journal,* May 8, 1975, p. 1; May 9, 1975, p. 1.

126. *New York Times,* September 11, 1975, p. 21.

127. *New York Times,* October 14, 1975, p. 26.

128. Northcott interview.

129. *New York Times,* July 27, 1975, p. 24; August 6, 1975, p. 30; *Saint Paul Pioneer Press,* July 27, 1975, p. 7, sec. 3; August 6, 1975, p. 32.

130. On the Mission case see *New York Times,* November 30, 1975, p. 54; on Sioux Falls see *Saint Paul Pioneer Press,* December 16, 1975, p. 14. Means was convicted before the same judge who in the previous trial had dismissed the cases

because he said it was impossible to select an impartial jury in Minnehaha County. On Wilson see *New York Times*, December 20, 1975, p. 48.

131. Nancy Zaroulis and Gerald Sullivan, *Who Spoke Up? American Protest Against the War in Vietnam, 1963–1975* (New York: Holt, Rinehart and Winston, 1984), pp. 414–415.

132. Kutler, *The Wars of Watergate*, p. 571.

133. Quoted in Carol Chomsky, "The United States–Dakota War Trials: A Study in Military Injustice," *Stanford Law Review* 43 (1990): 85.

134. The observation is from a memo written by Colonel Frank B. Oblinger, one of the "observers" at Wounded Knee. The Pentagon used the protest to test what it called operation "Garden Plot," a plan to combat civil disturbance. The others on the scene were Colonel Volney Warner, Chief of Staff, 82nd Airborne, and Colonel Jack Potter, Chief of Logistics, 6th Army; *New York Times*, December 2, 1975, p. 32.

135. *New York Times*, December 21, 1975, p. 1.

136. *New York Times*, December 30, 1975, p. 16; *Saint Paul Pioneer Press*, December 30, 1975, p. 2.

137. The comments came at a meeting with John W. Warner, the chief of the federal bicentennial agency; *New York Times*, January 31, 1975, p. 40.

10. RETELLING STORIES OF HISTORY AND POWER

1. Michel Foucault, "The Dangerous Individual," in *Politics, Philosophy, and Culture: Interviews and Other Writings*, ed. Lawrence D. Kritzman, trans. Alain Baudot and Jane Couchman (New York: Routlege, 1988), pp. 123–151; quote on p. 142.

2. *Minneapolis Tribune*, January 1, 1976, p. 1.

3. Jacques Derrida, "Force of Law: The 'Mystical Foundation of Authority,' " in *Deconstruction and the Possibility of Justice*, ed. Drucilla Cornell, Michel Rosenfeld, and David Gray Carlson (New York: Routledge, 1992), pp. 3–67, 34–35.

4. Stephen Cornell, *The Return of the Native: American Indian Political Resurgence* (New York: Oxford University Press, 1988), p. 217.

5. John Locke, "Of Civil Government" (1690); Jennifer Nedelsky, *Private Property and the Limits of Constitutionalism: The Madisonian Framework and Its Legacy* (Chicago: University of Chicago Press, 1990), p. 2.

6. *Johnson v. McIntosh*, 21 U.S. 543 (1823); see also Priscilla Wald, "Terms of Assimilation: Legislating Subjectivity in the Emerging Nation," in Karl Kroeber, ed., *American Indian Persistence and Resurgence* (Durham: Duke University Press, 1994), pp. 78–105, 81–87.

7. Frederick E. Hoxie, *A Final Promise: The Campaign to Assimilate the Indians, 1880–1920* (New York: Cambridge University Press, 1984), p. 15.

8. Alan Hunt, *Explorations in Law and Society: Toward a Constitutive Theory of Law* (New York: Routledge, 1993), pp. 25–34.

9. Gerald Torres and Kathryn Milun, "Translating *Yonnondio* by Precedent and Evidence: The Mashpee Indian Case," *Duke Law Journal* (September 1990): 652–653.

10. Testimony of Clyde Warrior, before the President's National Advisory Commis-

sion on Rural Poverty, February 2, 1967, quoted in Alvin M. Josephy, Jr., *Red Power: The American Indian's Fight for Freedom* (Lincoln: University of Nebraska Press, 1971), p. 72.

11. Hunt, *Explorations in Law and Society,* pp. 21–22.

12. Ibid., p. 29; see also Torres and Milun, "Translating *Yonnondio,"* pp. 628–632, 654–656.

13. See Wald, "Terms of Assimilation," pp. 81–87.

14. Clayton interview.

15. Hurd and Gienapp interviews.

16. Cohoes, Gallant, Hall, Tilsen, Kunstler, and Banks interviews.

17. "Disruption in the Courtroom and the Publicly Controversial Defendant," Justice Department Report (copy in Cavise files), pp. 8–9.

18. *Saint Paul Pioneer Press,* January 1, 1974, p. 4.

19. "Disruption in the Courtroom," p. 10.

20. Gienapp interview.

21. "Disruption in the Courtroom," p. 2. Hurd and Gienapp felt the *Saint Paul Pioneer Press* coverage was more accurate; Hurd commented that he thought the *Minneapolis Tribune* had given the defendants too much publicity, while sometimes ignoring important testimony. Hurd added that he believed this was typical press coverage for such trials. Hurd and Gienapp interviews. In Saint Paul the defense was pleased with the coverage in general (in particular the reporting of Dennis Cassano in the *Minneapolis Tribune)* but critical of the *Saint Paul Pioneer Press.* Banks, Tilsen, Gallant, Kunstler, Northcott, James, and Wiley interviews. Judge Nichol also praised the *Minneapolis Tribune'*s coverage. Nichol interview.

   In criticizing the Saint Paul papers, the defense points to the visit by the FBI at the beginning of the trial and examples like the paper's coverage of Louie Moves Camp, which was on page one throughout his testimony but moved to the inside pages when his credibility was challenged. See *Saint Paul Pioneer Press,* August 29, 1974, p. 19; September 4, 1974, p. 15; September 5, 1974, p. 21; September 6, 1974, p. 13; compared with August 22, 1974, p. 1; August 23, 1974, p. 1; August 24, 1974, p. 1. Other examples mentioned include the lack of coverage of the juror's letter to Saxbe and the release of Nichol's written opinion.

   See also Kevin McKiernan, "Wounded Knee: A Firsthand Review," *The Minnesota Leader,* December 30, 1974, p. 1. McKiernan, who covered the trial for Minnesota Public Radio (KSJN), praised the *Minneapolis Tribune* and criticized the *Saint Paul Pioneer Press,* claiming that their stories did not adequately cover the defense witnesses. McKiernan quoted a former employee of the paper who speculated that the visit by FBI agents had intimidated the editors and was responsible for their control over the coverage of the trial. McKiernan also accused the local press in general of not dealing with the political nature of the trial and of focusing on the sensational. For the latter he cites two examples: first, a local TV news report on July 19, 1974, which used an artist's sketch showing Means gesturing with a clenched fist as background for a report on an exchange between defense attorneys and Nichol, which McKiernan says Means never entered into; and second, a conversation with a local television reporter who was covering two trials, taking notes on one in the morning and the other in the afternoon, saying that they both were criminal trials and that he "didn't see the difference," pp. 9–11.

The *Sioux Falls Argus Leader* and the *Rapid City Journal* both relied on the Associated Press for their day-to-day coverage of Saint Paul, including a wealth of often colorful quotes from the participants. Reporters from South Dakota were rarely in the Twin Cities, though they did conduct interviews with the participants by telephone. There were almost daily stories on Indians, Pine Ridge, and AIM (which were not always negative), but often the focus was the sensational or controversial. McKiernan, who claims to have read hundreds of AP dispatches, also noted that the AP tended toward the sensational and contends that the AP "regionalized" the coverage, putting many of its Wounded Knee reports on the "B" wire, thus limiting its exposure in other regions of the country. "Wounded Knee: A Firsthand Review," p. 9.

In the national press, the *New York Times* was the only one with a reporter on the scene with any regularity. Network news, with a couple of exceptions—the lawyers' being held in contempt and the subpoenaing of the White House tapes—covered the opening of the trial and Nichol's decision at the end. See nightly news broadcasts of ABC, NBC, and CBS for 1974 at the Television News Index and Abstracts Archives, Vanderbilt University, Nashville, Tennessee. See also the *Washington Post,* on the opening of the trial, January 9, 1973, p. 2A; on the arrests of Kunstler and Lane, August 24, 1973, p. 8A; and the dismissals, September 17, 1973, pp. 1A, 4A; also the *Los Angeles Times,* August 24, 1973, p. 2; and September 17, 1973, pp. 1, 13.

The coverage by national news magazines was similar. See *Time,* September 30, 1974, p. 32; *Newsweek,* September 9, 1974, p. 26; September 30, 1974, p. 54–55. *Newsweek* did do a story on the state of Indian treaties which included a report on the hearing before Judge Urbom in Lincoln; January 13, 1975, pp. 58–59.

For comparison, see Judith Vick, "The Press and Wounded Knee, 1973: An Analysis of the Coverage of the Occupation by Selected Newspapers and News Magazines" (M.A. Thesis, University of Minnesota, 1974). Vick, who studied coverage in the *Minneapolis Tribune, New York Times, Washington Post, Newsweek, Time,* and *U.S. News and World Report,* argues that the press leaned toward personalities and drama and away from substantive issues. In particular she singles out the national news magazines (especially *Newsweek)* for what she terms "blatantly prejudicial" coverage. McKiernan levels similar criticisms at the press for its coverage of Wounded Knee, noting that it gravitated toward accounts of weapons and factionalism on the reservation, with less focus on the reasons for the protests and violence. "Wounded Knee: A Firsthand Review," pp. 9–11.

22. Stanley I. Kutler, *The Wars of Watergate: The Last Crisis of Richard Nixon* (New York: W. W. Norton, 1992), pp. 183, 161–162.

23. Todd Gitlin, *The Whole World Is Watching: Mass Media in the Making and Unmaking of the New Left* (Berkeley: University of California Press, 1980), pp. 1–18.

24. "Jackson Committee Report on Wounded Knee," submitted to the U.S. Senate

Interior Committee by the U.S. Department of Justice (undated copy in Cavise files), p. 31.

25. Banks interview. The defense read the papers daily—"religiously," in Kunstler's words. Tilsen, who went to the courthouse each morning with the New York attorney, said they would always stop on the way to pick up the *New York Times*. Kunstler stated: "It's our obligation to help the defendants reach the community." Kunstler and Tilsen interviews.

26. Stuart Ewen, *All Consuming Images: The Politics of Style in Contemporary Culture* (New York: Basic Books, 1988), p. 265.

27. Robert F. Berkhofer, Jr., *The White Man's Indian: Images of the American Indian from Columbus to the Present* (New York: Vintage Books, 1979), pp. 3, 71.

28. Gitlin, *The Whole World Is Watching*, p. 3.

29. DeCora Means and Gilbert Thunder Hawk interviews.

30. Trudell interview. Bill Means expresses similar sentiments, saying that the organization of AIM itself "deteriorated in direct proportion to the amount of fame that began to surface for leadership"; Bill Means interview.

31. Cornell, *The Return of the Native*, pp. 202–205.

32. Means interview. Pine Ridge has been called the poorest area in the country. See "The Spirit of Crazy Horse," a presentation of "Frontline," PBS, and WGBH, Boston, December 18, 1990. As Pine Ridge and other reservations face deep cuts in federal funding, unemployment on the reservation remains at 75 percent. *New York Times*, October 15, 1995, pp. 10–11.

33. Thomas, Trudell, Ted Means, Bill Means, DeCora Means, Gilbert Thunder Hawk, Vernon Bellecourt, Clyde Bellecourt, and Banks interviews. "There are different points of view," says Ted Means, "but we all feel a part of something." Ted Means, second interview, July 16, 1991.

34. In the documentary on Pine Ridge, "The Spirit of Crazy Horse," a former member of the "goon squad" gave credit to AIM for pushing Oglalas, including himself, to seek a greater awareness of their heritage and culture. A recent report, "The Indian Way," made similar comments; WCCO TV, Minneapolis, May 12, 1991. See also Cornell, *The Return of the Native*, pp. 187–218; Marla N. Powers, *Oglala Women: Myth, Ritual, and Reality* (Chicago: University of Chicago Press, 1988), pp. 194–195.

35. Quoted in Peter Nabokov, *Native American Testimony: A Chronicle of Indian-White Relations from Prophecy to the Present, 1492–1992* (New York: Penguin Books, 1991), p. 376.

36. Gilbert Thunder Hawk interview.

37. Peter Schrag makes a similar point about the dismissals in the Ellsberg case; see *Test of Loyalty: Daniel Ellsberg and the Rituals of Secret Government* (New York: Simon and Schuster, 1974), pp. 371–373.

38. Bill Means, Ted Means, DeCora Means, Banks, Trudell, and Vernon Bellecourt interviews.

39. See Tilsen, "Fair and Equal Justice," p. 7. According to Tilsen, another U.S. Attorney who took over the nonleadership cases at the time the failed plea bargain agreement was being negotiated in June 1974 classified the remaining cases in four categories: "dismissed"—those with no prosecution merit; "marginal"—those with little merit; "tolerable"—those which were thin; and

"acceptable"—those which were solid. To that, prosecutor Alan S. Kersham added a note to the effect that the cases designated as "acceptable" were, with few exceptions, cases which "when compared with ordinary cases, would be considered mediocre in strength." Added Kersham: "The scale goes downward from there." Tilsen, "Fair and Equal Justice," p. 7; note 5, p. 9. See also the transcript of the pretrial hearing for *U.S. v. Crow Dog, Camp & Holder,* pp. 527–529, copy in WKLDOC Records, MHS.

40. Gienapp interview.

41. Hurd interview.

42. The quote was used in a WKLDOC press statement and reported in the *Sioux Falls Argus Leader,* September 19, 1974, p. 20.

43. *New York Times,* July 16, 1975, p. 36; April 6, 1975, p. 39; *Sioux Falls Argus Leader,* September 17, 1974, pp. 1, 2.

44. Thomas, Trudell, Banks, Ted Means, Gilbert Thunder Hawk, DeCora Means, Tilsen, and Kunstler interviews. The classic essay on the rule of law is contained in E. P. Thompson's conclusion to *Whigs and Hunters: The Origin of the Black Act* (London, Allen Lane, 1975), pp. 258–269.

45. Trudell interview.

46. Theresa Hak Kyung Cha, *Dictee* (New York: Tanam Press, 1982), p. 33.

47. Derrida, "Force of Law," p. 60.

48. bell hooks, *Black Looks: Race and Representation* (Boston: South End Press, 1992), p. 193.

49. Torres and Milun, "Translating *Yonnondio,*" p. 627; William E. Forbath, Hendrik Hartog, and Martha Minow, "Introduction: Legal Histories From Below," *Wisconsin Law Review* (1985): 759–766.

50. A recent example took place in the spring of 1994, when the United States finally returned Kaho'olawe Island to Hawaii. Named for the god Kanalo, the island had been inhabited for more than a thousand years and regarded as a sacred place by native Hawaiians when it was seized by the United States during the overthrow of Queen Lilivokalani in 1893 and subsequently used as a bombing range by the Navy after 1941. During the 1970s Kaho'olawe became the focal point in the cultural revitalization campaign of the Hawaiian sovereignty movement. The fifteen-year campaign for the return of the island, which included numerous occupations and arrests, is regarded by many as "a time of cultural and political awakening" for Native Hawaiians. Christopher Merrill, "A Little Justice in Hawaii," *The Nation,* May 12, 1994, pp. 235–236.

51. Sidney L. Harring, *Crow Dog's Case: American Indian Sovereignty, Tribal Law, and United States Law in the Nineteenth Century* (New York: Cambridge University Press, 1994), pp. 287–291.

52. Cornell, *The Return of the Native,* pp. 209–213.

53. David William Cohen, *The Combing of History* (Chicago: University of Chicago Press, 1994), p. 244.

54. Murray Edelman, *Constructing the Political Spectacle* (Chicago: University of Chicago Press, 1988), p. 124.

55. Jean-François Lyotard, *The Differend: Phrases in Dispute,* trans. Georges Van Den Abbeele (Minneapolis: University of Minnesota Press, 1988), pp. 8–14.

56. Inspired by the writings of Gilles Deleuze and Felix Guattari, *A Thousand

Plateaus: Capitalism and Schizophrenia, trans. Brian Massumi (Minneapolis: University of Minnesota Press, 1987), pp. 295–297, and Walter Benjamin, "Theses on the Philosophy of History," in *Illuminations: Essays and Reflections*, ed. Hannah Arendt, trans. Harry Zohn (New York: Schocken Books, 1969), p. 261.

57. Michel Foucault, "Nietzche, Genealogy, History," in *Language, Counter-Memory, Practice: Selected Essays and Interviews*, ed. Donald F. Bouchard, trans. Donald F. Bouchard and Sherry Simon (Ithaca: Cornell University Press, 1988), p. 154.

58. Maurice Blanchot, *The Infinite Conversation*, trans. Susan Hanson (Minneapolis: University of Minnesota Press, 1993), p. xii; see also Foucault, *Language, Counter-Memory, Practice*, p. 164.

INDEX